National Hunt and Point-to-Point Racing in Ireland

Arkle with trainer Tom Dreaper at Greenogue stables in 1966.

National Hunt
and Point-to-Point
Racing in Ireland

A History

Frances Nolan

FOUR COURTS PRESS
in association with
The Irish National Hunt Steeplechase Committee

This book was published by
Four Courts Press
7 Malpas Street, Dublin 8, Ireland
www.fourcourtspress.ie
and in North America for
Four Courts Press
c/o IPG Books, 814 N. Franklin St, Chicago, IL 60610

© The Irish National Hunt Steeplechase Committee and Four Courts Press 2025

A catalogue record for this title
is available from the British Library.

Page vi: Honeysuckle and Rachael Blackmore jumping the last to win
the Fairyhouse Mares' Maiden Hurdle in 2018. © *Healy Racing*.

Page x: Punters queuing for the Tote at Thurles Racecourse in 2010. © *Healy Racing*.

ISBN 978-1-80151-188-9

All rights reserved. No part of this publication may be reproduced,
stored in or introduced into a retrieval system, or transmitted, in any form
or by any means (electronic, mechanical, photocopying, recording or otherwise),
without the prior written permission of both the copyright owner and publisher of this book.

Printed in Poland by L & C Printing Group, Krakow
Book design and typesetting by Anú Design, Tara

*Dedicated to the memory of my grandfather,
John McCarthy.*

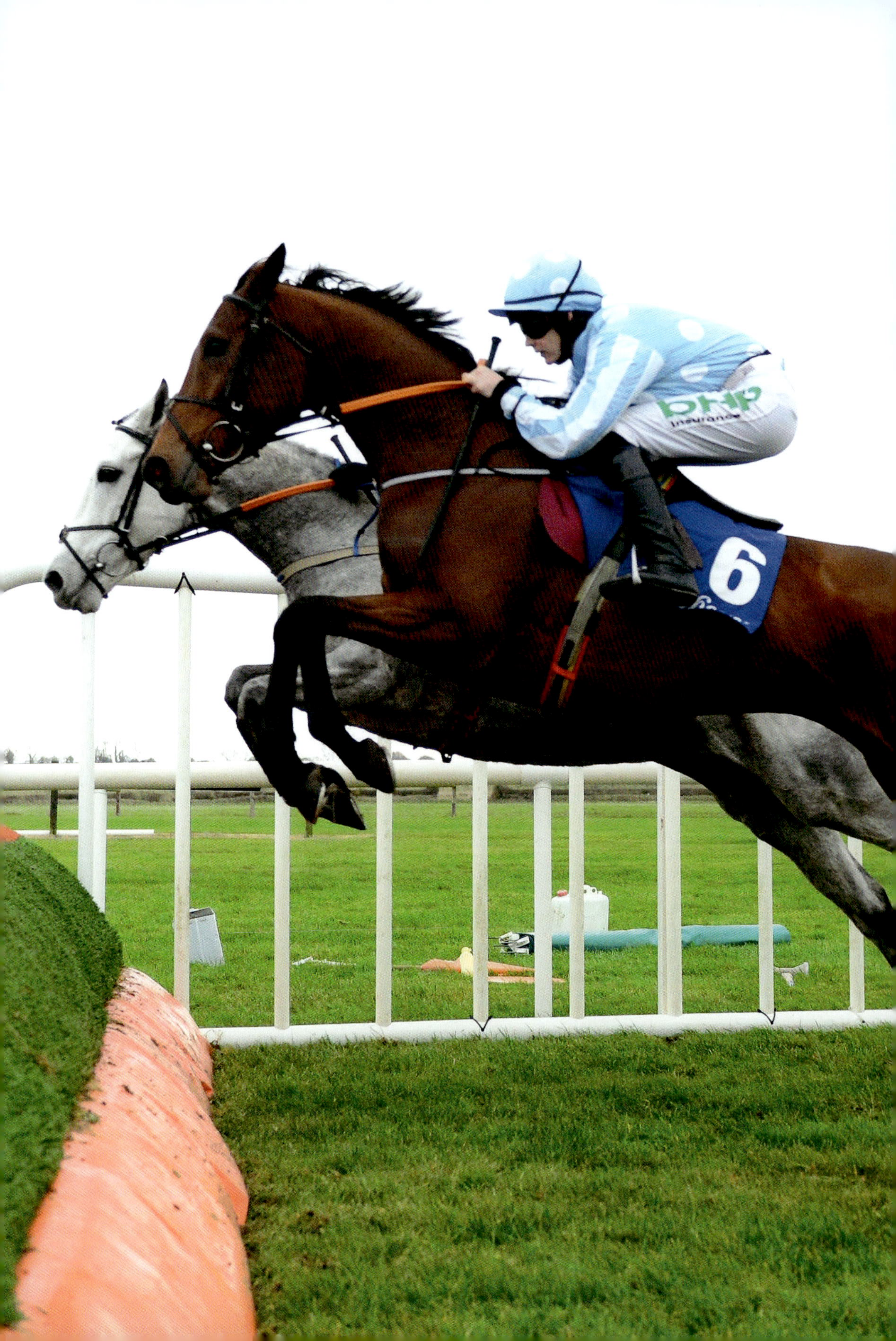
bhp
6

Contents

Abbreviations		viii
Acknowledgments		xi
Introduction		1
Chapter One	1752–1869: 'This truly Irish sport'	9
Chapter Two	1870–1921: 'The delight of Irishmen'	39
Chapter Three	1922–1945: 'A national industry and a national sport'	81
Chapter Four	1945–1969: 'For the first time, Ireland was the best at something'	129
Chapter Five	1970–1993: 'Where the "shoe pinches"'	177
Chapter Six	1994–2022: 'One of the distinguishing signs of "Irishness"'	225
Endword by Martin O'Donnell		271
Notes		275
Bibliography		287
Index		295

Abbreviations

AIR	Association of Irish Racecourses
BBC	British Broadcasting Corporation
CIÉ	Córas Iompair Éireann
CRAC	Central Racing Advisory Committee
DIB	*Dictionary of Irish biography*
EADP	Equine Anti-Doping Programme
EBF	European Breeders' Fund
EEC	European Economic Community
GAA	Gaelic Athletic Association
GPR	Guinness Park Royal
GRAI	Gambling Regulatory Authority of Ireland
GSWR	Great Southern and Western Railway
IBA	Irish Bookmakers' Association
IBOTA	Irish Breeders', Owners' and Trainers' Association
IHA	Irish Horseracing Authority
IHRB	Irish Horseracing Regulatory Board
INBA	Irish National Bookmakers' Association
INHS	Irish National Hunt Steeplechase
INHSC	Irish National Hunt Steeplechase Committee
IPREA	Irish Provincial Racecourse Executives' Association
IRA	Irish Republican Army
IRTA	Irish Racehorse Trainers' Association
ITGWU	Irish Transport and General Workers' Union
ITM	Irish Thoroughbred Marketing
MGWR	Midland Great Western Railway
NAI	National Archives of Ireland

NLI	National Library of Ireland
NPA	National Photographic Archive
PRONI	Public Record Office of Northern Ireland
QRAF	Qualified Riders' Accident Fund
RACE	Racing Academy and Centre of Education
RDS	Royal Dublin Society
REAI	Racecourse Executives' Association of Ireland
RHA	Royal Horse Artillery
RMG	Racecourse Media Group
RTÉ	Raidió Teilifís Éireann
S.I.	Statutory Instrument
SIS	Sports Information Services
SP	Starting Price
TIB	Thoroughbred Industry Board
UIR	United Irish Racecourses

TOTE TOTE
TOTE
TOTE
TOTE CUSTOMER SERVICE
TOTE
CUSTOMER SERVICE

Acknowledgments

In early 2021, I met with then INHS Senior Steward Martin O'Donnell, who had the idea of publishing a history of the Irish National Hunt Steeplechase Committee, to mark the 150th anniversary of its foundation in 1869/70. As Martin observed, it was an opportune moment to reflect on the long life of the Committee, which has had a central role in the success of National Hunt and point-to-point racing in Ireland. Originally established as the sports' governing body, the Committee has endured across a century and a half of profound change; that is largely a result of the passion and endeavour of its members, who have voluntarily served to promote and improve the standard of jump racing across the island of Ireland. I am incredibly grateful to Martin and the INHS Committee for their unwavering support for the project. I am also hugely indebted to the staff at the IHRB offices on the Curragh, and particularly Ray Bergin, who went above and beyond to help me access relevant records, images and interviewees.

This book could not have been written without the help of people whose knowledge of horse racing far exceeds my own. I owe a massive debt to Victor Connolly of Burgage Stud, who has been so generous in sharing his time and expertise with me. By reading and providing feedback on drafts of this book, Victor helped me to create a more detailed and characterful history of jump racing. He also took the time to meet with members of significant racing families, to gather together many of the photographs that now bring the book to life. Thank you Victor, and thank you Liz, for the fantastic hospitality I received at Burgage.

I have the great fortune to count a legend of the sport, Mr W.A. (Bill) McLernon, as a family friend. I am forever indebted to Bill – one of the all-time great amateur riders, a hugely experienced racing official and an absolute gentleman – for sharing such colourful memories of his time in the saddle and his deep understanding of the sport. Bill also demonstrated typical generosity in providing me with many wonderful images and artefacts.

My sincere thanks to former INHS Registrar Sean Barry, who so kindly imparted his extensive knowledge of the administration of Irish racing, and shared warm memories of past colleagues and INHS Committee members. Thanks also to Leo Powell for his help and advice, and to Guy St John Williams, who has written more than anyone on the history of Irish horse racing, and who very kindly shared his expertise and the contents of his library with me. I have, of course, relied on the work of others to augment and contextualise my research – in particular, I must acknowledge the contributions of S.J. Watson and Fergus D'Arcy, whose books have helped me to navigate the often labyrinthine history of horse racing in Ireland.

I have been helped at every turn in writing this book, which is testament to the generosity of the wider racing community. Thank you to the Brabazon, Hogan, Molony, Flood and Walford families, for sharing many of the photographs and mementos that now enliven its pages. Thank you also to Mr Jack Anderson and Mrs Marian Cave, for providing images and artefacts relating to racing in Ulster, to David Patterson for supplying an image of the Manifesto board game, and to Stephen Doherty for sharing his incredible collection of race cards with me.

I have also received ready support from the management and staff at racecourses across the island. My sincere thanks to Peter Roe, Orla Aaron and Marie Burke at Fairyhouse Racecourse; Jane Hedley and the staff at Leopardstown Racecourse; Niamh Byrne at Naas Racecourse; Ruth Morrison at Downpatrick Racecourse and the staff at Down Royal Racecourse.

Anyone involved in horse racing knows that the recent history of the sport in Ireland (and beyond) has been brilliantly and comprehensively captured by the photography of Healy Racing, which was founded by Liam Healy in the 1970s, and which continues today under the stewardship of his son, Pat. Healys have been incredibly helpful in making their archive available to me during the course of this project and I cannot thank Pat and Cathy enough for providing such beautiful and evocative images.

As a historian, I am used to annoying archivists and librarians, and I had ample opportunity to do so in writing this book. As per usual, I was met with the highest levels of expertise and professionalism, and with good-humour and kindness. My sincere thanks to Barbara Bonini and Nora Thornton at the National Photographic Archive; Berni Metcalfe and Glenn Dunne at the National Library of Ireland; Éilis

Crowe at the Guinness Archive; Stephen Weir at National Museums NI; and Selina Collard at UCD Archives.

I am fortunate to be able to rely on the support and good counsel of my colleagues. I am enormously grateful to Professor Paul Rouse, a pioneer of sport history in Ireland and a champion of other scholars' work, who kindly recommended me to Martin and the INHS Committee. Thank you to Professor Ivar McGrath, Mark Duncan, Dr Emma Lyons, Dr Eoin Kinsella, Niall O'Leary and Professor Bernadette Whelan for their help and advice on different elements of the project. And my thanks to the team at Four Courts Press, who have been an absolute pleasure to work with.

Last but by no means least, thank you to my family and friends. This book is most relevant to my mam's family, the McCarthys, who have a longstanding and deep attachment to the sport of jump racing. I am hugely grateful to my aunt, Mary Dinneny, for sharing her knowledge and her memories of Fairyhouse and the racing 'scene' around Ratoath. Thanks, too, to my lovely uncle Tom. I am very lucky to have a brother who is passionate about horses and horse racing – thanks Thomas, for explaining many of the technical aspects of jump racing and for always giving me sound advice. And I am eternally grateful to my parents, Tom and Rosaleen, who have always encouraged me to follow my own path and who never stop cheering me on. Lastly, thank you Denise, for your support in this and in everything I do.

Interested spectators at the Meath Hunt Point-to-Point, c.1914.

Introduction

'There where the course is,
Delight makes all of the one mind'

National Hunt – the branch of horse racing that encompasses steeplechasing and hurdle races – holds a special place in the Irish imagination. Before the establishment of the GAA in the late nineteenth century, horse racing was regarded as Ireland's 'national sport' and steeplechasing proved especially popular, with the achievements of Irish chasers celebrated across the island, by rich and poor alike.[1] The first recorded steeplechase took place in County Cork in 1752, to satisfy a wager made by two huntsmen over dinner one evening at Buttevant Castle. The following day, Cornelius O'Callaghan and Edmund Blake met on horseback in the shadow of Saint John's Church in Buttevant and from there they raced each other four-and-a-half miles across country, clearing stone walls, hedges, streams and ditches, to reach Saint Mary's Church in the town of Doneraile. Run from steeple to steeple, or point to point, the result of the race is not known, but the winner's courage was rewarded with a cask of wine.[2]

In the two-and-a-half centuries since O'Callaghan and Blake raced along the banks of the River Awbeg, jump racing has transformed almost beyond recognition. The actions and impulses that have driven this evolution are numerous and complex. To tell the story of Irish National Hunt and point-to-point racing, it is vital to trace the pedigree of its older stablemate: Flat racing. And it is necessary to situate horse racing's development within Ireland's wider sporting tradition, which has been shaped across centuries and in many ways by '[t]he evolution of Irish society – its politics, its culture and its economy'.[3] That evolution was fundamentally directed by the English

The Meath Hunt Point-to-Point Races by Letitia Marion Hamilton, RHA (1878–1964). This is a study for a painting that won Hamilton a bronze medal in the art competition of the 1948 London Olympic Games. That was the last Games at which medals were awarded for art inspired by sport.

colonization of the island in the sixteenth and seventeenth centuries, by the rise of an Anglo-Irish ruling class in the eighteenth and nineteenth centuries, by Ireland's resultingly complex relationship with Britain and by its historic position within the British Empire.

Horse racing has been shaped more acutely than any other modern sport by the peculiarities of Ireland's past. The Anglo-Irish community's passion for horses was 'almost … esteemed a satire on common sense' and their imprint on equestrian sport is undeniable.[4] It was not for nothing that Brendan Behan, writing in the mid-twentieth century, would define an Anglo-Irishman as 'a Protestant with a horse'.[5] Their adventures in the saddle made Ireland the birthplace of the steeplechase, they were responsible for the codification of Irish horse racing through the establishment of the Turf Club in 1784 and the Irish National Hunt Steeplechase (INHS) Committee in 1869/70, and they poured as lifeblood into the hunt clubs that sprang up across the island from the late eighteenth century. They also worked to improve the quality of Irish bloodstock and ensured that Irish horses were exported to every corner of the British Empire, from India to Ceylon (now Sri Lanka) and Australia.

The Anglo-Irish elite reinforced their power through bonds of association and the attendant marginalization of Catholics, and this was reflected in the development of equestrian sport in Ireland. Despite legal, social and economic barriers to ownership and participation in the eighteenth and nineteenth centuries, however, Ireland's Catholic population demonstrated an enduring passion for horses and equestrian sport.[6] The involvement of wealthier Catholics in the top tier of racing and hunting was limited but it was not entirely prevented; indeed, in some cases it was facilitated by their Protestant neighbours and friends. For the Irish peasantry, meanwhile, horses retained a distinct historical and cultural resonance. They attached their own traditions and folklore to the animals, worked with them in different capacities, and viewed horse ownership as a desirable status symbol, even when it was financially unviable.[7]

It was a near-universal enthusiasm for horse racing that ensured its popular and commercial success from the mid-nineteenth century, when the expansion of the railways caused the number of Irish racecourses to increase rapidly. Rich and poor, young and old, Protestant and Catholic – all travelled to thrill at a sprint on the Flat, or to exalt in the frantic procession of a steeplechase. Many also gathered to drink, to dance and, if they could afford it, to gamble. Their shared passion for racing ensured its survival through a period of great economic and social change in the late

'Studying the form' at Punchestown in 1986.

(clockwise from top) A series of stamps produced by An Post in 2002, to commemorate the 300th anniversary of the first recorded steeplechase; the menu card (cover and interior) from a dinner held at the Gresham Hotel in Dublin on 7 April 1953, to celebrate Early Mist's Grand National success; race cards from the Galway Festival in the 1970s and 80s.

Winner of the 1958 Grand National, Mr What, being welcomed home by schoolchildren from Rathcoole, County Dublin, where he was trained by Tom Taaffe. A novice chaser who went to post at odds of 18/1, Mr What powered to a 30-length victory in heavy conditions – this was the longest winning margin in the race since 1893.

nineteenth and early twentieth century, as the power of the Anglo-Irish ebbed away and a new Catholic middle class emerged. In 1908, amid this slow revolution, W.B. Yeats sat down to write 'At Galway Races'. Lamenting Ireland's lost bardic tradition and the aristocratic society that made it possible through patronage, Yeats saw in horse racing what he so desired for the arts: a 'unity of culture'.[8] Summoning to mind the popular summer meeting at Ballybrit, he immortalized the irresistible power of sport and of horse racing specifically, writing that 'There where the course is/ Delight makes all of the one mind/ The riders upon the galloping horses/ The crowd that closes in behind.'[9]

Racing's broad appeal endured through the turbulent years of the First World War and Ireland's revolutionary decade and helped to ensure its continuation on an all-island basis after partition in 1921. That cross-border accommodation reflected another vital ingredient in horse racing's modern success: economic pragmatism. Since the foundation of the Free State in 1922, horse racing has benefitted from the support of successive Irish governments, who have recognized its importance as a shop window for the valuable bloodstock industry. It has also become a profitable industry

INTRODUCTION

in its own right, with the establishment of the Racing Board in 1945, the Irish Horseracing Authority in 1994 and Horse Racing Ireland in 2001, marking signal moments in the story of its commercial success.

Throughout the twentieth century and right up to the present day, both the sport and the industry have developed in innumerable and fascinating ways, by responding to moments of political and economic crisis and opportunity, adapting to significant social change, and embracing technological advancements. More importantly, on an island that has struggled to find common ground, horse racing has brought people together. And within Ireland's storied sporting tradition, jump racing has its own rich heritage. It is this branch of the sport – which is often looked upon as the 'poor relation' of Flat racing – that has most completely captured hearts across generations. On some of Ireland's darkest days, its people could look to racetracks at home and in England to find examples of Irish excellence. It is for this reason that Vincent O'Brien remains a towering figure in Irish sporting and cultural memory, and the exploits of horses like Arkle and Dawn Run are still recalled with giddy awe.

Born of the land, this gloriously uncertain sport is embedded in Ireland's history, culture and identity. From the shadow of a church's steeple in County Cork in 1752, to the dazzling spectacle of the island's modern racing festivals, the story of 'the jumps' is – at its core – the story of a people, a place and their horses.

Horses racing up the hill at Downpatrick, undated.

INTRODUCTION

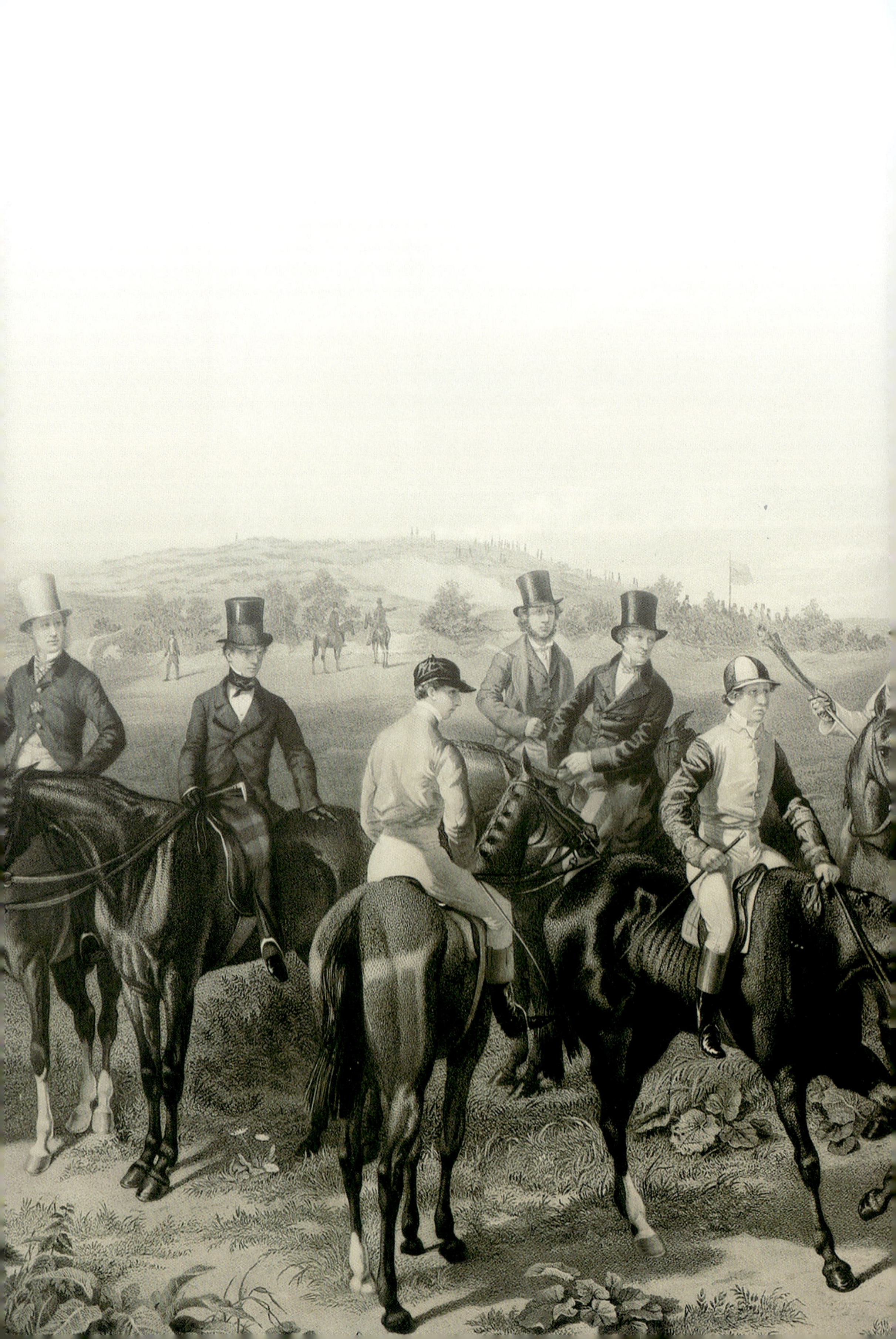

CHAPTER ONE

1752-1869

'This truly Irish sport'

THE HORSE RACES THROUGH every chapter of Ireland's history. From the Iron Age settlements at Newgrange through medieval Gaelic lordships, across centuries of plantation and settlement and into the modern era. In this long history, horses have served the Irish people as a means of transport and agricultural production, as symbols of wealth, status and power, and as companions on the fields of battle and sport.[1] Long before horse racing was formalized through English interventions in the seventeenth century, Irish people gathered in great numbers to watch as horses and riders charged across plains and strands in search of glory. It was through the English conquest of Ireland, however, that horse racing was first formalized on the island, and it was through the rise of the Anglo-Irish elite in the eighteenth century that the sport came to be codified. Racing's formal development in Ireland imitated Britain, where the growth of associational culture resulted in the foundation of the Jockey Club in 1750. This was followed, five years later, by the establishment of an Irish Jockey Club, and that body was succeeded in the 1780s by the Turf Club. At the same time that Flat racing developed in form and popularity, another branch of the sport began to emerge. The steeplechase, which was a high-tempo evolution of a more static jumping contest known as a 'pounding match', quickly captured the imagination of the Irish people. While British steeplechasing began to formalize in the first half of the nineteenth century, with the creation of man-made racecourses, in Ireland the sport was slower to develop. By the mid-nineteenth century, however, jump racing in Ireland began to modernize. This process was accelerated by the expansion of Ireland's rail network, which precipitated an explosion in the building of racecourses and provided horse racing with its first form of commercial sponsorship. The Turf Club initially took responsibility for the regulation of Irish National Hunt racing, with a distinct set of rules set down by Henry Francis Seymour Moore, third marquess of Drogheda, in the 1860s. And it was that reforming lord who acted to establish a separate governing body for jump racing, the Irish National Hunt Steeplechase Committee, in 1869. By doing so, he turned the page on the first chapter of jump racing's colourful history and began to write the second.

'Horses in Ireland are like a drug'

Sport is woven tightly into the fabric of any society and its evolution reveals much about the political, social and economic conditions of the past. Equestrian sports have a long history on the island of Ireland, with both hunting and horse racing enjoyed by the Gaelic Irish and by the Old English (Anglo-Norman) nobility who had achieved a partial colonization of the island in the twelfth century. The ubiquity of pattern (holy) days and fairs in Gaelic Ireland point to 'the antiquity of the tradition of horse racing' on the island. These 'great occasions of sociability [were] replete with music, dance, drink and play'.[2] This included sport and gambling, which were both well-established features of medieval Irish society.[3] It was in the seventeenth century, however, through the English plantation of Ireland, that the antecedent to modern horse racing was established. As New English Protestant settlers sought to assert control over Gaelic Irish and Old English Catholic communities, sport served as a powerful marker of ethnicity and identity and 'there was little agreement on what constituted acceptable sporting activity'. The New English regarded the favoured pursuits of the Gaelic Irish – like hurling – with suspicion, and the bear and bull baiting beloved of the Old English with unease, and instead pursued sports like tennis, bowling, archery, hunting and horse racing.[4] Race meetings of varying value and quality occurred across the island in the seventeenth century, with evidence of horses being raced on Carrickfergus Strand in County Antrim in 1622, at Bellewstown in County Meath in the 1630s, on Youghal Strand in County Cork in the 1650s and in Belfast in 1668.[5]

It was the Curragh in County Kildare, however, that 'emerged early as the country's premier racecourse because it appealed to the leaders of government and society'.[6] In 1634, Baron Digby and the earl of Ormond raced their horses over four miles across the plains there, having laid a wager on the result.[7] While horse racing – and the gambling that accompanied it – proved popular with the elite in Ireland, it was first formalized in England, with the Restoration of Charles II in 1660 precipitating the development of a racecourse at Newmarket.[8] Racing in Ireland only began to formalize in the 1670s, when Sir William Temple, a former MP for Carlow, introduced a scheme to address a lack of quality horses across the island. Observing that 'Horses in Ireland are like a drug', Temple conceived of a scheme to encourage breeding and the development of a domestic and export trade in both working and pedigree horses. He proposed the organization of a week-long horse fair and race meeting at the Curragh, the success of which would be guaranteed by the daily attendance of the Lord Lieutenant or his deputy.[9] Temple's overall plan was too ambitious, but his suggestion that the Irish Exchequer should endow a series of plate races to encourage the breeding of high-quality horses did bear fruit, as Charles II agreed to provide £100 for the purchase of a King's Plate, which was to be run for annually at the Curragh.[10] In 1685, James II extended the royal patronage of racing to Ulster, when he issued a patent for races to the Down Royal Corporation of Horse Breeders, and a three mile horseshoe course was laid out one mile south of the town of Downpatrick. Five years later, while at war with James in Ireland, William III granted the Down Royal meeting £100 annually for a King's Plate.[11] It was on the hills of Downpatrick that a race was won by the Byerley Turk, one of the foundation sires of the modern thoroughbred, who had travelled to Ireland with his owner, to fight for William.[12]

'a great diversion in the country'

While racing began to develop in Ireland in the 1670s and 80s, it was after William III's defeat of James II in 1691 that Anglo-Irish identity coalesced and the ruling elite fully 'aspired to pursue English games', which were '[c]onsistent with their geographical and ethnic origins, and their sense of themselves as English, albeit the English of Ireland'. Equestrian sports – which were rooted in the land – ranked first among these 'English' pursuits and formed the basis of Anglo-Irish sporting identity, which in turn reinforced political, social and economic hierarchies.[13] The importance of the horse in this divided society was underlined by the introduction of a penal law in 1695, permitting the requisition of Catholic-owned horses worth £5 or more. This security measure was designed to prevent a meaningful military threat to the State but, contrary to belief, it did not allow Protestants 'to purchase any horse they might fancy in Catholic ownership for £5'. It did, however, serve to discourage Catholics from maintaining good quality horses.[14] Evidence suggests that some members of the surviving Catholic gentry colluded with Protestant friends and neighbours to hold onto high quality bloodstock in the eighteenth century. In one instance, the Catholic owner of 'one of the most celebrated racers in Ireland' prevented the seizure of the horse by presenting him to a Protestant friend.[15]

Economic realities and the limiting impact of the penal laws meant that Catholics typically raced inferior horses for smaller purses or non-cash prizes. In 1712, at a time when the penal laws were being strictly enforced, a notice was given that 'at Garriston in the County of Dublin, will be a fair the 16th of August next, Custom Free, here a saddle and bridle is to be run for; no horse to be above 5 pound price. A mantua is to be run for by women, all free.'[16] Before 1760, the prize money for races held in Dublin and beyond rarely reached £20, compared to stakes of between 60 and 100 guineas at the Curragh. The popularity and proliferation of low-value race meetings prompted concerns among the Irish government over the moral corruption of the peasantry, particularly in respect of gambling. While the elite enthusiastically laid wagers on horse races and other sporting contests, they did not tolerate the same behaviour from working people. A 1739 Act for the more Effectual Preventing of Excessive and Deceitful Gaming included a clause prohibiting low-value races, which were believed to encourage 'idleness and debauchery among … farmers, artificers and day-labourers … to the frequent ruin of their families'.[17] The legislation had little effect, however, as low-value race meetings continued to be organized. This included a highly popular meeting at Crumlin, which drew large crowds of working people from Dublin city and which was derided in the *Freeman's Journal* as occasioning 'the idleness of the lower orders of the working manufacturers, the calling of industrious artificers from their occupations, to attend where dissipation, club law and tumult only exist'.[18]

The Irish peasantry enjoyed the entertainments that accompanied race meetings, including gambling and drinking, but their love of horse racing was also deeply rooted in custom and tradition. Ireland's folklore is replete with stories of horses and

'The Byerley Turk, held by a Syrian Groom', attributed to Thomas Spencer (active c.1730–c.1763). The Byerley Turk was one of three Arabian stallions brought to England in the late seventeenth and early eighteenth centuries that would become one of the foundation sires of the modern thoroughbred racehorse.

the Irish people's deep connection to them.[19] This includes the tale of James Sullivan from County Cork, who worked as a horse-breaker in the late eighteenth century and was described as 'an ignorant awkward rustic of the lowest class'. Sullivan reportedly earned 'the singular epithet of Whisperer by an extraordinary art of controlling in a secret manner and taming into the most submissive and tractable disposition, any horse or mare that was notoriously vicious and obstinate.'[20] The cultural attachment of the Irish people to horse racing, meanwhile, is found in the story of Irish Lass, who became widely known as the 'Podareen Mare' after a well-wisher hung Rosary beads (*paidrín*) around her neck ahead of her success in a match against Othello – a horse popularly referred to as 'Black and all Black' – in 1760. This 'incident seized on popular fancy, and grew in the imagination until Black and all Black came to be regarded as the Arch-fiend himself; for even Satan could not be painted blacker than the horse was. The victory of Irish Lass was ascribed to the efficacy of the Rosary Beads.'[21]

Horse racing was slow to develop in Ireland in the first years of the eighteenth century, in part because it lacked sufficient royal patronage, but by 1731 it had 'become a great diversion in the country'.[22] It only grew in popularity thereafter, with the number of meetings rising from the mid-teens prior to 1730 to 95 by 1760. This increase indicated the transformation of the sport 'from a regional to a national activity', with meetings held regularly and in every corner of the island.[23] Racing's expansion in this period was driven largely by a growth in the circulation of newspapers, with race organizers frequently publishing details of meetings and accompanying diversions, like hunting and cockfighting. Race meetings often ran over several days and coincided with local fairs or pattern days; this allowed working people to attend, although different social groups were kept apart. While eighteenth-century racing was an overwhelmingly male pursuit, women were increasingly encouraged to attend race meetings by the promise of attractive entertainments, with notices advertising balls, as well as 'plays and assemblies for the diversions of ladies every night'. With a resulting demand for accommodation and places to dine, innkeepers and tavern owners often acted as patrons of local meetings, alongside members of the gentry.[24]

Horse racing was popular at every level of Irish society, but the formal development of the sport was dictated by the Anglo-Irish elite. They were guided fundamentally in their actions by developments in Britain, where the rise of associational culture led to the formation of countless clubs and societies and helped to make sport the province of wealthy men.[25] Associational culture was slower to emerge in Ireland, where the political, economic and social environment was less conducive, but clubs and societies nevertheless emerged from the early eighteenth century and reflected a broad range of interests, including sport and (relatedly) gambling. This was a significant development, as it augmented the authority of the Anglo-Irish elite and rooted them within the much broader cultural context of empire. From the mid-eighteenth century and especially from the 1770s, hunt clubs were the most visible expression of association through sport, but horse racing was similarly exclusive.[26] The foundation of the Jockey Club in England in 1750 provided an obvious template for the Anglo-Irish lords of the turf and so it was, on St Patrick's Day in 1755, that an Irish Jockey Club sat down to dinner at the Rose and Bottle tavern on Dame Street, Dublin.[27]

Led by Tom Conolly of Castletown House, the body established the Curragh Coffee House as a hub for racing in the 1760s. From there, it organized racing on the

Kildare course and shaped the sport in fundamental ways – this included the vesting of authority in three Stewards and the appointment of the first Keeper of the Match Book. The Irish Jockey Club also agreed and published a code of regulations, which outlined the administrative, adjudicatory and disciplinary powers of the Stewards. This was a significant development in the regulation of racing in Ireland but the body was defunct by the early 1780s, so it is not clear to what extent it was able or willing to enforce its code. It was replaced by the Turf Club, which, like its predecessor, was formed from a small community bound 'by bonds of marriage, friendship, political connections and shared military service'.[28] The Turf Club was established in 1784 but it failed to thrive until 1790, when Patrick Sharkey established the *Racing Calendar*. The *Calendar* met with the approval of the Turf Club from the outset, as it allowed the Stewards to reach a broad audience and to promote the Club as the foremost racing authority on the island. The Turf Club did not produce a unified code of racing in Ireland overnight, but by using the *Calendar* to provide advice to those who sought it out, the Stewards amassed 'a certain gravitas and informal authority' over time.[29]

'in the effort to "pound" an opponent the most dreadful obstacles were attempted'

While the Turf Club presided increasingly over the regulation of racing on the flat, jump racing began to develop in form and popularity. The steeplechase negotiated by Blake and O'Callaghan in 1752 was not a wholly new invention, but a variation on the 'pounding match' – a slow-moving contest between two riders, who took turns selecting obstacles for their horses to jump, until one or the other had been 'pounded' to exhaustion. The elite's enthusiasm for gambling meant that significant amounts of money were often waged on these matches and 'in the effort to "pound" an opponent the most dreadful obstacles were attempted'.[30] The pounding match endured throughout the eighteenth century, but the thrill of racing over jumps to an agreed finish line proved increasingly popular. It would take time for steeplechases to be incorporated into race meetings, however, with jumping contests first used as a means of qualifying for Flat races. In Derry in 1775, for example, a hunters' race worth £50 was staged in three heat races of four miles and, to qualify, horses had to appear four days before the race and 'leap back and forward over a wall made from stone and lime, 4ft 2ins high and 9ins broad at the top, and also over a drain 10ft wide, carrying 12st, before judges that were appointed'.[31] Fifteen years later, fences were included in a race for the first time. At a meeting in Roscommon in April 1790, a 'drag chase of 5 miles across country over many high leaps' took place. This was followed by other races over other courses, which typically required hunters to jump walls and ditches in the first heat.

A meeting at Kilcock, County Kildare, in August 1790, advertised a prize of £30 'for hunters that have been fairly rode last season to the death of two brace of foxes or three brace of hares, to be rode by gentlemen'. This race represented an important development in handicapping – a system that enabled horses of different ability to race against each other through the allocation of weights. The organisers of the meeting at Kilcock considered horses' historic performance alongside the better-established weight-for-age scale, and it was stipulated that 'Any horse ... that has ever won £50 or upwards [was] to carry 10lbs more than any other horse (matches excepted)'. Four-year-olds, meanwhile, were limited to 12st, five-year-olds to 13st, six-year-olds to 13st 7lbs and aged horses to 14st. The innovation was not wholly successful, as it was asserted that the winner, Mad Tom, 'did not carry sufficient weight as required by the Articles for a former winner, which is to be determined by the Turf Club'. As a result, the first ever dispute adjudicated on by the Turf Club concerned a jump race. In September 1790, the Stewards convened and found in favour of Mad Tom.[32] It was also in the first decades of the nineteenth century that the Turf Club's authority across the island was augmented. Members had not actively sought to impose their authority beyond The Curragh, but their influence grew over time, as more and more race organizers looked to the Stewards to fix the weights for meetings, to give their approval on the standard of racecourses, and to adjudicate in any disputes that arose.[33] Thus, within two decades of the Turf Club's formation, 'a code of conduct was securing assent throughout the land and a court of appeal was being resorted to more frequently'. This circumstance endured until the 1850s, when the Turf Club began to revise and expand on the *Rules of Racing* – a general code of conduct for racing in Britain and Ireland. By so doing, the Stewards 'moved from being a mere influence, to possessing a positive power over racing folk beyond The Curragh'.[34]

The eighteenth century ended in violent upheaval, with the outbreak of the French Revolution in 1789. In Ireland, the growth of republicanism and the prospect

Horses and riders showing four different leaps in a steeplechase. Lithograph.

of popular unrest alarmed the British administration. In 1790, fears of disturbances led to the cancellation of the race meeting at Crumlin, with cavalry and infantry sent in to disperse the assembled crowd. One year later, an Act to Prohibit Horse Races in the Neighbourhood of the City of Dublin was introduced by the Irish Parliament.[35] The underlying tensions in Irish society erupted into a rebellion against British rule in 1798. That uprising caused racing to be put aside across the island, as horses were drafted from racecourse to cavalry regiment. Only three meetings were recorded in

Pencil sketch of a steeplechaser by James Henry Brocas, created between c.1810 and 1846.

the Irish *Racing Calendar* for 1798 and the sport was resumed with some caution. In June 1799, Wills Hill, first marquess of Downshire, informed Robert Stewart, Viscount Castlereagh, who was then the Chief Secretary of Ireland, that the Down Royal Corporation of Horse Breeders would hold two meetings at Downpatrick that year, but expressed concern that 'a drop of whiskey may revive the ideas of Yeomen and Orangemen, and Union Irishmen and Papists, when racing is over'.[36]

The 1798 Rebellion led to the passage of the Act of Union, which abolished the Irish Parliament and brought Ireland under the legislative control of Westminster from 1801. Union would have profound consequences for Ireland, not least because it encouraged absenteeism among Anglo-Irish landlords, many of whom were MPs in the Westminster Parliament. Difficult political conditions did not hinder horse racing in Ireland for long though, and the sport flourished again in the early nineteenth century. This was partly due to the Napoleonic Wars, which buoyed the Irish economy by increasing demand for the export of Irish goods, including horses.[37] Between 1805 and 1811, the Irish *Racing Calendar*'s subscriptions exploded, rising from 438 to 1,659.[38] This was good news for the *Calendar*'s new owner, Robert Hunter, who also served as joint Keeper of the Match Book (with a Mr Dease) between 1811 and 1817, before his son J.R. Hunter assumed the role. It was in this period that the term 'steeplechase' came into common usage, with the Irish *Racing Calendar* reporting on a six-mile 'steeplechase' that was run across country from Ballybrophy in Queen's County in 1807.[39] War with France also had an impact on membership of the Turf Club, which had been slow to increase since 1790. The Club's ranks began to swell in 1805, at the same time that a military encampment was established at the Curragh in response to the threat of French invasion.[40] That threat aroused significant fear and suspicion among the ruling elite and in 1807, spies were deployed to the Curragh to report on a game of hurling played by 'exercising boys belonging to the gentlemen of the Turf'.[41]

'the peasantry assemble in crowds, and generally have a favourite into whose cause they enter heart and hand'

The end of the Napoleonic Wars in 1815 was followed by a prolonged period of economic depression across Europe. This exposed many of the flaws in Irish society, not least the enormous gulf between rich and poor.[42] The Irish population had exploded between 1791 and 1821, and the demand for land meant that rents stayed high as the economy stagnated. Landowners pursued rent arrears more doggedly and cleared tenants from their estates if they were unable to pay.[43] At the same time, a succession of bad harvests in the 1810s and 20s hit the Irish poor hard, with the failure of the potato crop resulting in a famine in the West of Ireland in 1822.[44] The economic downturn was felt in a different way in Dublin, as the aristocracy and gentry abandoned their great Georgian houses, and the city fell into decline. Racing did not escape the general trend: membership of the Turf Club fell from 34 to 24 between 1819 and 1824, while subscriptions to the Irish *Racing Calendar* tumbled from 1,166 in 1815 to 381 just ten years later.[45] By 1840, fewer people subscribed to the *Calendar* than had in 1791, one year after it was first issued.[46]

STALLION.

THAT SUPERIOR HORSE

YOUNG ARTHUR,

EIGHT YEARS OLD,

THE PIOPERTY OF

THE HON. CHARLES W. MOORE,

Will stand this Season at Springmount, Templemichael, and Youghal, on Saturdays, within 4 miles of Youghal, 6 of Tallow, and 9 of Lismore.

At the low price of £1 Farmers Mares, and 2s. 6d. to the Groom.

Young Arthur is a beautiful Bay, stands 15 hands 3 inches high, a perfect beauty, good symmetry, bone and sinew, that defies competition. He is the strongest Horse of his breeding in Ireland. His Sire Arthur, his grand-sire Hercules, out of Whalebone, out of Peri, by Wanderer, the sire of Carnation, the winner of the Derby in 1841, and Discount the winner of the great Liverpool National and the Worchester Steeple Chase, this year, and Brunnette the best Steeple Chase Horse in Ireland, Birdcatcher, Maria Longford, Cruiskeen, Hillus, Corsair, and many other first-rate Horses, in England and Ireland. Arthur's Dam was Angelica, by Sir Harry Dimsdale, out of Lady Gray, by Stamford,—sister to Viscount the best Horse of his year in England. Angelica, was purchased from King George the Fourth, out of the Hampton Court Stud, as a Brood Mare, for the sum of £500.

Young Arthur's Dam was got by Black Lock the sire of four winners of the Great Anglesea Stakes, his grand-dam the celebrated Kitten, the winner of four of His Majesty's Plates ; also, the dam of the Speedy, White-foot, Blackfoot and Magpie, by the Sligo Waxy, grand-dam Eclipse mare, great-grand-dam own sister to the Juniper, by Snap who covered at 50 guineas a mare, being on an equality as a Race-Horse, if not superior to any Horse of his time.

Arthur's performance as a Racer has been first-rate, having won 22 Races, including 3 Queens Plates in Ireland and one in England, one Hurdle Race, (the only one he started for) beating the best Horses in England, ran second for the Great Liverpool National Steeple Chase in 1840, and was only beaten by a length after meeting with an accident that lost him more than 500 yards. Groom's Fees to be paid at first service.

Ballynatray, May, 1855.

R. F. Lindsay, Printer, "Old Youghal Press."

Broadside dating from May 1855, advertising that the stallion Young Arthur was to stand for the season at various locations in County Cork. The horse boasted a strong pedigree: his grandsire, the compact Sir Hercules, was the son of one of the most influential sires in history, the Derby-winning Whalebone. Sir Hercules also had an impressive career at stud, producing the two-time leading British sire, Birdcatcher; the Derby-winning Coronation; the first Irish-bred St Ledger winner, Faugh-a-Ballagh; and the Grand National-winning Discount. Young Arthur's own sire – a diminutive grey named Arthur – finished second by a length in the 1840 Grand National.

In England, meanwhile, the commercial appeal of jump racing meant that its formal organization had become a necessity by the 1830s. The Grand Annual Steeplechase was run for the first time in 1834, around Andoversford, near Cheltenham. Two years later, the Grand Liverpool Steeplechase – subsequently known as the Grand National – began at Aintree in an unofficial capacity, before being officially recognized in 1839. The Irish preoccupation with steeplechasing was evidenced by the participation of Irish-bred and Irish-trained horses in the Grand National from its first running. The County Cork-bred Mathew, who was trained by John Murphy on the Curragh, became the first Irish winner of the official race in 1847. This achievement was bettered by the 'pintsized' Abd-El-Kader, who stood around fifteen hands high and became the first horse to win back-to-back Grand Nationals in 1850 and 1851. Nicknamed 'Little Ab', he was bred by Henry Osborne of Dardistown Castle in County Meath, out of a brown mare that had been bought out of service on the Shrewsbury Mail Coach.[47] While Irish horses competed in England, man-made courses were not enthusiastically embraced in Ireland, where the unpredictability of natural courses was still celebrated as a chief thrill of the steeplechase. There was also little impetus to develop the sport commercially in the first half of the nineteenth century. Participation remained largely the province of the Anglo-Irish hunting community, who owned and bred high-quality horses, organized meetings and matches, set the rules and lay sizeable wagers on the outcome of their personal sport. They did not race to entertain the Irish peasantry and considered it more important to stop crowds from interfering with a race than to encourage them to watch it.[48]

Ireland's economic conditions had a direct impact on the development of horse racing in the nineteenth century. While Britain's rapid industrialization created a working class capable of paying to be entertained, Ireland was home to a large rural peasant class who did not have the money to spend on entertainment and leisure activities. In order to bet, the Irish poor would 'first have to beg', but this did not dampen their enthusiasm for the sport.[49] In 1833, a correspondent for *The Sporting Magazine* remarked of Irish steeplechases that

> the peasantry assemble in crowds, and generally have a favourite into whose cause they enter heart and hand. Riding a steeple-chase is [in England] considered to be a sufficiently dangerous thing … but here a man has to run the gauntlet at the risk of martyrdom – to put himself in the way of becoming a second St Stephen or, in plain language, being stoned to death. These self-elected and active partisans stick at nothing, and are no respecters of person.[50]

Before the Great Famine, horse racing was regarded as 'Ireland's "national sport"',[51] and steeplechasing was a significant draw. By the late 1830s, the *Racing Calendar* regularly advertised steeplechases, which continued to be run in the traditional fashion, in heat races and over natural courses. While Irish steeplechasing continued on a more informal path than its English counterpart, it nonetheless required regulation in the nineteenth century, not least in respect of handicapping. As well as a growing jurisdiction over the flat, the Turf Club 'assumed *de facto* responsibility for such steeplechasing as took place at race meetings' with both branches 'equally covered by its rules and orders'.[52]

'the horses will gallop all the faster with the blessing of the poor'

Those who attended race meetings in the nineteenth century were not always focused on the course. An account of a meeting in Kilkenny in 1844 shines a light on the pageantry found at meetings across the island, even as Ireland stood on the brink of disaster. As well as observing the throngs of spectators on the field, in stands and in 'a crowded city of carriages', the German travel-writer Johann Georg Kohl wrote about the myriad entertainments that sprang up 'a short distance from the course, behind a hill'. There,

> a city of tents was erected, where every earthly desire an Irishman could form might be gratified. These tents were all long and large, and all constructed

in the same manner – an alehouse in front, a large room with benches and tables behind, and in the middle a dancing-floor. This dancing-floor generally consisted of a door, or planks fastened together like a door, and placed over a hole in the ground so as to render it more elastic under the feet of the dancers, who were usually four in number, and jumped about to their heart's content.

The gaiety of the scene described by Kohl was undercut by the visible poverty of the Irish peasantry, who gathered around Kilkenny 'all clad in the strangest costume of rags and tatters, all waving their printed ballads in the air. Some of them were literally misery personified: hunger and want were too evident on their haggard features, and care and anxiety sat in their sunken eyes'.[53]

One year after Kohl visited Kilkenny, in the autumn of 1845, potato blight was first discovered in Irish fields. The country had experienced episodes of famine before, but the scale of mortality and displacement caused by the Great Famine was unprecedented. The population had increased significantly from the latter half of the eighteenth century and reached a peak of 8.5 million by the mid-1840s. A large peasant class survived on poor, densely populated and increasingly over-cultivated land and relied heavily on the potato for nourishment. The failure of the potato crop in successive years was calamitous, particularly in the west and south of Ireland, and matters were made worse by the inconsistent and ineffectual policies of the British government. The responsibility for providing relief fell increasingly on Irish landlords, some of whom refused to help, while others were unable to meet the demands placed upon them. There were those who worked to alleviate distress and preserve the lives of their tenants, however, including the well-known horse breeder and trainer, George Henry Moore, whose family estate was in County Mayo, one of the worst-affected counties in Ireland. Moore – whose brother Augustus died after a fall in the 1845 Grand National – laid a wager on his horse Coranna in the Chester Cup in May 1846 and used some of his £17,000 winnings to help his Irish tenants. Writing to his mother Louisa, he explained that 'No tenant of mine shall want for plenty of everything this year, and though I shall expect work in return for hire, I shall take care that whatever work is done shall be for the exclusive benefit of the people themselves.' Moore also disclosed his intention to give £500 'in mere charity' to the poorest of his tenants, being sure that 'it will be well expended, and the horses will gallop all the faster with the blessing of the poor'.[54]

It was in this sad chapter of Irish history that steeplechasing made significant strides toward becoming a codified and commercial sport in Ireland. While the number of meetings declined during the Famine, racing continued across much of the Irish countryside. Attendance at meetings regularly reached into the thousands, with steeplechases proving 'especially attractive to racegoers'.[55] The attraction of the sport was laid out in the *Kerry Examiner*, on 23 April 1846:

> A steeple chase is a grand essay of human skill and courage – it is a break-neck attempt to ride over every barrier that comes in the way, without calculating difficulties, or pausing about danger… there must be … no flunking, no scheming out of the way, no jack-a-dandy riding – all is honest and above board. We would, however, advise every steeple-chaser to make his will, if he don't think proper to make his soul, before he takes the field.[56]

Some of the meetings organized in this period provided the foundation for the most famous meetings on today's steeplechase calendar. In 1843, the Ward Union Hunt advertised a 'Grand National Steeple Chase' at Ashbourne, County Meath, although the name at this point referred to two races – the Hunt Race and the Kilrue Cup. By 1851, the Hunt had moved their race meeting to a new course at Fairyhouse, which lay just outside the village of Ratoath.[57]

A watercolour sketch of a meeting at the Maze (Down Royal) Racecourse in County Down, dated 1852. *Maze* (1852) by James Moore, MD, 1819–83.

Elsewhere, Punchestown was first mentioned in the *Racing Calendar* as the venue for the Kildare Hunt Club's annual steeplechase in 1850, although the race had been organized by the Hunt Club since 1837.[58] The first meeting at Punchestown did not augur well, with the *Leinster Express* reporting that the morning of 1 April 'broke hazy and threatening and caused an exceedingly thin attendance from Dublin, the assemblage at Punchestown being chiefly composed of persons from the surrounding neighbourhood'. The Dublin crowds were right to stay away, because '[a]s the day advanced the wind and rain increased in violence, and the sports, which did not commence 'till a quarter past two o'clock, were carried on amid a perfect hurricane'. The facilities provided were also met with little enthusiasm, as '[t]here was no Stand House, the view of the running was limited, and the course very badly kept'.[59]

'a mighty multitude ... filled the fields of Punchestown'

The less-than-ideal conditions encountered at Punchestown in 1850 did not prevent the future success of the meeting. By 1854, Punchestown had become a two-day event, a development immortalized in a watercolour titled 'The Corinthian Cup', by Michael Angelo Hayes. Hayes' painting is a 'who's who' of Irish steeplechasing in the mid-nineteenth century and includes three noblemen who were founding members of the Irish National Hunt Steeplechase Committee in 1869/70 – Lords Drogheda, St Lawrence and Conyngham.[60] Working with the civil engineer Thomas G. Waters, both Drogheda and Viscount St Lawrence (who was heir to the earldom of Howth) were instrumental to the development of Punchestown from 1861, overseeing the construction of enclosures, stands and facilities, and the expansion of the race programme. The festival at the Kildare course quickly became a glittering social spectacle, attracting members of the nobility and gentry, as well as throngs of spectators from the lower rungs of the social ladder. The Kildare Hunt Ball was first held in 1867 and was an immediate success, with over 350 guests making merry in a 'spacious ballroom, hung in pink and white' and dancing 'until an advanced hour of the morning'.[61] Punchestown's place on the Irish social calendar was confirmed in 1868, with the visit of the Prince of Wales to the April meeting. The heir to the throne attended against the wishes of his mother, Queen Victoria, who believed that the excursion would only strengthen the belief – 'already far too prevalent' – that her son's

The Race for the Corinthian Cup, 1854. This engraving by William Henry Simmons is after a painting by Michael Angelo Hayes, RHA (1820–77). It depicts a number of the leading figures in National Hunt racing in nineteenth-century Ireland, including Lords Drogheda, St Lawrence, Waterford, Howth and Conyngham.

'chief object is amusement'. She further cautioned that 'races have become so bad of late, and the connection with them has ruined so many young men, and broken the hearts thereby of so many fond and kind parents, that I am especially anxious that you should not sanction or encourage them'.[62]

In response, the Prince insisted that he did not attend for his own personal pleasure, 'but as a duty'. He also noted that Lords Mayo and Abercorn were anxious for him to attend because 'such a large concourse of people would be gathered together from all parts of the country, who look upon those Races as a kind of annual national festival, and would have better opportunity of seeing me there than in Dublin, and give them an occasion to display their loyalty to you and our family, if (as it is to be hoped) such a feeling exists'.[63] In the end, the Prince and Princess travelled to the Kildare course on 16 and 17 April and were met by an estimated crowd of 150,000 on the first day.[64] It was reported that a 'mighty multitude … filled the fields of Punchestown and thronged round every break-neck jump, and swarmed to the top-most branch of every tree, and packed the Grand Stand, tier on tier, with a black phalanx of male spectators, and spread beside it a flood of light and colour on the ladies' stand'. Even with such a crowd in attendance, Punchestown – like other racecourses developed in the late nineteenth century – was a largely segregated public space.

Beyond the grandeur of the stands, farmers ate picnics with their families in the fields, while the poor were occupied with music and dancing in tents erected out of sight. There was an 'unusually large number of card-sharpers, roulette players and the like on the ground', but they struggled to find business from any segment of the assembled crowd.[65] While reports often describe the enjoyments offered by race meetings, the sudden growth of horse racing as a spectator sport in the mid-nineteenth century was not without incident. The convergence of crowds and the consumption of alcohol gave rise to crime, including violence and theft, and reports of trouble at race meetings appeared in the press with some regularity in the 1850s and 60s. Hooliganism was not unheard of and the results could be fatal,

Grand National Steeplechase at Cork Park Racecourse. From the *Illustrated London News*, 29 May 1869.

CHAPTER ONE: 1752–1869

Advertisement for a Great Northern Railway's Special Train from Drogheda to Portmarnock, servicing the Dublin Metropolitan Meeting at Baldoyle, 26 May 1885.

as at the Howth and Baldoyle Races in the 1850s, when a young man was killed by a gang while trying to protect his father from attack. Crowd trouble contributed to Baldoyle's closure in 1861 and – tellingly – the sale of spirits in racecourse tents was banned when the course was reopened by William, Viscount St Lawrence in 1865. The terrible apex of crowd disorder came at Limerick in 1867, however, when on the second day of the meeting, excessive drunkenness resulted in 'scenes of so revolting a character', which culminated in the murder of a child by their father. The owner of the land used for the Newcastle racecourse was so disgusted by what had occurred that he refused to allow racing to take place there again and the organizers were forced to look for a new location.[66]

Punchestown's place at the centre of the Irish sporting and social calendar demonstrated the growing popularity of steeplechasing. It also evidenced the importance of Ireland's growing transport network to the commercialization of horse racing. An *Irish Times* report on the royal visit described the crowded scene at Sallins station at the end of the first day's racing as 'grand, exciting, almost terrible'.[67] Improvements in the rail network from the mid-nineteenth century allowed horses – and more importantly, *good* horses – to travel further to compete, and made meetings across the country more accessible to the public. A 'sudden growth' in railway building began in 1843, with lines reaching Carlow by 1846, Thurles and Limerick Junction by 1848, and Mallow, Cork and Dundalk one year later. The 1850s brought the 'Iron Horse' to Galway, Killarney and directly to Belfast, while a decade later, Roscommon, Claremorris and Sligo had been connected to the network. This represented an exciting opportunity for Irish racing, and before long 'the roll-call of railway stations was like a roll-call of contemporary racecourses'. The commercial relationship between racing and the railways developed further in subsequent decades, as rail companies began sponsoring races. The first instance of such sponsorship came in June 1844, when the Dublin and Drogheda Railway Company contributed 25 sovereigns to a sovereign handicap sweepstakes run at Bellewstown. The railway companies clearly understood the commercial potential of racing and such contributions grew in frequency and amount in the years that followed. Alongside Waterford and Limerick rail companies, the Midland Great Western Railway (MGWR) had a policy of allowing horses to travel for free to race meetings. However, the Great Southern and Western Railway (GSWR), which was the most significant financial contributor to race meetings in

Ireland, was slow to adopt a similar policy.[68] One contributor to the *Irish Sportsman and Farmer* – who was disgruntled by the company's insistence on charging members of the press to travel to race meetings – argued that the GSWR should provide free transport to horses, noting that

> Race-meetings can't be got up without horses; if horses won't come in sufficient numbers, neither will sightseers. The latter means excursionists, travellers, who, without the attraction of horse-racing, had remained at home, thus depriving the company of a large amount of accidental income. To be generous is, in such cases, to be prudent.[69]

The GSWR were eventually persuaded to provide free passage for racehorses from 1874.[70]

'some reformation is sadly needed at many of the steeplechase meetings, now so very numerous in Ireland'

The codification of jump racing in Britain in the nineteenth century was reflective of a wider trend for regulating sport. Developments in steeplechasing there had a clear impact on Ireland, as the top tier of the racing fraternity was tightly bound, not just by their love of steeplechasing, but by familial ties, and a shared identity and status, which were galvanized by bonds of association. While the Turf Club was entirely independent of the Jockey Club, in some cases the Irish body referred cases to its British counterpart. Irish owners, breeders, trainers and riders were common features of the racing scene in England, in particular, and concerned themselves with the development of the sport there. This was evidenced by the success of Irish horses in some major English races, but it was also made apparent by the esteem in which prominent members of the Irish racing community were held. In 1845, printer Henry Wright published the first ever *Steeple Chase Calendar* in London, dedicating it to Henry de la Poer Beresford, third marquess of Waterford, a keen horseman who had won numerous steeplechases in Ireland and England, before his death in a hunting accident in 1859. Wright's *Calendar* was a landmark publication, providing the first advisory list of rules for steeplechasing. While this was a positive development,

British steeplechasing faced challenges that were not evident in the Irish context. This was tied to the rapid commercialization of the sport there in the nineteenth century. The ability of the British working class to spend money caused a rise in the popularity of gambling, and by the mid-century concerns were raised over a decline in the standard of both Flat and steeplechase meetings.[71] While the Jockey Club undertook a sustained and successful effort to restore the reputation of Flat racing, no such effort was made with steeplechasing, with the effect that it remained 'the refuge of all outcasts, human and equine, from the legitimate turf'.[72]

Further attempts to establish a set of rules to regulate British steeplechasing were followed, in 1863, by the foundation of the Grand National Hunt Steeplechase Committee. Two years later, the Jockey Club assented to the establishment of the National Hunt Committee. The same impetus for the regulation of steeplechasing did not exist in Ireland, where widespread poverty prevented the same scale of malpractice from developing. Until the late 1860s, the principal Irish steeplechases were supervised by the Turf Club Stewards, with smaller provincial meetings overseen by local officials. This circumstance might have endured beyond 1869, but the Victorian impulse for regulation was not easily ignored and, in the history of Irish racing, Lord Drogheda stands as a regulator without equal. Lord Drogheda left an indelible imprint on the development of Irish Flat racing, but his contribution to Irish National Hunt racing was fundamental and unparalleled. He was the driving force behind its modernization in the 1860s, through his efforts to develop Punchestown and the codification of the sport. Influenced by developments in Britain, he first drafted a set of rules for steeplechasing in Ireland in 1862–3. He elaborated on this effort in 1867, when he prepared and had printed copies of the Irish National Hunt and Steeplechase Rules. He sent these to R.J. Hunter, then Keeper of the Match Book and owner of the *Racing Calendar*, 'for sale and circulation' at the price of 5*d*., which covered his expenses. Hunter also published the Rules in the *Calendar*.[73] Drogheda altered and added to the Rules in 1869, before they were again printed in the *Calendar*. In the summer of that year, Drogheda asked Hunter to send a circular to a cohort of noblemen and gentlemen, asking them to join a new body, to be known as the Irish National Hunt Steeplechase Committee, which would be 'similar to the Grand National of England'.[74] The circular received an enthusiastic response: Henry Fitzwilliam replied that 'it is a thing much needed in Ireland',[75] while H.S. Croker remarked that it would

Lord Drogheda and the first INHS Committee

The establishment of the INHS Committee in 1869/70 was of fundamental importance to the development of Irish jump racing. The Committee's founding father was Henry Francis Seymour Moore, third marquess of Drogheda. Born in 1825, Drogheda succeeded to his uncle's Irish title and County Kildare estates while still a boy. His career in Irish racing began in 1848, at a time when both branches of the sport were at a low ebb. Drogheda enjoyed moderate success as a trainer of horses for both Flat racing and steeplechasing. He won the Kildare Hunt Cup five times – including on four occasions between 1849 and 1852, with his horse Westmeath. Having registered his colours with the Turf Club in 1852, he was elected to that body eleven years later and became 'the unquestioned patriarch and guardian of the sport in prosperity.' During his long association with the Turf Club, Drogheda served as Steward for twenty-five years (1866–70; 1873–92), and as Senior Steward on eight occasions. He also enjoyed membership of the Jockey Club, which allowed him to represent Irish interests at Newmarket.[1] As the long-serving Ranger of the Curragh, he was instrumental in securing land for racing against the infringement of the British army. By the time Drogheda took the fateful first step to form the INHS Committee in 1869, he had already made a significant contribution to National Hunt racing in Ireland, most notably through his drafting of INHS Rules and his involvement in the development of Punchestown Racecourse. Drogheda's enlisting of Robert J. Hunter, a skilled administrator who was the third generation of

(right) A caricature depicting Lord Drogheda. Captioned 'Punchestown', it was published in Vanity Fair on 30 March 1889. (opposite page, top right) R.J. Hunter, Keeper of the Match Book and owner of the Irish Racing Calendar, was instrumental in helping Drogheda to establish the INHS Committee. (opposite page, top left) A copy of the circular sent by Hunter, at Drogheda's request, to enquire whether various lords and gentlemen of the turf would be interested in joining the INHS Committee.

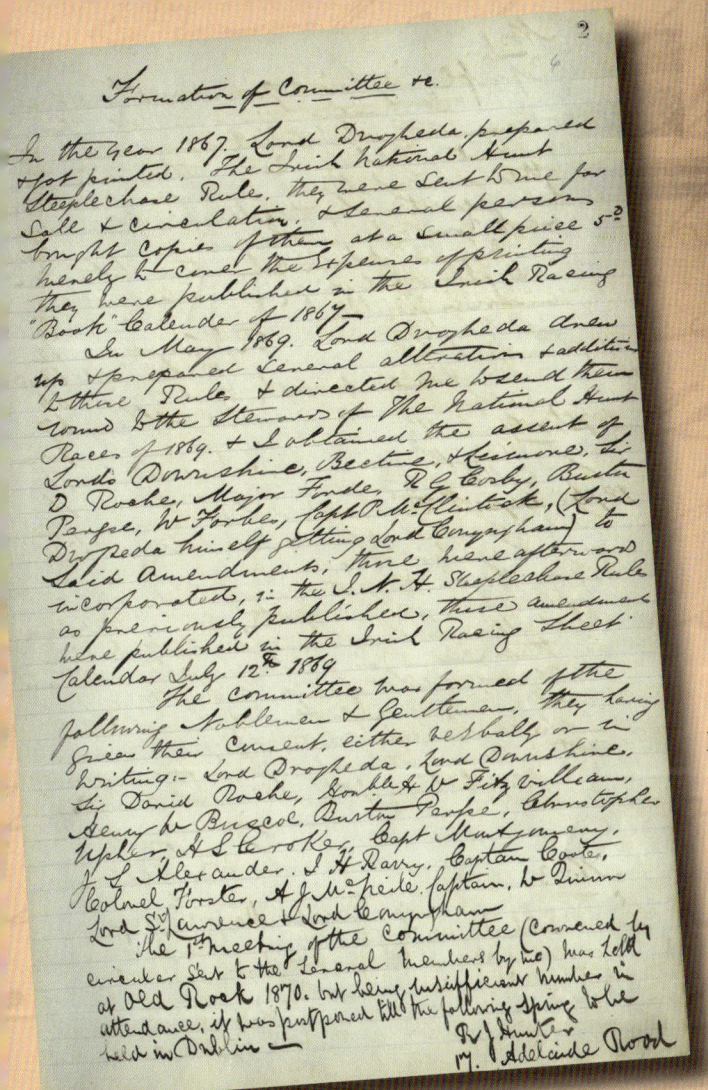

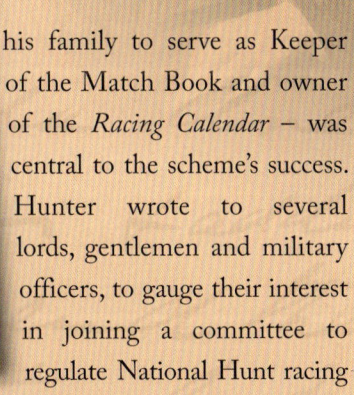

his family to serve as Keeper of the Match Book and owner of the *Racing Calendar* – was central to the scheme's success. Hunter wrote to several lords, gentlemen and military officers, to gauge their interest in joining a committee to regulate National Hunt racing in Ireland. The response was positive and the first INHS Committee comprised Drogheda, Lord Downshire, Sir David Roche, H.W. Fitzwilliam, Henry W. Briscoe, Burton Persse, Christopher Ussher, H.S. Croker, Captain John Montgomery, J.S. Alexander, J.H. Barry, Captain Richard Coote, Lt Col. F.R. Forster, A.J. McNeile, Captain W. Quinn, Lord St Lawrence and Lord Conyngham. Drogheda also occupied the role of Steward, alongside Forster and Montgomery, who served as the first Senior Steward.[2] The appointment of Hunter as Secretary to the Committee was vital to its early success, as his presence 'regularised' its 'relationship with the Turf Club'.[3] After a false start in October 1870, when a meeting at the Old Rock Races was abandoned due to insufficient attendance, members first assembled at Hunter's home at 17 Adelaide Road in Dublin, on 2 December 1870.[4]

CHAPTER ONE: 1752–1869

35

'no doubt … be of great use in this country, where some reformation is sadly needed at many of the steeplechase meetings, now so very numerous in Ireland'.[76]

Drogheda formed the INHS Committee at an exciting moment for Irish jump racing, with Irish people 'thronging to … meetings in scorching summer, as well as in dreary March' and demonstrating 'their love for this truly Irish sport'.[77] The success of Punchestown underlined the public appetite for the sport and it was no coincidence that the end of 1860s witnessed the establishment of a number of courses across Ireland, catering to both branches of racing. In 1865, St Lawrence reopened the Baldoyle course after a four-year closure, having carried out extensive upgrades. Nine years later, with assistance from businessman John Arnott, Baldoyle was relaunched again as a fully enclosed course.[78] In the south, Arnott and others took a five-year lease on a portion of slobland from Cork Corporation and opened a racecourse. The inaugural meeting at Cork Park took place in May 1869, leaving the city 'completely deserted' and causing a 'partial cessation of business, the population having for once given themselves up to pleasure'.[79] At Ballybrit in Galway, a course was established through the efforts of Thomas St Lawrence, third earl of Howth, and his son, Viscount St Lawrence (then MP for Galway), who had previously worked with Drogheda to expand Punchestown and shortly afterwards became a member of the first INHS Committee. The first meeting at Ballybrit took place in August 1869, with the MGWR carrying large crowds from Dublin, Athlone and Tuam.[80] The meeting was an immediate success: a report in the *Connaught Telegraph* described how 'The streets were crowded with people anxious to participate in the pleasures of an event the like of which they never had an opportunity of witnessing there before.' The programme opened with the Connaught Pony Race, valued at £10, and this was followed by the main attraction: the Galway Plate of £100, which was run over two-and-a-half miles on the steeplechase course. Thirteen horses started in the inaugural Plate and the race was 'beautifully contested' before being won by the mare, Absentee, whose name was a provocative reference to those landlords who resided outside Ireland, but profited from their Irish estates.[81] A ball was held at the Railway Hotel on the evening of the first day of the meeting, under the patronage of the nobility and local gentry, including St Lawrence.[82]

Fairyhouse was improved by the Ward Union Hunt in this period, too, and the programme for its April meeting was expanded in 1870 to include the Grand National

Steeplechase. The inaugural Grand National took place at the County Meath course on 4 April 1870, as part of a six-race card. The meeting was a considerable success, with crowds travelling by train from Dublin to a temporary station erected just beyond Dunboyne, two miles from the course. Among those in attendance were Lord Drogheda and the Lord Lieutenant, Earl Spencer. The weather was 'as soft and balmy as in midsummer' and traditional music 'rattled' out from the booths that studded the ground behind the newly erected stand, which was built to the highest standard to accommodate 800 spectators. The man who designed and supervised the construction of the new Fairyhouse course was Thomas G. Waters, the engineer who was responsible for the development of Punchestown, Galway and Cork Park. The saddling paddock at Fairyhouse was on the same plan as Punchestown, with dressing rooms for professional jockeys and gentlemen riders and 'a small shedded place … set apart for weighing'. Waters' skill was also apparent on the near-three-mile track, where thirteen obstacles were constructed with 'the greatest care' so that they were 'made as safe and complete as possible'. The only issue was with the ground, with poor drainage in places making the going unpredictable. The card consisted of six events, with Mr L. Dunne's grey gelding Sir Robert Peel (named for the former British Prime Minister) racing into the history books as the first winner of the Irish Grand National.[83]

By the 1870s, steeplechasing, which began as a means for elite men to test the strength and stamina of their horses, had grown into a semi-codified and commercial concern in Ireland. While Flat racing remained the more valuable and exclusive branch of the sport, jump racing became more popular. It captured the imagination of the Irish people, rich and poor, who flocked on foot, by train, in carriages and on jarveys, to newly appointed racecourses in every corner of the island. With this growth in popularity came a growing need for regulation, and it was into that breach that Lord Drogheda and the INHS Committee stepped. The Committee's ambition to regulate and modernize the sport would not be easily realized, as Ireland's economic underdevelopment and the febrile political climate on the island made for heavy going. As in any good nineteenth-century steeplechase, Drogheda's assembly of lords and gentlemen would have to overcome many and varied obstacles to succeed.

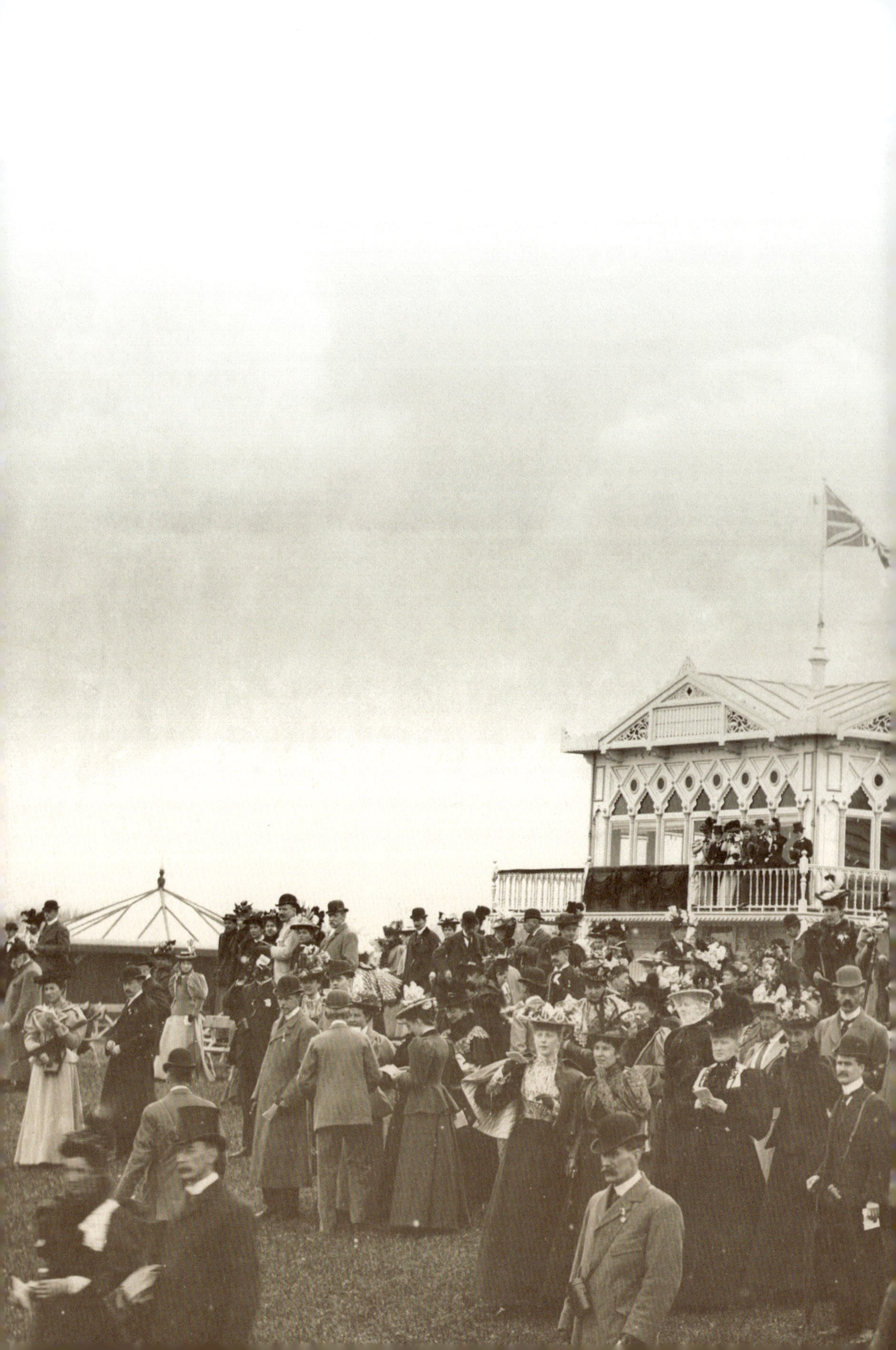

CHAPTER TWO

1870-1921

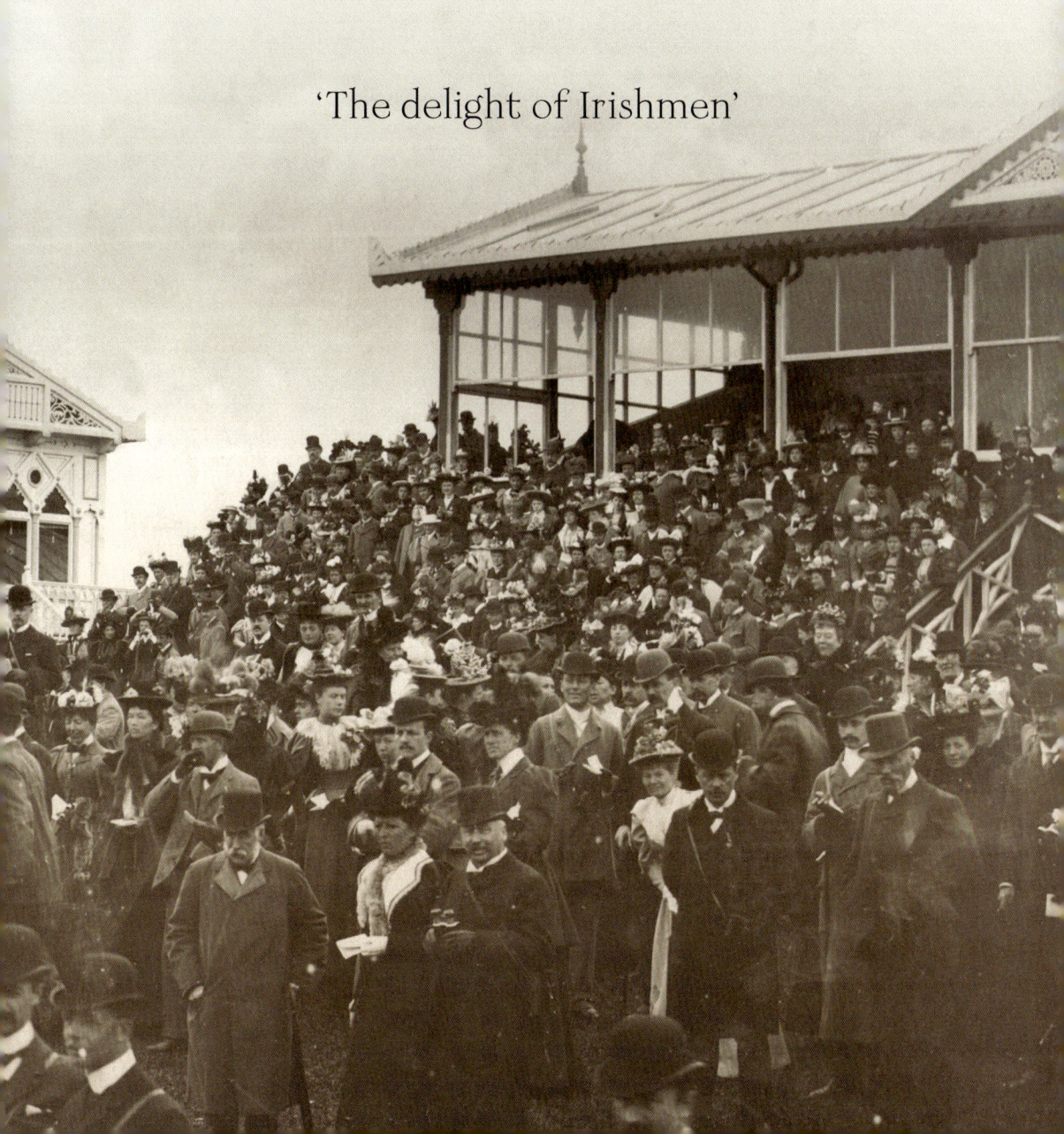

'The delight of Irishmen'

THE FORMATION OF THE INHS Committee in 1869/70 was a pivotal moment in the history of jump racing in Ireland. For the first time, National Hunt racing had a distinct governing body, concerned with its advancement through regulation, adjudication and promotion. Helmed by a rotating panel of three Stewards, the Committee gradually extended its authority and transformed the sport across the island. The Committee's early reforms were numerous and included the regulation of handicapping and the improvement of fences and racecourse facilities. These and other interventions were generally welcomed, but the Committee (like the Turf Club) was not immune from criticism. As the nineteenth century drew to a close, prominent breeders, owners and trainers began to coordinate to make their voices heard, while hunt clubs across the island reacted to increased regulation by organizing traditional steeplechases for their members; it was from these contests that modern point-to-point racing emerged. A period of economic growth after the Great Famine, meanwhile, led to the increased participation of small owners – typically farmers who kept one or two horses to race and sell at a profit. Expansion did not amount to a democratization of the sport, however. In fact, the Committee's establishment formalized racing's traditional hierarchy, which itself was a reflection of Ireland's highly stratified society. This meant that, as the twentieth century dawned, the men who bred, owned and raced the best horses continued to shape the sport in their own image and interest. It was in this moment too, however, with the disestablishment of

Church of Ireland in 1869 and the passage of the first Land Act in 1870, that the pillars upholding the Anglo-Irish elite began to crumble. As deep-rooted tensions in Irish society bubbled to the surface, racing, and especially hunting, became targets of violence and dissent. At the same time, National Hunt racing remained highly popular, with hard-run steeplechases drawing crowds of every class and creed, and with public demand met by a rising number of metropolitan and provincial race meetings. In the end, it was a combination of Anglo-Irish and popular passion for the sport that ensured its survival in a decade of turmoil, as the First World War and the campaign for independence from Britain unmade and remade Irish society.

'These conditions may suit English requirements, but are unjust & ill-suited to Ireland'

The INHS Committee formed at a time when the popularity of steeplechasing easily exceeded that of Flat racing. An article on Irish racing in the *Irish Sportsman and Farmer* in February 1870 noted that racing on the flat 'has lost considerable ground in public estimation, and is by no means as well suited to the tastes of the great majority of the population, as it lacks all the concomitant excitement of steeplechasing … The exciting nature of the sport is the delight of Irishmen, who alone can fully appreciate the many casualties that occur.'[1] This love of steeplechasing crossed social and economic boundaries, and was often linked to its seeming lawlessness, which was understood to appeal to the 'innately' wild Irish character. In 1870, a contributor to the *Irish Times* observed that 'the peasantry know the pedigree of every famous animal, and could tell you who was his trainer, who was his groom, and his chances of success. They have fully as much enjoyment in a vigorously contested race as the owner of the most promising horse can hope to obtain.'[2] An 1874 report in *The Field*, meanwhile, attributed the popularity of jump racing in Ireland to the 'gentle and simple' nature of the Irish people, who typically eschewed Flat racing at the Curragh, but would travel *en masse* to see 'a couple of jackasses … "lep" over four sticks'. At the same time, the *Field*'s correspondent envied the development of National Hunt racing in Ireland, observing that the prize for the Irish Grand National had increased from £100 in 1870, to 'the handsome sum' of £500 in 1874.[3] At this point, the prize money that could be won for Irish steeplechases was equal to that awarded for many Flat races, which in part caused the number of chasers to grow to 'about three times the number of performers on the flat'.[4]

While National Hunt racing thrilled the masses, the INHS Committee remained an exclusive body, populated by the Anglo-Irish elite. Members of the Committee were eager to advance its authority, but they were not always agreed on the best way forward. This was partly because the social and economic conditions of nineteenth-century Ireland were unlike those in Britain. In late 1870, disagreements arose over a number of issues. This included proposals to ban horses that had raced at meetings not advertised under INHS Rules, and to improve the standard of Irish horses by abolishing heat races and fixing the minimum handicap weight at 10st.[5] These proposals were intended to improve the standard of Irish horses, but St Lawrence argued that while they might 'suit English requirements', they were 'unjust & ill-suited to Ireland'. The issue, as St Lawrence saw it, was 'the primitive state of … sporting civilization in country parts of Ireland', which was home to many 'humble' horse owners and inexperienced 'rustic officials'. St Lawrence also believed that a growth in the Committee's authority would threaten the authority of local hunts, which were historically responsible for the organization of steeplechase meetings in Ireland. For their authority to be accepted, St Lawrence argued, the Committee would have to avoid enforcement and instead frame 'rules and conditions so wise in their provisions and so suitable to the requirements of Irish Races [that] they will be accepted all over the country'.[6] It was clear that a compromise had to be reached between the Committee's desire to improve standards and the bread-and-butter reality of steeplechasing in Ireland. This was soon achieved by the passage of a motion acknowledging that the Committee's authority was 'not as yet … sufficiently recognized throughout Ireland', with some owners of horses and organizers of race meetings still entirely unaware of its existence.[7]

'to banish weedy sires from the country'

The INHS Committee worked tirelessly in its first years to become the recognized authority for National Hunt racing in Ireland. While some meetings remained beyond the Stewards' control, an increasing number looked to the Committee to promote the best interests of the sport through regulation, recommendation and fair adjudication

Henry Eyre Linde of Eyrefield Lodge was the outstanding Irish trainer of the nineteenth century, winning two Grand Nationals, three Irish Grand Nationals, and two Grand Steeple-Chase de Paris. Tall and somewhat severe-looking, he was rarely seen without a top hat at race meetings and was known for his dry wit.

on cases of alleged malpractice. Drogheda's initial 74 Rules swelled to 187 by 1889,[8] but the speed and scale of change meant that criticism from the wider racing community was not uncommon. Debate was near-constant on the subject of handicapping, which was integral to the health of the sport. The Committee took early steps to establish a weight-for-age scale, and acted against St Lawrence's advice to introduce a 10st minimum handicap.[9] The introduction of the minimum weight was understood to be a positive development in some quarters, with a contributor to the *Irish Times* suggesting that it gave 'the hint to breeders to look out for bone and substance ... to banish weedy sires from the country'.[10] Others echoed St Lawrence's concern that the minimum was too high for Irish steeplechasing, which relied to a great extent on the participation of poorer quality horses. Colonel Graves, who owned and managed the Cork and Metropolitan meetings, wrote to the Committee in 1874 to complain that the 10st minimum had caused a reduction in the number of horses contesting Irish steeplechases.[11]

There were also complaints that the handicap was inconsistently applied, including from Henry Eyre Linde, 'the outstanding Irish trainer of the nineteenth century', who operated a stud farm and stables out of his family home, Eyrefield Lodge, on The Curragh. Linde was hugely successful in Ireland, where his monopoly of meetings at Punchestown earned him the nickname 'Farmer'. He also trained three Irish Grand National winners – the aptly-named Grand National in 1876, Thiggin-thue in 1877 and Controller in 1880.[12] Linde also claimed the major prizes of English and French National Hunt racing, training Empress (1880) and Woodbrook (1881) to win the Grand National, and Too Good (1882) and Whisper Low (1883) to win the Grand Steeple-Chase de Paris.[13] Many of his most celebrated victories were delivered by the gifted gentleman rider, Tommy Beasley, whose three brothers – Harry, Willie and Johnny – also enjoyed success in the saddle.[14] In 1878, Linde wrote a letter to the *Irish Times*, claiming that certain horses had won 'race after race since the beginning of the season without being proportionately penalized; whilst less favoured animals, occupying the unenviable position of second, have been denied adequate allowance in subsequent events'. Linde anticipated an exodus of owners from steeplechasing, as they would 'begin to grow tired of such a one-sided game … where, at least for them, there seems to be all blanks and no prizes'.[15]

Handicapping was not the only cause for concern in National Hunt racing in this period. The condition of racecourses across Ireland was one area that required the Committee's early and repeated attention. In May 1875, members 'unanimously and strongly recommended' to the clerks of the course and managers of meetings 'the advisability of making the fences larger'. This was urged because of a growing tendency to furnish courses with smaller fences, which were more dangerous and tended 'to deteriorate the quality & merit of Steeplechase horses'.[16] The problem was not easily solved and in 1888, the *Irish Times* reported that 'there can be no doubt that on many of our courses at present the fences are absurdly small and equally dangerous. In several places they consist of nothing more than a few furze bushes and a gripe at the landing side.'[17] The Committee initially encouraged improvements by offering advice, but this approach made little difference. Rules were eventually introduced stipulating that all meetings had to be sanctioned by the Stewards of the Committee, and that a licence had to be secured for every scheduled meeting. The Stewards had the authority to withhold or withdraw licences if the Inspector of Courses reported unfavourably on the construction of fences on the course in question. They were not afraid to exercise their power in this respect. In August 1897, for example, the Inspector made an unfavourable report about the racecourse in Slane, County Meath, and the Stewards refused the organizers a licence until the fences were properly constructed and met with the Inspector's approval.[18] In order to advance National Hunt racing in Ireland, the INHS Committee had to be sensible of the concerns of the wider racing community. By engaging with breeders, owners and trainers, the Committee was able to develop a set of rules that were suited to Irish circumstances. This was evidenced in the contributions made by owners and trainers to the handicapping debate, and in the fallout from a Committee proposal to abolish Farmers' races in 1877. At a meeting on the Curragh in October that year, owners and trainers spoke in favour of these low-value contests, with John Hubert Moore arguing that their abolition would debar many farmers 'from having a try with their horses in public', which would lead many small meetings to be 'crushed'.[19] Taking heed of the owners' concerns, the Committee preserved Farmers' races, but altered the Rules in 1892 to limit participation to farmers and residents of the county in which the races were held.[20]

'a happy night or a lonely homeward journey'

The proposal to abolish Farmers' races resulted from a desire to improve the standard of Irish steeplechasing, and it was for the same reason that the Committee worked to bring an end to £4 19s. races, also known as flapper races. Run outside INHS Rules, these contests were highly popular across Ireland in the late nineteenth century, with many farmers using them to blood young horses. By the 1890s, however, reports of malpractice were widespread, and the Committee received complaints that owners and trainers commonly ran horses 'under names different from those borne by them under INHS Rules'. As a result, flapper meetings were perceived to be 'irresponsible to any authority whatever', so the Committee resolved that 'the existence of these meetings as at present carried on is inimical to the best interests of racing in Ireland'.[21] After some deliberation, it was decided to bar any horse that took part in a flapper race from subsequent meetings run under INHS Rules.[22] While the Committee acted to advance the sport, there was a clear appetite for flapping across the island. Flapper races were not likely to enrich those involved, but 'they were looked forward to as if the prizes were as valuable as the Derby or Grand National'.[23] As well as offering small owners and trainers a means to test their horses, they carried on in the tradition of the small-purse races of the eighteenth century, providing important sporting and social occasions for poor rural communities across the island.

This was apparent in Clare, where the principal meetings were held at Ballycoree, Ennis, Kildysart and Kilrush. It was customary for the people of these towns to organize dances and to

> invite their friends to remain overnight for the second days race. This was a problem for the young people who wished to stay in the town as the cash given in those days would not have been much use to keep one in pocket money for two days and a night. The trainer, therefore, was the most sought man in the town to try and get a tip, as the winning of a few shillings would mean a happy night or lonely homeward journey … This applied especially to the islanders who could not return to the town.[24]

Flapper meetings were part of a long tradition of Irish horse racing and their decline had a negative impact on already struggling rural communities. At the same time, the Committee was not focused on the sporting and social habits of the rural poor and it was justified in its belief that flapping undermined the standard of National Hunt racing in Ireland. In a stratified and otherwise divided society, 'progress' did not mean the same thing to everyone. Having initially allowed for honest mistakes, in March 1893 the Stewards decreed that it was 'to be clearly understood that in future … disqualification will under no circumstances be removed from any horse running at a meeting not held in accordance with [INHS Rules]'.[25] While flapping endured (and found a modern equivalent in pony racing), it was in a greatly reduced state, with the Committee's efforts causing many meetings to fall into abeyance.

'when the storm clouds have passed away … the old sports … will be restored'

While the INHS Committee took steps to improve the standard of National Hunt racing, hunt clubs across Ireland played an integral part in the evolution of jump racing

Point-to-points became a fixture on the Irish hunting scene in the late nineteenth and early twentieth centuries. The production of sound horses for hunting and point-to-point races required great care and attention to detail. This book of bloodstock records belonging to Tom Levins Moore (father of trainer Dan Moore) contains descriptions of every horse bred, purchased and sold by him, including details of their physique, temperament, subsequent owners and point-to-point careers.

in the late nineteenth century. They did so through the organization of Redcoat races, which – along with military race meetings – were the antecedent of modern point-to-pointing. Redcoat races (also known as Sportsman races) were run over natural terrain, incorporating obstacles like banks and ditches, with riders keeping their horses 'between the flags' that marked out the course. The Ward Union Hunt held the first Redcoat race in Ireland in early 1873, after a similar contest organized by

48   NATIONAL HUNT AND POINT-TO-POINT RACING IN IRELAND

Lord Waterford's Curraghmore Hunt was cancelled owing to severe frost. Redcoat races quickly became popular as an end-of-season event for several hunts across the island. As one observer put it, there were no 'horse nor jockey aspirants to Grand National laurels, [but] every man did his best to win, which we do not always see even in the Grand National'.[26] The INHS Committee did not rush to regulate Redcoat meetings and they were first included in the INHS Rules in 1889, following the passage of a resolution put forward by Lord Drogheda. These meetings were defined as including 'only four races, all of which are hunters steeplechases to which not more than £20 is added (Farmers' races excepted)' and were 'confined to horses the property of members of, or subscribers to a specified Hunt, or of Farmers residing within the limits of that Hunt'. Drogheda's resolution also sought to achieve a measure of regulatory control over the sport, as organizing Hunts were now required to have each meeting sanctioned by the INHS Stewards. Sanction was only 'granted on payment of a fee of £1, and on satisfying the Stewards of the INHS Committee that such a Meeting is to be held under the management and control of some specified Hunt Club, and that a licensed Clerk of the Course & Scales has been appointed'.[27] Over a decade later – in 1900 – six rules governing point-to-point racing were introduced to the INHS Rule Book.[28]

While hunting contributed to the development of jump racing through point-to-point races, its ubiquity as the sport of the landlord class made it an obvious target for agrarian protests in the 1880s. It was observed that 'During the season 1880–81 unpleasant manifestations began to be shown … by certain sections of the farmers'. The following year, Lord Waterford and his hunting party were 'absolutely stoned out of it' by a large mob, who also ran through some of the hounds with pitchforks.[29] Hunt meetings were targeted more frequently than race meetings but the land campaign impacted upon the racing calendar, too. After the attack on his Curraghmore Hunt, Lord Waterford closed his steeplechase course at Williamstown and decamped to England until the unrest died down.[30] The actions of Land League

A snapshot from the point-to-point meeting at Carroll's Cross in County Waterford, c.1901.

members caused the Kildare Hunt to cancel the Punchestown meeting in 1882. The League attempted to organize an alternative meeting but was unsuccessful, with a correspondent in *Bell's Life* expressing relief that 'the contemplated steeplechases … intended to take the place of Punchestown, are almost certain to be a complete failure' because 'respectable farmers have declined to subscribe'.[31] The lack of support from 'respectable farmers' for a Land League-backed alternative to Punchestown hints at the complex dynamics within Irish society. The rise of a Catholic middle class of large farmers and professionals in the decades after the Famine blurred social boundaries and it appears that some supporters of the Land League also wanted to preserve and enjoy the spectacle of Punchestown. The power of competing personal and ideological interests was apparent in Tralee in the 1880s, where nationalist urban traders were 'actively involved in organizing popular horse racing events with members of the town's highest orders'. Indeed, the County Kerry Steeplechase Committee comprised two founding members of the Tralee Land League – Edward Harrington and Thomas Lyons – who served alongside several members of the local gentry.[32]

In this complicated landscape, the nationalist *Freeman's Journal* could express the hope that 'when the storm clouds have passed away … a mighty crowd on the stand and a mightier crowd on the hill will rejoice over the pleasures of a restored and a rejuvenescent Punchestown'.[33] Crowds did return to the Kildare course in 1883 but anxieties over Ireland's political distemper provoked a royal visit in 1885, with the Prince and Princess of Wales deployed to ease tensions in the country. The royal party travelled to a rain-sodden Punchestown after receiving a mixed reception on their progress through Ireland. The royal couple were generally welcomed at the Kildare course, but it was reported that 'a few insignificant hisses were heard in the vicinity of the Royal Enclosure which were promptly rebuked and silenced by loud cheers'.[34] One young man in the public enclosure was sent 'head-over-heels' after his hissing caused 'a dapper little man wearing a covert coat and billycock hat' to rebuke him with a 'sock-dolloger' punch.[35] The 'sock-dolloging' in the public enclosure may have provided more excitement than the racing programme. On the occasion of the last royal visit in 1868, the average field numbered 16, while in 1885 the average was six, with only two entries for the Drogheda Stakes. The *Irish Times* reported that the runners for the famous Conyngham Cup 'were below the standard in point of quality which we had been accustomed to see contesting this event'.[36] The Cup was won by

John Kane, owned by a Kildare-based large farmer, William Hanway, who trained his horses 'by letting them loose in a big field, and setting collie dogs after them to make them gallop'.[37]

The programme at Punchestown in 1885 reflected something of a downward trend in steeplechasing in Ireland. Agrarian unrest had an impact in the 1880s but it did not explain a prolonged disenchantment with the sport at the end of the nineteenth century. It is likely that the INHS Committee's increased regulation had an impact on the number of steeplechases and the number of horses entered. This was the view of Lord Howth (formerly Viscount St Lawrence), who maintained that 'excessive interference on the part of the [I]NHSC' had resulted in the decline of Irish steeplechasing.[38] Howth took a short-term view of a long-term process, however, as the Committee's interventions demonstrated the many ways that Irish steeplechasing needed to improve in order to thrive. Howth also overlooked the great successes enjoyed by Irish steeplechasers in England between 1879 and the early 1900s. The importance of England to Irish jump racing was evident in the INHS Committee's decision, in 1890, to work toward regulatory alignment with the National Hunt Committee, and to exchange lists of suspended owners, trainers and riders with Messrs Weatherby, the publisher of the English *Racing Calendar*.[39] These developments made it easier for Irish horses to compete in English races and vice versa. Irish success in high-profile English steeplechases was essential, not only to the sport, but to the breeding industry, which had grown in scale since the 1860s. It was at that point that Robert J. Goff was appointed official auctioneer to the Turf Club, beginning a relationship that would help to develop the reputation and value of Irish bloodstock. Breeding was an important feature of the Irish economy by the late nineteenth century; this was underlined by the appointment of a parliamentary commission to inquire into the Irish breeding industry in 1897, following the Congested Districts Board's introduction of poorer-quality Hackney horses to impoverished areas of Ireland.[40] Concern over the introduction of Hackneys aside, the 1890s and 1900s witnessed significant progress in Irish breeding, with the establishment of a number of large stud farms, including Colonel William Hall Walker's property at Tully in County Kildare (later the National Stud) and J.J. Parkinson's enterprises on the Curragh.[41]

If the decline in Irish steeplechasing in the late nineteenth century was partly a result of the INHS Committee's regulation, it was also a result of the Turf Club's efforts to provoke Irish interest in Flat racing. In 1890, a contributor to the *Irish Sportsman and Farmer* considered whether 'it may be that flat racing has no charms for the Irish people … perhaps the Turf Club has no desire to have its meetings attended otherwise than at present by the select handful … the Turf Club needs a lot of waking up, and overhauling and general reformation'.[42] This reform was achieved in large part by Thomas Brindley, who was appointed Keeper of the Match Book in 1891. The son of a Ward Union huntsman, 'Judge' Brindley had a reputation for energy and efficiency, and his appointment was widely welcomed in racing circles. As well as rescuing Baldoyle in the early 1890s, Brindley had remarkable success in turning around the fortunes of the Curragh, where he inaugurated the Drogheda Memorial Stakes, oversaw the first running of The Oaks in 1895 and increased the value of the Derby and King's Plate. The result was an upsurge in interest and enthusiasm for Irish Flat racing that extended beyond the plains of Kildare, with new and revived meetings being organized across the island.[43] By 1904, members of the INHS Committee were alarmed by the decline in the popularity of steeplechasing in Ireland, attributing it to the rise of low-stakes Flat races across the island. In the Committee's view, these Flat races were 'of insignificant value and being in many cases contested on courses which are quite unsuitable for Flat racing, cannot tend in any way to promote the interests of the Turf in general, while their existence obviously has a prejudicial effect on the sport of steeplechasing'.[44]

The Committee proposed to address this circumstance by reaching an agreement with the Turf Club, whereby Flat races would be run on courses certified for that purpose and by increasing their minimum value from £20 to £50. The Stewards of the Turf Club were slow to take action, but in 1905 it was decided to inspect all Flat courses in the country, with the result that licences were withdrawn from and refused to several provincial courses. Two years later, Percy La Touche – who served almost continuously as an INHS Steward for thirty years and was Senior Steward on ten occasions – proposed that Flat courses should be required to meet a certain standard to qualify for a licence. This proposal resulted in the appointment of Arthur Blennerhassett as the Turf Club's first Inspector of Courses in 1907. A fixture in hunting and racing circles, Blennerhassett worked with racecourse executives to impose a standard for safety and facilities.[45] Meanwhile, the INHS Committee took steps to

Wild Man from Borneo, winner of the 1895 Grand National, with Joe Widger up and owner Tom Widger at the head. Wild Man was bred in Nenagh in County Tipperary and was bought by Joe Widger and his brother, Michael, who trained the horse in England in the 1890s. The Widger family ran a successful equestrian business at Railway Square in Waterford city.

encourage the public's interest in jump racing, providing an annual grant of £200 for the running of an Irish National Hunt Plate. The first edition was awarded to the Louth Hunt meeting of 1906,[46] reflecting the Committee's commitment to improve provincial race meetings, many of which relied on 'exceedingly unsatisfactory' courses, stands, dressing rooms and weighing rooms.[47] While interest in Irish steeplechasing dipped in the late nineteenth and early twentieth century, the period nonetheless 'constituted a minor golden age' in breeding, in racecourse development, and in the performance of Irish horses in major Flat races and steeplechases across the Irish Sea.[48] Success on the flat was achieved largely through the interest of the colourful Irish-American Richard 'Boss' Croker, who established a successful stud and racing stables on his Glencairn Estate near Leopardstown.

Before returning to Ireland in the early twentieth century, Cork-born Croker was a powerful figure in Tammany Hall, the Democratic machine that dominated New

York city politics from the mid-nineteenth century. Croker bred Orby, who in 1907 became the first Irish-trained horse to win the Epsom Derby and the first horse to win the Epsom Derby-Irish Derby double.[49] While Orby raced to glory on the flat, the quality of Irish-bred chasers was also evident in England in the first years of the twentieth century. Ireland's reputation as both a producer and an exporter of exceptional chasers was underlined by the Grand National success of several Irish-bred horses. In 1900, Ambush II won the most coveted prize in steeplechasing for his royal owner, the Prince of Wales (the future Edward VII). The Prince's horse was trained by G.W. Lushington at Eyrefield Lodge, which was bought by Eustace 'Lucky' Loder after Henry Eyre Linde's death in 1897, and was ridden to victory in the Grand National by Algy Anthony. In the years following, the Grand National was dominated by Irish-bred animals who were English-owned and English-trained; this included Shannon Lass (1902), Drumcree (1903) and Kirkland (1905). Having won the Irish Grand National in 1904, meanwhile, Ascetic's Silver (the son of super sire, Ascetic) was bought by the German Prince von Hatzfeldt and put into training in England before winning the Grand National in 1906.[50]

'The riding of those days was of the toughest description'

Horses needed riders to win or lose and Ireland had a tradition of turning out gifted horsemen for Flat racing and steeplechasing. Professional jockeys became a more common feature of the sport in the late nineteenth century, but 'gentlemen riders' – later known as 'amateurs' – continued to race against each other. With the exception of military races, which were limited to Army officers, there were very few gentlemen's steeplechases in Ireland in the nineteenth century, however. Gentlemen could pay jockeys to give them their mounts, but this practice was discouraged by the meting out of 'unpleasant' treatment during races. As Harry Sargent recollected, 'The riding of those days was of the toughest description'. In a race with only two starters, for example, a professional jockey named Chiffney waited until he and his gentleman rival 'reached a part of the course out of view of the primitive structure that did duty for a stand' before 'seizing his opponent by the collar and dexterously throwing him out of the saddle and then going on to win the race at his leisure'.[51] Chiffney's actions were unsporting, but they reflected the economic disparity and resultant tension between

The Brothers Beasley

Racing has always been a family affair, but few clans can claim to have been as successful as the Beasleys – Tommy, Harry, Willie and Johnny – a family of gentlemen riders from Athy in County Kildare. The Beasleys apprenticed under some of the great figures of nineteenth-century steeplechasing; Tommy under Allen McDonough, Harry under Henry Eyre Linde, and Willie and Johnny under John Hubert Moore.[1] The brothers took up residence in Linde's Eyrefield Lodge, where Tommy was appointed stable manager to protect his amateur status. The supremely talented Tommy rode in twelve Grand Nationals, winning with the Linde-trained Empress (1880) and Woodbrook (1881), and with Frigate (1889), who was trained by Baldoyle chairman and INHS Committee member, Matt Maher. The only other Beasley to win the National was Harry, who trained and rode Come Away to victory in 1891. Tommy and Harry were also successful in France, where both won the Grand Steeple-Chase de Paris.[2] It was in Ireland, however, that the Beasleys were held in the highest regard, with one profile proclaiming that 'never in all racing history has there been a record of so many of one family possessed of such perfect horsemanship'.[3] Tommy won two Irish Grand Nationals, two Galway Plates, two Conyngham Cups and a Prince of Wales' Plate between 1876 and 1886, before retiring from steeplechasing in 1892. He had significant success on the flat, too, winning the Irish Derby three times.[4] Johnny and Willie also claimed some of the major prizes of Irish steeplechasing, with one Grand National, three Conyngham Cups and one Galway Plate between them. Willie Beasley died in 1892 when he was struck by a stray hoof after falling at Punchestown's infamous double bank.[5] It surely cast a shadow over the Kildare course for Harry, who achieved

Tommy Beasley

(above) The eldest Beasley brother, Tommy, was a highly talented horseman who enjoyed a glittering career as an amateur rider; winning three Grand Nationals, the Grand Steeple-Chase de Paris, two Irish Grand Nationals and two Galway Plates. (top opposite page) Tommy's younger brother, Harry, was no less gifted in the saddle. He won major races in England and Ireland but it was at Punchestown that he reigned supreme. He rode his last winner as a 71-year-old at the County Kildare course in 1923.

Harry Beasley

incredible success there before and after his younger brother's death. While Harry claimed major prizes elsewhere – including two Irish Grand Nationals and two Galway Plates – his achievements at Punchestown were legion and included seven Prince of Wales Plates and six Conyngham Cups. He rode his last winner there at the age of 71, steering Pride of Arras to victory in the Maiden Plate some 45 years after his first win at the Kildare course.[6] The Beasleys became one of racing's great dynasties, with Harry's son H.H. becoming a highly successful Flat jockey. It was H.H.'s son Bobby, however, who added to the family's glittering National Hunt legacy, winning the Grand National, the Gold Cup and the Champion Hurdle by the time he was 26. Bobby struggled with alcoholism for a number of years before being persuaded to join Alcoholics Anonymous. He won a second Gold Cup in 1974, aged 38, on board Captain Christy. Beasley later credited 'Christy' with giving him back his self-respect, saying 'He made a huge difference to my life and was a hell of a horse.'[7]

Harry Beasley on Come Away, whom he partnered to win the Grand National in 1891.

One of the leading gentlemen riders of his day, Garrett 'Garry' Moore (1851–1908) was six foot tall and solidly built, which made it difficult for him to maintain weight – a task made even more difficult by his hell-raising lifestyle. He nonetheless enjoyed significant success in the saddle in the 1870s, when he combined with his trainer father, John Hubert Moore, to win the Irish Grand National on Scots Grey (1872, 1875) and the Grand National on The Liberator (1879).

those who rode for fun and those who rode to make a living. The success of Irish gentlemen was all the more remarkable because there were so few of them in the field. What lacked in quantity was more than made up for in the quality of gentlemen like Allen McDonough, who won the last unofficial Grand National (run at Maghull) on Sir William in 1838 and rode in his last steeplechase at Punchestown in 1872, at the age of 64. One of the top gentlemen riders in the late nineteenth century was Garrett 'Garry' Moore, who rode many winners for his father, John Hubert. This included The Liberator, who earned a famous victory in the Grand National in 1879 – a race that was otherwise notable for including the four Beasley brothers.

Moore and the Beasleys occupied an interesting space between amateur and professional, riding full-time, but as gentlemen. They were jockeys in all but name, but their economic and social circumstances were not the same as those who took rides to earn a living. The INHS Committee regulated the participation of professionals to ensure that malpractice did not proliferate as it had in England, issuing licences and taking disciplinary measures against any rider found to have acted in an unsporting fashion. At the same time, the Committee was conscious of the dangers that jockeys faced, with the poor standard of courses, in particular, making steeplechasing highly treacherous in the late nineteenth century. One year after Willie Beasley died in a fall at the double bank at Punchestown, well-known jockey Terry Kavanagh suffered a serious fall at the same fence. Kavanagh's mount, Dark Girl, was killed and it also appeared that the jockey had suffered a similar fate, as

> He was shot over the horse's head and flung with a frightful force against the top of the double, and from this he fell limp and apparently lifeless over the brow of the ditch into the gripe. He lay unconscious for some minutes, when he was revived ... He was able to walk over to the stand after a little time, but it was simply inhuman to allow a man after getting such a fall to do so.[52]

Kavanagh recovered and four years later, in 'a triumph of Irish jockeyship', rode Manifesto to victory in the 1897 Grand National, one week after the death of the man under whom he had served his apprenticeship – the great Henry Eyre Linde.[53] At the suggestion of Lord Drogheda in 1891, the Irish Trainers' and Jockeys' Benevolent and Provident Fund was established to provide support to professional jockeys (or

The Herd Garden double bank at Punchestown. Banks were a feature of steeplechases in Ireland in this period, but the double at Punchestown was a particularly challenging obstacle for horse and rider. From F.H. Bayles, *The race courses atlas of Great Britain and Ireland* (London, 1903).

'The Immortal Manifesto'

The success of Irish-bred horses in the Grand National has always been a source of pride in Ireland. Among the many Irish success stories at Aintree, there are few who could claim to match the career of Manifesto, one of the best horses to ever contest the National. Bred by solicitor and landowner Harry Dyas in Athboy, County Meath, Manifesto was sired by Man O'War out of Vae Victus and was foaled in 1888. Trained by Dyas, Manifesto had his first run in the Grand National in 1895, partnering with the Irish jockey, Terry Kavanagh. He finished fourth in a race that was won by Wild Man from Borneo and Irish gentleman rider, Joe Widger. Manifesto returned to Aintree the following year – this time with Dyas onboard – but failed to make it past the first fence. In 1897, Dyas enlisted the services of trainer Willie McAuliffe and,

The Irish-bred Manifesto won twice and placed third three times in eight Grand National appearances between 1895 and 1908. His fame was such that he featured on a boardgame and a whisky advert, and was held up as the greatest of Grand National winners in the 1944 MGM feature film, *National Velvet*.

'Manifesto', a boardgame by Jean Jacques of London, dating from 1911.

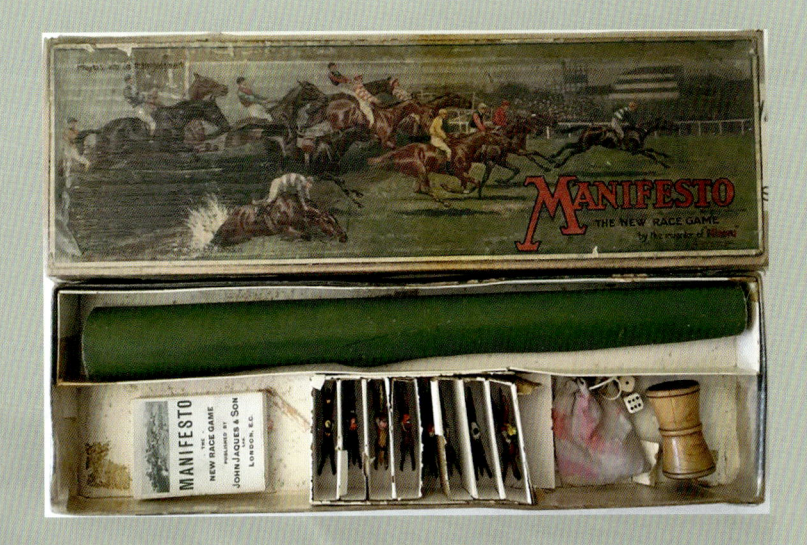

with Kavanagh back in the saddle, Manifesto made it third time lucky. Carrying 11st 3lbs, Manifesto was in a two-horse race at the third-last fence when his rival Timon unseated his rider, and he cantered to a twenty-length victory. Dyas sold Manifesto to Mr J.G. Bulteel for £4,000 in 1898 and he was sent into training with Irishman Willie Moore, who had already won the National with Why Not and The Soarer. Based in England, Moore was the son of the celebrated trainer John Hubert and brother of the 'hard-riding, hell-raising and happy-go-lucky' gentleman rider, Garrett.[1] Manifesto missed the 1898 edition of the race, however, when he got free from his stable and injured his fetlock jumping a gate. He returned to Aintree the following year and made history under jockey George Williamson, carrying 12st 7lbs to a five-length victory. Now a two-time National winner, Manifesto was far from finished at Aintree; he placed third in the race in 1900, 1902 and 1903 and his eighth and last appearance came in 1904, at the remarkable age of sixteen. He carried 12st 1lb and finished eighth behind Moifaa.[2] Manifesto was a steeplechasing superstar – the bay gelding made such an impression on the public that he lent his name to a board game and appeared in whisky advertisements. He was also lauded in Edith Bagnold's 1935 novel *National Velvet*, with Velvet – played by Elizabeth Taylor in a 1944 feature film of the same name – announcing her ambition to win the Grand National on her horse, 'The Pie', and to thus be added to the 'roll-of-honor books where they put down the winners and call them the Immortal Manifesto.'[3]

CHAPTER TWO: 1870–1921

their families) who suffered an accident or otherwise fell on hard times. Following Drogheda's premature death from a heart attack in June 1892,[54] the Committee passed a resolution changing the name of the Benevolent Fund to the 'Drogheda Memorial Fund'. It was a fitting tribute to a man who had worked tirelessly to improve the conditions of all who were involved in the sport.[55] The Committee's provisions did not tackle the immediate dangers faced by jockeys, however, and serious and even fatal accidents continued to occur. It would be some years before significant strides were made on jockey welfare, but as time went on racecourses began to provide and improve medical facilities. This included the Baldoyle Metropolitan Meeting, where a motor ambulance was introduced 1912. This innovation drew praise from a contributor to *Irish Life* magazine, who suggested that it was 'only fair to give injured jockeys every chance of speedy attention in hospital'.[56]

A fashionable crowd watches horses race by the finishing post at Leopardstown in the late nineteenth century. The horses are racing right-handed, contrary to the course layout today.

'princely Punchestown … was lacking in the usual splash of colour'

While the standard of Irish racecourses was a persistent concern in the late nineteenth century, there were some positive developments, most notably the opening of a park course at Leopardstown in 1888. Built by Captain George Quin and modelled on Sandown Park in England, the course lay conveniently near the Dublin and South-Eastern Railway line, just six miles outside the city, and was built to accommodate both codes of racing. Leopardstown was a quick success and six annual meetings were held there by 1897. That year, a visit to the course was included in the itinerary of the Duke and Duchess of York (later George V and Queen Mary), who attended the Second Summer Meeting in August. With royal patronage, Leopardstown became a fixture on the Irish social calendar and its popularity confirmed that racing had become a viably commercial sport in Ireland. It also underlined the importance of the racecourse as a public space, where the social and political order could be reinforced through ceremony and spectacle. As the prospect of self-government loomed in the background, the visibility of the royal family and the British administration –

The first motor ambulance at Baldoyle Racecourse, 1912.

including successive viceregal couples – assumed a new significance. To that end, it was expected that the Prince and Princess of Wales would visit Punchestown in 1901, but all plans were abandoned after the death of Queen Victoria on 22 January.

The elderly queen had made a last visit to Ireland one year earlier, as her reign stretched into a new century; now, with her death, came the end of an era. In April, 'princely Punchestown was … lacking in the usual splash of colour', but the meeting still attracted a large crowd and 'maintained a certain festive air'.[57] Edward VII and Alexandra eventually visited Ireland in July 1903, arriving as the Wyndham Land Act, which heralded the end of the landlord system, passed through Parliament. The success of that visit prompted the royal couple to return the following year, when their itinerary included race meetings at Punchestown, the Phoenix Park and Leopardstown. On a sunny day in Kildare, people came 'pouring in from all directions – some by railway, some by motor car, some in brakes and coaches, and a host upon the side car', to catch a glimpse of the royal couple. Edward VII's past Grand National-winner Ambush II disappointed by finishing seventh in the Prince of Wales Plate, but the King could otherwise be satisfied with his visit, as evidence of Irish affection was everywhere to be seen.[58] At the south Dublin course, meanwhile, the king and queen and their daughter Princess Victoria were welcomed by a sizeable portion of the Irish peerage, making for 'a gala day of fashion'.[59]

Edward VII made a last visit to Ireland in 1907, during which he attended Leopardstown and again received a warm reception. He died three years later and the esteem in which he was held by the Irish racing community was made plain by the votes of condolence passed by both the Turf Club and the INHS Committee. Stewards and Members of the Committee expressed 'profound sorrow at the death of our late beloved Sovereign King'.[60] Edward's successor George V visited Ireland with his queen, Mary, in July 1911, as talk of Home Rule filled the air and Irish nationalism grew on the ground. The royal couple received a warm welcome in Dublin, including at the Phoenix Park Racecourse – which had opened through the contrivance of Sir John Arnott in 1902 – and at Leopardstown. There was also clear political opposition to the visit, however: in Dublin, nationalist and socialist groups protested in the streets and the Corporation refused to present a loyal address to the king and queen; in Limerick, meanwhile, tensions flared when a group forcefully entered a premises on Mungret Street and tore down a Union Jack flag.[61]

The royal visit demonstrated that Ireland was a changed and changing place, but it also highlighted the endurance of order and tradition amid a complex political, social, cultural and economic landscape. While the landlord system had been effectively dismantled by 1911, Ireland remained a hierarchical society and racing continued to provide a space for the nobility, gentry and large farmers to demonstrate their wealth and status. Ornament and spectacle were not confined to racecourses in and around

The Union Jack flying for the visit of Edward VII and Queen Alexandra to Leopardstown in 1907.

Dublin. This was evident in August 1912, when 'a large and fashionable attendance' was reported at the reopening of Tramore Racecourse in County Waterford. The encroaching sea had robbed the popular resort town of its racecourse and golf course, at considerable cost to owner Martin J. Murphy. The man known as the 'Napoleon of Tramore' was not cowed, however, and was rewarded with a bumper crowd at the course's reopening, with many attending 'to show the proprietor how Irishmen appreciate pluck'. Murphy's new enclosed course lay in a 'commanding position', and those travelling to the meeting could still glimpse the stands and other buildings of the old course, now half-submerged by the tide.[62]

The reopening of Tramore was a great success, not least for trainer James J. Parkinson, a Waterford native based at Maddenstown Lodge in Kildare, who had five winners across the three-day meeting.[63] Parkinson was the outstanding figure in early twentieth-century Irish racing. As a trainer, he achieved 2,577 wins across both Flat and National Hunt racing, a record only equalled in 2000 by Dermot Weld. In 1923 alone, he trained the winners in 137 Irish races and this record stood until 1990, when it was broken by Jim Bolger. Such was Parkinson's dominance, in fact, that on twenty-three occasions between 1906 and 1937, he recorded more winners than any other Irish trainer. Parkinson was also the foremost breeder in Ireland and exported horses widely, and often to different parts of the British Empire, including India, Malaya

The entertainment that accompanied race meetings often proved to be an attraction for racegoers, with the Amusement Field in Tramore proving popular in 1901. The town, which became a popular seaside spa and resort in the eighteenth century, hosted a four-day race festival every August from 1807.

Lady Kathleen Lindsay 'has a fancy' at the reopening of Tramore Racecourse.

J.J. Parkinson (centre) deep in conversation outside the parade ring at Tramore Races, c.1913. He was the leading Irish trainer a remarkable twenty-three times and dominated as an owner. Parkinson, who was also the foremost breeder and exporter of bloodstock on the island, was nominated to the first Seanad by W.T. Cosgrave in 1922.

and the Union of South Africa. He could indulge quantity to identify quality, and this underpinned his remarkable success as a trainer and owner. In his long reign, 1914 was perhaps his most remarkable year; as well as winning the title of leading trainer, with winnings totalling £10,292, he was also the most successful owner in Ireland and his eighteen-year-old son, Billy – who had previously professed little interest in the sport and had never ridden racehorses – was crowned champion amateur and champion jockey. Billy pipped the reigning champion and fellow amateur, Leslie Brabazon, to the title, and was even more successful in 1915, with 72 winning rides, an amateur record that was only surpassed by Patrick Mullins in 2012.[64]

CHAPTER TWO: 1870–1921

(left) The son of trainer J.J., Billy Parkinson (1896–1941) initially wanted to be an engineer and showed little interest in riding competitively, only sitting on a racehorse for the first time in 1914. He won the first of three consecutive champion jockey titles that year, despite being restricted to riding his own or his father's horses. He also won five amateur titles (1914–17, 1919 joint). (right) A headshot of leading amateur rider, Leslie Brabazon. Born in Westmeath in 1885, Brabazon enjoyed great success in the saddle, winning four amateur titles (1910 joint, 1911, 1912 and 1913) and becoming one of only three amateurs to top the overall jockeys championship in the twentieth century (1913).

An 'English invasion'

While the Parkinsons wrote their names in the annals of horse racing, the course of history changed direction. In Ireland, the growing prospect of Home Rule resulted in the formal establishment of the Ulster Volunteers in January 1913. Irish nationalists responded by forming the Irish Volunteers, adding to fears of violence and even civil war. Events in Ireland were overtaken in the summer of 1914, however. News of the assassination of Archduke Franz Ferdinand of Austria reached Ireland on the first day of the June meeting at Baldoyle, but gave rise to little alarm. The clouds of war quickly gathered over Europe, however, and on 4 August Britain entered the fray. Two days later, racing in Ireland was temporarily suspended when the Turf Club and the INHS Committee jointly announced that:

> Owing to the mobilization of the Army, and the consequent inability of the Irish Railway Companies to guarantee the dispatch of horses to the various race meetings, permission is granted to have the following meetings abandoned – Powerstown Park, Carnew, Tramore, Ennis and Miltown Malbay.[65]

The break was brief, with racing resumed at Leopardstown on 22 August, but any hopes that war would be short-lived were quickly extinguished, and Europe entered a new and savage reality. By the end of August, the war had claimed thousands of lives, and the INHS Committee voted to donate £100 to the Prince of Wales National Relief Fund, to support the families of soldiers.[66]

Both the Turf Club and the INHS Committee were fully supportive of the war effort but, with very few corners of life left untouched by the conflict, it was not long before the Irish racing authorities had to answer some existential questions. In May 1915, the Turf Club met to consider whether their programme should be abandoned, with one concern being the demand racing placed on the rail network. In the end, it was decided that Flat and National Hunt races should continue. Some 95 meetings took place across the island, with four held in aid of the Red Cross, and with Billy Parkinson again riding the most winners.[67] While racing continued largely uninterrupted in Ireland, the war caused significant disruption to British fixtures. At Aintree, the Grand National was run in 1914 and 1915 but the course was then requisitioned by the War Office, for use by the Army. Other English courses were proposed as venues for a 'War National', but there was some concern that an alteration to agreed fixtures there would not be allowed and the *Irish Field* concluded that in the circumstances, one could 'only look to Ireland'. Brief consideration was given to Leopardstown, where the fences might be built up to the required standard,[68] but in the end the 'War National' was run at Gatwick from 1916 to 1918, before returning to its Liverpool home. Two of the Gatwick winners – Vermouth and Ballymacad – were bred in Ireland. The latter was bred by J.J. Maher, a farmer's son who left a Benedictine monastery and was an amateur rider before enjoying success as a trainer and breeder. Maher also bred the winner of the 1913 Grand National, Covertcoat, but by then he had focused his attention almost exclusively on Flat horses. He nonetheless retained a deep interest in National Hunt racing and served as INHS Senior Steward on three occasions in the 1920s and 1930s.[69]

In Britain, the government did not initially move to curtail racing in wartime. That was because it served as an engine for the valuable bloodstock industry and helped to keep the British public entertained. A press campaign stoked public opposition to the carrying on of the sport, however, with participation in and attendance at race meetings characterized as unpatriotic. In 1915, the Jockey Club agreed to the abandonment of all race meetings beyond Newmarket, and there was only a small increase in permitted fixtures the following year.[70] Allied with the aggressive curtailment of British fixtures, the Army's relentless need for soldiers had significant implications for both branches of racing in Ireland. On 3 January 1916, in the expectation that Parliament would introduce conscription for single men in Britain, the INHS Committee postponed any decision on granting licences to jockeys.[71] Conscription of single men resulted in an increase in marriage rates, but it also contributed to an influx of racing professionals from Britain into Ireland, and this had implications for both National Hunt and Flat racing: the number of licenced trainers increased in both branches, while the number of licenced jockeys under INHS Rules rose from 129 in 1910, to 155 in 1915 and to 195 in 1920.[72] The arrival of English horses, jockeys and trainers was accompanied by the arrival of English spectators. At Leopardstown in August 1916, the crowd included 'a large number of English racing folk, who now that meetings are denied them across the Channel are delighted at the idea of enjoying the splendid sport provided in this country'. The benefit was not just to Irish racecourses, with many visitors looking to 'important sales of Irish bloodstock to occupy their attention during the week'.[73]

There was some debate over the impact of this 'English invasion', with those in favour arguing that it helped the 'gates' and improved the standard of Irish racing. Those against the increased English presence complained of a rise in training costs, particularly around the Curragh, where rents, labour charges and fodder prices all went up.[74] There was also an increase in crime, with 'a following of unusual desirables' travelling from England to Irish meetings, to pick the well-lined pockets of the assembled crowd.[75] The war had other and longer-lasting consequences for Irish racing, as the government took steps to divert domestic revenue to the Allied campaign. In 1915, the Excess Profits Duty was introduced, imposing a 50 per cent (and later 80 per cent) levy on any profits exceeding antebellum levels. While this tax was not welcomed, it was not as long-lasting nor depleting as the Entertainment Tax, which imposed a levy on admissions to places of public entertainment from 1916.

Race card for the Ward Union Hunt Steeplechases meeting at Fairyhouse Racecourse, which took place on Easter Monday 1916.

This levy continued to have a detrimental effect on racing throughout the 1920s; a period in which many courses struggled to survive.[76] While the Irish racing authorities worked to ensure that the sport continued throughout the war, they were also mindful of the sacrifices being made by members of the racing community on the battlefield. In April 1916, the INHS Committee's attention was drawn to the plight of British jockeys and stable boys interned in Germany. Lord Enniskillen 'promised to lay the details of a scheme for their relief before the Turf Club at the next Curragh Meeting and the Stewards were empowered by the Committee to deal with the matter'.[77]

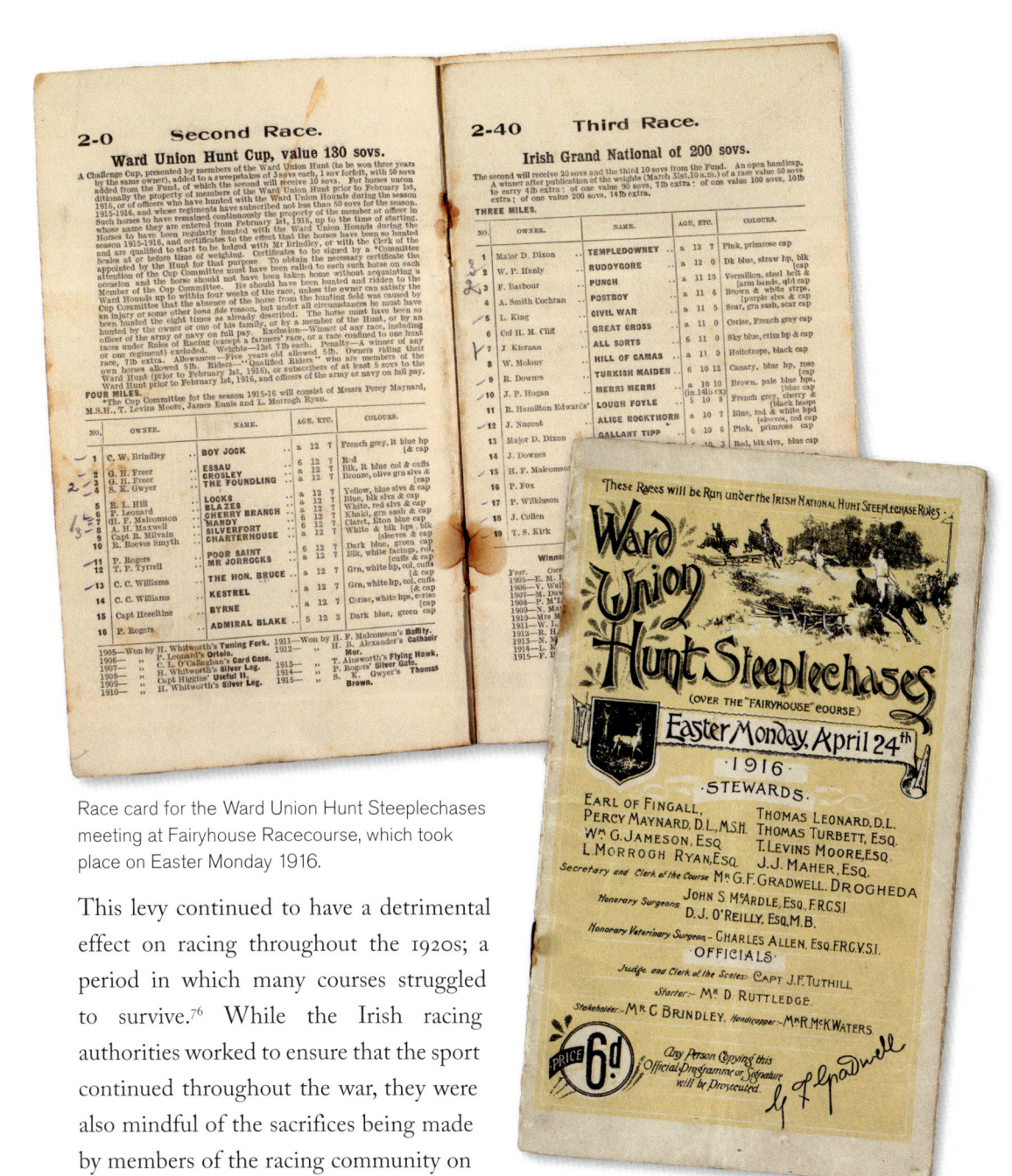

CHAPTER TWO: 1870–1921

71

The war effort was supported by the majority of Irish people, who accepted the deferral of Home Rule following the outbreak of the conflict in 1914. For those committed to Irish independence, however, Britain's difficulty was understood to be Ireland's opportunity. On Easter Monday 1916, thousands of people – including members of the British administration and a large contingent of British Army officers – travelled to the annual meeting at Fairyhouse. As trains and motor cars snaked out of Dublin, members of the Irish Volunteers, the Irish Citizen Army and Cumann na mBan began an armed insurrection. Most of the fighting took place in the city centre, where the rebels quickly gained control of the General Post Office on Sackville Street (now O'Connell Street). It was from that building that Patrick Pearse emerged at 12:45p.m. and read aloud the Proclamation of the Irish Republic. Racegoers who left town late carried reports of rebel activity in the capital, but news arrived piecemeal and accounts conflicted, leading British officials and officers to dismiss the threat and remain at Fairyhouse. Half an hour after Pearse proclaimed Irish independence in Dublin, racing got underway in County Meath, with the Grand National featuring as the third race on the programme. The field included two former National winners – Punch and Civil War – but it was the 'workmanlike' All Sorts who finished first past the post under jockey Jackie Lynn. All Sorts was an unlikely champion: owned by James Kiernan and trained by Dick Cleary in County Westmeath, his granddam had been 'a plain little pony whose success in a couple of the £4 19s. races … encouraged her owner to breed from her'.[78]

Racing continued through the afternoon, but it soon became clear that the events unfolding in Dublin were serious. The Army commandeered the trains, forcing anyone who had travelled by rail to walk home – including the National-winning All Sorts.[79] By evening-time on Easter Tuesday, the Lord Lieutenant, Viscount Wimborne, had declared martial law. One week later, long-serving INHS and Turf Club Steward Percy La Touche armed himself with revolvers and drove his motor car to Dublin. By then, the rebels had surrendered, and La Touche learned that several rebel leaders had been court martialled and executed.[80] The British response to the Rising stoked public support for the Republican cause and resulted in the replacement of General John Maxwell as Commander-in-Chief of the British Army in Ireland. Maxwell's successor was General Bryan Mahon, a Galwayman who had commanded the 10th Irish Division during the ill-fated Gallipoli campaign, before being appointed Commander of the British forces at Salonika. Mahon's transfer to Ireland reflected the British government's belief that, as an Irishman, he was better-equipped to restore calm to the country. His reputation as a passionate horseman meant that his arrival was welcomed by the Turf Club and the INHS Committee, with both bodies admitting him to their membership.[81]

Only time would reveal the profound consequences of the Easter Rising, but for racing its immediate impact was the suspension of fixtures by the Turf Club and INHS Committee until 9 June, when action resumed at Leopardstown. By the end of the year, a total of 86 meetings had been held across the island. This included the inaugural meeting at Limerick Junction, in September 1916.[82] The continuation of racing in Ireland came under threat in 1917, however. A curtailment of fixtures was expected, but by May the War Cabinet had resolved that horse racing in Britain and Ireland was to end for the duration of the conflict.[83] The Stewards of the Turf Club were instructed to make an announcement to that effect. This caused alarm beyond racing circles, with Galway Urban District Council passing a resolution calling to 'the attention of the Lord Lieutenant of Ireland and the Chief Secretary that the order with the object of prohibiting racing, if it applies to the Galway Races, will mean a loss of about £10,000 to the people of Galway, who are already very hard hit by the war, that it will be disastrous to hotels and other public places in Galway'.[84] The Turf Club were also directed to make arrangements to limit the supply of oats to race horses in Ireland, to avoid a depletion of grain stocks. Senior Steward Lord Decies travelled immediately to London to appeal to Henry Duke, Chief Secretary for Ireland, and Lord Devonport, the Food Controller. Decies argued that the complete abandonment of fixtures would be disastrous for those involved, not only in racing, but in horse breeding – an industry already impacted by the demands of the Army Remount Department and a reduction in the government subsidy.[85]

Many small Irish breeders relied on racing to advertise the quality of their animals and the Stewards of the Turf Club eventually persuaded the War Cabinet to permit a limited fixture list in Ireland.[86] This was not an unqualified success, however, as members of the Irish Breeders', Owners' and Trainers' Association (IBOTA) – which was formed in the 1890s but began to act in concerted fashion during the war – believed that the Stewards had sought preferential treatment for the Curragh and 'one or two other places'. At a meeting to protest the fixture list, IBOTA Secretary Edward Kennedy told attendees that the Irish bloodstock and racing industries provided employment to between 15,000 and 20,000 people and that Irish breeders had provided 300,000 horses for export since the outbreak of the war. IBOTA demanded that the Stewards seek sanction for meetings at Gowran Park, Limerick Junction and Thurles, alongside the Curragh and metropolitan courses, but only Gowran Park was permitted to go ahead in June. The crisis was short-lived, however, as the government ended its ban on race meetings one month later. In the end, a total of 112 race days across 81 meetings were held in Ireland in 1917.[87]

A 'misguided and destructive policy'

The unprecedented casualties inflicted by the war meant that by 1918, the conscription of Irish men had become a very real prospect. The political landscape had altered significantly in the years following the Easter Rising and Irish Republicans were supported in resisting the introduction of conscription by the trade unions and the Catholic Church. A general strike was organized and took effect on 23 April 1918 – the first day of the Punchestown meeting. The *Irish Field* concluded that

> the fact that Punchestown should be badly hit was of minor importance compared with the total dislocation of the business of the country for a whole day; but the great Kildare steeplechasing carnival has come to be regarded as a national institution, endeared by association and tradition of all creeds and classes, and it was a pity so many should have been debarred from participating in the opening stage as the result of the suspension of the railway service.[88]

Less than one month after the Punchestown meeting, political tensions escalated further, as the Lord Lieutenant, Field Marshal Viscount French, ordered the arrest of prominent Republicans, including Eamon de Valera and Arthur Griffith, who were alleged to have 'conspired to enter into, and had entered into, treasonable communication with the German enemy'. By this point, the tide of popular opinion had turned in favour of an independent Ireland, free of British influence, and hopes for the peaceful introduction of Home Rule had all but disappeared. The end of the First World War in November 1918 was followed by a general election in which the unambiguously Republican Sinn Féin won a landslide victory. Newly elected Sinn

Féin MPs refused to take their seats in Westminster, instead forming Dáil Éireann on 21 January 1919. On the same day, two policemen escorting explosives to a quarry were shot dead by the Irish Volunteers (soon renamed the Irish Republican Army (IRA)) at Soloheadbeg, County Tipperary. With this action, the War of Independence began and rumours quickly began to circulate that the Irish Railway Executive would request a curtailment of Irish racing because of a shortage of coal. This would have a direct impact on racing, as trains remained the primary means of transporting horses to meetings across the island. These fears were not without foundation: coal shortages and a reduced rail service had already negatively impacted the 1918 programme, with the government only sanctioning 85 days racing for the year, a reduction of 27 days on 1917. Provincial courses struggled more than their metropolitan counterparts and this fuelled resentments toward the Turf Club and INHS Committee, who had refused executives the chance to hold meetings without a rail service.[89]

Difficulties encountered in powering the 'Iron Horse' would continue to impact on Irish racing during the War of Independence, and served to compound a difficult period for the sport. Following the eruption of the war in early 1919, Sinn Féin and the IRA began a targeted campaign against hunt clubs across Ireland. This had obvious parallels with the campaign undertaken in the 1880s, and demonstrated the enduring perception of hunting as the preserve of the elite. Hunt meetings and point-to-points were cancelled, and the IRA's campaign resulted in the abandonment of five race meetings advertised under INHS Rules, including both Fairyhouse and Punchestown. On 19 March 1919, the Committee met to discuss the 'general situation in regard to racing under the INHS Rules in different parts of the country … owing to the action of the Sinn Féin Executive'. The Committee 'unanimously recorded their unqualified endorsement of the decision of the [local] Stewards, and expressed the strongest condemnation of the misguided and destructive policy that had left the Stewards no alternative but to act in the manner aforementioned'.[90] A week before the INHS Committee met, all remaining Sinn Féin members interned in Britain were released. On 1 April, the Dáil met privately and elected Eamon de Valera as its President. The War of Independence carried on, with the IRA employing guerrilla tactics to target policemen and British troops. The biggest disruption to horse racing in 1919, however, was a continued shortage of coal, which was exacerbated by miners' strikes in Britain. Racing was postponed because of shortages in early October but resumed mid-month at Gowran Park. In all, 85 meetings were held in 1919, with J.J. Parkinson again finishing as leading trainer. Joseph Canty was leading jockey, with 65 winners, while Joe Manly and Billy Parkinson shared the amateur honours, with seven winners each.[91]

Irish horses were particularly successful in Britain after the First World War, meanwhile, with Troytown claiming the Grand National at Aintree in 1920. Bred in County Meath and trained by Algy Anthony at Westenra Lodge on the Curragh, Troytown was a late starter, making his first appearance as a six-year-old in the Maiden Plate at Baldoyle in January 1918. He won the Silverpark Maiden Steeplechase at Leopardstown in March 1919, before finishing outside the places in the Stanley Steeplechase at Aintree. He did not leave Liverpool empty handed, however, as he claimed the Champion Chase. That year, the hard-mouthed brown gelding also won the Grand Steeple-Chase de Paris, making him only the second horse in history, after the great Jerry M., to claim both that prize and a Grand National win. Like Jerry M., Troytown followed up his French victory by winning the Grand National, pulling winning amateur rider J.R. 'Jack' Anthony around the course to victory. After the race, Anthony – who had previously won the National with Glenside (1911) and Ally Sloper (1915) – described Troytown as a 'bloomin' steam engine'. The horse's success was followed by tragedy, however, when he broke his leg in the Prix des Drags at Auteuil the following June, and had to be destroyed. A year after Troytown's Aintree success, another Irish-bred horse claimed the 'Blue Riband of Steeplechasing'. Shaun Spadah was bred in Streamstown, County Westmeath, by Patrick McKenna – a large farmer who twice failed to win a seat for the Irish Parliamentary Party in Westminster, before being elected to the Dáil on the Farmers' Party ticket in 1923. From a sire that once changed hands for the small sum of £3, Shaun Spadah was an unlikely success story. He was trained as a two-year-old by Algy Anthony, who rejected him in the belief that he lacked sufficient speed for racing on the flat. He was successful in his first steeplechase at Downpatrick, and won three of four steeplechases in Ireland as a four-year-old, before being sold to the Scottish civil engineer and construction magnate, Sir Malcolm McAlpine. Shaun Spadah completed the Grand National without falling in 1919, but finished unplaced. It was solid jumping that won him the race in 1921, when he cantered home under jockey Fred Rees as the only horse in a field of thirty-five not to fall.[92]

The War of Independence increased in bloodshed and bitterness in 1920, as the guerrilla tactics of the IRA were met by the violent reprisals of the Black and Tans and

"Jerry M"
Grand National, 1912

Player's Cigarettes

A cigarette card depicting Jerry M., a big, handsome horse who was one of the great National Hunt performers of the early twentieth century. Bred in County Limerick by Kate Hartigan, Jerry M. became the first dual winner of the Grand Steeple-Chase de Paris (1910) and the Grand National (1912). Owned by Sir Charles Assheton-Smith and trained by Bob Gore, he was ridden by Ernie Piggott, grandfather of the famous Flat jockey, Lester.

Auxiliaries. A general strike in support of Republican prisoners caused Punchestown to be cancelled, but 80 meetings were held throughout the year. The war made a violent intrusion upon the sport on 30 July 1920, however, when Frank Brooke, chairman of the Dublin and South Eastern Railway, was assassinated in his office at Westland Row Station. Brooke was Senior Steward of the Turf Club, a member of the INHS Committee and a Steward at both Leopardstown and the Phoenix Park.[93] While not a particularly prominent unionist, he had served as a Privy Councillor and acted as an advisor to the recently departed Lord Lieutenant, Viscount French, and this connection may have sealed his fate. Brooke was replaced as Senior Steward of the Turf Club by Percy La Touche, who had been a leading figure in both the Flat and National Hunt authorities for thirty years and for whom a storied cross country race at Punchestown is named. La Touche, who was vice-president of the Irish Unionist Council, died less than one year later, in April 1921, and Captain H. Dixon proposed a resolution of sympathy to his family at a meeting of the INHS Committee that month. La Touche was 'a great Irishman, a good sportsman, and the most outstanding personality in the world of sport of his generation. As a

Turf legislator he had no equal, and as an authority he was everywhere recognized.'[94]

In May 1921, one month after La Touche passed away, the Government of Ireland Act came into effect, partitioning the island and creating Northern Ireland. On 22 June, the King opened the Parliament of Northern Ireland and appealed to 'all Irishmen to pause, to stretch out the hand of forbearance and conciliation, to forgive and forget, and to join in making for the land they love a new era of peace, contentment and goodwill'.[95] In early July, members of Dáil Éireann agreed to enter formal negotiations with the British government; fighting was soon suspended and, on 6 December 1921, the signing of the Anglo-Irish Treaty brought an end to the war and provided for the establishment the Irish Free State. This was a critical moment for National Hunt racing in Ireland. In the decades since the formation of the INHS Committee, it had evolved into a coherent and modern sport and it proved increasingly to be a valuable commercial concern – primarily as an adjunct to the

A powerful performer, Troytown was another National Hunt star of the early twentieth century and is the only horse other than Jerry M. to have won the Grand Steeple-Chase de Paris (1919) and the Grand National (1920). His career was brought to a sudden and tragic halt in 1920, when he suffered a fatal fall at Auteuil. Bred near Navan in County Meath, he is remembered by the annual Troytown Chase at Navan Racecourse.

Stable lads at Westenra Lodge near Kildare town in 1920. This was where Algy Anthony trained the great Troytown to win the Grand Steeple-Chase and the Grand National.

Shaun Spadah (which translates to 'John the Bogman') was the only one of thirty-five horses to complete the Grand National course without falling in 1921, when he cantered to a comfortable victory. He was bred in County Westmeath by Patrick McKenna, who was a Farmers' Party TD for Longford–Westmeath between 1923 and 1927.

breeding industry but also in its own right. It had survived a decade of devastating conflict and bitter recrimination, but the new political reality left the Anglo-Irish arbiters of the sport in a vulnerable position. As the island descended into civil war, the traditionally unionist INHS Committee, like the Turf Club, had to navigate new and unpredictable terrain to ensure the survival of the sport they had nurtured to the brink of maturity.

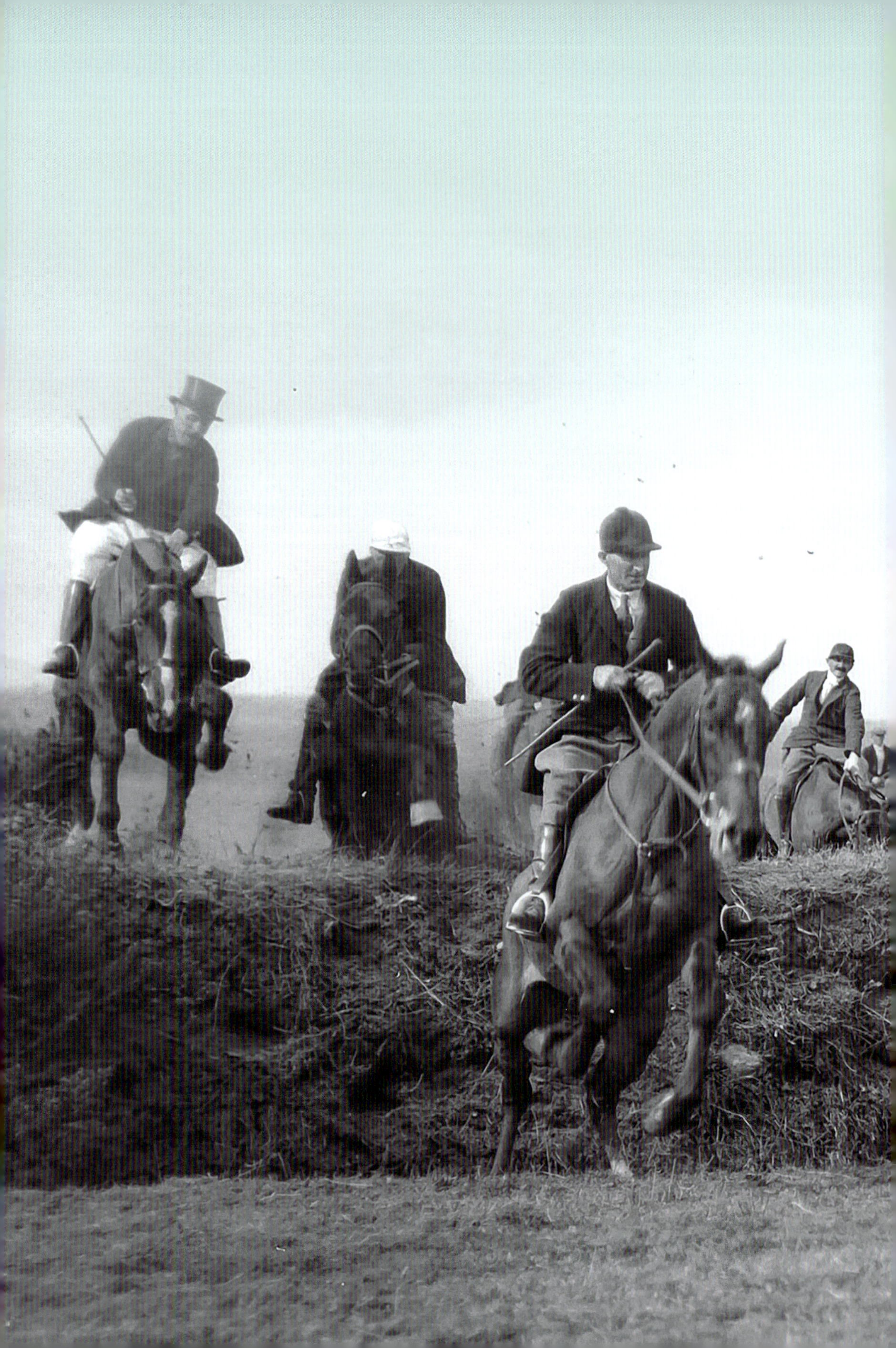

CHAPTER THREE

1922-1945

'A national industry and a national sport'

BY 1922, IRELAND WAS TRANSFORMED. A near-decade of change, forged in the fire of global and domestic conflict, resulted in partition and the creation of Northern Ireland and the Irish Free State. The end of the War of Independence did not signal an end to bloodshed, however, and between June 1922 and May 1923 the pro-Treaty Free State forces and the anti-Treaty IRA fought a bitter civil war over what might have been and what was to come. The old ruling class found themselves 'rather exposed' following the ratification of the Treaty, but W.T. Cosgrave's Cumann na nGaedheal government recognized the importance of plurality and sought to include members of the Anglo-Irish elite in the establishment of the State. For their part, the Anglo-Irish community understood that the surest path forward was to accept the new reality, whatever that might look like. This attitude extended to racing's governing bodies, who approached Ireland's changed circumstances with pragmatic resolve. The 1920s and 30s were replete with challenges for both branches of the sport, as the Free State 'grew into a particularly unpromising youth' and went 'awkwardly through its "tedious years of adjustment".'[1] But this was also a moment of unmistakable opportunity. Irish horses continued to perform at the highest level, with chasers in particular thrilling crowds across Ireland and Britain and underlining the quality of the island's bloodstock. With the Free State government seeking to shape its economic identity, racing was recognized as a shop window for the valuable

Photograph of W.T. Cosgrave mounted on a black horse in full riding gear. Horse racing and breeding benefitted from the support of successive Irish governments, and few political leaders were more supportive than Cosgrave, who was President of the Executive Council of the Irish Free State, 1922–32.

breeding industry and, increasingly, as an important industry in its own right. For this reason, successive Irish governments took steps to develop the sport, and while these efforts did not immediately transform its flagging fortunes, they did provide a solid foundation on which to build. By surviving the challenging political and economic climate of the 1920s and 1930s and the impecunity of the Emergency (the Second World War), National Hunt racing in Ireland would climb, by 1945, to the brink of something truly transformational.

'North and South mingle on the common field of sport'

As Ireland descended into civil war, members of the Turf Club and the INHS Committee understood the importance of acknowledging the new political order. This pragmatic attitude was demonstrated in remarkable fashion in July 1922, when the executive of the Phoenix Park Racecourse hosted 'The IRA Meeting', an event organized to raise funds for disabled Republican soldiers. There is no record of the Turf Club Stewards' views on the meeting, but they allowed it to go ahead and in doing so, they demonstrated a willingness to look past political differences to ensure the future success of their sport.[2] The determination of racing's governing bodies to adapt and accommodate different political perspectives was underlined again in September 1922, when both the Turf Club and INHS Committee passed resolutions of sympathy following the death of the President of the Executive Council of the Free State, Arthur Griffith, and the assassination of General Michael Collins.[3] Given the pace and scale of change in Ireland after the First World War and the preponderance of unionists in racing circles, this was an extraordinary development. On the other side, the fundamental importance of the Anglo-Irish community to breeding and racing could not be overlooked by the Free State government. While 'the joy of racing and its rivalry continued to transcend ancient enmities', the impulse to overlook those enmities was also rooted – deeply – in economic concerns.[4] These concerns combined with the Free State government's desire for a representative Oireachtas to ensure that a number of men involved in racing and breeding were installed in the first Seanad in 1922. The twin industries were helped by W.T. Cosgrave's position as President of the Executive Council, as he had a deep love of horses, was a member of the Kildare Hunt, and was committed to the success of Irish breeding and racing. As well as the earl of Mayo and Sir Bryan Mahon, Cosgrave's nominations to the first Seanad included the earl of Granard, who was a Steward of the Turf Club; Captain Henry Greer, Director of the National Stud and a member of the Jockey Club and the Turf Club; Colonel Maurice Moore (son of George Henry); and J.J. Parkinson.[5]

For their part, the Turf Club and INHS Committee demonstrated that horse racing could be a powerful agent of continuity in a period of seismic change. The two bodies also proved that cross-border co-operation on sport was possible, as Flat and National Hunt racing continued to be governed on an all-island basis. In this respect, the Turf Club and INHS Committee resembled the Irish Rugby Football Union, which also had a strong unionist contingent and continued to control their sport north and south of the new border. Unlike horse racing, however, rugby union was played and supported by a relatively small section of the Irish population. While members of the Anglo-Irish elite continued to dominate, racing – and specifically National Hunt racing – attracted a significant number of small owners and trainers

A large crowd at Down Royal in 1931. Racing in Northern Ireland remained under the purview of the Turf Club and the INHS Committee after the partition of the island in 1921.

across the island. National Hunt also continued to attract a broad base of spectators, with large numbers of 'ordinary' Irish people attending meetings. As a shared social space, race meetings had an obvious value to the Free State government. The sport had long served as a platform for the social and political elite, with viceregal couples in regular attendance at major meetings, and occasionally at point-to-points. In April 1923, Cosgrave and the new Governor-General of the Free State, T.M. Healy, attended Punchestown, where they enjoyed the social habits of the old order. By adopting this tradition, they advertised the new political reality in Ireland. A contributor to *Irish Life* noted that 'Punchestown is a national event that recognizes no polities and no partition. There North and South mingle on the common field of sport, as we hope they will eventually in the more serious field of politics'. The presence of the two men was, the commentator added hopefully, 'a happy omen of coming good and peaceful times'.[6]

A correspondent for the *Kildare Observer* took a more partisan view, noting that 'we are having Punchestown this week under altered conditions. For the first time it is being held in a purely Irish atmosphere – with not even a lord lieutenant to pay a visit official or unofficial.'[7] Cosgrave and Healy's attendance at Punchestown came five months after the formation of the Free State government. This historic moment was not followed by 'good and peaceful times', however. The anti-Treaty IRA's threat to the racing community was underlined by the presence of Free State soldiers on patrol at point-to-point meetings and by the mining of a bridge on the railway line to Fairyhouse on Easter Monday 1923.[8] Away from the racecourse, anti-Treaty forces intensified a campaign to burn many of the 'big houses' that punctuated the landscape. The homes of a number of senators with ties to horse racing were targeted, including Lord Mayo, Colonel Maurice Moore and Sir Bryan Mahon. Throughout the violent climax of the Civil War, however, the racing community continued to work in the interest of their sport and they were supported by the of Free State government, who recognized the value of their endeavours to the Irish economy.

Those who attended Punchestown alongside Healy and Cosgrave in April 1923 would have had the pleasure of watching one of the greats of Irish steeplechasing, Harry Beasley, ride Pride of Arras to victory in the Maiden Plate. In jubilation, the

Governor-General of the Irish Free State, T.M. Healy, inspecting the cups at Punchestown in 1923.

'huge crowd rose to the wonderful veteran in a spontaneous tribute unparalleled in Irish racing. A mighty roar of cheering followed Pride of Arras past the post and the scenes of enthusiasm in the paddock when horse and rider returned to scale beggars description.'[9] The then 71-year-old's winning ride served as a reminder of 'halcyon days' of Irish jump racing, when the sport stood on the precipice of commercialization but still retained the lawless edge of the nineteenth-century steeplechase. By 1923, horse racing in Ireland had transformed into a regulated concern. After an unspectacular start to the twentieth century, racing began to prosper in 1911–12, and by the outbreak of the First World War it was a booming business, with the opening of new courses like Gowran Park (1914) and the improvement of others, like Down Royal.[10] This period of prosperity continued immediately after the war, even as domestic conflict impacted on the calendar, and taxation – in the form of the Entertainment Tax and Excess Profits Duty – took a healthy share of racecourse profits. At the same time, the increasing commercialization of racing resulted in a concentration of recognized meetings in metropolitan courses and a falling away of provincial meetings. This circumstance was highlighted by INHS Steward J.J. Maher in November 1922, when he proposed that the Committee 'should give out of their funds say four races of the value of 50 *sovs.* each to some of the Country Meetings, who find it most difficult to carry on'.[11]

'the condition of racing in Ireland at the present time is far from perfect'

Despite the ongoing War of Independence and the first signs of discontent among provincial racecourse executives, the decade began optimistically. The inaugural meeting at Proudstown Park in Navan took place in September 1921, Naas Race Company was formed the following year and the racecourse there was opened in June 1924. In April 1923, Turf Club Senior Steward, Sir William Goulding, felt confident enough to congratulate members on 'the results we have achieved considering the very troublous times we have passed through … racing has progressed in a wonderful manner … in spite of the many difficulties that have had to be faced, caused by strikes, political unrest, postponements and abandonments following the want of racing facilities'.[12] Racing's ascendance was evident in a Dáil debate on a failed Sweepstakes Bill in 1923, when TD Vincent White's observation that 'the three great divisions of

Some founder members of Naas Race Company at the inaugural meeting at the racecourse on 19 June 1924. General Francis Waldron, the Senior Handicapper, and Thomas Whelan, the first chair of Naas Race Company, are on the left, while Edward 'Cub' Kennedy, who bred The Tetrarch and was chair of Goffs from 1922 to 1925, is on the right.

any nation – the three most important services – are the Church, the State –' was interupted by the rejoinder, 'And the Turf'.[13] It was a comment made in jest, but it revealed an underlying truth: as the Free State struggled to find its economic feet, both horse breeding and racing assumed ever-greater importance.

The breeding industry in Ireland was well-established, but its development was distinct in both structure and composition. Large studs, like those owned by Colonel William Hall Walker at Tully and J.J. Parkinson on the Curragh, operated alongside a large number of small breeders; typically farmers in possession of a good mare, who bred, raced and sold high-quality horses on a much smaller scale. The First World War impacted significantly on Irish breeding, as the Army Remount Department worked to replace high numbers of equine casualties and so reduced the population of good quality Irish horses. Particular concern was expressed over the large number

Being Seen, Tuning In: Horse Racing and Early Media

Media has long played an important part in horse racing, with newspapers printing advertisements for race meetings from the early eighteenth century and contributing significantly to the sport's growth in popularity. Photography became a feature of Irish race meetings in the late nineteenth century, with the first photographic image of an Irish race meeting dating from 1868, when the Prince of Wales' visit to Punchestown was captured for posterity. This new medium quickly gained in popularity and by the 1910s photographers were a regular feature at racecourses across Ireland, capturing the excitement on the track and the fashionable attendances off it. Many such photographs appeared in the society periodical *Irish Life*. In May 1916, however, the governing bodies issued the following notice to clerks of the course: 'The Stewards of the Turf Club and of the INHS Committee strictly forbid the taking of photographs at race meetings. Clerks of course are instructed not to admit

The first photographs of an Irish race meeting were taken in 1868, when James Simonton and Frederick Holland Mares captured scenes from the Prince of Wales' visit to Punchestown.

Cameras were a common feature at race meetings by the early twentieth century. Used to capture events at the reopening of the racecourse at Tramore in 1912, the Wonder Photo Canon was a magazine camera for one-inch ferrotype plates produced by the Chicago Ferrotype Company.

to enclosures etc., persons with photographic outfits in their possession.'[1] On foot of the Easter Rising, this directive may have been issued to stop unknown persons from gaining access to areas populated by members of the Anglo-Irish elite and the British administration in Ireland. Photographers nevertheless continued to document Irish race meetings and did so during both the War of Independence and Civil War.[2] By then, a new form of technology had arrived at Irish racecourses: the film camera. Operators captured the excitement of the inaugural meeting at Proudstown Park in Navan in 1921 and Punchestown in 1926.[3] The arrival of film cameras marked a new and exciting era in Irish racing. Now – in grainy black and white – the thrilling exploits of horse and jockey could be captured and replayed to audiences in newly constructed cinemas across the island. The 1920s also saw the advent of radio broadcasting, which raised the possibility of 'tuning in' to horse racing on the wireless. This was a hard-won pleasure for Irish people, however. In August 1926, the newly established 2RN (later Radio Éireann) became the first station in Europe to broadcast a field game – the All-Ireland hurling semi-final. The Irish government was less enthusiastic about proposals to report on racing, however.[4] In 1924, responding to a suggestion that racing results might be broadcast on 2RN, Minister for Posts and Telegraphs J.J. Walsh replied, 'No, not under any circumstances', adding that he considered 'racing to be the deadliest element in the life of this country.'[5] By 1928, however, it was acknowledged that the broadcasting of racing results was 'a matter which may have to be reconsidered', and that there was a need 'to get some idea of what public opinion generally is on the matter.'[6]

of mares being allowed to go barren, a situation that caused some smaller studs to shut down, but the industry endured and there was a 'pronounced increase' in the number of Irish stud farms, and the number of broodmares kept in each stud, after the First World War. By 1927, there were 40 large and 200 smaller stud farms across the island. This included the National Stud at Tully, which was donated by Hall Walker to the British government in 1916. It also included two of the most valuable studs in the world in the mid-1920s: Gilltown Stud, then owned by Viscount Furness; and the Aga Khan's nearby Sheshoon Stud. Other successful operations included Ballykisteen, Straffan, Greenfields, Adare, Balreask, Cloghran, Ballylinch, Old Connell, Knockainey, Moyglare, Glascairn and Slane Castle.[14]

The boom in Irish stud farms was underpinned by a boom in Irish racing in the post-war period. Racing's chief importance to the State was as a shop window for the valuable breeding industry: the sport advertised the quality of Irish horses, which were exported widely and in great numbers, and it also allowed owners to ascertain the value of their animals for stud purposes. The success of Irish-bred chasers in England, in particular, made them an attractive prospect to British and to wealthy American owners, who increasingly took an interest in winning the Grand National.[15] In 1922, another Irish-bred chaser won the famous steeplechase. Music Hall was bred in County Kildare by Mrs Freddie Blacker, who broke the gelding to hunt while her husband was serving in the First World War. He was sold into England, as a hunter to Miss Molly Stokes, and won the Scottish Grand National before being sold to Hugh Kershaw. Trained by Owen Anthony, Music Hall was ridden to victory at Aintree by Lewis Rees, the brother of Fred Rees, who had piloted Shaun Spadah home one year earlier.[16] In 1923, the spoils went to the thirteen-year-old Sergeant Murphy, who was bred in County Meath by G.L. Walker and – as the property of Stephen 'Laddie' Sanford – became the first American-owned horse to win the famous steeplechase. The chestnut Sergeant Murphy competed in the Grand National a total of seven times, beginning with the War National at Gatwick in 1918, and ending in 1925, when the then fifteen-year-old was remounted to finish tenth. The Sergeant's exploits made him 'one of the truly great stalwarts of the race', but his legacy was tinged with tragedy, as three of the men who rode him in the National – William Smith, Charles Hawkins and winning rider Captain G.H. 'Tuppy' Bennet – were all killed within a period of two years, after racecourse falls.[17]

Seargent Murphy, with trainer George Blackwell at the head and Captain G.H. 'Tuppy' Bennet up. Bred in County Meath, Sergeant Murphy ran in seven Grand Nationals and, in 1923, became the first horse owned by an American (Stephen 'Laddie' Sanford) to win the race.

Master Robert – a gentle-natured, thick-winded chestnut bred by Robert McKinlay in County Donegal – added to the list of Irish-bred Grand National winners in 1924.[18] At the same Aintree meeting, Ballinode, who was commonly referred to as 'the Sligo Mare', won the Grand Sefton Steeplechase. The following year, she became the first Irish-trained horse and the first mare (of four in total) to win the Cheltenham Gold Cup, delivering a famous victory for her Curragh-based trainer, Frank Morgan, and owner Joss Bentley.[19] These achievements further advertised the quality of Irish chasers to British, American and other international buyers. In Ireland, meanwhile, the success of racing after the First World War meant that racecourses were able to turn healthy profits, even while subject to high levels of taxation. This was sustainable as long as meetings attracted large enough crowds. For a time they did, and then they didn't. By September 1923, there were rumblings in the press that all was not well, with a contributor to *Irish Life* observing that it was an 'open secret' that the 'condition of racing in Ireland at the present time is far from

A cartoon by Gordon Brewster titled 'The "G" Man – a proposal to tax betting is under consideration by the government', for publication in the *Evening Herald* on 28 January 1926. It depicts Minister for Finance, Ernest Blythe (on the right), glaring at an anxious-looking bookmaker.

perfect'. Owners complained about the cost of keeping and running horses, while the expense of a day at the races had increased because of the duties introduced during the war, and because of the 'exorbitant' train fares that resulted from the removal of rail subsidies.[20] The growing feeling of unease around racing was not helped by inclement Irish weather, with heavy rainfall resulting in the suspension of eighteen meetings between 1 May and 31 December 1923.[21]

While the opening of courses at Mallow and Naas in 1924 suggested that racing remained in rude health, it could not escape the Free State's general economic malaise, as the pragmatic and conservative Cumann na nGaedheal government imposed austerity and presided over a period of economic depression.[22] The Excess Profits Duty was repealed in 1921, but the Entertainment Tax took a greater toll, as the Irish population grew more reluctant to spend their money at race meetings. Matters were not helped by the introduction of a Betting Tax in 1926.[23] The Free State Minister for Finance, Ernest Blythe, sought to include the measure in the 1926 Budget, but it was racing's great friend, Cosgrave, who signed the tax into law; he was persuaded, no doubt, by the State's ailing finances and the argument that the sport's problems were a consequence of too many race meetings.[24] The tax was designed to generate revenue by imposing a 2.5 per cent levy on all on-course wagers and a 5 per cent levy on those made in betting offices. It was deeply unpopular in the racing industry but it proved to be a healthy revenue stream for the government, yielding £120,863 within eight months of its introduction.[25]

The legislation that brought the Betting Tax into existence also introduced measures to curb illegal street betting, which had become a significant problem in impoverished urban areas. The problem was particularly acute in Dublin, where betting offices

> are conducted in a noisy and disorderly manner; crowds congregate and loiter in them; lists of runners and odds are displayed as on a racecourse; backers wait on from one event to another, payments being made immediately after results, which are obtained immediately by special telephone service; children, and women accompanied by children, are present in the crowd, with a consequent increase in juvenile gambling; these evils are increased in poorer class areas in the cities; the gambling craze has affected all classes down to persons in receipt of unemployment benefit and home assistance, and the total results are demoralising, disorderly, uneconomic, thriftless.[26]

The law did much to reduce the epidemic of illegal betting by requiring bookmakers to hold licences, have certification for their premises and limit their hours of business.[27] The government could feel some satisfaction at the increase in revenue and the regulation of betting, but the racing community was convinced that the Betting Tax would make a bad situation worse. Both the Turf Club and IBOTA – the representative body for breeders, owners and trainers – lobbied Blythe to abolish the on-course levy, but the Minister for Finance refused to do so until 1931.[28]

Unsurprisingly, the poor health of Irish racing was an ongoing concern for the governing bodies. In January 1926, retiring Senior Steward of the Committee, Sir

Walter Nugent, urged members to promote the sport in Ireland. He pointed to the success that the National Hunt Committee had made of the Cheltenham Festival – which expanded to three days in 1923 and inaugurated the Gold Cup in 1924 and the Champion Hurdle in 1927 – and urged that it be replicated at Punchestown. He advised the Committee to work closely with the Kildare Hunt and suggested that the recently appointed Manager of Punchestown, Sir Bryan Mahon, be made Senior Steward, as he was uniquely placed to pursue an Irish equivalent to the meeting at Prestbury Park.[29] Mahon was duly appointed, but by then National Hunt racing required more than an Irish Cheltenham to reverse its fortunes. The challenges facing the industry were significant and the situation was fast becoming dire. Among other issues, the exodus of yearlings to England at low prices, the decline and disappearance of provincial meetings and the scourge of betting shops gave trainer Hubert Hartigan cause for despair. In 1927 Hartigan travelled around the traditional racing strongholds of Meath and Westmeath and found that he 'could not see a steeplechase horse between two and four years old'. This circumstance was all the more upsetting because 'it was that horse that made this country the best horse country in the world'.[30]

'a national industry and a national sport'

The pressures placed on horse racing and breeding during the war and in the 1920s resulted in disagreement between the governing bodies and different stakeholder groups that emerged within the industries. In 1919, IBOTA criticized the prevalence of low stakes, high forfeits and registry charges, but unsuccessfully sought to have some of their members elected as Stewards of the Turf Club. One year later, however, IBOTA successfully compelled the Turf Club to institute an inquiry into the expense of racing in Ireland. While the resulting report made little impact, it demonstrated the growing power of representative groups, which formed to martial and advance the interests of stakeholders in the thoroughbred industry. IBOTA was dissolved in January 1923, to be replaced by the Thoroughbred Breeders' and Owners' Association.[31] The Trainers' Association came into being one year later, and quickly found itself at odds with the Irish Transport and General Workers' Union (ITGWU) over trainers' plans to cut the pay of stable staff to satisfy owners' demands for a reduction in charges. Stable staff at the Curragh moved to strike and their sudden unemployment meant that most experienced hardship. The strike ended in April 1924, when staff agreed to return to work with no improvement to their pay, which at that point amounted to £2 per week for lodgers and boarders, £1 per week for those who 'lived in' and £2 to a winner's groom.[32] With hostilities ended, the chairman of the Trainers' Association, J.J. Parkinson, stated that trainers 'are not desirous of making capital out of the boys who were on strike coming back to work. Our regret is that the strike should have taken place at all. Our outlook on the situation is that it was a victory without cheers and a defeat without tears.'[33]

The Curragh strike came to a quick conclusion, but there were other grievances growing in the industry. Dissatisfaction over a decline in revenues at provincial courses, along with an increase in the share of meetings held by Dublin-area executives resulted in the formation of the Irish Provincial Racecourse Executives' Association (IPREA) in 1924. Many blamed the Turf Club and the INHS Committee for racing's woes, and tensions between the IPREA and the governing bodies boiled over when Mallow Racecourse was refused a renewal of an Easter Monday meeting for 1927, despite its success the previous year. Mallow's manager, F.F. McCabe, blamed the influence of National Hunt interests at Fairyhouse and, when the Turf Club refused to bring his complaint before a general meeting, he called on the IPREA to protest. The IPREA believed that there was a bias toward metropolitan courses in deciding the fixture list and they also resented the charges levied by the governing bodies, including officials' fees and the cost of advertising meetings in the *Racing Calendar*. On the other side, the Turf Club and INHS Committee believed that the provincial executives had played a significant part in creating their own difficulties, by paying generous dividends to shareholders during the post-war boom. This view was shared, to an extent, by the government.[34]

With divisions deepening, the IPREA took the unprecedented step of sending a deputation to meet Ernest Blythe at the Department of Finance in May 1927. They asked the Minister to consider abolishing the Entertainment Tax, imposing a £10 levy on course bookmakers and introducing the totalisator to Irish racecourses. The totalisator was a device designed to calculate the bets in a *parimutuel* betting system, with the total stakes on all competing horses divided *pro rata* to the stakes on the race winner, determining an agreed starting price (SP) and the amount paid out on winning tickets. The Tote was the great white hope of Irish racecourse executives, who believed that a percentage of the profits derived from its use would help them to survive. Significantly, the Tote had the early support of the government, with provisions for its introduction included in the legislation for the Betting Tax in 1926. The system's introduction was wholeheartedly supported by the Turf Club and INHS Committee, after they formed a committee to investigate its merits.[35] The governing bodies saw themselves as the logical choice to control the Tote, but this view was not shared by the IPREA, who urged Blythe to consider other options.[36] The IPREA's extraordinary actions represented the first real challenge to the governing bodies authority and helped to convince Blythe of the need to convene an Interdepartmental Committee on Irish Racing.

Appointed in June 1927, this body was tasked with exploring 'thoroughly from the financial and other points of view the present position of Irish racing, both Metropolitan and Provincial'.[37] The Committee sought to identify what, if any changes, had occurred in Irish racing since the pre-war period; explore the impact of the entertainments and betting duties on attendances at race meetings; enquire into the relationship between racecourse executives and the Turf Club and INHS Committee (including the revenues derived by the two bodies from the executives); and examine the possible benefits of introducing the totalisator system to Irish racecourses. Following a period of inquiry and engagement with major stakeholders, including the INHS Committee and the Turf Club, the Committee published its report in 1928. It underlined the importance of horse racing, which in Ireland was 'both a national industry and a national sport'.[38] The evident quality of Irish horses made them desirable, with close to 1,200 yearlings produced annually for sale in Dublin, and at Doncaster and Newmarket, producing an aggregate turnover of £550,000. A similar figure was derived from the sale of horses-in-training, broodmares and foals, placing the value of bloodstock sales to the Irish economy at over £1 million. Beyond Britain, Irish horses were exported to Europe, to the United States and to British dominions and colonies across the globe, including Australia, Ceylon, India, Canada and South Africa. While the sale of horses for the flat was recognized as important, Ireland's reputation for producing exceptional chasers was highlighted in the report, which observed that Irish-bred horses' 'most noticeable successes have been achieved in steeplechasing; so much so that it is generally recognized that practically all the best steeplechasers abroad are recruited from this country'.[39]

National Hunt racing was essential to the health of the Irish bloodstock industry and its decline was alarming.[40] The sport's perilous position was in part a result of commercialization. Until the turn of the twentieth century, hunt clubs and local voluntary committees were responsible for the majority of rural race meetings, which were funded by subscriptions and small entry fees and were typically free to attend. As well as bringing valuable business to towns around the country, these meetings encouraged local farmers, small owners and others to keep one or two horses in training. With the rise of profit-seeking racecourse companies and enclosed courses, however, the meetings organized by local committees began to disappear. As the Interdepartmental Committee noted, these meetings had been 'responsible for the discovery of some of the most noted steeplechasers, whose subsequent performances advertised the potentialities of this country as a breeding-ground for this type of horse'. The shift toward a corporate system had entirely altered the nature of racing and – by extension – breeding in Ireland. Racecourse companies relied on entrance fees for revenue and provincial executives became increasingly reliant on attracting racegoers from Dublin, so much so that the success of a meeting was entirely dependent on the size of the crowds arriving on special race-trains from the capital.[41]

The problem for the majority of courses was that, amid an economic depression, the crowds stopped coming. The fall-off was apparent even at metropolitan meetings. At Baldoyle, for example, attendance fell from a high of 68,390 across nine meetings in 1919 (a daily average attendance of 7,598), to 24,208 at ten meetings in 1927 (a daily average of 2,420). Limerick tumbled from 42,027 attendees at a total of eight meetings in 1916, to 8,276 at three meetings in 1927.[42] Unsurprisingly, given the collapse in attendance, revenue figures provided to the Committee by racecourse executives made for stark reading. It was acknowledged that practically all racecourse companies in the Free State were in a precarious financial position, with none being able to pay a dividend for 1927, with some forced to abandon meetings for lack of funds and with all bar two making losses on the year previous. With a fall-off in attendances, the yield from the Entertainment Tax fell significantly, from £21,000 in 1924–5, to approximately £10,700 in 1927–8.[43] In his Budget address in April 1928, Blythe admitted that the situation was unsustainable and moved to exempt horse racing from the tax. Speaking in the Dáil, Blythe confessed that 'I have been only twice at race meetings in my life and I am not interested in race meetings at all', but acknowledged that 'an enormous number of race meetings will collapse if some aid is not given to them'. He concluded that 'In giving this concession to horse racing we are supporting an important industry.'[44]

One of the major accusations made by the IPREA against the Turf Club (and by extension, the INHS Committee) was that the disinterest of non-resident members was at the root of Irish racing's problems. Under unprecedented scrutiny, the Turf Club and INHS Committee were stirred to action, and they launched a joint inquiry into the state of racing across the island. In October 1927, they presented a report, which included proposals to limit the number of metropolitan meetings and charge bookmakers for oncourse pitches, to a general meeting. This went some way toward proving that they had the energy to revive the sport in Ireland. Crucially, the two bodies retained the support of important stakeholders, even the disgruntled IPREA. Deference did not preclude dissent, however. While the report was generally welcomed, the IPREA challenged it on a number of fronts. The group took issue with the report's recommendation that the Turf Club and INHS Committee be given sole responsibility for the Tote and accused the governing bodies of failing to tackle the government on taxation. The Association also repeated complaints about officials' fees and *Racing Calendar* charges, and the prioritization of metropolitan meetings. The standard of local Stewards proved to be another bone of contention, as the governing bodies believed they should do more and the IPREA believed they were under-resourced. The Interdepartmental Committee saw merit in both sides of the argument. Their report concluded that there was 'considerable laxity in the supervision exercised by ... local stewards', which gave rise to malpractice and a 'good deal of public dissatisfaction'. At the same time, the Report recognized that local Stewards were under-resourced and urged the Turf Club and the INHS Committee to give the matter 'immediate and careful consideration', with one recommendation being the appointment of a Stipendiary Steward – a proposal also put forward by the IPREA.[45]

The crisis reached its apex when the IPREA agreed not to apply for any fixtures in 1928, resulting in a fall in the number of meetings to 92, down from 157 the previous year. The Association also sent the Minister of Finance a fulsome critique of the Turf Club–INHS Committee Report. Cracks began to appear in the provincial executives' united front, however, when the Claremorris Racing Club suggested that IPREA's anger was misdirected and that the real enemy was taxation. The Listowel

Executive then resigned from the Association, announcing that 'we have always been treated with kindness and courtesy whenever we had occasion to put forward any grievance to a [Turf Club/INHS] steward and we have no reason to withdraw our confidence from them'. At the same time, IBOTA – which was dissolved in 1923 but had been reformed by 1926 – pushed to find a resolution, sending a proposed list of reforms to Blythe at the Department of Finance, ahead of a meeting with the Turf Club on 2 January 1928. This included a proposal that IBOTA be represented on various Turf Club committees; that the Club and INHS Committee extend *ex officio* membership to the President of the Executive Council and Minister for Agriculture; that a joint delegation from IBOTA, the Turf Club and the INHS Committee meet with IPREA representatives to find a solution to the ongoing crisis; and that a deputation be sent to meet the government to advise on the measures required to save racing. IBOTA largely approved of the Turf Club–INHS Committee Report, but they felt that breeders, owners and trainers should have a say in the governance of the Tote.[46] In the end, a compromise was reached. The Totalisator Act of 1929 gave control to the governing bodies, but they were required to appoint a Committee of Management, which was comprised of three members from the Turf Club, three from the INHS Committee, one each from the metropolitan and provincial racecourse executives, and two representing breeders, owners and trainers.[47] In October 1928, INHS Committee members elected Sir Bryan Mahon, Sir Walter Nugent and Major Gerrard as their representatives.[48] The first mechanical bet taken in Ireland was at Fairyhouse on Easter Monday 1930.[49] The breach between the governing bodies and the provincial executives was not easily mended, but some overtures were made to effect reconciliation. At the January 1928 meeting, the Turf Club and INHS Committee agreed to submit some of IBOTA's recommendations on taxes, betting and the general reform of Irish racing to the government, but rejected proposals to admit other bodies to various committees in an advisory capacity. The decision was also taken to elect W.T. Cosgrave an *ex officio* member – the only political figure ever afforded that honour.[50]

    The decline of racing from the mid-1920s had resulted in deep rifts in the industry and culminated in a very public crisis and government intervention. Amid this crisis, however, Irish horses and jockeys continued to deliver notable successes on the track. From the mid-1920s, furthermore, there had been a small but significant revolution

Red Park being led in by owner Lady Helen McCalmont (née Conyngham) after winning the Irish Grand National in 1933. Dan Kirwan – later a successful trainer who handled Nicolaus Silver early in his career – is in the saddle.

in the province of horse breeding and ownership in Ireland, as women began to make their presence felt. In 1923, Mrs Freddie Blacker's Be Careful claimed the Irish Grand National and her success was followed by Lady Eva Forbes, who owned the 1924 winner, Kilbarry. The following year, Miss E.L.M. Barbour's horse Blancona was ridden to victory by Charlie Donnelly in the Galway Plate, while at Punchestown, Mrs H. Smyth's Pop Ahead claimed the honours in the Conyngham Cup. The most successful Irish woman owner in this period, however, was Lady Helen McCalmont, the youngest daughter of the fourth Marquess and Marchioness Conyngham. 'A first flight woman to hounds', she was a fixture of the Meath Hunt up until her marriage to Major Dermot McCalmont in 1918, at which point she joined her husband's pack, the Kilkenny Foxhounds. She was also the joint-Master of the County Limerick Hounds between 1934 and 1936.[51] Major McCalmont had enjoyed considerable success on the track before the First World War, as the owner of The Tetrarch. Widely known as 'the spotted wonder' because of his unusual markings, The Tetrarch established himself as one of the fastest two-year-olds of all time, winning all seven of his starts before injury forced his premature retirement in 1913. Seeking to stand his famous stallion, Dermot McCalmont purchased Mount Juliet Estate in County Kilkenny, where he established Ballylinch Stud.

While her husband preferred Flat racing, Lady Helen McCalmont was known to favour racing under National Hunt Rules and it was over jumps that she enjoyed significant success as an owner. At Punchestown, she won the Conyngham Cup (a trophy named for her forebears) on five occasions, as well as the Prince of Wales Plate. She also claimed the Irish Grand National and the Galway Plate with Red Park in 1933, five years before her death aged 46.[52] By then, Helen and her husband had established a racing dynasty; their son, Major Victor McCalmont, was a successful breeder and owner of thoroughbreds and followed in his father's footsteps to become Senior Steward of the Turf Club and a Steward of the INHS Committee.[53] His son, Harry, was appointed Senior Steward of the Turf Club in 2018.[54]

'not a healthy sign'

The 1920s proved to be one of the most challenging periods in the history of horse racing in Ireland. The Turf Club and INHS Committee's dispute with the IPREA highlighted the pressure placed on the sport and the industry and suggested that the two bodies would face greater scrutiny in the future. At the same time, those involved in Irish racing could enter the 1930s with some reason for optimism. Crucially, Irish horses continued to achieve notable success in England as the 1920s drew to a close. In 1928, Tipperary Tim was the only one among forty-two horses not to fall on his way to an unlikely victory in the Grand National at Aintree. It was in this period, too, that Easter Hero – one of the greats in chasing history – made his mark. Bred in County Meath by Larry King and owned by the American Jock Whitney, in 1929 he won the Cheltenham Gold Cup and finished second carrying 12st 7lb in the Grand National, before winning the Gold Cup again the following year.[55] These successes advertised the enduring quality of Irish horses and underlined racing's importance to the state, as the shop window for Irish bloodstock. While Ernest Blythe was not a racegoer, he recognized that improving the sport's fortunes was a fiscal necessity. The abolition of the Entertainment Tax in 1928 was a positive step, as was the introduction of the Totalisator. Income from the Tote and the ability of courses to charge bookmakers for their pitches, among other developments, allowed courses to reduce admission charges. And the operational needs of the Tote helped to resolve the longstanding issue of declarations, as it required horses to be declared for entry twenty-four hours in advance of a race.

Beyond these improvements, the industry was given a major boost in 1931, when the government abolished the contentious Betting Tax.[56] The same year, a new Betting Act was introduced to better define the legal parameters of off-course bookmaking within the Free State. The legislation reflected the political influence of Irish bookmakers, as the terms under which registered premises were licensed and operated was given strict statutory definition. The Betting Acts of 1926 and 1931 were intended to stamp out illegal betting shops through regulation but – by prioritizing bookmakers' interests – they also limited the influence of the Tote. This was a hugely consequential intervention: by denying the Tote a monopoly, the Irish government diminished its direct revenue from gambling and prevented the horse racing industry from becoming self-sufficient. This has left Ireland and Britain in a minority of two, as bookmaking has become 'subordinated to *pari-mutuel* betting in almost every part of the world'. Britain sought to stamp out illegal activity by legalizing off-course betting in 1961, with the government eschewing the chance to establish a Tote monopoly by passing the Betting and Gaming Act. As in Ireland, British horse racing has remained reliant on the government and private investment for funding. By contrast, in France, Australia and elsewhere, the industry controls the Tote and the Tote holds a monopoly, and this provides horse racing with a consistent revenue stream and security.[57]

While betting dominated the legislative agenda in this period, the INHS Committee and Turf Club were kept busy regulating and improving the sport. In early 1931, the Jockeys' Accident Fund was established. The fund was derived from a one shilling fee paid by owners for each mount ridden by a professional jockey and

Horses jumping a bank at Wexford Hunt Point-to-Point, 1925. Point-to-point racing remained a popular source of entertainment in rural communities, but standards had become a concern by the late 1920s and members of the INHS Committee resolved to increase supervision at meetings.

The Early Evolution of Fences

The INHS Committee had sought to impose some kind of standard on National Hunt fences from its foundation in the nineteenth century, with the Inspector of Courses appointed to report on bad practice and impose a sort of quality control.[1] Despite the Committee's efforts, however, standards continued to be mixed in the early decades of the twentieth century. Frank Barbour (who established Westmeath Point-to-Point's celebrated Barbour Cup) took an active interest in the improvement of fences and in 1926 he asked that the INHS Stewards 'acquaint the Clerks of Courses to build the fences at each meeting to a uniform size, as … fences at meetings varied considerably.' The Stewards duly instructed Registrar F. Harold Clarke to write to the clerks of the course and inform them that the 'ordinary fly fences should be 4' 6" in height and 2' in width.'[2] In 1932, Barbour went further, producing a circular with instructions on how to build fences, which was to be provided to clerks of the course across the island. The Committee also responded to complaints from trainers about provincial meetings and it was decided to 'send a competent man, on application from the Management of any Race Course, to give advice and build one ordinary fence in accordance with the requirements of the Rules.'[3] Fences continued to be improved throughout the twentieth century; some important developments included the introduction of hurdles with the top bar rubber protected, and of warning discs,

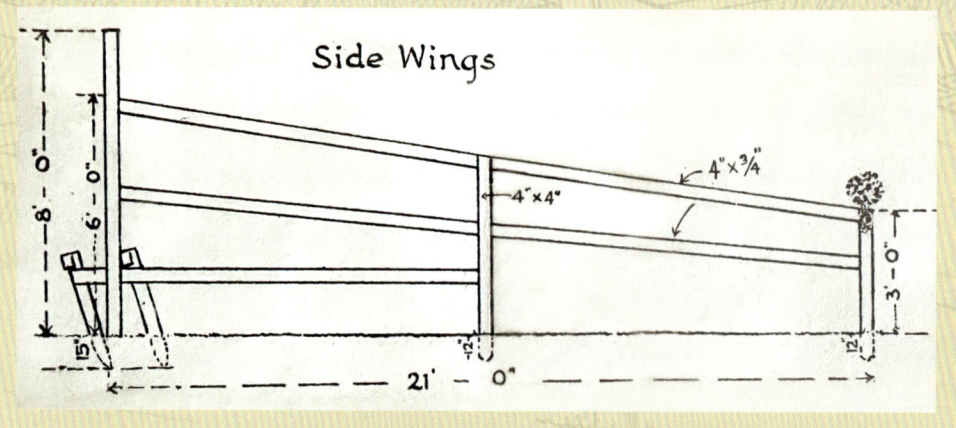

A drawing of sidewings from Frank Barbour's circular on fence building, 1932.

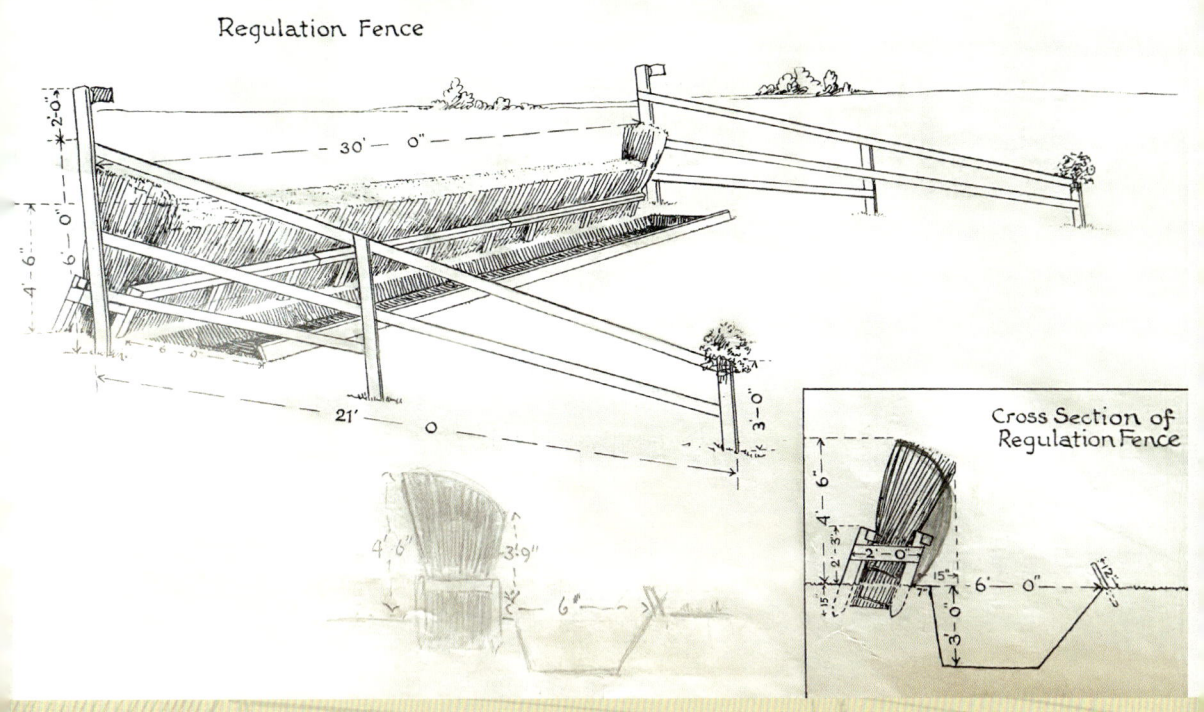

A drawing of a regular fence from Frank Barbour's circular on fence building, 1932.

to alert riders to any obstruction behind a fence, followed later by by-passing.[4] The standard of fences at point-to-point races was slower to improve, partly because of an initial reluctance from the INHS Committee to assume responsibility for standards at meetings, and partly because standards were more difficult to impose. A significant development came in the 1950s, when brush fences were first introduced to point-to-point meetings; this was the first time non-natural obstacles were included in the sport.[5] John Welcome lamented this development in the *Irish Times*, writing 'Gone are the days when the fences were made by sticking a flag in a bank and cutting away the worst of the "skeoghs" with a bill-hook.' This was part of the wider evolution of point-to-pointing, however, as the hunters that had traditionally raced over natural fences were being replaced in the running by thoroughbreds.[6]

Three important racing officials: former INHS Senior Steward, Col. Stephen S. Hill-Dillon (centre), with Captain Gerald Dunne (left), who served briefly as Senior Steward after the death of Captain G.A. Boyd-Rochford in 1940, and sat on the first Totalistor Board with Judge W.E. Wylie (right).

from a levy on the sale price of the winner of every selling race run under INHS Rules. The fund was jointly administered by Trustees appointed by the INHS Committee and the Turf Club and initially only extended to fatal accidents.[58] One of the most significant developments in jump racing in the early 1930s was the introduction of a set of rules governing point-to-point meetings, drafted by the Stewards in consultation with a delegation from the Masters of Foxhounds Association. Point-to-pointing was popular, particularly in the south of the island, but there was growing concern over the standard of meetings, in respect of animal welfare, fences, and the attendance of Stewards. In 1928, it was resolved that a veterinary surgeon be in attendance at every meeting and that a humane killer also be provided; that Stewards' names be displayed prominently in the weighing room; and that natural fences be maintained, with man-made bush fences not permitted under any circumstances.[59] Soon after, the Stewards barred racecourse executives from allowing their stands, offices and enclosures to be used for point-to-point meetings.[60] The 'unsatisfactory' state of Irish point-to-points warranted further action, however. In 1937, a comprehensive code was drafted by Senior Steward Colonel Stephen S. Hill-Dillon, bringing point-to-point meetings 'under stricter supervision of the INHS Committee'; this was met by the approval of the Hunts.[61]

While the world still reeled from the Wall Street stock-market crash of 1929, the political and economic trajectory of the Irish Free State changed radically in 1932, with the election of Eamon de Valera's Fianna Fáil, in coalition with the Labour Party. The policy of protectionism under Fianna Fáil had immediate and lasting consequences for the State, as tariffs became the central pillar of an economic programme designed to deliver decentralization and self-sufficiency. Ideology fused with protectionist impulses to start the Economic War in 1932, as the government refused to repay land annuities to Britain. Westminster retaliated by imposing a 20 per cent import duty on Irish agricultural products, which amounted to 90 per cent of all exports. In return, the Irish government placed tariffs on British imports, including coal, cement, electrical goods, iron and steel manufactures and sugar.[62] De Valera secured an outright majority in a 1933 snap election and the prospect of a long-term economic standoff with the UK hardened into a miserable reality. The Economic War was calamitous for breeding and racing in Ireland. Westminster imposed a 40 per cent special import duty on Irish livestock and the resulting decline in revenue from the export of horses was significant: in 1933, £626,974 was realized for sales into the UK, a figure that contrasted starkly with the £1,943,590 achieved in 1930.[63] Racing remained in poor health, meanwhile, as income from the Tote failed to match expectations, with turnover for the executives never rising above £4,000 in a given year between 1930 and 1937.[64]

The Economic War had a more immediately obvious impact on Irish breeding, however, as a number of valuable stallions were moved from studs in Ireland to England. Increasingly concerned, the Irish government was spurred into action and introduced the Horse Breeding Act in 1934, to provide a system for licensing stallions. For some, however, the damage was already done, with W.T. Cosgrave remarking in a Dáil debate that the Horse Breeding Bill would 'not remedy the disadvantage which we have suffered during the last month or two by reason of the loss to this country of the sires Tredennis, Blandford, Trigo and Stratford. A dozen Bills such as this would not remedy that.'[65] Another step to improve the situation was taken in 1935, when the Commission of Inquiry into the Horse Breeding Industry was established under the chairmanship of Mr Justice William E. Wylie, reporting to the Minister for Agriculture, James Ryan. Among the Commission's recommendations to improve the breeding industry was the purchase of ten stallions and the establishment of a National Stud to house them – reflecting the fact that Tully was still owned by the British government.[66] While not focussed on racing, its 'essential' value to the breeding industry was impossible for the Commissioners to ignore. Their report acknowledged the loss of race meetings across the State, noting that the stakes run for had declined by 50 per cent since the mid-1920s. There was 'a grave danger' that further race meetings would close down, doing 'incalculable harm' to the breeding industry and to exports.[67] Racing could not thrive if it was not profitable or even sustainable for owners and trainers; this was underlined by the retiring Senior Steward of the INHS Committee, Major (later Lt Col.) Evelyn Shirley, in 1935, when he reminded members that the majority of owners in Ireland were 'not rich and mainly race with a view to selling their horses at some period of their career'. With a healthy demand for chasers outside Ireland, there was an obvious temptation to sell horses before they had run over fences. Shirley further remarked that it was 'not a healthy sign to see that five races at the Leopardstown Christmas Meeting and three at the Baldoyle New Year Meeting failed to fill at the first time of closing, and that runners in many chases during the past season were not as numerous as one would like to see'.[68]

The Commission agreed, and concluded that the best way to save racing was to encourage the participation of small owners, who 'would race, particularly in steeplechasing, if the expense of running a horse could be minimized'. With bigger and better fields, 'the public would be attracted in greater numbers and the increase in attendances would provide funds out of which stakes could be increased and entrance fees reduced'. Significantly, the Commission also queried the feasibility of privately owned racecourses, and suggested vesting ownership of all courses in the Turf Club or a similar body. This would help to effect greater control, standardize admission charges, and allow for a subsidy system. Profits accruing from metropolitan meetings could then be used to help less financially secure provincial meetings, which were in danger of decline and extinction, and of being replaced by flapper meetings. The Commission urged the government to confer with the Turf Club and INHS Committee to ascertain the most effective means of acquiring various racecourses in the Free State. While recognizing 'the great work that has been done in the past' by the Turf Club and the INHS Committee and the 'absolute necessity of having an independent governing body with absolute autocratic power', the Commission believed that both bodies required reform. The main concern was with representation. The Commission recommended that owners and those 'keenly interested in provincial and metropolitan racing' be given a seat at the table. Echoing the IPREA's earlier complaints, it was noted that the Turf Club and INHS Committee comprised 'many' members 'who had ceased to be active participants of the sport and the business of the Saorstát'. By admitting those who were active participants, it was suggested, the 'prestige' of the two bodies would only be increased.[69]

'on sound if not on spectacular lines'

The Commission did not recommend a grant to reverse racing's decline, as this would only amount to a 'temporary palliative'. Instead, it urged the introduction of legislation to divert a majority of wagers from betting shops to the Tote, with profits derived used to reinvigorate Irish racing. Change was slow to materialize at government level but there were some developments on the ground. In January 1938, retiring INHS Senior Steward Colonel Stephen S. Hill-Dillon informed members that steeplechasing was progressing 'on sound if not on spectacular lines'. While the number of races had not changed significantly, the number of horses running increased from 2,237 in 1936 to 2,400 in 1937, with an increase in the average field from seven horses to eight. Racecourse executives had played their part, providing £752 more in stake money than in 1936; this increase would have been higher still if four days racing at Navan, Down Royal and Baldoyle had not been lost to bad weather in the Spring.[70] Further green shoots were in evidence in 1938: in Galway, the value of the Plate increased to 1,020 *sovs*, bringing it in line with the value of the Irish Grand National. That year, the race attracted a field of twenty-three horses and was won by the unfancied Symaethis, owned by a surprised Hill-Dillon, who asked the INHS Stewards to conduct an enquiry into the legitimacy of the mare's success.[71] This was Hill-Dillon's second win in the race, after Yellow Furze claimed the honours in 1936.[72]

In his January 1938 address to INHS Committee members, Hill-Dillon also expressed optimism over the extension of the Jockeys' Accident Fund and the

Golden Miller, with Gerry Wilson up, being led in after winning the 1934 Grand National in record time, carrying 12st 2lbs. Golden Miller also won the Cheltenham Gold Cup a record five times between 1932 and 1936.

introduction of new point-to-point regulations.[73] He concluded by commenting on the 'exceptional' performance of Irish horses in England and elsewhere, as Irish breeders continued to sell heavily for export. This was a sign of an industry still under pressure, but it was also further proof of the superior quality of Irish chasers. It was an Irish-bred chaser that dominated the 1930s and became one of the giants of steeplechasing. Bred by Laurence Geraghty (grandfather of jockey Barry) in Pelletstown, County Meath, Golden Miller was sired by the five-guinea stallion Goldcourt, out of an ex-hunter named Miller's Pride. Geraghty was left in possession of the mare when her soldier owner was killed on a tour of duty in France. Matching Miller's Pride with the unraced Goldcourt, Geraghty bred two useful chasers in May Court and May Crescent; then, in 1927, the same union produced Golden Miller. Bought first as a yearling at the Ballsbridge Sales, as a three-year-old Golden Miller caught the eye of English hunter dealer, Captain Farmer, who convinced trainer Basil Briscoe to buy him for 500 *guineas*.[74] Briscoe acted without seeing the young horse and his impression on their first meeting was not good; he described the bay gelding – who had endured a long journey by sea and rail – as possessing 'a wet bear-like coat (above) An Ogden's Cigarette card depicting Golden Miller, alongside the racing colours of owner Dorothy Paget. (below) Horses racing in the Feale Plate at Listowel Racecourse in 1940. Bookmakers' pitches and a crowd of spectators stand on the inside of the track, which was typical of past race meetings. The track at Listowel was right-handed at this point but was subsequently changed to a left-handed track.

sticking up in places like a porcupine and plastered in mud from head to tail'.[75] After a disappointing performance in a hurdle race, Briscoe sold Golden Miller to his friend and patron Philip Carr for £1,000. Carr retained Briscoe as Golden Miller's trainer and the trio had quick success over hurdles. A second-place finish in a steeplechase at Newbury hinted at Golden Miller's glorious future, but Carr died before the horse's potential was realized.[76]

In 1931 therefore, the talented four-year-old was sold for £6,000 to Dorothy Paget, daughter of the first Baron Queenborough and Pauline Payne Whitney, a member of a famous American racing and breeding family. One of the most successful owners in Flat and National Hunt racing in the interwar period, Paget also owned a breeding operation at Ballymacoll Stud, just outside Dunboyne in County Meath, where Arkle was foaled in 1957. One of the biggest gamblers in England in this period, the enormously wealthy and eccentric Paget sometimes slept all day and placed bets at night, on races that had already taken place. Trusting that she did not know the outcome of a given race, bookmakers would take and – when she was successful – pay out on Paget's wagers.[77] Briscoe remained as Golden Miller's trainer after the sale to Paget and in 1932, the horse delivered the first of five consecutive Cheltenham Gold Cups. In 1934, he became the first horse to achieve the Gold Cup–Grand National double, underlining his exceptional ability by completing the Aintree course in record-breaking time while carrying 12st 2 lbs. This was Golden Miller's first and last Grand National triumph, however; his dislike for the Aintree fences was such that, on three subsequent appearances, he either unseated his rider, refused to jump, or fell.[78] At Cheltenham, the most remarkable of Golden Miller's five-in-a-row came in 1935, when he faced an 'exceptionally fast, tough, little horse' named Thomond II, who was owned by Paget's cousin, Jock Whitney. With an eye on the more valuable Grand National, Golden Miller appeared at Prestbury Park just short of full fitness. He was also unsuited to the hard ground but, having matched Thomond II stride for stride, he showed his strength when outstaying his talented rival up the hill to the finishing post, to win by ¾ of a length.[79]

The outstanding Golden Miller was a powerful advertisement for the quality of Irish steeplechasers, which continued to be exported in great number. In 1939, retiring INHS Senior Steward John E. O'Brien remarked to Committee members that 'Ireland always has been, and will continue to be, the best breeding ground for chasers in the world, and as long as there is a demand in England and in other countries for good chasers they will have to come to us for them'. O'Brien underlined the importance of sales to smaller breeders and owners, noting that 'Ninety per cent of the people who race horses in this country mainly race with a view to selling their horses at some period in their career'.[80] This was true of Dick Ball, who bred the double Grand National winner, Reynoldstown, a horse named for the townland

Prince Regent being led in after winning the Irish Grand National at Fairyhouse in 1942, with Tim Hyde up. One of the greatest Irish chasers ever, his career was limited by the Second World War, which prevented him from running in England until 1946 – he won the Gold Cup at Cheltenham that year.

where he was foaled, near Naul in County Dublin. The jet black gelding was the son of My Prince, who was one of the best National Hunt sires of the twentieth century. He sired Grand National winners Gregalach (1929) and Royal Mail (1937) and Cheltenham Gold Cup winners Easter Hero (1929 and 1930) and Prince Regent (1946), and was also the sire of Arkle's granddam. Described as a 'long-backed, narrow-gutted brute', Reynoldstown was a temperamental horse, but this did not deter Major Noel Furlong, an Irish Protestant who had moved to England amid the violence of the Civil War. Hoping to train a Grand National winner, Furlong bought Reynoldstown for £1,500 in 1932; three years later, his ambition was realized, when his son Frank rode the horse to victory at Aintree, in a field that included returning champion Golden Miller.

Prince Regent's owner, J.V. Rank (centre), pictured with the horse's jockey, Tim Hyde (left), after the 1942 Irish Grand National. On the right is P.P. Hogan, who romped home on another Rank-owned horse, The Slacker, in the Joseph O'Reilly Memorial Cup.

Then, in 1936, Reynoldstown became just the third horse to win the race twice in succession, after Abd-El-Kader (1851) and The Colonel (1870). On that occasion, he was ridden to victory by Fulke Walwyn, after the long-odds race leader Davy Jones ran out after his reins broke at the last fence.[81] In Ireland, meanwhile, Prince Regent thrilled race-goers during the years of the Emergency and heralded the arrival of trainer Tom Dreaper on the domestic scene. Prince Regent was bred by A.M. Maxwell at Corduff Stud in County Dublin and sold to J.V. Rank – brother of the film magnate J. Arthur Rank. Prince Regent won a Flat race at Naas in 1940 and the following year he claimed a maiden hurdle at the Phoenix Park, before registering his first steeplechase victories in the Mickey Macardle Memorial Cup at Dundalk and the Webster Cup Handicap Chase at Navan. He carried 12st 7lbs to victory in the 1942 Irish Grand National at Fairyhouse and carried his imperious form into 1943, when he won or placed in every one of the eight races he contested, including seven steeplechases and one weight-for-age Flat race.[82] Having enthralled Irish crowds during the Emergency, Prince Regent was given an opportunity to prove himself in England after the Second World War, and began by winning the Bradford Chase at Wetherby in December 1945. In the spring of 1946, the eleven-year-old demonstrated his imperious talent by winning the Cheltenham Gold Cup by twenty lengths. He followed this with a courageous performance carrying 12st 5lbs in the Grand National. The veteran overcame

A cartoon depicting Dan Moore's prowess as a jumps jockey in the 1930s and 40s. It dates from 1948 – the same year Moore had to retire from race riding after injuring his leg in a fall at Punchestown.

several jumping errors to land in front over the last fence, but he struggled on the run in and was beaten into third place by Lovely Cottage and Jack Finlay. His age showed further the following year, when he finished fourth.[83] The interruption of racing during the Second World War meant that Prince Regent was denied the opportunity to prove his outstanding ability, but his initial performances in post-war England and his race record in Ireland place him in the ranks of the all-time jumping greats. Indeed, Arkle would have to achieve the near-impossible to overtake Prince Regent in Tom Dreaper's estimation.[84]

Irish jump jockeys continued to make a name for themselves in this period, too. Often riding in the colours of Dorothy Paget, Dan Moore became a fixture in winner's enclosures across Ireland and Britain in the late 1930s and 40s. In 1938, he lost by a short head on Royal Danieli in the Grand National at Aintree, although he maintained that he had beaten seventeen-year-old Bruce Hobbs on the declared winner, Battleship, a diminutive entire horse by the American 'racing machine' Man O'War.[85] Moore was Irish Champion Jockey in 1940, taking the title by a 'street', after claiming 58 wins from a total of 231 mounts – all under National Hunt Rules.[86] That triumphant year was not without incident for Moore, who was involved in a dispute arising out of a hurdle race at Gowran Park on 30 May. The race was won by Mr Wolf, owned by the Duchess de Stacpoole and ridden by J.C. Parkinson, who finished ahead of Tim Molony on Prospect Lad and Moore on the Paget-owned Disney. The local Stewards disqualified the three horses, however, believing them to have run the wrong course, and awarded the race to the fourth-placed Another Consul. Parkinson, Molony and Moore, meanwhile, were fined 5 *sovs*. each. Shortly afterwards, the INHS Stewards invoked their right to conduct their own investigation and concluded

On Portmarnock Strand: Dan Moore is second from left on Royal Danieli, a horse he rode into second place in a tight finish in the 1938 Grand National. Moore maintained that he had won the race from Battleship, an American-bred 40/1 shot ridden by 17-year-old Bruce Hobbs. Without photo finish cameras, there was no way for Moore to prove his case.

that the three riders had gone the wrong course, but only because it had not been flagged correctly. The result was upheld, but Moore and his colleagues had their fines overturned.[87] Described in the *Irish Horse* as 'one of the first steeplechase horsemen of any age', Moore continued to excel over jumps until 1948, when he retired to become a trainer after injuring his leg in a fall at Punchestown.[88] That same year, his engagement to Joan Comyn was announced, marking the beginning of one of the great Irish racing dynasties.[89]

'the gain to the greatest number is more important than preservation of the vested interests of the few'

Away from the track, the Irish public voted to adopt a new constitution in July 1937. *Bunreacht na hÉireann* brought the Irish Free State to an end and established the state of Éire, or Ireland. It also removed the Oath of Allegiance to the Crown and scrapped the Office of the Governor-General, replacing it with the Office of the President; the President of the Executive Council, meanwhile, was replaced as head of government by the Office of the Taoiseach. This period also marked the beginning of a shift in the balance of power in Irish racing. The government's increasing involvement in the sport made it impossible for the Turf Club and INHS Committee to maintain exclusive control, or to resist changes to their membership. In 1938, the bodies welcomed the racehorse-owning Minister for Justice, P.J. Ruttledge; the Secretary of the Department of Agriculture, Daniel Twomey; Mr Justice W.E. Wylie; and Captain Gerald Martin of the Horsebreeders' Association to their ranks. Perhaps the most significant addition was Wylie, who had served as both prosecutor and defender of W.T. Cosgrave at the military tribunals that followed the 1916 Rising, and who might also have prosecuted Eamon de Valera.[90] A member of the RDS from 1910, Wylie recognized the importance of equestrianism and breeding to the Irish Free State and was the driving force behind the introduction of international competitions to the Horse Show in 1926. He served as both vice-Chair of the Board of Control for Mechanical Betting (Tote Board) and Chair of the Horse Breeding Commission before being appointed to the Turf Club and INHS Committee. He was instrumental in animating both branches of Irish racing in the late 1930s and early 1940s and was appointed to the Racing Board on its creation in 1945.[91]

Any misgivings felt by the existing members of the Turf Club and INHS Committee over these appointments were quicky overcome by the award of a significant government grant in 1939. Following consultation with the two bodies, Agriculture Minister James Ryan provided a sum of £10,000 for the development of both branches of the sport on an all-island basis. The grant was intended to improve the stake money offered across the island, particularly to encourage the greater participation of small owners, who were an indispensable feature of the sporting landscape and – ultimately – the bloodstock industry. Both the Turf Club and the INHS Committee were tasked with the distribution of the grant and this resulted in the first classification of Irish races. To ensure success, this process required 'unique cooperation between the State, the Turf Club and the INHS Committee, and the Tote Board, and represented a considerable healing of old wounds'.[92] In the end, it was agreed that races would be divided into three classes, based upon the number of day's racing held at individual courses in 1938. The money awarded was proportionate to each class: Class I meetings were to receive £900; Class II meetings, £400; and

Red Cross Steeplechase at Leopardstown in 1940. Between 1940 and 1945, with the Second World War ongoing, the Irish Hospitals' Trust organised ten steeplechases in aid of the Irish Red Cross. The Trust – which administered the Irish Hospitals' Sweepstake – raised £184,000 for the organzation. Similar races were held in aid of the Red Cross during the First World War.

Class III meetings, £100. To qualify, executives were required to match the stakes they had provided for the relevant race one year earlier, and to add the money awarded from the grant to the prize pot. In the end, the grant was divided almost evenly between Flat and National Hunt racing, with the latter receiving a total of £4,900.[93]

The impact of the grant was almost immediate. The stakes run for in 1939 amounted to £38,891, which represented an increase of £8,331 over the previous year.[94] A correspondent for the *Irish Press* observed that improvements had 'been most noticeable at the country meetings and it will not be denied that a new interest was created amongst the people of the South and West in racing'. This reinvigoration was also demonstrated by the turnover of the Tote, which beat all previous records.[95] The grant assumed even greater importance in September 1939, as Britain declared war on Germany and the Irish government passed the Emergency Powers Act – legislation that gave special powers to the government, including internment, censorship of the press, and control of the economy. Irish neutrality was not welcomed by the British, who began a supply squeeze in 1941, stopping the export of agricultural fertilizer, feedstuffs, coal and petrol to Ireland.[96] While the government renewed the grant to Irish racing annually up to and including 1944, the Emergency presented the sport with a number of challenges. The increase in stake money proved to be short lived; in National Hunt racing it reached a high of £47,026 in 1940, before plummeting to £27,964 in 1941.[97] This collapse was the result of the cancellation of race meetings and closure of courses across the island, as the impact of the war – including significant fuel shortages – was exacerbated by an outbreak of foot and mouth disease. All racing stopped in Northern Ireland, while racing and point-to-pointing in Éire was temporarily suspended, leading to the abandonment of both Punchestown and Fairyhouse. Despite these adverse circumstances, racing proved to be highly popular with the Irish public, with high attendances allowing the Tote Board to completely clear its overdraft in September 1941. The success of the slimmed-down fixture list proved an argument first put forward in the 1920s, namely that there was too much racing in Ireland.[98] The popularity of National Hunt racing was used to generate funds for the war effort, too. Between 1940 and 1945, the Irish Hospitals' Sweepstake – a lottery established in 1930 to fund hospitals in the Free State – organized ten steeplechases in aid of the Irish Red Cross, generating £184,000 (41 per cent) of the organization's revenue in that period.[99]

One of the issues facing Irish racing during the Emergency was a shortage of oats. In March 1942, as the full force of rationing began to be felt, it was announced in the *Racing Calendar* that, in light of expected restrictions, the Minister for Agriculture 'strongly' advised anyone with an interest in thoroughbreds 'to make immediate arrangements to grow the oats they require'.[100] Matters were made even worse by the behaviour of some Irish farmers, who elected to hold up supply in order to secure higher prices. There was also considerable (and related) anxiety around the prospect of British horses being permitted to relocate to and race in Ireland, as they had been during the First World War. In 1939, the Stewards resolved that 'Irish interests must not be overwhelmed by the peculiar conditions produced by the war'.[101] It was decided, therefore, to initially reserve two races in each days programme for horses in training in Ireland before 1 September 1939.[102] In 1941, the Stewards introduced restrictions on the entry of British horses that were not located or trained in Ireland on 1 June that year. In late 1942, however, the Committee was asked to consider rescinding the restrictions. The resulting debate underlined some of the concerns felt in National Hunt circles at the time. Those against rescinding argued that the presence of British horses would only increase the competition for oats, and that an influx of wealthy owners and high-class chasers would 'strike a blow against Irish racing' and make it 'very hard for the small man to win a race'. Those in favour, meanwhile, argued that the presence of British chasers would 'put more money in the game' and increase the value of any winning Irish horse.[103] The restrictions were upheld, but the Committee met again the following month to reconsider the matter. Some members continued to voice concerns, with Captain (later Major) J.H. de Burgh suggesting that a British migration would not be of 'any use in this country, [because] they are only birds of passage'. In the end, an amendment was passed to restrict the number of British horses competing and to limit the type of races open to them. This appeased any remaining concerns and allowed the Irish National Hunt community an opportunity to support their beleaguered British counterparts.[104]

In March 1942, the government introduced severe petrol rationing and Seán Lemass, the Minister for Supplies, requested a meeting with the governing bodies, to discuss the position of racing. The Turf Club and the INHS Committee understood the government's position, with INHS Steward Sir James Nelson telling a meeting of Committee members that 'they had found the government ready to listen to and

Irish Hospitals' Sweepstake draw, March 1933. Founded by Richard Duggan, Spencer Freeman and Joe McGrath, the Sweepstake was a government-backed lottery established in 1930, to raise money for Irish hospitals. It proved to be very popular among Irish emigrant communities, with significant funds raised (illegally) in the US and UK.

consider any suggestions made by them and had treated them very fairly'. The Turf Club and the INHS Committee were ready to help the government 'in every way',[105] and their meeting resulted in the creation of the Central Racing Advisory Committee (CRAC), through Emergency Powers Order 167 of 1942. Ruttledge served as chair of the new body, with Nelson chosen to represent the INHS Committee, Wylie the Turf Club, and P.J. Murphy the Tote Board, while the newly established Bloodstock Breeders' and Horse Owners' Association and South and West of Ireland Breeders' and Owners' Association were represented by Joe McGrath and T.A. Morris, respectively. McGrath was a member of the IRA during the War of Independence and took the pro-Treaty side in the Civil War, serving as the National Army's director of intelligence. He subsequently assumed control of the Criminal Investigation Department, which was the Free State's intelligence service. A founder member of Cumann na nGaedheal, McGrath served as Minister for Labour (1922) and for Industry and Commerce (1922–4) before resigning from the party in 1924. He was also a founder of the Irish Hospitals' Sweepstake and one of the greatest all-round figures in twentieth-century Irish racing. He purchased and developed Brownstown Stud on the Curragh in the 1930s, securing the services of Michael Collins to train his Flat horses and manage the stud. By the 1940s, he was established as one of the leading breeders and owners in Ireland. While McGrath's primary focus was on Flat racing, he also owned National Hunt horses, many of whom were trained by his son Seamus at Glencairn Stables, which was 'Boss' Croker's former base of operations near Cabinteely in County Dublin. Seamus McGrath's development of Glencairn and his success as a National Hunt trainer convinced his father to part company with Michael Collins in 1947, and to entrust his more valuable Flat horses to his son.

Joe McGrath's impact on Irish racing extended into the administration of the sport and development of the industry. This was apparent in his involvement in the CRAC, as well as by his later service as a Steward of the Turf Club and chairman of the Racing Board.[106] While the CRAC was a short-lived body, its creation 'represented a decisive shift in the balance of power within racing'.[107] With fuel rationing resulting in a complete ban on the use of motor transport to race meetings, the CRAC were vested with the power to draft a curtailed calendar – in so doing, they assumed one of the major functions of the Turf Club and INHS Committee. This was not without its problems. In 1943, for example, Punchestown was cancelled when agreement could not be reached between the Racecourse Executive and the CRAC.[108] While the CRAC's role in determining the calendar provoked displeasure in some corners of the Turf Club and INHS Committee, it was generally well-regarded and its work had important implications for the future of horse racing in Ireland. Through a Special Racing Fund, the CRAC used some of the monies generated by permitted race meetings and the Tote to assist those racecourse executives impacted by the reduced racing calendar. In this lay the foundation of the Racing Board.[109] The creation of the CRAC was not the only important development in Irish racing in 1942, as the Turf Club and INHS Committee established an inquiry into the 'present and post-war conditions of racing' in September that year. This body, which was helmed by Lord Adare and also included Major Dermot McCalmont, Captain J.H. de Burgh, Paddy Dunne Cullinan, Duc de Stacpoole, Captain E.A. Gargan

A prominent figure in Ireland's revolutionary generation, Joe McGrath was a founder member of Cumann na nGaedheal, a Free State government minister, and a founder of the Irish Hospitals' Sweepstake, before becoming a driving force in the creation of the Racing Board and one of the principal architects of the horse racing industry in twentieth-century Ireland.

and Major A.H. Watt, would become known as 'The Adare Commission'.[110] The Commission's inquiry was concluded by November 1942 and Adare presented its Report to the Turf Club and the INHS Committee in January 1943, recommending 'Sweeping changes in the control, administration, and practical management of racing in Ireland'.[111]

Proposed improvements included the appointment of a Stipendiary Steward, the election by ballot of Turf Club and INHS Stewards, a Tote monopoly on betting, the delegation of tasks to committees, and the acquisition of country racecourses 'to ensure

CHAPTER THREE: 1922–1945

uniform control'. It was also proposed to replace eight absentee members of the Turf Club and INHS Committee with individuals who were resident in Ireland and to amalgamate the two bodies.[112] The Report was discussed at a joint meeting of the Turf Club and INHS Committee in March 1943 and some of its recommendations were quickly adopted, either directly or in a modified form. The suggested amalgamation of the Turf Club and INHS Committee was not pursued, but the two bodies agreed to meet no less than four times annually, to ensure greater cooperation. Both also agreed to alter procedures for the election of Stewards and Committee members and to establish both joint committees and sub-committees. The latter commitment quickly bore fruit: in June 1943, Wylie successfully moved to establish a six-man sub-committee to consider what amendments 'were necessary or advisable to the Rules and Orders of the INHS Committee'. This improving impulse extended to point-to-point racing. In September, a sub-committee was appointed to attend meetings across Ireland, to 'look after the racing details, and the qualification of horses and riders and generally clean up point-to-point meetings'.[113]

Not all of the Adare Commission's recommendations were adopted by the Turf Club and INHS Committee but the Report proved to be prescient, as many of its proposals for the improvement of horse racing in Ireland would be instituted over time. In this respect, it proved to be more successful than its more detailed and comprehensive British counterpart, the Ilchester Report, which was published in April 1943.[114] This period also saw a major step taken toward improving the standard of Irish bloodstock, with the government's acquisition of the National Stud at Tully in 1944. The Free State government had tried to claim the stud in 1922, but the British government 'would not recognize the claim at that time on the grounds that the stud was a gift to the United Kingdom and that under the deed of gift it could not be alienated'. Further discussions over the transfer of the property took place between the Irish and British governments in 1935, as tensions eased in the Economic War. It was not until 1943, however, that an agreement was reached, with the Irish government taking possession of Tully on 31 December. The British agreed to pay a sum in lieu of rent on the premises, backdated to the foundation of the Free State on 6 December 1922. Once the cost of livestock and equipment left to the use of the Irish State had been deducted, this amounted to £21,300. The British retained ownership of the bloodstock that had stood at Tully, so the Irish government put in place plans to purchase high-quality stallions and broodmares. A public liability company was formed to run the new National Stud, with funds provided by the State.[115]

The statutory creation of the Irish National Stud in 1945 demonstrated the State's commitment to the success of the racing and breeding industries. This development, alongside the provision of the government grant and the move to create the Racing Board, indicated that Irish racing was on a new and exciting path. Writing in the *Irish Horse* in 1944, the well-known breeder and trainer Roderic More O'Ferrall underlined the irresistible nature of progress, noting that 'Changes will come, to the chagrin of those who fail to read the writing on the wall; because human beings are not fools forever, and the gain to the greatest number is more important than preservation of the vested interests of the few.'[116] The challenges facing the sport in the 1920s and 1930s, and in the difficult years of the Emergency, had also created an impetus among the major stakeholders in the sport, including the governing bodies, breeders, owners and trainers, racecourse executives and, of course, the State. The infrastructure required to revolutionize Irish racing and breeding was put in place and the result was transformational. Out of adversity came a new dawn, full of opportunity and promising success.

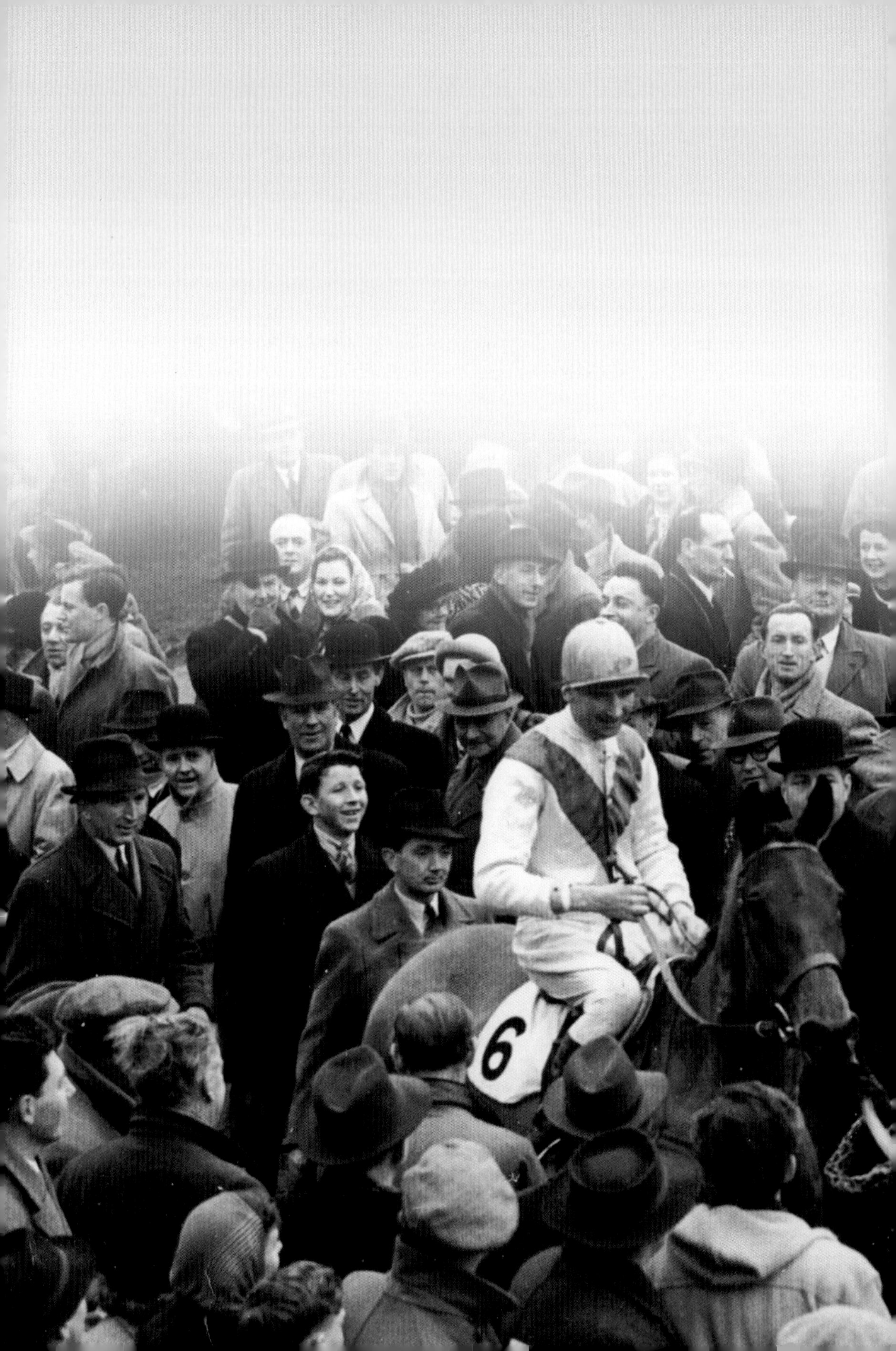

CHAPTER FOUR

1945-1969

'For the first time,
Ireland was the best at something'

THE PROGRESS MADE IN IRISH racing during the difficult years of the Emergency would culminate in the foundation of the Racing Board in 1945. Reform had been slow to materialize, but the importance of the racing industry to the stagnant Irish economy meant that the sport was eventually transformed through inquiry, investment and reorganization. This process had begun under Cumann na nGaedheal in the 1920s and was continued by Fianna Fáil in the 1930s and 1940s. Tensions around the Anglo-Irish complexion of the governing bodies would endure, but the need to promote Irish racing and bloodstock provided political common ground. With the Racing Board serving as a centralized authority, providing consistent financial support, racing thrived in Ireland from the mid-1940s. And this was no false dawn; even amid the turgid economic climate of the 1950s, jump racing delivered moments of magic to the beleaguered Irish people. The progress made in the 1950s served as a foundation for a golden age in National Hunt racing. The 1960s were defined by increasing prosperity and the modernization of social and cultural practices. They were also defined by Arkle. Ireland had always been the cradle of National Hunt champions, but in Arkle it produced a superstar. The bay gelding achieved a rare fame, becoming a national hero and, to the world, a symbol of Irish excellence. With 'Himself' to the fore and with more money to spend and car ownership increasing, the public flocked to race meetings and point-to-points across the island. Radio and television brought racing into Irish homes, sponsors were drawn to the sport and the commercial foundations of modern National Hunt racing were laid down. Even in this period of success, however, there were challenges to overcome.

'if there is one thing that is going to blend the various elements in this divided country it is the sportsmen'

The establishment of the Racing Board in 1945 marked the beginning of a revolution in Irish racing. Relevant only to the 26 counties of Éire, the Board was created to improve the standards of horse breeding and racing, to better control racecourses and to fund essential elements of the sport, for example stake money and supplements for the transport of horses to meetings. This latter function was to be achieved using money that was raised through a levy on bookmakers, and by assuming control of the Tote. Responsibility for bringing the Racing Board into being lay with then Minister for Finance, Seán T. O'Kelly, and his department. A veteran of the Revolutionary period and a future President of Ireland, O'Kelly would later become a racing enthusiast and racehorse owner, but he did not have any real knowledge of the sport at this point. He nevertheless understood racing's importance, particularly in relation to the breeding industry, and was committed to making the eleven-man Board 'a business-like' and representative body.[1] This was easier said than done, however. Six seats on the Board were to be divided equally among the Turf Club and the INHS Committee, which were to be given statutory recognition for the first time in their history. This reflected the governing bodies' regulatory importance to the sport but as the *Irish Times* reported, they would 'be expected, no doubt, to pay attention to the reports and recommendations of the Board'.[2] Statutory recognition of the Turf Club and INHS Committee also revealed some of the enduring tensions around racing in Ireland. In the Dáil, some Fianna Fáil TDs complained about the enduringly Anglo-Irish complexion of the two bodies. Addressing the Minister for Finance in March 1945, P.J. Fogarty suggested that the members of the Adare Commission, whose recommendations contributed to the establishment of the Board, were 'more reminiscent of a British courtmartial [*sic*] than of a board interested in Irish racing'. His party colleague Robert Briscoe went further, arguing that 'these two bodies are controlled mainly by persons who, from a national point of view, are very far away from us'. Naming every member of both bodies, Briscoe noted that 'the gentlemen with military titles are gentlemen who hold these titles from a foreign army … These are the people who are going to be given statutory rights and supreme control.' The comments were refuted by Fine Gael's George Cecil Bennett, who accused Briscoe of 'unintentionally' drawing 'a national and an anti-national outlook into the discussion'. In Bennett's view, members of the governing bodies 'were all "sports"' and he suggested that 'if there is one thing that is going to blend the various elements in this divided country it is the sportsmen'.[3]

A new Board was appointed by the Minister for Finance every five years, with the first edition comprising W.T. Cosgrave, Lord Adare, W.E. Wylie, Joe McGrath, I.J. Blake, W. Dwan, Lt Col. Sir Cecil King-Harman, J.M. Martin, F. O'Beirne, A.P. Reynolds and Lt Col. Evelyn Shirley. A shared political ambition for the success of racing and breeding was underlined by Cosgrave's acceptance of an invitation to become a member of the inaugural Board, despite his 'intense antipathy' toward de Valera.[4] Cosgrave would become the Racing Board's first Chair, but McGrath was recognized as the driving force in its creation. Having helped to draft the Racing Board Bill, McGrath used his political connections to ensure its smooth passage through the Irish Parliament. There was some debate in the Dáil, with certain TDs giving voice to bookmakers' concerns over the extent of a levy on their turnover. These concerns were unfounded, as the levy was reduced from 5 per cent to 2.5 per cent, and a growing public appetite for racing ensured a healthy turnover from betting in the years that followed.[5] This included takings from point-to-point meetings, where bookmakers were allowed to do business. The growing public interest in racing was also reflected in the Tote, from which the Board deducted 10 per cent to fund the development of the sport, and which increased its turnover from £659,536 in 1945 to a comparatively staggering £1.6 million in 1950 (an average of £11,248 per meeting).[6]

The Board put income from the levies to immediate and effective use, with stake money increasing significantly in both codes. The stakes provided for National Hunt racing in 1949 amounted to £121,643, compared to £150,000 for Flat racing – a gap that was reduced to nothing if the highly valuable Classics were excluded from consideration.[7] The healthy condition of National Hunt stakes was justified, as it enjoyed 'greater popularity' among the Irish people, with 528 races run under INHS Rules in 1949 and 374 under the Rules of Racing. By 1950, there were 2,065 and 2,360 starters in steeplechases and hurdle races, respectively. The Board also contributed financially to point-to-point racing, with a sum of £40 awarded to every meeting in its jurisdiction in 1949.[8] The Board pursued other initiatives to improve the health of racing overall. This included the provision of financial supplements for the carriage of horses to race meetings across the 26 counties. Between 1945 and 1950, the Board provided almost £130,000, which encouraged 'bumper entries and runners' at country meetings.[9] While a boom in residential, public and industrial construction hampered schemes for the improvement of racecourses, the Board still provided £250,000 to executives for capital works between 1946 and 1949. This figure had increased to £350,000 by 1950 and the majority of executives, particularly in rural Ireland, improved their facilities and tracks. With sustained financial support, National Hunt racing was in rude health by the middle of the twentieth century and bucked the general economic trend.[10]

'racing is in an astonishingly healthy condition'

The Racing Board was responsible for transforming Irish racing from the mid-1940s, but it began its work at a 'propitious' moment.[11] The Emergency had presented significant challenges but racing had shown strong signs of life in the early 1940s, owing significantly to the government grant. In January 1945, retiring INHS Senior Steward A.L. Moore informed members of the Committee that 'racing is in an astonishingly healthy condition' and it was reasonable to 'look forward to the future with confidence'. The only concern Moore had was 'the apparent lack of high-class young chasers', with owners and trainers instead choosing to enter their top prospects in bumpers or maiden hurdles.[12] This was a result of a reduced demand for Irish chasers in Britain during the Second World War, a circumstance that was not helped by a temporary ban on Irish horses running in National Hunt races in England, when the sport resumed there in 1944.[13] The ban was short-lived, but at the time the INHS Committee considered it to be a 'very serious matter' and it was decided that Committee member and Fianna Fáil TD, P.J. Ruttledge, should bring their concerns to the government – a move that demonstrated the enduring political access and influence of racing's governing bodies.[14] The door to England was reopened in early 1945 and – while the end of the war marked the beginning of the end of the great Prince Regent's career – Ireland's position as a pre-eminent producer of steeplechasers was quickly reaffirmed. In the decade after the Second World War, seven of the ten winners of the Grand National were Irish-bred, with the winner of the 1948 edition, Sheila's Cottage, becoming the first mare to win the race since Shannon Lass in 1902. Four of those post-war winners were Irish-trained, and only one among them was not trained by Vincent O'Brien. That exception was Caughoo, a 100/1 long shot who became one of the most unlikely success stories in the history of the Grand National. Bought for 50 guineas as a two-year-old by Herbert McDowell, a County Cavan-based vet who had never trained a racehorse before, the small, bad-tempered Caughoo made an unpromising start on the flat and over hurdles, before proving he was a stayer with a surprisingly comfortable win in the 1946 Ulster National. Herbert sold the horse to his brother Jack – a jeweller and owner of the famous Happy Ring House on Dublin's O'Connell Street – and together they set their sights on Aintree in 1947. Caughoo's victory was so unlikely that some refused to believe it had even happened, suggesting instead that jockey Eddie Dempsey had used the foggy conditions to hide behind a fence, before emerging on the second circuit to race home 20 lengths in front. That myth was only dispelled in the 1990s, after film footage of the race was discovered.[15] Irish-bred horses dominated at Cheltenham in the post-war era, too. Prince Regent delivered his greatest moment when winning the Gold Cup in 1946, but the Irish-bred Distel also made the headlines that year, delivering the Champion Hurdle to trainer Charlie Rogers and owner Dorothy Paget. Rogers delivered another

Caughoo, with Aubrey Brabazon up, led in by Miss Mary McDowell after winning the Ulster National at Downpatrick in 1946. Caughoo became one of the most unlikely Grand National winners in history in 1947, romping home under jockey Eddie Dempsey at odds of 100/1.

CHAPTER FOUR: 1945–1969

A packed Gowran Park on 2 June 1949 – the first meeting after its reopening. Gowran's revival was led by the charismatic Kilkenny businessman Jack Duggan, who served as the new race company's first Managing Director.

Irish-bred winner for Paget, with Dunshauglin taking the honours in the inaugural Festival Trophy Handicap Chase.[16]

The unprecedented financial support provided by the Racing Board and the success of National Hunt racing in Ireland and of Irish chasers in Britain was welcomed by the INHS Committee.[17] The growing scale of the sport was evidenced by the expansion of some race meetings and the resuscitation of others. Killarney, which had been revived in 1936, became a three-day meeting in 1947 and Roscommon returned after a twelve-year absence in 1948. Gowran Park, which had shuttered in 1940, was also resurrected that year, primarily through the efforts of Kilkenny businessman Jack Duggan. A salesman and an innovator, Duggan transformed Gowran's fortunes, working with Michael O'Hehir to introduce on-course commentary to Irish racing, adding the Thyestes Chase to the race programme in 1954, and securing the visit of President Seán T. O'Kelly to the course in October 1955. A member of the Racing Board, he also arranged for the Tote Jackpot to debut at Gowran Park in 1966.[18] The opening of a new course in Wexford in October 1951, meanwhile, brought racing to that part of the country for the first time since the early twentieth century.[19] Racing's growing popularity placed greater demands on the INHS Committee and it was no surprise that Lord Fingall ended his third term as Senior Steward in 1949 by observing that the role 'has got more difficult and complicated each time and needs more work every year'.[20] While the Stewards and the Committee remained dedicated to the success of jump racing in Ireland, a growing workload meant that they relied increasingly on their staff. This included the Keeper of the Match Book and INHS Registrar. Both roles were occupied by the 'faithful and untiring' F. Harold Clarke for over twenty-five years. An Englishman, Clarke worked at Leopardstown for many years, and was eventually appointed Secretary and Manager at the south Dublin course, where he 'caused all the old glories … to be restored'. His talent as a businessman, along with a reputation for industry, courtesy and tact, made him a widely respected figure among the Irish racing community.[21]

Clarke retired in September 1945 and was replaced by Brigadier E.T. Boylan of Hilltown, County Meath. Boylan had served in the Royal Artillery in the First World War and re-joined the British Army on the outbreak of the Second World War. He was posted to the Royal Horse Artillery (RHA) and was at the evacuation of Dunkirk in 1940, before being promoted to the rank of Brigadier. As part of the

(left) The presidential visit to Gowran Park in October 1955. Pictured from left to right are Mrs Phyllis O'Kelly, Mr Jack Duggan, President Sean T. O'Kelly, Mrs Jack Duggan, Mr T.A. Connolly (Director of Gowran) and an unidentified man, possibly an aide-de-camp to the president. (right) An Englishman, F. Harold Clarke came to Ireland after he was appointed assistant manager to Captain George Quin at Leopardstown. He took over as manager on Quin's death in 1917, moving with his family into a house on the course. He was appointed Keeper of the Match Book in 1921 and held that position until 1945.

CHAPTER FOUR: 1945–1969

Capt. Denis Baggallay succeeded Brigadier E.T. Boylan as Keeper of the Match Book in 1959. An amateur who rode on either side of the Second World War, Baggallay most notably steered the Dorothy Paget-owned Astrometer to victory in the Kim Muir Chase at Cheltenham in 1946. He trained horses for a time but it was as a racing official that he had a major impact on the sport.

RHA, in 1926 Boylan represented England at the first international jumping competition at the RDS and he later served as a judge at the Horse Show.[22] He served as INHSC Registrar until 1958 and Keeper of the Match Book until his death in 1959,[23] when he was succeeded by Captain Denis Baggallay, who had served as acting Keeper since 1956. Baggallay had success riding in point-to-points before the Second World War, and became a qualified rider at the conclusion of that conflict. He was appointed the first professional Steward of the Turf Club in 1973, passing his duties as Keeper of the Match Book and Receiver of Entries to Lord HolmPatrick. Baggallay's sudden death in December of that year shocked the racing world. The 56-year-old was so highly esteemed that the door of the governing bodies' office was painted in his registered racing colours of black and yellow.[24] Alongside Clarke, Boylan and Baggallay, May Lennon served as Assistant Keeper and Assistant INHSC Registrar and was 'a tower of strength in the Office' for forty-eight years, until ill-health forced her retirement in 1964.[25] The governing bodies' increasing responsibilities resulted in some important additions to the established staff in this period. In the late 1940s, the position of Stewards' Secretary was created to help manage the workload, with Dan Bulger appointed to the role. This appointment proved 'very useful and helpful to local Stewards' and by the 1960s, four Secretaries were employed.[26] The governing bodies also found a new home in 1958, moving from Hume Street, where they had been located since 1924, to a larger premises on Merrion Square.[27]

'Racing was no longer merely a rich man's sport, but becoming more democratic every day'

Tensions around the demographic make-up of the Turf Club and the INHS Committee endured into the mid-century and both bodies understood the importance of strengthening their connection to the Irish State. Ireland became a republic in April 1949 and the following November, the Committee 'unanimously decided to ask the President of Ireland to become an Honorary Member'. The invitation was declined, not on ideological grounds, but to avoid the Office of the President being named in any future litigation involving either body.[28] As the Irish Republic celebrated its first birthday in 1950, 'princely Punchestown' prepared to mark its centenary year. Writing in the *Irish Independent*, Michael O'Hehir contemplated its evolution and concluded that 'Modern amenities may have brought the course and its enclosures up-to-date but the old spirit of the gathering remains.'[29] The first meeting in Punchestown in 1850 was marred by bad weather, with the racing 'carried on amid a perfect hurricane'; one hundred years later, racing was delayed after a blizzard 'swept the countryside and left the fields mantled in over two inches of snow'.[30] The meeting got underway one day later than planned, attended by the great and the good of Irish politics. President Seán T. O'Kelly was a notable absentee, as he was visiting the Vatican, but Taoiseach John A. Costello, the leader of the first inter-party government, made the journey to Kildare. Costello's wife, Ida, was tasked with presenting the cups on the opening day of the meeting and was succeeded in that role on the second day by Mrs C.A. Garrett, wife of the US Ambassador. Labour Party leader and Tánaiste William Norton also attended, accompanied by his wife Helen.[31] All watched proceedings from the Stewards' Stand, alongside other members of the Dáil and representatives from the Diplomatic Corps.[32]

The visibility of the Irish political elite at Punchestown's centenary meeting represented a significant shift in the attitude of the racecourse executive. A decade earlier, President Douglas Hyde had been asked to attend the meeting in a purely private capacity, in sharp contrast to Dorothy Maffey, wife of the British representative to Ireland, who received an official invitation. The slight did not go unnoticed in the Áras, with Secretary to the President, Michael McDunphy, labelling the racecourse executive 'anti-national'.[33] While progress had been made at Punchestown by 1950, discomfort around the membership of the governing bodies lingered. In 1956, the Senior Steward of the Turf Club Dermot McCalmont was summoned to an interview with Minister for Finance, Gerard Sweetman. In the course of their meeting, Sweetman informed McCalmont of a perception that 'the present members of the Turf Club were, for the most part, out of touch with Irish affairs and were not representative of those interested in and connected with the sport'. Sweetman pointed out that times had changed and that 'Racing was no longer merely a rich man's sport, but becoming more democratic every day. It was the shop window of an important national industry and … it was from that angle that he had to consider the matter.' The minister did not reveal the specific reason for his sudden anxiety, but he did tell McCalmont that if the Turf Club membership did not change, 'questions might be asked in the Dáil which it might be difficult for him to answer and which might do infinite harm to racing and everything connected with it'. The Turf Club heeded Sweetman's warning and suggested Mr Justice Cecil Lavery and Lt General P.A. Mulcahy as suitable candidates for membership; the Minister agreed and both men were elected members shortly afterwards.[34] Tellingly, Lavery and Mulcahy were also elected to the INHS Committee.[35]

'For the first time, Ireland was the best at something'

By the late 1940s, the growing number of entries to Irish steeplechases and hurdle races gave 'an idea of the immense amount of "jumping material"' in Ireland.[36] But, great horses would achieve nothing without great trainers and riders, and it was in this period that some of the major figures of twentieth-century Irish National Hunt racing began to make their mark. Alongside Dan Moore, who retired from riding to focus on training in 1948, other exemplars of Irish jockeyship emerged, including Aubrey Brabazon, Pat Taaffe and brothers Martin and Tim Molony. Martin Molony was an exceptional dual-purpose rider and was crowned Irish champion jockey six times (1946 joint–51) before an injury from a fall brought his career to a premature end in 1951. His elder brother Tim spent most of his career in Britain, where he was a five-time champion jockey (1948/9–1951/2 & 1954/5). Ireland also boasted a number of talented amateur riders in this period, including P.P. Hogan and Bunny Cox. At Greenogue in County Meath, former amateur rider Tom Dreaper built on his early success as a National Hunt trainer. In Churchtown, County Cork, meanwhile, Vincent O'Brien began to establish a reputation as a highly astute trainer, frequently turning out horses that landed major gambles. Following in the footsteps of his father (left) Martin and Tim Molony pictured at Sandown Park in 1950. The brothers were two of the most talented jockeys of the twentieth century. (right) Trainer Dan Moore and his wife Joan (née Comyn) with their son, Arthur, in the 1950s. The Moore family owned Old Fairyhouse Stud, which was located across the road from the racecourse. The stud was later sold to Frank Hillman, before being purchased by Tattersalls Bloodstock Auctioneers in 1986.

Dan, O'Brien – who rode as an amateur until 1941 – started training in 1943. He had quick success on the flat, with wins in the Irish Cambridgeshire and the Irish Cesarewitch the following year, and soon proved his great talent for training jumpers. It was not until 1948, however, that he introduced the world to a true steeplechasing star. Cottage Rake was bred by R.J. Vaughan in County Cork, but struggled to find a buyer because of a respiratory issue. He was eventually bought by Frank Vickerman, on O'Brien's recommendation. The gamble soon paid off: in 1946, Cottage Rake won a Naas November Handicap and the following year he was first past the post in the Irish Cesarewitch. He faltered as the strong favourite in the Leopardstown Chase and finished runner-up in the Irish Grand National in 1948, but more than redeemed himself in England, where he won the first of a remarkable three consecutive Gold Cups at Cheltenham (1948, 1949 and 1950), before adding the Emblem Chase at Manchester and the King George VI Chase at Kempton.

Amateur Legends of the Mid-Twentieth Century

The changing character of point-to-point racing was reflected in the growing status of qualified riders. There had been some outstanding amateurs in the inter-war years, including Welshman Willie Rooney, who moved to Ireland in the 1930s and rode 401 point-to-point winners.[1] Rooney was succeeded in the next decade by P.P. Hogan and John Richard 'Bunny' Cox. A legend of hunt and point-to-point circles, Hogan hailed from Limerick and was champion amateur on five occasions, riding countless point winners and steering Cottage Rake to victory in two bumpers for Vincent O'Brien. He subsequently became a bloodstock agent and established himself as one of the finest trainers of point-to-pointers and hunter chasers in the sport's history. His most successful horses included Under Way, Fearless Fred, Any Crack, No Other Way and Ah Whisht.[2] Bunny Cox also claimed five amateur championships across the 1940s and 50s, sharing the title with another great – Francis Flood – in 1958. His greatest success on the track came at Cheltenham, where he delivered for Dan Moore on Quita Que in the 1959 Champion Chase.[3] From the late 1950s and throughout the 1960s, however, Cork native Bill McLernon was the amateur rider without equal, riding 257 winners at a time when there was far less racing.[4] A nine-time amateur champion, McLernon dominated the period in which point-to-point racing ceased to be a 'sportsman's' event (where hunters were ridden over entirely natural fences), and became a nursery for National Hunt racing. Like Cox before him, his success was not confined to the point-to-

P.P. Hogan on his mount, ahead of the Downshire Plate at Punchestown.

142 NATIONAL HUNT AND POINT-TO-POINT RACING IN IRELAND

(right) Born into a family of farmers, huntsmen and horse dealers from County Limerick, P.P. Hogan rode his first race at the age of 12 and became one of the leading amateur riders of the twentieth century. (below) Bill McLernon (right) on Susan at Clonakilty Point-to-Point, 1960.

point circuit, and he also had significant success as an amateur on the track. During a twelve-year period, McLernon was Phonsie O'Brien's first-choice rider for all but the Galway Hurdle and Plate, which were ridden by professional jockeys Fred Winter and Stan Mellor. He won the Kerry National on Baxier in 1968, rode Bonne and Musty Penny to victory in the Player Wills Amateur Handicap at Galway in 1968 and 1969, respectively, and claimed the Sweet Afton Cup at Dundalk on Fearless Fred in 1968 and Royal Flush in 1971. He also rode in five Grand Nationals, completed the course on three occasions and registered a race-best eighth-place finish on Baxier in 1964. In Ireland, McLernon's dominance of the amateur scene in the 1960s was such that the governing bodies were compelled to introduce a rule limiting him to just fifteen mounts per year in 1968. He retired in 1972 but represented Ireland in eventing at the Munich Olympics the same year. He was appointed Inspector of Courses by the Turf Club in the mid-1980s and held that position for almost twenty years.[5]

Remarkably, Cottage Rake was O'Brien's first runner in England when he won the 1948 Gold Cup, with Cheltenham becoming the first English racecourse that the great trainer set foot on. Indeed, O'Brien later recalled that he was unsure of where to stand and was unable to see the race's finish from his spot at the last fence. And it was a pulsating finish: Happy Home – ridden by Martin Molony – came to the last a length-and-a-half in front, but Cottage Rake charged home under Aubrey Brabazon to win by the same distance.[37] Molony didn't have long to wait to claim Gold Cup honours, however, as he steered Silver Fame to victory in the marquee race in 1951.[38] By then, Cottage Rake had achieved his remarkable Gold Cup hat-trick and his exploits had inspired a short verse: 'Aubrey's up, the money's down/ The frightened bookies quake,/ Come on, lads and give a cheer – / Begod, 'tis Cottage Rake!'[39] And the bay gelding was a history-maker in more than one way. Ahead of his second Gold Cup win in 1949, he became one of the first horses to travel to a race meeting by aeroplane, with O'Brien making use of an old RAF transport to fly him, Hatton's Grace and Castledermot from Shannon to Cheltenham.[40] This was not the only important development in transporting horses in the mid-twentieth century, as the rationalization of the rail network by Córas Iompair Éireann (CIÉ) in the 1950s and 1960s brought an end to the use of trains. In 1952, CIÉ reported that over 18,000 horses had been carried via rail, in horseboxes, but this number declined to 11,706 by 1956, with road haulage replacing trains as the primary means of carrying horses to race meetings or bloodstock sales.[41]

Vincent O'Brien continued to dominate National Hunt racing in the early 1950s, with Brabazon piloting the unlikely Hatton's Grace to three successive Champion

Cottage Rake, with Aubrey Brabazon up, before winning the King George VI Chase at Kempton in 1948. Cottage Rake failed three veterinary examinations because of a wind problem but O'Brien learned that this would not affect his race performance and convinced Frank Vickerman to buy the horse. It was not long before the versatile and consistent bay claimed a hat-trick of Gold Cups.

(clockwise from top left) Vincent O'Brien after riding his first winner, Hallowment, in a two-mile bumper at Limerick Junction on 7 November 1940. The horse was owned and trained by O'Brien's father, Dan. O'Brien rode three winners as an amateur, before deciding not to renew his licence in 1941; Tom Dreaper loading horses into a Great Southern Railway's horsebox at Kingsbridge Station (now Heuston Station) in the 1940s. The rationalization of the rail network in the 1950s and 60s made road haulage the preferred means of carrying horses to race meetings and bloodstock sales; Jackie O'Brien leading in his point-to-point winner, China Cottage, with P.P. Hogan up. The Fermoy man had a major impact on Vincent O'Brien's early career as a trainer, after meeting him at Limerick Junction Racecourse in 1943. It was through Jackie that Vincent met Frank Vickerman, who later bought Cottage Rake; Vincent O'Brien's transformational impact on horse racing was not limited to the track. In 1949, he pioneered the transportation of horses by air, using an old RAF transport aircraft to fly Cottage Rake, Castledermot and Hatton's Grace to Cheltenham. All three horses won their races.

CHAPTER FOUR: 1945–1969 145

The Tóstal Steeplechase

In 1953, an annual festival celebrating Irish life was inaugurated. An Tóstal ('The Gathering') was organised at the suggestion of the President of Pam Am Airlines, who conceived of the idea after seeing the 1951 Festival of Britain. Devised to boost tourism in the off-peak season, An Tóstal was primarily aimed at the Irish diaspora in the US. The festival was not a resounding success and was wound down in 1958, but it nonetheless left a significant imprint on Irish culture, originating the Cork Film Festival, the Dublin Theatre Festival (and, relatedly, 'The Rose Tattoo' controversy), the Tidy Towns competition and the Rose of Tralee.[1] An Tóstal also comprised events organised by local committees and, in 1954, Buttevant's programme included a steeplechase to commemorate Blake and O'Callaghan's race from that town to Doneraile in 1752. The twentieth-century event was not a facsimile of the original, as thirty riders in hunting attire raced four miles across a marked course in the reverse

The winning team from Killeagh Harriers: Brian McLernon, John Twomey and W.A. (Bill) McLernon. The McLernons are descended from Cornelius O'Callaghan, one of the participants in the 1752 steeplechase.

The programme for the Buttevant Tostal Committee Steeplechase, which was run in 1954 to commemorate Blake and O'Callaghan's 1752 steeplechase. It was part of the town's programme for An Tóstal, a series of festivals held between 1953 and 1958 to boost tourism through a celebration of Irish culture.

direction going from Doneraile to Buttevant. Four teams from the Duhallow Hunt competed against representatives from the Kildare Hunt, the Black and Tans, the Avondhu, the Tipperary, the Killeagh Harriers and the United Hunt. Eight women competed, as did the legendary film director, John Huston, and actor Tim Durant, both of whom represented Kildare. They were joined in the field by brothers Bill and Brian McLernon, who were descended (on their mother's side) from Cornelius O'Callaghan.[2] The McLernons and John Twomey won the team event for Killeagh Harriers. Bill would go on to have a stellar amateur career, but it was another legend of the non-professional ranks, P.P. Hogan, who won the individual race on Baypark II.[3] In 2002, a re-enactment of Blake and O'Callaghan's famous match was staged to mark its 250th anniversary, with a number of top Irish jockeys – including Ruby Walsh, Barry Geraghty and Paul Carberry – taking part. The event raised €20,000 for the creation of a plaque by artist James McCarthy, to commemorate the first recorded steeplechase in history.

CHAPTER FOUR: 1945–1969

(left) Early Mist being led in by owner Joe 'Mincemeat' Griffin, after winning the Grand National under jockey Bryan Marshall in 1953. Vincent O'Brien's head lad, Maurice O'Callaghan, is in jubilant form on the left, while the great trainer is on the right. British-bred but Irish-trained, Early Mist was the first of O'Brien's famous trio of consecutive National winners, followed by Royal Tan and Quare Times.

(below) Hatton's Grace led in by owner Moya Keogh after winning the Champion Hurdle at Cheltenham in 1949.

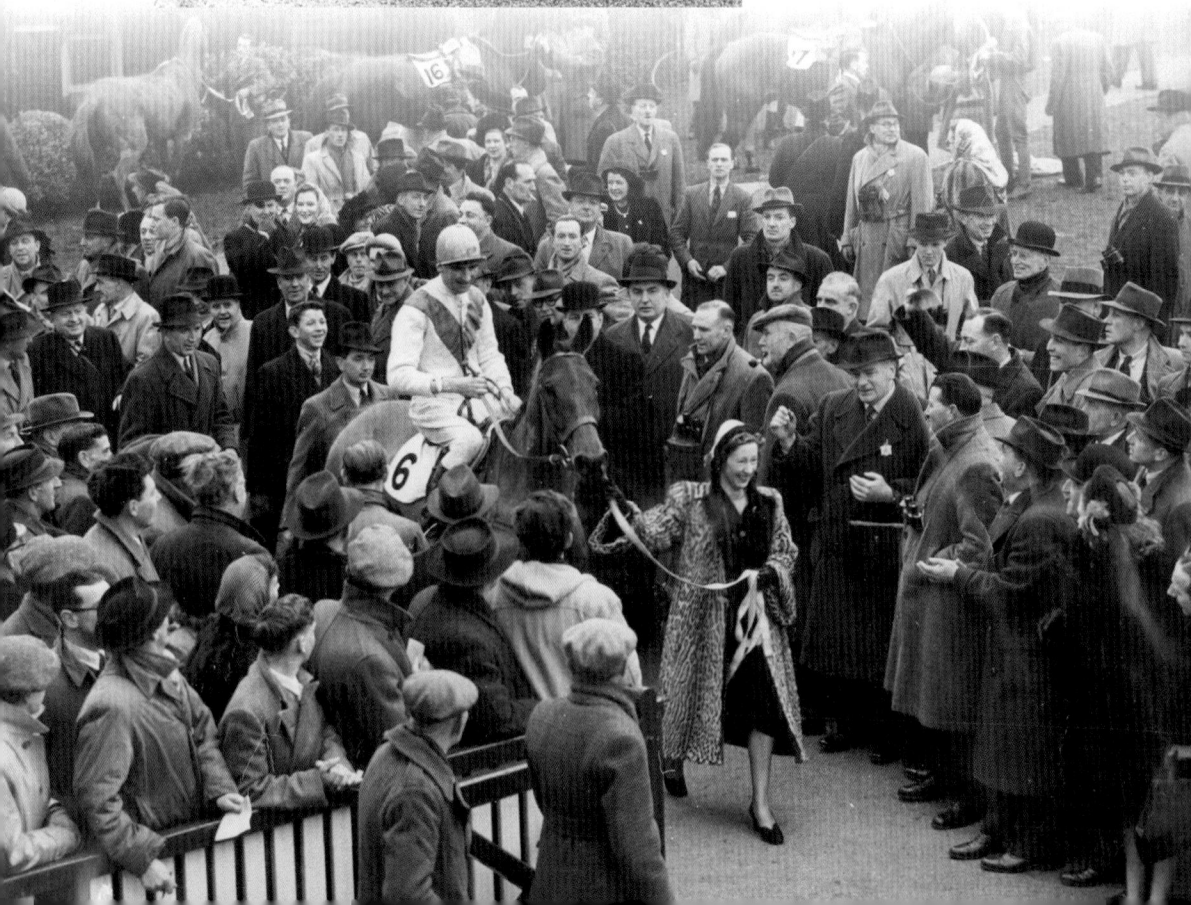

Hurdles between 1949 and 1951. During this remarkable period, O'Brien moved from Churchtown to Ballydoyle House, near Cashel in County Tipperary and there, over time, he converted a working farm into a state-of-the-art training facility. O'Brien was already establishing himself at Ballydoyle when he became the only trainer in history to achieve a consecutive hat-trick in the Grand National, with Bryan Marshall riding Early Mist and Royal Tan to victory at Aintree in 1953 and 1954 respectively, and Pat Taaffe delivering on Quare Times in 1955.[42] It was a good Grand National for the Taaffe family, as Pat's brother Thomas finished third on Carey's Cottage, a horse trained by their father at Rathcoole.[43] By then, O'Brien had already added a fourth Gold Cup to his resumé, with Tim Molony riding Knock Hard into the history books in 1953. Knock Hard was a long way off the leading pack when they emerged out of the mist and raced down the hill but – as O'Brien recalled – 'Tim was at him, driving him, kicking him, pushing him all the way', and the horse accelerated up the hill to win by five lengths.[44] O'Brien's record at Prestbury Park was staggering; as well as four Gold Cups and three Champion Hurdles, he also achieved an incredible ten wins in the premier novice hurdling event, the Gloucestershire Hurdle (later the Supreme Novices), which was sometimes run in two divisions to accommodate large entries.[45] The trainer's wife, Jacqueline, later reflected on the importance to the Irish people of O'Brien's successes in England:

> For the first time, Ireland was the best at something – I think that every Irish parish priest followed him to Cheltenham. He had an immense following there, it was a great boost for Ireland, Irish people were able to put their shoulders back, beating the English, it was an astonishing state of affairs. He won three Gold Cups, three Champion Hurdles and three Grand Nationals – all in succession. So it seemed as though he was invincible, and Ireland too.[46]

O'Brien was not only focussed on the major English National Hunt races. In Ireland, Alberoni took the Irish Grand National at Fairyhouse in 1952 and found summer success at Galway, where he beat stablemate Lucky Dome by a head in the Plate.[47] Lucky Dome gave O'Brien another notable success over jumps the following year, when he won the Leopardstown Chase.[48] Having conquered National Hunt racing, the Ballydoyle supremo began to turn his attention to the flat, with Chamier claiming

From one winner to another: Quare Times (left), winner of the 1955 Grand National, looking at Royal Tan, who won the same race one year earlier, at Vincent O'Brien's stables in Ballydoyle.

the 1953 Irish Derby.[49] O'Brien was also active in advancing the interests of Irish trainers in this period. In September 1950, he joined with eleven other Flat and National Hunt trainers – Michael Collins, Darby Rogers, Charlie Rogers, W.J. Byrne, Gerald Wellesley, Martin Quirke, Dan Moore, Paddy Sleator, Danny Morgan, Hubert Hartigan and Cecil Brabazon – to form the Irish Racehorse Trainers' Association (IRTA).[50] The formation of a representative body for Irish trainers in 1950 reflected their growing success and stature in the sport and in the industry, which was largely a result of the State's greater investment in Irish racing from the early 1940s. The IRTA was established with the immediate aim of lobbying the protectionist Fianna Fáil government to import higher quality oats from Canada, but its overarching object was

> To consider all questions affecting the interests of the profession and to initiate and watch over and if necessary to petition Dáil Eireann or promote deputations in relation to matters affecting the profession and to procure changes of laws or regulations affecting the profession and the promotion of improvements in matters relating thereto.[51]

'NO INTOXICATING LIQUOR MAY BE TAKEN INTO JOCKEYS' DRESSING ROOMS'

The formation of the IRTA came at the beginning of a dark decade for the Irish people. Among other things, a series of deflationary budgets and limited growth and productivity caused income *per capita* to fall further behind the west European average. Living standards declined and emigration rocketed, with Ireland entering a period of recession in the mid-1950s that lasted into the next decade.[52] Civil War politics aside, there was no meaningful difference in the main political parties' policies and this meant that changes in government did little to improve Ireland's economic and social decline. The development of political consensus stymied innovative thinking and prevented radical approaches to tackling Ireland's problems. High emigration rates and political stability also resulted in a conservative society, resistant to change and unsympathetic to the issues that often attended economic and social disadvantage.[53] And yet, as historian Paul Rouse notes, 'For all that the 1950s were suffused with misery and cataclysm, people also had to live. And, in the midst of all that living, a lot of people had an awful lot of fun.'[54] It was in the difficult decades of the mid-twentieth century, during and after the Emergency and throughout the 1950s, that the crowds attending sporting events increased. Attendances at GAA, rugby union and association football matches grew, as did those at regattas and athletic events.[55] Similarly, racing's importance to the Irish people was undiminished; for the State, meanwhile, the industry became even more significant.

In this moment of unlikely opportunity, the Racing Board and the governing bodies were

Aubrey Brabazon takes a moment to have a drink and a cigarette after falling from Luan Casca at Becher's Brook in the 1947 Grand National.

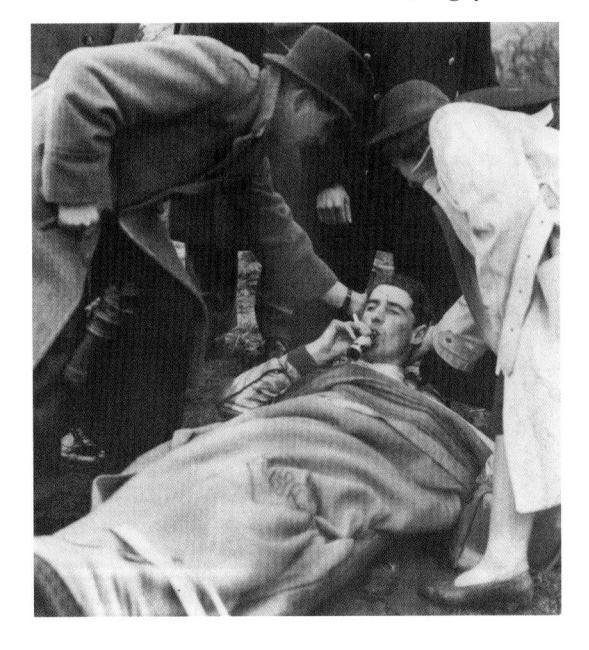

anxious to ensure the sport's success. The impulse to advance racing was evident in the introduction of technology to the racetrack and in the expanding media coverage of meetings. The first significant development was the introduction of a photo finish camera, which was employed by the Jockey Club for Flat races from the mid-1940s. The Turf Club changed their rules to allow the use of official photographs to adjudicate on close finishes in 1950 and after a trial period, cameras were installed at a number of Irish racecourses.[56] Three years later cameras were used at Baldoyle, the Curragh, Leopardstown, Naas and Phoenix Park, which accounted for about 44 per cent of meetings held in Ireland. Concerns that the inclement Irish weather would impact the quality of photographs were dispelled, as cameras were used at meetings held exclusively under National Hunt Rules and 'despite winter conditions including humidity, fog, etc.' results were 'uniformly good'.[57] The INHS Committee's early adoption of cameras was in contrast to its English counterpart, which declined to use the photo finish until 1957. At the Curragh the following April, the Turf Club became a European pioneer in the use of patrol cameras, which allowed the Stewards to monitor the race at most points around the track, providing them with the evidence to immediately investigate improper or dangerous riding. The INHS Committee also recognized the potential of this new technology and it was not long before they were employed in National Hunt races.[58]

Alongside efforts to modernize racing, there was an impetus to stamp out corrupt practice, which became more common as money flowed into the sport. Vincent O'Brien may have been used as an example by the INHS Committee, when it brought the Ballydoyle juggernaut to a halt in 1954. On 22 March that year, the trainer was requested to attend an INHS Stewards' inquiry into the alleged inconsistent running of four of his horses – Royal Tan, Early Mist, Lucky Dome and Knock Hard. Nine days later, the hearing concluded and the Stewards informed O'Brien that they did not accept his explanations, stating that he had been 'warned and cautioned on several previous occasions', and were withdrawing his licence for three months.[59] O'Brien afterwards told the press that 'I am completely in the dark as to what, if any offence I am alleged to have been guilty of', adding that 'no specific charges in respect of the running of any of the horses in any of their races have been made'.[60] In some ways, the trainer was an easy target because he did not come from the traditional 'racing establishment', his success was unprecedented and he had a reputation for laying wagers on his own horses.[61] The suspension had an immediate impact on O'Brien, as both Royal Tan and Quare Times were prevented from running in the 1954 Irish Grand National.[62] The INHS Committee's ruling was extended by the Turf Club to the flat, so O'Brien was compelled to send prospects in both codes to other trainers until the suspension ended.[63] The ban did not have a long term impact on O'Brien's career. His first success after returning to action came at Tramore in August, where his brother, amateur rider Phonsie, rode Blue Mosque – a horse owned by Vincent's wife, Jacqueline – to victory in a bumper.[64] By October, he was 'back into his stride' and registered four winners in one day at his local racecourse, Limerick Junction (now Tipperary Racecourse).[65] In the years that followed, however, O'Brien shifted his focus to Flat racing.[66]

Inconsistent running was not the only concern for the governing bodies in this period. The safety of jockeys and amateur riders was a growing preoccupation. Safety standards on nineteenth- and early twentieth-century racecourses were 'virtually non-existent' and riders – many of whom were physically diminished by wasting to keep weight down – wore no protective equipment. Silk caps had been worn by jockeys for centuries, but skull caps made from cork were not worn until the early twentieth century, with the National Hunt Committee in Britain making them compulsory in 1924, after the death following a fall of leading amateur, Captain G.H. 'Tuppy' Bennet.[67] The INHS Stewards followed suit in 1931, stipulating that 'No rider shall be weighed out for, or ride in, any race unless he is wearing a skull cap of the pattern approved by the Stewards of the Irish National Hunt Steeplechase Committee'.[68] The British and Irish National Hunt authorities acted long before the Jockey Club and the Turf Club, both of which made the wearing of skull caps compulsory under the Rules of Racing in 1956.[69] It was not until 1962, however, that the use of chin straps to keep skull caps in place was made compulsory in National Hunt racing on both sides of the Irish Sea, with the INHS Committee altering its rules so that riders no longer had to weigh in or out with their skull caps. The Committee also made it compulsory for riders to wear a specific type of crash helmet, which weighed about one pound and included a chin strap.[70] The 1960s marked a turning point in attitudes to rider safety and the use of effective helmets, as the governing bodies in Britain and Ireland looked to developments in Australia and the US and began to improve standards domestically.[71] A greater emphasis on rider welfare in point-to-point racing, meanwhile, resulted in the compulsory wearing of approved skull caps in that branch of the sport from 1974.[72]

As well as working to ensure rider safety, the INHS Committee also provided financial support to those who sustained serious or fatal injuries while racing. This included jockey Francis Shortt, who 'suffered considerable hardship' in 1965, after breaking his leg twice in seven months.[73] The same year, the Committee also contributed £500 to the fund being raised for the widow of J.J. Rafferty.[74] Consumption of alcohol was another problem among riders. Aubrey Brabazon recollected that during his riding career,

> there were few jump jockeys who didn't know how to enjoy themselves properly. We could be revelling and partying until dawn and still, when it came to race time the next day, we could be one hundred per cent fit for the job. There is no doubt that it takes a certain degree of madness to ride horses over fences in the first place, so it's only to be expected that the lifestyle of a jump jockey should be something other than the disciplined 'nine to five' model.[75]

Besides its social function, alcohol was consumed by jockeys to keep weight down and as a source of 'Dutch courage' on the track.[76] In 1952, the INHS Committee and the Turf Club tackled the problem by issuing a notice, which was 'to be placed in a prominent position in Jockeys' Dressing Rooms at all Meetings'. It stated clearly that 'NO INTOXICATING LIQUOR MAY BE TAKEN INTO JOCKEYS' DRESSING ROOMS'.[77]

As racing became more competitive, there was also growing concern over the administering of banned substances to horses. This was not the first time that doping posed a problem for the governing bodies in Ireland and Britain. The administering of substances to fix a race by diminishing a horse's performance was well-established in British racing by the mid-nineteenth century. In 1865, John Mills described the practice of 'nobbling' a horse by drugging it to prevent it racing at its full potential; these concoctions comprised bitter aloes and opium, which would cause the horse to feel drowsy and faint.[78] Substances were also provided to enhance horses' performances – the arrival of American trainers on the British racing scene in the late nineteenth century led to the widespread use of cocaine, for example, which had 'marvellous

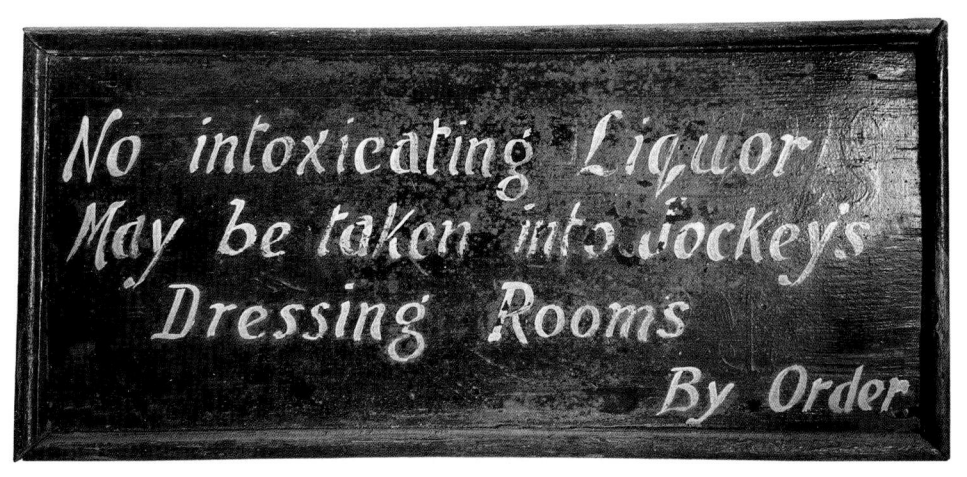

Many jockeys used alcohol as a source of 'Dutch courage' or a means of making weight, a practice that caused the INHS Committee to ban it from jockeys' dressing rooms in 1952.

properties … for the jaded horse'.[79] In Ireland, meanwhile, one sporting correspondent claimed that he had 'put his shirt' on a horse ridden by Garrett Moore, after he spied the famous gentleman rider pouring a pint of Jameson whiskey down the mare's throat.[80] Both the Jockey Club and the Turf Club introduced rules to punish doping in 1903, with the English National Hunt Committee following suit in 1910. It was not until 1947, however, that a similar provision was added to the INHS Rules.[81] The INHS Committee went further in 1954, stipulating that:

> If in any case it shall be found that any drug or stimulant has been administered to a horse for the purpose of affecting its speed in a race, the licence or permit of the trainer of the horse may be withdrawn and he may be declared a disqualified person.[82]

By placing responsibility for doping offences on the trainer – whatever the extent of their knowledge or negligence – the rule encouraged better discipline, greater compliance and an improvement in security around stables. On the other hand, it also raised the possibility that a trainer could be treated unfairly. This is what happened in April 1960, when the Vincent O'Brien-trained Chamour tested positive for a banned substance after winning a Flat race at the Curragh. No one believed that O'Brien was directly involved in administering the substance but because the greatest share of responsibility lay with the trainer, the Turf Club banned him for eighteen months. Trouble arose, however, because the Turf Club's ruling implied that O'Brien was the individual responsible for administering the substance.

The Turf Club Stewards issued a clarification in the *Racing Calendar*, stating that they 'did NOT find Mr O'Brien had administered the substance or knew of its administration ... any other impression given by the wording of their previous decision is incorrect.'[83] This only served to highlight their error, however. O'Brien took matters to the High Court and was vindicated in July 1961, when the Stewards agreed to a settlement. The Stewards issued a full apology, while O'Brien acknowledged that they had found evidence of a banned substance and were entitled to suspend him because he was Chamour's trainer.[84] The fallout from the case meant that the governing bodies could not expect their authority to go unquestioned in future. Recognizing the need for greater transparency in dealing with cases of suspected doping, in July 1960 the Stewards of the Turf Club arranged for Dr George William Pennington, head of Trinity College Dublin's Department of Pharmacology, to analyse samples of urine and saliva taken from all Flat and National Hunt race winners. Under this arrangement, which was funded by the Racing Board, samples were taken in the presence of the horse's trainer, who could nominate another analyst to receive a second sample, which would serve as a 'check' on the primary test.[85]

'a schooling ground for horses, riders and administrators'

While the INHS Committee negotiated the evolution of National Hunt racing in the mid-twentieth century, it also took a greater interest in the regulation of point-to-point racing after the establishment of the Racing Board, most notably through the establishment of a Point-to-Point Committee. In 1952, that Committee made a series of recommendations on issues of 'paramount importance' to the sport of point-to-point racing; this included the stricter segregation of the weighing scales area; the separation of the judges 'box', with no members of the public to be admitted; the provision of a suitable meeting place for the Stewards to conduct enquiries; and the better control of the crowd in the finishing straight.[86] This was followed by the decision to allow members to nominate individuals from outside the Committee, to help at point-to-points across the island, reducing the burden on the Stewards and (above) Over the famous double bank at Kellistown Point-to-Point in County Carlow in 1946. From l–r: Mr Jim Mullins on Carlingford Lough (finished 2nd), Mr Paddy Mullins on Jurisprudence (finished 3rd), and the eventual winner, Mr A.S. "Wren" O'Donnell on Ballyfoyle (owned by Mr T.A. Connolly). (below) A scene from a point-to-point meeting at Bartlemy in County Cork in 1951. Point-to-point racing still takes place there, under the auspices of the United Hunt Club.

Committee members and allowing reforms to be enacted.[87] In early 1961, the retiring Senior Steward N.W. Waddington noted that while there was still 'considerable room for improvement … the standard of management of point-to-points and their courses have improved a great deal in the last few years'.[88] The same year, stake money was raised from £25 to £40. Even this increase was debated, with some members maintaining their belief that it would put point-to-points in competition with National Hunt racing. As A.L. Moore pointed out, however, some increase was necessary because the ratio between point-to-point and National Hunt prize money had grown exponentially since the 1940s.[89]

The need to maintain a clear distinction between point-to-point and National Hunt racing was an ongoing concern for the INHS Committee. This was evident in restrictions on the use of racecourse amenities for point-to-point meetings. In April 1964, for example, the Kilkenny Hunt struggled to find a suitable venue for its point-to-point meeting and requested the use of the stands at Gowran Park, which would allow for the easier control of the crowds in attendance. The proposal was not without precedent – the Ward Union Hunt had made use of Fairyhouse in exceptional circumstance – and it drew the support of some Committee members, who felt it was more important to keep good meetings going. On the other hand, Lord Fingall argued that 'if people could go to a course and enjoy its amenities free for a point-to-point they might think twice before going there to pay a few weeks later for an ordinary race meeting'. Another Committee member, Mr S.W.N. Collen, added that it might create an 'even bigger gap between the good and bad point-to-point meetings and perhaps kill off the lesser meetings'. These discussions highlighted the uneven development of point-to-point racing across the island, but they also underlined its changing character and its growing popular appeal. By the mid-1960s, it had 'gone so far from the old ideas that they should be viewed in a new light', as 'junior race meetings run as efficiently as possible as a schooling ground for horses, riders and administrators'.[90] The growing importance of point-to-point racing as a production line for National Hunt racing was underlined in 1965, when the Racing Board pledged to increase its annual grant to individual meetings from £50 to £100 and to provide money to fund the inspection of all courses.[91]

'between the king and crown prince of chasing'

While point-to-point racing evolved, Irish horses, trainers and jockeys continued to perform at the highest levels of National Hunt racing, both at home and in Britain. By early 1965, retiring INHS Senior Steward Major J.H. de Burgh could reflect with satisfaction that 'There can seldom have been a greater number of really top-class horses trained in this country and, most important, we have been able to convince them to do most of their racing in Ireland.'[92] Among the most successful trainers

(right) Based at Grangecon in County Wicklow, Paddy Sleator was a champion amateur rider before becoming a successful trainer. He was a dominant presence at Galway, where he won the Plate a remarkable nine times.
(below) The Tom Dreaper-trained Fortria winning the 1961 Irish Grand National under Pat Taaffe. Fortria was bred by Alec Craigie and was by Fortina – the only entire horse to win the Gold Cup – out of Senria.

was Paddy Sleator, from Grangecon in County Wicklow, who began riding in point-to-points and was amateur champion in 1934, 1937 and 1938, before turning his attention to training. Sleator was crowned champion trainer in 1958 and he was primarily known for his dominance at Galway, where he won 24 races, including the Plate nine times and the Plate/Hurdle double with Knight Errant and Tymon Castle in 1957. But his success wasn't confined to Galway, nor was it limited to jump racing. The winning performances of Sword Flash, Havasnack and Another Flash in the Irish Cesarewitch prompted the Turf Club to ban bumper winners from Flat races. It was the classy Another Flash who delivered Sleator's greatest victory, when he raced home under Bobby Beasley to win the Champion Hurdle at Cheltenham in 1960. This was one year after Beasley's Gold Cup success aboard the English-bred, Irish-trained Roddy Owen – the first Irish winner of the race since Knock Hard in 1953.[93]

If Sleator dominated Galway, Tom Dreaper reigned at Fairyhouse, where he won the Irish Grand National ten times. Dreaper started saddling horses in 1931 but his

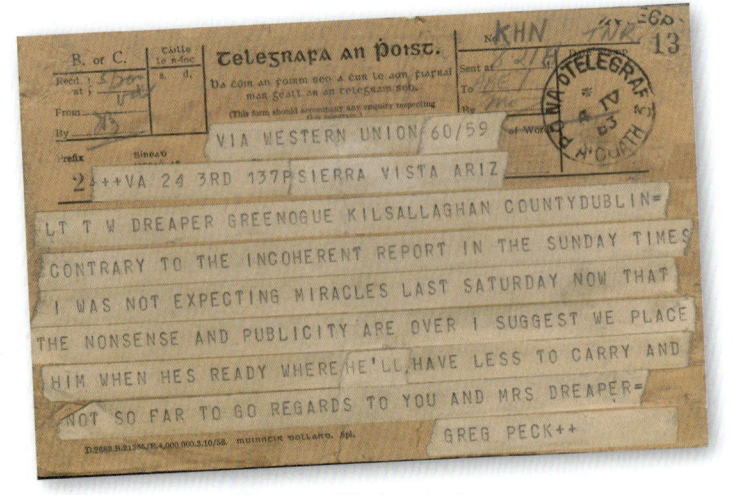

A telegram from film star Gregory Peck, who owned Owen's Sedge, asking trainer Tom Dreaper to ignore an 'incoherent report' published in the *Sunday Times* after the horse finished seventh in the 1963 Grand National. Peck would win an Oscar for his role in *To Kill a Mockingbird* the following week.

career really took off when he became trainer for the American owner, J.V. Rank, who made his fortune in flour milling.[94] His success with Prince Regent was followed by Irish Grand National victories with Shagreen in 1949 and Royal Approach in 1954, but he surpassed all expectations by training seven successive winners of the race between 1960 and 1966. Among this stable of champions was the talented Fortria, who was bred by Dreaper's neighbour, Alec Craigie, and won the Irish Grand National in 1961, with Pat Taaffe on board. Fortria had a first notable success when winning the Cotswold Chase at Cheltenham in 1958 – a then-record year for Irish-trained horses, with eight winners at the Festival. Fortria subsequently became the first dual winner of the Champion Chase (1960 and 1961), was runner-up to Mandarin in the Cheltenham Gold Cup in 1962 and Mill House in 1963, and became the inaugural and first dual winner of the Mackeson Gold Cup (1960 and 1962).[95] By that point, Dreaper's reputation was such that film star Gregory Peck numbered among the owners at the Greenogue stables. Peck's horse – a grey named Owen's Sedge – placed seventh in the Grand National in 1963, one week before the actor won an Oscar for his role as Atticus Finch in *To Kill a Mockingbird*.[96]

In 1966, the last of Dreaper's seven-in-a-row in the Irish Grand National was delivered by the British-bred Flyingbolt, a tall, highly-strung, white-faced chestnut, who is still rated as the second-best steeplechaser of all time. A star from the beginning, in 1964 Flyingbolt claimed both the Gloucestershire Hurdle at Cheltenham and the Irish Champion Hurdle at Leopardstown. One year later, he won the Cotswold Chase and romped home fifteen lengths in front in the Massey Ferguson Gold Cup. Following that dominant performance, the *Irish Field* reported that 'There are many who thought that before the big race Flyingbolt was a little behind Arkle; while

Liam McLoughlin exercising Flyingbolt at Dreapers' Greenogue stables, with Betty Dreaper following behind. McLoughlin was the first rider to win on Arkle and won the Irish Grand National and the Thyestes Chase on the mare Kerforo in 1962. His son, Dermot, has trained two Irish Grand National winners – Freewheelin Dylan in 2021 and Lord Lariat in 2022.

after his resounding victory they are in no doubt that he is as good.'[97] Flyingbolt continued his impressive form in 1966, winning the Thyestes Chase at Gowran Park by over thirty lengths. He then raced to an emphatic victory in the Champion Chase at Cheltenham, before placing third in the Champion Hurdle the following day. A few weeks later, he became the first horse since Golden View II in 1946 to carry 12st 7lbs to victory in the Irish Grand National, beating Height O'Fashion, who received 40lbs, by two lengths. Reflecting on Flyingbolt's Irish National win some years later, Pat Taaffe commented that he was 'Once again … reminded that I was alternating between the king and crown prince of chasing. More than ever, it now seemed only a matter of time before he took over from Arkle.'[98] Flyingbolt never got the chance. In the summer of 1966, the then seven-year-old contracted brucellosis, a bacterial disease that caused inflammation of the joints and muscle soreness, and he never achieved the greatness for which he was destined.[99] In the end, Flyingbolt's was a story of unfulfilled potential, the tragedy of which was underlined by his complete omission from a 2004 list of *Racing Post* readers' top 100 all-time favourite horses.

'Himself'

If Flyingbolt is jump racing's greatest unsung hero, then his stablemate (and the winner of that *Racing Post* poll) remains the sport's biggest star.[100] In 1962, the *Irish Horse* made reference to a 'promising young jumper', a five-year-old gelding who had been bought by the Duchess of Westminster at Goffs' Ballsbridge sale two years earlier, and who had recently won the President's Hurdle at Gowran Park. Bred by Mary Baker of Malahow House near Naul in County Dublin, Arkle was sired by Archive out of Bright Cherry.[101] Between 1962 and 1966, he recorded 22 wins in 26 steeplechases and 27 wins from 35 starts overall, with all of his steeplechase victories achieved under jockey Pat Taaffe.[102] After posting mixed results in bumpers and hurdle races across 1961 and 1962, Arkle was immediately successful in his chasing career, finishing twenty lengths ahead of the field in the Honeybourne Chase at Cheltenham in November 1962. In February the following year, he raced to an eight-length victory in the Milltown Novice Chase at Leopardstown (which would later be renamed as the Arkle Novice Chase) and followed that performance with wins in the Broadway Novices' Chase at Cheltenham, the Punchestown Gold Cup and the Powers Gold Cup at Fairyhouse. In November 1963, Arkle faltered in the Hennessy

The 'crown prince of chasing': Flyingbolt and Pat Taaffe on the way to winning the Cotswold Chase at Cheltenham in 1965. A highly strung white-faced chestnut, Flyingbolt was arguably as good as (if not better than) Arkle, but his career was cut short by brucellosis and he did not fulfil his undoubted potential.

Gold Cup at Newbury and finished third behind his great rival, Mill House.[103] That was his only defeat of the season; after wins in the Christmas Handicap Chase, the Thyestes Chase, and the Leopardstown Chase, on 7 March 1964 he recorded the first of his three consecutive Cheltenham Gold Cup victories.

Despite Tom Dreaper's absence through illness, Arkle arrived at Prestbury Park 'absolutely full of himself' and justified that confidence by racing home five lengths ahead of a tired Mill House. Journalist Hugh McIlvanney would later recall that:

> As Pat Taaffe, who had planned it all that way, began to close on the turn at the top of the hill, the incredible Irish support, the farmers and stableboys and priests, roared in unison 'Here he comes.' It was like a beleaguered army greeting the hero who brings relief. He came all right, to run the heart out of Mill House, and that great horse was never the same again.[104]

Arkle was given a 'tremendous' reception by the crowd, as three cheers were called and a spontaneous round of applause followed him out of the winner's enclosure. Taaffe told reporters that 'This was the best race he has run yet, but I think he needed it and will improve'.[105] At this point, Arkle was unstoppable. Ahead of the 1964 edition of the Irish Grand National at Fairyhouse, the handicappers took the unprecedented step of creating two handicaps – one to be employed when Arkle was running and one to be used in his absence. The new system made a difference, as Arkle won by only one length from the 'wonderfully game little mare' Height O'Fashion (who was beaten – even more impressively – in 1966 by Flyingbolt), but his dominance was underlined by the fact that he conceded 30lbs to his competitors.[106] Arkle began the 1964–5 season with a win in the Carey's Cottage Handicap Chase at Gowran Park and was then

Arkle jumping to win the Leopardstown Chase in 1966.

Arkle beating reigning champion Mill House in the Gold Cup at Cheltenham in 1964. Theirs was one of the great rivalries of National Hunt racing, with Arkle's brilliance ultimately outshining Mill House's considerable talent.

successful in the Hennessy Gold Cup at Newbury, where he avenged his previous defeat by posting a ten-length victory over Mill House. With owners and trainers reluctant to race to a foregone conclusion, Arkle faced small fields in the next two editions of the Cheltenham Gold Cup; he cantered home twenty lengths ahead of Mill House in 1965 and was in even more dominant form the following year, when he started the race as the 1/10 favourite and beat the second-placed horse, Dormant, by thirty lengths.[107]

Mill House (Pat Taaffe up) jumping the last to win the Osberstown Maiden Hurdle by five lengths at Naas Racecourse, 5 March 1961. Bred by Mrs Bridget Lawlor in County Kildare, Mill House was broken in by Pat Taaffe and trained by his father, Tom, before being sold into England. At over 17 hands high, the Gold Cup and King George winner was known affectionately as 'the Big Horse.'

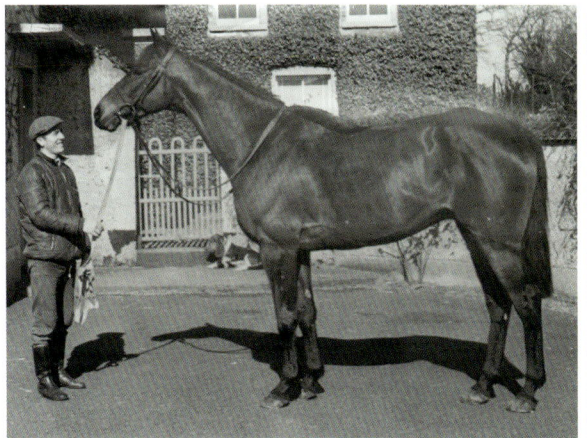

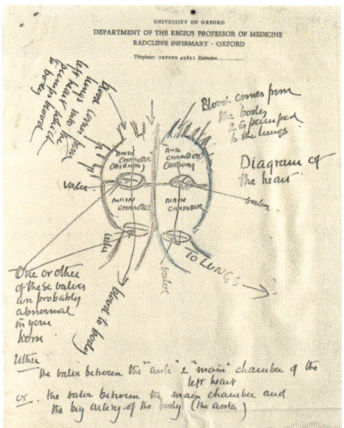

(left) Tom Dreaper had an embarrassment of riches at Greenogue in the 1960s. The talented Fort Leney won the 1967 Leopardstown Chase and the 1968 Gold Cup, despite having a heart defect. As Pat Taaffe later would fondly remark, Fort Leney's 'heart may have been unsound, but on a racecourse it became the heart of a lion'. (right) A diagram of a horse's heart, drawn by a faculty member at Oxford Medical School and sent to Fort Leney's owner, Colonel John Thomson. Thomson, who was very fond of the horse, also sought advice on his condition from UCD Veterinary School. He sent the findings to Betty Dreaper, who ran Greenogue while Tom was ill, and expressed his thanks for the care she had taken with Fort Leney.

Prestbury Park was not the only venue graced by Arkle's genius in this period: across 1965 and 1966 he won another two Leopardstown Chases, the Whitbread Gold Cup and Gallaher Gold Cup at Sandown, another Hennessy Gold Cup at Newbury, the King George VI Chase at Kempton and the SGB Handicap Chase at Ascot. Like Flyingbolt, it was not time but misfortune that brought an end to Arkle's dazzling career. He returned to Kempton for the King George VI Chase on 26 December 1966 and jumped the last clear, but Dormant caught him 'stride by stride' on the run in and while the great horse 'fought back gamely … there were some miracles that were beyond even him'.[108] It was subsequently confirmed that he had fractured a pedal bone.[109] Arkle appeared to make a good recovery and was put back into training, but it was decided to retire him after a lacklustre racecourse gallop at Naas. The Duchess of Westminster stated that 'he has been off the course for two years and is now eleven years old, and I feel that possibly not even Arkle, for all his immense courage, could be expected to reproduce his old brilliance'.[110] The equine superstar lived the rest of his life on the farm at Bryanstown House, the Duchess' residence in County

Kildare. By 1969, he started to show signs of arthritis and one year later he was put to sleep for humane reasons, with Pat Taaffe recalling that the thirteen-year-old 'died quietly and peacefully, thank God'.[111] Debates about Arkle's status as the greatest ever steeplechaser have endured, with some arguing that his Timeform rating is inflated and others suggesting that if given the chance, Flyingbolt would have beaten him in a race.[112] Racing doesn't run on hypotheticals, but it is difficult to imagine any of the great horses that raced after the 1960s beating either of Dreaper's remarkable charges, given the huge amount of weight they gave away in handicaps at that time.

In some ways, the question of Arkle's superiority as a steeplechaser is irrelevant. Referred to with great affection by the public as 'Himself', Arkle's popularity was such that he passed into legend during his own lifetime. He regularly received fan mail, was the subject of a song by Dominic Behan (brother of Brendan) and one admirer went so far as to daub 'Arkle for President' on a wall in Dublin.[113] His legend was such that when Muhammad Ali came to Ireland to fight Alvin (Al 'Blue') Lewis in Croke Park in 1972 – two years after Arkle's death – he was asked to sign a portrait of the great horse. This picture was bought by the Irish supermarket mogul Pat Quinn in a charity auction, for the sum of £1,000.[114] The fond feeling that Arkle evoked in Ireland and beyond was a product of his exceptional talent, but it also resulted from the commercialization of sport, the development of sports broadcasting, the changing shape of celebrity and popular culture in the 1960s, and the evolution of Irish identity – particularly in relation to American and British cultures and identities. Television was 'the great agent of social change in the modern world' and was a driving force in a changing Ireland. In the decade after the Second World War, television ownership rose rapidly in the US and by 1961, sets could be found in eighty-five per cent of American homes. At the same time in Britain, some ten million homes owned a television. The new media grew in popularity in Northern Ireland in the 1950s, with BBC Northern Ireland making its first broadcast in 1953 and with Ulster Television launching six years later.[115] In the Republic, TVs first appeared in well-to-do homes in the 1950s. By the time Teilifís Éireann launched on New Year's Eve in 1961, Ireland was more prosperous than at any point in the previous decade. This was a result of a change in the country's political leadership and economic policy. After replacing Eamon de Valera as Taoiseach in 1959, Seán Lemass recognized that deflation and lower living standards would not remedy Ireland's ailing economic health, and instead increased expenditure and looked

Michael O'Hehir, the pioneering figure in sports broadcasting in twentieth-century Ireland. O'Hehir is pictured here at the Leopardstown Chase meeting in 1965.

outward for investment. The Lemass government was helped by trends in Britain and Europe, which proved favourable to Irish economic growth.[116] The launch of the new national broadcaster thus coincided with an increase in Irish families' incomes and led to a boom in television-ownership. In 1963, forty-four per cent of households owned a TV and this rose to seventy-six per cent by the end of the decade.[117]

Along with radio and film, television transformed Irish society and helped to shape youth culture, which from the late 1950s began to reflect American and British influences. This shift was evident in the rise of showbands, which were a 'specifically Irish musical response to American and British rock'n'roll and pop music'.[118] The Irish public wanted to be entertained and an increase in car-ownership in the 1960s facilitated travel to racecourses, stadia and other venues, but sport – with its immediacy, unpredictability and sense of spectacle – was also a good fit for television. In Ireland, the development of sports broadcasting can be largely attributed to one man: Michael O'Hehir. Two days after the patrol camera was first used at the Curragh in April 1958, O'Hehir was appointed Stewards' Secretary in control of cameras. By then, he was already a household name. In the 1940s, he was appointed the *Irish Independent*'s sports sub-editor and racing correspondent, and in the middle of that decade he began broadcasting the Irish Grand National for Radio Éireann. In 1946, the BBC

'Himself' and 'The Black Stuff'

As horse racing opened up to modern corporate sponsorship, Arkle became an early brand ambassador. Horses and jockeys had long featured in advertisements for commercial products and Guinness had previously featured the sport in its advertising, but the 'black stuff's' association with 'Himself' was different.[1] Following Arkle's victory in the Cheltenham Gold Cup in March 1966, Elisabeth Guinness, Lady Moyne, wondered whether the fact that the celebrated chaser enjoyed two pints of the famous stout in his oats every day had 'been sufficiently publicised.' Writing to a company employee, Bryan Guinness, Lord Moyne, noted that 'In the ordinary way one would not give more than a little publicity to a racehorse having some Guinness in his diet, but it seems

(above) Arkle drinking Guinness with the Managing Director of Kempton Park, Henry Hyde; (right) 'Himself', with Pat Taaffe up, parading in front of a large crowd at Tolka Park in 1966, ahead of a soccer match in aid of St Andrew's, an athletics club based in Ashbourne that was raising funds to build a pavilion on land donated to them by Tom Dreaper. Horse and rider are preceded by a man carrying a prop bottle of Guinness.

Arkle's performances are so amazing as to deserve some special publicity – perhaps.'[2] The brewer decided to provide Tom Dreaper with a free supply of the drink, to make the most of the 'pleasant publicity', with one executive remarking that 'it is fortunate that the horse they are now calling the greatest steeplechaser in the world is a loyal Guinness drinker.'[3] Arkle's association with Guinness was highlighted in the press and at public events, including at a charity soccer match at Tolka Park, the home of League of Ireland team, Shelbourne FC. The match was arranged to benefit St Andrew's Athletic Club, which was based in Arkle's hometown of Ashbourne, with members of that club togging out against a team of jockeys. After it was announced that the great horse would not run in the Whitbread Gold Cup at Sandown, it was arranged to have him parade in front of the crowd before kick-off. With jockey Pat Taaffe onboard, Arkle trotted around the pitch behind a man carrying a giant bottle of Guinness - much to the delight of his adoring fans.[4]

invited him to be part of their broadcast of the Grand National.[119] It was the forward-thinking O'Hehir who introduced racecourse commentary to Ireland in 1952. On 20 March that year, crowds assembled at Gowran Park heard the crackle and pitch of a tannoy system coming into life. For the first time, a single voice reigned over the usual hubbub of an Irish racecourse, carrying spectators along, mile after mile, fence by fence, into the final furlong and the thrilling race for the finishing post.

One of O'Hehir's greatest moments as a racing commentator came at Aintree in 1967, when long-odds outsider Foinavon won the Grand National after emerging from a pile-up at the fence after Becher's Brook. O'Hehir made a habit of entering the weigh-room before the famous race and it was there that he confirmed a colour change with Foinavon's jockey, John Buckingham. Recognizing Buckingham in his new black and red silks, O'Hehir carried on the commentary without pause, telling millions of BBC viewers that 'now, with all this mayhem, Foinavon has gone off on his own'.[120] O'Hehir was also responsible for the first televised broadcast of racing in Ireland, providing coverage of the Leopardstown Gold Flake Meeting in May 1961.[121] Three months after that pioneering broadcast, he was appointed head of sports programmes for radio and television at Radio Éireann.[122] The Leopardstown meeting demonstrated the growing presence of sponsorship at Irish race meetings. The sponsorship of races was not new – rail companies had provided stake money to a number of racecourses in the nineteenth century. By the 1960s, the success of Irish horses and the sport's popularity with the Irish public made both Flat and National Hunt racing attractive to companies like Guinness, Powers, and Player's Cigarettes, among others. The first instances of modern commercial sponsorship in Irish racing occurred in April 1960, with the running of the Player's Navy Cut Stakes at the Phoenix Park and the Powers Gold Cup at Fairyhouse.[123] One month later, the tobacco firm Messrs W.D. and H.O. Wills sponsored the entire Gold Flake Meeting, with a programme of races named for their products. The meeting drew an 'enormous' crowd and 'proved to be an outstanding success'.[124] The commercial suitability of racing was further underlined in 1962, by the success of the Irish Sweeps Derby at the Curragh, which received an endowment of £30,000 from the Hospitals' Trust. The Sweeps Derby was responsible for the reinvigoration of Ireland's premier Flat meeting and, to an extent, the boom in Irish breeding that occurred in the 1960s.[125]

Alongside the stimulating effects of commercial sponsorship and media coverage, a growth in motor vehicle-ownership in the 1960s helped to transform the public's relationship with racing. Motor cars first came to Ireland in the late nineteenth century and grew in popularity in the early 1900s, with ownership largely restricted to the landed and professional classes. Cars and motorbikes played an important role in the 1916 Rising, the War of Independence and Civil War, but the majority of the Irish population continued to travel over distance by train. The increased prosperity of the 1960s made car-ownership more achievable; this, along with the closure of many railway lines in the mid-twentieth century, made the Irish public almost entirely reliant on motor vehicles for transport to and from racecourses. Owners and trainers, meanwhile, depended increasingly on trucks and trailers to transport their animals to meetings across the island. This shift was felt at point-to-point meetings too. In 1965, a meeting jointly organized by the Ward Union Hunt and Fingal Harriers at Oldtown in Dublin was sponsored by the British oil company, Lobitos.

Like Burmah Castrol's annual sponsorship of a Phoenix Park (and later Leopardstown) meeting from 1972, Lobitos' sponsorship of the Oldtown Point-to-Point reflected and reinforced the changed nature of Ireland's transport infrastructure. In addition to providing each competing owner with fifteen gallons of petrol free of charge, the company raffled off a further 225 gallons of fuel at the meeting, while the organizers provided a free car park and a motor enclosure from which to view the races. Lobitos' sponsorship of the Oldtown meeting demonstrated the commercial potential of larger point-to-points in the 1960s. While the sport had traditionally benefitted (and would continue to benefit) from local sponsorship, its growing popularity with the Irish public made it a more attractive prospect for companies seeking to advertise goods and services. The public and commercial appeal of the 1965 Oldtown meeting was underlined by the presence of Michael O'Hehir, who provided the on-course commentary.[126]

'Arkle-itis'?

While racing was now a highly valuable and increasingly commercial concern, the early 1960s were not without difficulty. The Racing Board's ability to support the industry was threatened in 1963, when the government introduced a highly unpopular 2.5 per cent turnover tax (a forerunner of VAT). The Board initially chose to pay the turnover tax from its own resources, but this quickly depleted its funds. Eventually, the Board informed Minister for Finance James Ryan that they would have to pass the tax onto punters by increasing both the Tote levy and the on-course bookmakers' levy, which would negatively impact racecourse attendances. The government could not afford a decline in racecourse revenues and quickly changed tack. Speaking to the Dáil in 1964, Ryan stated that the turnover tax already collected from the Board would be returned to it, via a grant-in-aid. The measure did not meet with unqualified praise, however, as Fine Gael's Gerard Sweetman suggested that the Minister was 'posing as Santa Claus'.[127] Perhaps the only individual more famous than Santa Claus in 1960s Ireland was Arkle, whose celebrity was interwoven with the evolution of Irish identity in the 1960s. If the old Ireland was insular and isolated, the new Ireland was outward-looking and growing in confidence. As Declan Kiberd put it, there was an emerging belief that it was possible to be 'Irish and modern at the same time'.[128]

Of course, excellence in Irish breeding and racing was nothing new and National Hunt racing, in particular, had long been understood in relation to its English counterpart. The tradition of Irish horses being sold into England was evidence of an economic dependence that had its roots in political subjugation. This difficult reality was tempered by the predominantly Anglo-Irish character of the racing community and by the ability of sport to transcend political divisions. The performance of Irish horses at English racecourses had long been a source of pride in Ireland, of course. Irish excellence was characterized, in part, by an ability to compete with and beat the wealthier and more powerful neighbours. This dynamic was amplified by developments in broadcast media, a growth in prosperity and the remarkable achievements of Arkle in the 1960s. At the same time that Arkle was 'Ireland's hero on what might be called a personal national level', however, the unifying power of sport meant that he 'had long been taken to the hearts of British racegoers'. As in Ireland, Arkle's appeal in Britain transcended sport. In December 1965, the horse was included in the *Evening Standard*'s list of the '12 most glamorous people in the world', alongside Queen Elizabeth II, Jacqueline Kennedy, John Lennon, and others. Of Arkle's inclusion, the author of the list, Angus McGill, remarked that 'Anyone misguided enough to complain that horses aren't people is not a true born Englishman'.[129]

Arkle's success was something of a double-edged sword, however, as his dominance caused a reduction in entries to major races. Along with increasing television ownership, 'Arkle-itis' (as one *Irish Field* contributor termed it) may have contributed to a fall in public attendance at race meetings in the mid-1960s.[130] Working with the Turf Club and INHS Committee, the Racing Board made some significant interventions to bolster the popularity of the sport more generally. This included an increase in prize money; the provision of £200 in travel expenses to French horses competing in Ireland; the introduction of evening race meetings; the expansion of the winter fixture list and the inauguration, at Gowran Park in January 1966, of a new form of betting, known informally as the Tote Jackpot Pool.[131] The Board's report for 1966 underlined the health of Irish racing, with prize money reaching a record high, a rise in bookmakers' turnover and an increase of over half a million pounds in the Tote's takings, largely due to the success of the Tote Jackpot.[132] Racing's appetite for money was insatiable, however. Speaking to INHS Committee members in 1968, retiring Senior Steward R.W. McKeever remarked that National Hunt racing was 'in a healthy position' but

> The one thing that seems to be in short supply is money. Money to increase the prize money for owners, and money to enable executives to provide amenities for the racing public. The Racing Board does everything possible in this matter, but its resources are stretched to the limit … Many executives are finding it increasingly difficult to meet the ever rising cost of maintaining their racecourses and I appreciate the sacrifices that have been made by their shareholders … to keep racing going.[133]

The following year, as well as increasing its contribution to prize money, the Board published their Rationalisation of Racing plan, which threatened a number of unprofitable racecourses with extinction at the end of 1971. The Racecourse Executives' Association queried the lack of consultation prior to the announcement and there was a feeling that smaller courses were being unfairly targeted.[134] Rationalization would become a hotly debated topic in Irish racing in the next decades, as the industry sought to create the optimal supply to meet demand.

'a great blow to everybody concerned with the sport'

Racing's problems were compounded in 1967 by an outbreak of foot and mouth disease in England. Fears over its spread resulted in the complete abandonment of Irish racing in mid-November. Addressing INHS Committee members in January 1968, R.W. McKeever remarked that the shut-down was 'a great blow to everybody concerned with the sport' and expressed the 'greatest sympathy for all those who are suffering financially or otherwise'. The Committee was keen to provide support to jockeys, who were hit hard by the shutdown, and the Stewards made contact with the Jockeys' Association in late 1967, to discuss 'the possibility of giving some financial assistance to National Hunt jockeys suffering hardship under the ban'.[135] In the end, foot and mouth was not as damaging to racing as might have been expected. Ten meetings were lost at the start of 1968 but racing resumed on 14 February and seven extra days were added to the calendar to offset earlier losses. In total, 275 hurdle races and 186 steeplechases were run. The robustness of Irish racing was signalled by the fact that 1968 would almost certainly have been a record financial year if a labour dispute had not resulted in the suspension of Tote operations between late June and early September.[136]

In January 1969, it was announced that a new event would be added to the National Hunt calendar. Like the Sweeps Derby at the Curragh, the Sweeps Hurdle was backed by the Irish Hospitals' Trust, with thousands of tickets sold to the public and generous prize money attracting the best hurdlers in Ireland and from across the Irish Sea. The Hurdle had been allocated to Leopardstown but was held at Fairyhouse until 1971, while new stands were constructed at the south Dublin racecourse. Aside from the switch from a left-handed to a right-handed track, the move to Fairyhouse was not expected to have any real impact, as the County Meath course was used to welcoming huge crowds to its Easter festival.[137] With the eruption of violence between Northern Ireland's nationalist and unionist communities in the late 1960s, however, the visibility of major sporting events made them vulnerable to disruption. There were real concerns over the possibility of a paramilitary attack on the meeting, after a spate of small bombings by loyalists in 1969, including at RTÉ's Montrose studios, the O'Connell monument in Dublin, and the Garda Central Detective Bureau at Dublin Castle.[138] A 24-hour security watch was imposed on Fairyhouse, with course foreman, John McCarthy, closely supervising the construction of all hurdles, while course secretary Norman Colfer conducted a 'final pre-Christmas' check on arrangements, and staff slept on camp beds in the course bars, to protect the valuable stock from 'potential hi-jackers'.[139] In the end, the Fred Rimell-trained Normandy won the Hurdle, and the

Race card for the Irish Sweeps Hurdle, run at Leopardstown: 1983.

meeting was carried off without incident and the whole enterprise was 'an unqualified success'.[140]

The founder of the Irish Hospitals' Sweepstake did not live to see the inaugural running of the Sweeps Hurdle. Joe McGrath passed away in March 1966, four months after W.T. Cosgrave, and one year before Jack Duggan. These early architects of Irish racing departed from a golden age in their sport, with the horizon bright and full of possibilities. This success was a product of the financial support provided by the Racing Board since 1945, allied with a widespread passion for the sport and ambition in the Irish equine industries. Horse racing brought joy to an Ireland that struggled to find hope in the darkness of the 1950s and by the 1960s, developments in broadcast media and a growth in prosperity meant Irish people could watch race meetings on television at home. With car-ownership increasing and amenities improving, National Hunt and point-to-point meetings across the island drew large crowds. Many of the major figures in Irish jump racing in this period are still remembered and revered, not only in racing circles, but in the public consciousness. Foremost among them is Arkle, who served as an emblem of Irish excellence, enjoying a rare celebrity in his lifetime, and becoming a legend before his death. As is still the case, however, the success of Irish racing was not built on a handful of star attractions, but on the thousands of people working behind the scenes, in the governing bodies and the Racing Board, in racecourse executives, in stud farms and in racing yards across the island. This cohort's contribution is largely unheralded, but it was essential to the continued success of Irish racing in the challenging climate of the 1970s, its survival in the cataclysmic conditions of the 1980s and its reinvigoration in the 1990s.

CHAPTER FOUR: 1945–1969

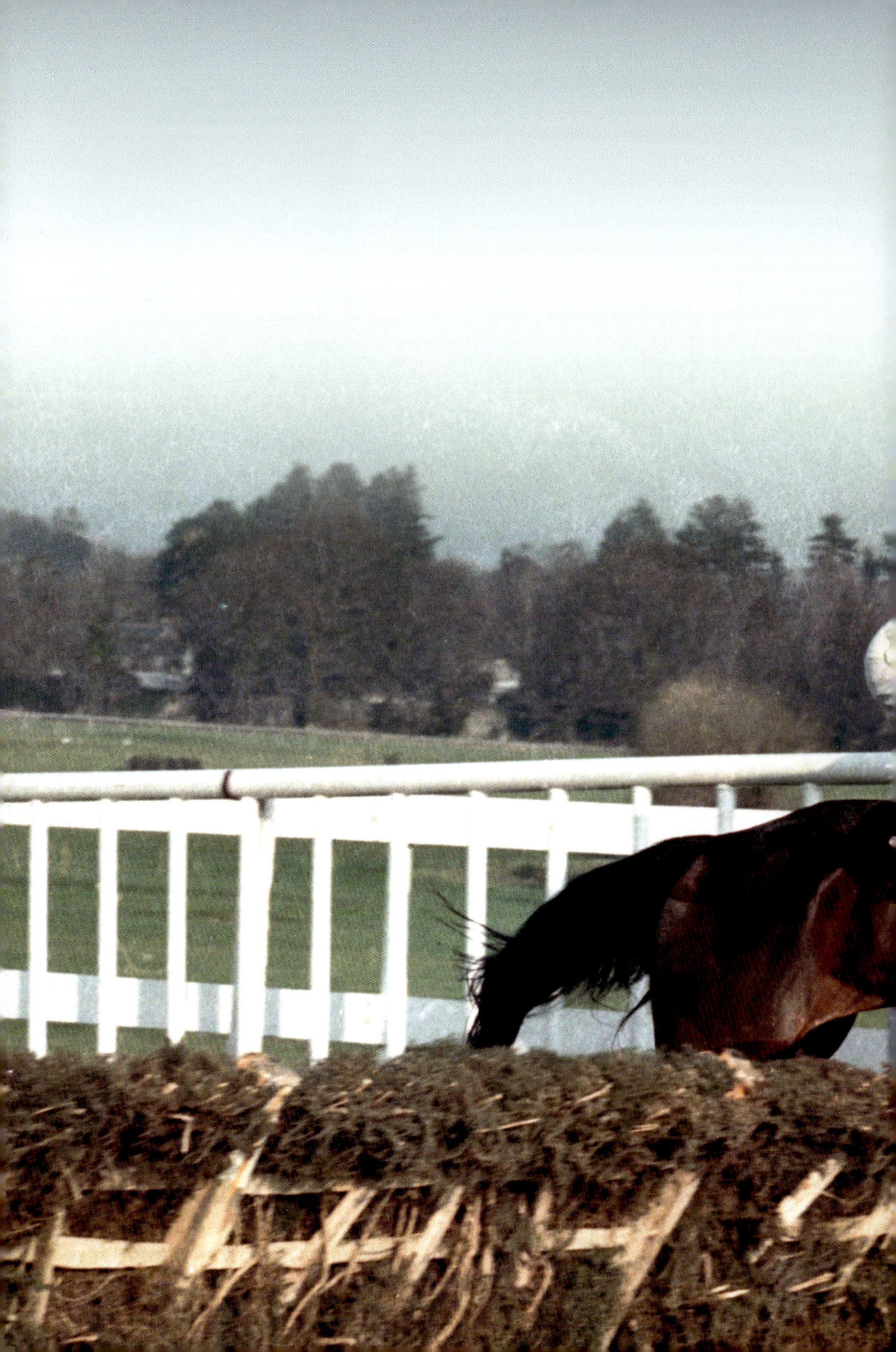

CHAPTER FIVE

1970-1993

'Where the "shoe pinches"'

As the INHS Committee prepared to celebrate its centenary year with a meeting at Punchestown in 1970, the body could reflect with satisfaction on the progress made in National Hunt and point-to-point racing in Ireland. Flat racing continued to be afforded greater prestige, but jump racing continued to captivate the Irish people. While the era of Arkle had come to an end, there was every reason to hope that the next decade would deliver more success. In the end, Irish horses, owners, trainers and riders delivered moments of sporting magic throughout the 1970s, while money continued to flow into the sport, attendances grew, and the number of race and point-to-point meetings increased. The continued success of Irish racing required the INHS Committee and the Turf Club to expand and to work more efficiently and effectively; their expansion and reform proved essential to its modernization. At the same time, the impact of wider social change could be felt in the growing presence of women in racing, not just as owners, but as trainers and riders, and in a greater emphasis on rider and animal welfare. These successes were achieved in increasingly adverse conditions, however. From the late 1970s, domestic and international economic trends worked against Irish racing. With inflation rising rapidly, the Racing Board struggled to provide prize money and to improve standards at Irish racecourses. By the early 1980s, the country had plunged into recession and the racing industry slid into a state of financial and existential crisis. Irish chasing talent left the country in great numbers and National Hunt racing entered a period of evident decline. In Northern Ireland, meanwhile, racing's problems were compounded by the enduring violence of the Troubles. Good news days were rare, but the brief and brilliant career of Dawn Run gave the Irish public something to be proud of. By the end of the 1980s, and on foot of the Killanin Report, the industry began to turn a corner, as the government, the governing bodies and the wider racing community endeavoured to reform and reinvigorate the sport in Ireland.

'such sport and such spectacle'

To mark one hundred years since its foundation, the INHS Committee commissioned Colonel S.J. Watson to write a commemorative history of jump racing in Ireland. Watson's book, *Between the flags*, was well received, with the INHS Stewards congratulating him on a 'masterpiece of information and entertainment', and thanking him for diverting profits from the sale of the book to the Drogheda Memorial Fund.[1] The Committee also organized a Centenary Meeting at Punchestown, which took place on Saturday, 24 October 1970. A period of hard ground in Britain meant that no horses travelled from there, but the meeting was nevertheless 'an unqualified success', with INHS Senior Steward John Brennan remarking that 'we were able from the strength of our own steeplechasing resources adequately to fill all the races and to provide such sport and such spectacle as I am sure will remain in the minds of those who were there for some time to come'. Prize money was provided by the Racing Board, while the Turf Club made a donation to the entertainment fund, the Punchestown Executive supplied a trophy and members of the British and French racing authorities travelled in numbers to attend.[2] All bar one of the races on the programme were named after nineteenth-century Irish winners of the Grand National. The only exception was the £5,000 added Irish National Hunt Centenary Handicap Steeplechase. This race was won by the Francis Flood-trained Glencaraig Lady, a chestnut mare who cost just 800 guineas and would become, in 1972, only the third mare to win the Cheltenham Gold Cup.[3] Other big name trainers registered winners on the day, including Paddy Sleator, Tom Dreaper, Dan Moore and Clem Magnier, another shrewd operator whose National Hunt successes in Ireland included four Galway Hurdles, an Irish Grand National and a Thyestes Chase.[4]

The third-placed horse in the Woodbrook Hurdle, the first race on the card, was a five-year-old bay gelding named Vulforo, owned by one Charles J. Haughey.⁵ A rising star in Jack Lynch's Fianna Fáil government, Haughey served as Minister for Finance until May 1970, when he was demoted to the backbenches for his suspected involvement in the Arms Crisis – a conspiracy to supply weapons to the IRA in Northern Ireland.⁶ Haughey's interest in equestrian pursuits was well known. Like W.T. Cosgrave before him, he enjoyed hunting, which provided him with 'a way into another part of Dublin society ... as a public representative'.⁷ He also dabbled

(top) Vulforo, owned by Charles J. Haughey, winning the Powers Gold Cup at Fairyhouse in 1973. (above) Charles Haughey (centre), with (from left to right), Richard Dunwoody, Barbara Finlay, Maureen Haughey and Jimmy Finlay, after Flashing Steel won the Bambury Bookmakers Novice Chase at Fairyhouse in 1992. Flashing Steel was trained by Haughey's son-in-law, John Mulhern, and would go on to win the Irish Grand National in 1995.

CHAPTER FIVE: 1970–1993

in breeding and had success as an owner of racehorses. The Jim Dreaper-trained Vulforo won thirteen races in all, including the Powers Gold Cup at Fairyhouse in 1973. Haughey also owned Flashing Steel, who was trained by his son-in-law John Mulhern and claimed the Irish Grand National in 1995.[8] He had less success on the flat, although his horse Aristocracy – trained by Vincent O'Brien – won the Group 3 Whitehall Stakes at the Phoenix Park in 1977. During his tenure as Minister for Finance, Haughey made a significant contribution to the Irish breeding and racing industries by securing cross-party support for the introduction of a tax exemption for stallion fees in the Finance Act in 1969. Over time, the exemption would transform Ireland's standing in the bloodstock and racing world, making it the 'destination of choice' for stallion owners and breeders, who established stud farms across the country. As a result, 'some of the best broodmares in the world were sent to Ireland to be covered, and many of the best racehorses in the world carry the IRE suffix in their name'.[9] Haughey also introduced legislation to increase the share capital of the Irish National Stud from £500,000 to £2 million in 1969, and he supported a further increase to £5 million in 1976.[10]

This financial injection enabled the visionary Michael Osborne to transform operations at Tully. A native of Naas in County Kildare, Osborne practiced as a veterinary surgeon for twelve years before being appointed Managing Director of the Irish National Stud in 1970. As well as putting the National Stud 'back in the forefront of Irish commercial farms', Osborne instituted what would become a world-renowned stud management course in 1970.[11] He also worked with Stan Cosgrove, Derek O'Sullivan and others to establish the Racing Academy and Centre of Education (RACE) in 1973, which provided apprentice jockeys with training and support. Osborne's impact on Irish racing was not confined to the National Stud; after a period in the US, he was employed by Sheikh Mohammed to purchase and develop Kildangan Stud in County Kildare. The success of this venture led to Osborne being installed as the Chief Executive of the Emirates Racing Association, and he was tasked with establishing international racing in Dubai.[12] Osborne enjoyed a stellar reputation internationally, but his commitment to racing and breeding in Ireland endured and he served as Senior Steward of the Turf Club, a director of the Irish Horseracing Authority and Horse Racing Ireland, and as chairperson of both Punchestown and the Curragh.[13]

'where the sandwiches often look part of the permanent fixtures'

Charles Haughey's controversial legacy has somewhat obscured his contribution to Ireland's equine industries, but as Brian Kavanagh (then CEO of Horse Racing Ireland) commented on the former Taoiseach's death in 2006, he was 'a true friend of Irish racing'.[14] Irish racing would need true friends in the difficult economic climate of the late 1970s and 1980s, but when the racing community came together at the INHS Committee's centenary meeting at Punchestown in October 1970, the future seemed bright. The 1960s had ended on a positive note for both codes of Irish racing. The Racing Board's 25th annual report evidenced a small but steady increase in attendances in 1969, as well as record growth in betting on the Tote and with bookmakers, who increased their take to almost £4.1 million and £9.83 million, respectively. The Board's net revenue from betting was £871,873, and its contribution toward prize money – which also set a new record – was £959,163.[15] From 1969, furthermore, the government provided the Racing Board with a £100,000 annual grant, which was used with their general surplus to pay capital grants or loans for buildings, equipment and other amenities at racecourses.[16] Racing continued to attract money and the relative prosperity experienced in Ireland in the 1960s was bolstered by Ireland's entry into the European Economic Community in 1973. EEC membership would transform Ireland's economic fortunes, providing capital funding to build necessary infrastructure and accelerating the inflow of Foreign Direct Investment. This positive trajectory in turn contributed to the transformation of Irish society, which began to push against the strictures of Catholic moral teaching and a pervading culture of intolerance and oppression. While membership of the Common Market would fundamentally alter the country's future, accession came just as Ireland's economic progress was threatened by international developments. In October 1973, the first oil crisis caused fuel prices to quadruple overnight and destabilized an already over-heated global economy. In reaction to world events, a newly elected Fine Gael–Labour coalition, under Taoiseach Liam Cosgrave (W.T.'s son and, like his father, a keen supporter of horse racing), would pursue a deeply unpopular programme of austerity and tax hikes, with the satirical television series *Hall's Pictorial Weekly* reflecting public displeasure by lampooning Finance Minister Richie Ryan as 'Richie Ruin', the 'Minister for Hardship'.[17]

The economy was not the only challenge for the horse racing industry. Television had become ubiquitous and from 1972 armchair punters could enjoy racing in full technicolour. By then, TVs popularity was a 'mounting concern' for racecourse executives, prompting the Irish Racecourse Executives' Association to take 'a hard look at the whole structure of Irish televised racing'. The principal issue at stake was whether the money paid by RTÉ to broadcast Irish racing was enough to offset the drop in on-course revenue.[18] This concern coincided with a period in which the number of horses registered to run increased, necessitating a rise in the number of meetings held. With a large number of chasers being sold into Britain, many of those competing were of a poor standard, while the declaration of a high-quality chaser frightened off most of the competition. And while it was assumed that 'crowds will come to see a class horse even if the race is only an exercise canter with their idol starting at unbackable odds', none of the leading jumpers of the 1970s achieved the same level of celebrity as Arkle.[19] An inflation in the number of horses was a focal point of retiring Senior Steward T.C. Vigors' speech to INHS Committee members in 1972. Vigors noted that the total number of runners in 1961 was 3,741, excluding bumpers, whereas the total ten years later was 6,767; this explained 'why some marathon programmes are inevitable, in spite of the extra meetings which have been provided'.[20] The issue endured throughout the decade and into the next. In 1977, retiring INHS Senior Steward John Brennan admitted that there were problems in National Hunt racing, and that 'Probably the greatest is that which has almost become endemic in recent years – too many moderate horses in hurdles and too few good ones in steeplechases'.[21] The high number of entries resulted in the division of races and this caused a dramatic increase in the number of National Hunt races, the vast majority of which were over hurdles. A much-detested system of balloting was also introduced to deal with large entries, whereby officials randomly selected the horses that would run, or determined the field based on ratings for handicaps.[22]

A predominance of ordinary horses and a slip in the standard of amenities impacted on attendances. In 1975, for example, attendances rose by 10 per cent and the number of meetings across both codes was 236 – 22 more than in 1974 – but this growth was uneven, with big meetings often drawing bumper crowds and posting record profits, but smaller ones struggling to maintain profitability.[23] Racing now had to compete with the 'increasing leisure time selectivity of the general public' and it wasn't just the action on the track that needed to be of a higher quality.[24] For one thing, Irish people now expected better racecourse amenities. One article in the *Irish*

Field compared the standard of catering at meetings to 'a wet Sunday in Belfast' and took particular issue with 'certain country meetings, where the sandwiches often look part of the permanent fixtures'.[25] Overall, however, racing remained popular with the Irish public, who still attended meetings across the country and still spent money. Tote takings rose and fell throughout the decade, but the Jackpot continued to stimulate public interest, as evidenced by a record attendance at the Mallow Easter meeting in April 1972, when the prize pot reached £3,000.[26] Ireland's 'colourless betting offices' and a high percentage levy on off-course betting (which was paid into the exchequer and did not benefit the Racing Board) also incentivized attendance at race meetings, which reached over 1 million annually.[27] The off-course levy – which was increased from 15 per cent to 20 per cent in 1975 – was a source of some debate, however. Those against the high percentage argued that it diverted punters to off-course bookmakers in Belfast or Britain, where the levy was 7.5 per cent.[28]

The money spent with on-course bookmakers continued to climb throughout the 1970s, even when adjusting for inflation, and dwarfed the takings from the Tote (although the percentage deduction from the Tote was far higher). Between 1970 and 1974, the sums staked with bookmakers at race meetings increased from £11.8 million to £18.4 million. This easily exceeded the Tote's increase from £4.4 million to £5.8 million in the same period.[29] The government sought to capitalize on bookmakers' popularity and to offset the impact of inflation by introducing the Racing Board and Racecourse (Amendment) Bill 1975; this increased the 'ceiling' for the on-course bookmakers' levy to 10 per cent, with an immediate rise to 6 per cent, in order to provide greater stakes. During a debate on the bill in the Dáil, Taoiseach Liam Cosgrave underlined the importance of 'bookies' to the culture, as well as to the financial health of the sport in Ireland, remarking that 'racing would be much poorer without these colourful characters who operate at race meetings'.[30] Racing would have been significantly poorer without sponsorship, too. Commercial support for the sport was typically the province of alcohol and tobacco companies, including Guinness, Irish Distillers, Player Wills and P.J. Carroll & Co. While sponsors often spread their patronage across Flat and National Hunt racing, Irish Distillers focused exclusively on the latter and did so 'in a lavish way', topping up the prize money for the Irish Grand National and the Powers Gold Cup at Fairyhouse, and the John Jameson Cup Chase at Punchestown, among others.[31] Sponsorship money came from other (above) Sean Graham at his pitch at Punchestown in 1983. A flamboyant and popular bookmaker from Belfast, Graham was known for his catchcry 'let them in and let them out'. His sponsorship of racing was hugely important to the sport in the 1970s and 80s. (left) Race card for the Sean Graham Meeting at Leopardstown, 1977.

sectors, too: Kerry Co-op sponsored 'holiday' meetings at Tralee, Listowel and Killarney; Waterford Crystal sponsored a number of races; and the popular Northern Irish bookmaker, Sean Graham, who was known to be fearless in taking big wagers, was a generous sponsor of the sport. He also funded the publication of the *Sean Graham Irish Racing Annual*, which was first published in 1976 and provided racing enthusiasts with a colourful and informative yearly review.[32] Graham's premature death at the age of 49 in April 1986 represented a major loss to Irish racing.[33]

'Sunday is the only day we have for the family'

Amid an uncertain economic climate, the INHS Committee and the Turf Club worked to regulate, advocate for and improve horse racing across the island. A significant concern for both bodies was the survival of Irish racecourses, particularly in light of the Racing Board's proposed rationalization scheme. Mullingar – the site of Arkle's racecourse debut – closed its gates in 1967. The course had opened in 1852, after the completion of the Dublin to Mullingar railway line, but had 'started to canter into decline' when the Racing Board reduced its annual programme to six meetings in the early 1960s. Efforts were made to revive the course after its closure: along with his bandmates in The Drifters, Joe Dolan proposed a plan to construct an entertainment centre alongside the racetrack. That plan did not come to fruition, however, after the Racing Board refused to increase Mullingar's programme to twelve meetings a year. The racecourse site was sold in 1972 and subsequently developed into an industrial estate.[34] The prospect of further closures caused members of the INHS Committee to fear that 'flapping might spread if orthodox racing ceased in any area'.[35] With particular concern for country meetings, it was decided 'that any Racecourse prepared to give the necessary financial guarantees to cover the stakes and other essential payments should be allowed to stage a meeting or meetings independently of the Racing Board'.[36] Owing to strong local opposition, the Board's rationalization scheme did not go ahead. Instead, a combination of the issues rationalization proposed to address – including rising costs, ageing infrastructure and dwindling crowds – resulted in the closure of Baldoyle on 26 August 1972. The loss of the historic metropolitan course was greatly regretted. In March 1972, the *Irish Field*'s 'Pandora' reported that 'a glorious sunny afternoon highlighted the bracing Edwardian allure of Baldoyle, where Dubliners thronged on St Patrick's Day, following the example of their grandfathers and great-grandfathers before them'. Now, with Baldoyle's fate sealed, 'everyone suddenly began to realize its attraction as *the* Metropolitan course', preferable even 'to swanky new Leopardstown and to the Phoenix Park'.[37] Baldoyle's dates were subsequently transferred to Leopardstown, which had been bought and revamped by the Racing Board in the late 1960s and needed to expand its programme to cover the cost of its refurbishment.[38] Mullingar and Baldoyle were not the only courses to disappear from the calendar in this period, as Tuam closed its gates in 1973 after failing to reverse a decline in attendances.[39]

Alongside the Racing Board and the Turf Club, the INHS Committee sought to stimulate attendances at race meetings and accommodate a growing number of entries by proposing a trial of Sunday racing in 1971. Senior Steward John Brennan informed members that the six Sunday meetings had been

> provisionally authorized ... in order to test reaction throughout the country. Interested parties such as the Trainers' Association, the Jockeys' Association, CIÉ and the Group of Unions for the Racing Industry had all been written to and when their answers had been received if it appeared that there was general demand for Sunday Racing the whole matter would be put before a Joint Meeting of the two bodies.[40]

The absence of Sunday meetings from horse racing was a legacy of sabbatarianism (the prohibition of sport on the Sabbath), which was a feature of Irish and British sport in the nineteenth and early twentieth centuries, with rugby, soccer and cricket barring Sunday play, though in general it was 'discouraged rather than prohibited'. The GAA was a notable exception, with Gaelic games fixtures on a Sunday proving instrumental in attracting large crowds, as people sought amusement in their free time.[41] Sunday

The new stand at Leopardstown under construction in 1970, three years after the racecourse was purchased by the Racing Board.

point-to-point meetings were introduced on a trial basis in 1970 and they quickly became a popular feature on the fixtures list, with the number of authorized meetings rising from 11 in 1971 to 24 in 1972.[42] The proposed introduction of Sunday meetings to National Hunt and Flat racing met with resistance, however. This was not on grounds of religion, but from a 'hard core of opposition' in the industry and particularly among unions, trainers and stable lads. One unnamed trainer complained to the *Irish Times* that 'Sunday is the only day we have for the family', while Tom Dreaper commented that he 'would have fallen in with Sunday racing with great reluctance. The labour troubles would have been immense as our staff would have been working on Sundays when all their friends would be free.'[43] In the end, it was not until 21 July 1985 that Sunday racing came to Ireland, with the first meeting – primarily sponsored by bookmaker Sean Graham – taking place at Leopardstown.[44] In Northern Ireland, where opposition endured on sabbatarian grounds, punters would have to wait until 2004. Even then, protests took place outside the first meeting at Downpatrick.[45]

'they bring to light areas where "the shoe pinches" and are often productive of fresh ideas'

From its establishment, the INHS Committee enjoyed a good working relationship with the Turf Club, which became even more important as racing expanded and faced new challenges. With greater workloads and more staff, the two bodies outgrew their offices on Merrion Square. At the end of 1976, the newly appointed Keeper of the Match Book, Cahir O'Sullivan, oversaw their move into a purpose-built office on the Curragh. The Registry Office opened for business there on 22 November and Taoiseach Charles Haughey presided over the official opening on 10 December.[46] In the 1970s, the two bodies worked together to remove any duplication in their rules, and avoided further confusion by making the majority of amendments at joint meetings. The Turf Club also agreed to place bumpers under the regulatory control of the INHS Committee. The bodies' mutual regard, and in some cases shared membership, was useful in liaising with the Racing Board and with British and international racing authorities. While the INHS Committee and the Turf Club enjoyed an amiable and productive relationship, the former was nonetheless wary of any possible threat to its autonomy. In 1976, retiring INHS Senior Steward Lord Hemphill told members that liaison with the Turf Club was essential, but the 'Committee must retain its complete independence as a body'.[47] This position was restated by John Brennan in 1977, when he stressed 'that we must above all preserve our own control of our own sport and see that our voice is heard in the general administration of racing'.[48]

Controlling National Hunt and point-to-point racing was no small task. The Committee's regulatory duties became more complex with every passing year, a circumstance that was exacerbated by the introduction of extra meetings, some of which carried marathon programmes to accommodate the large number of entries. While the Stewards' workload increased, they could look to a growing number of sub-committees for assistance, including the Point-to-Point Committee, the Programme Committee and the Special Committee on Betting. At race meetings, meanwhile, they were aided by local stewards and racing officials, a cohort that included clerks of the course, stewards secretaries, handicappers, starters, clerks of the scales, judges, veterinary and medical officers, and investigations officers. In his retirement address in 1972, Senior Steward T.C. Vigors acknowledged the fundamental contribution this group made to the sport, noting that 'Their work is essential to the smooth running of racing ... It is they who really have to bear the brunt of these extended meetings, but they carry on with their usual efficiency, which is sometimes taken too much for granted.'[49] The INHS Committee was also helped by ancillary associations, many of which were formed in the 1960s and 70s.

As INHS Senior Steward A.D. Wingfield observed, regular meetings between the Stewards and the racing associations 'are of the utmost value, as they bring to light areas where "the shoe pinches" and are often productive of fresh ideas'.[50] This was in evidence in the mid-1970s, when the Committee formed a Fences Commission comprising representatives from the jockeys, amateur riders, trainers and racing officials' associations, and the Racing Board. The purpose of the Commission was to get as much detailed information as possible on the standard of fences throughout the country, both through an official survey and by inviting feedback on individual courses from trainers, jockeys and amateur riders. It was hoped that the Commission would use the information gathered to improve fences where necessary and establish certain standards.[51] The Commission demonstrated the value of cooperation, as the INHS Committee sought to use the knowledge and experience of those 'on the ground' in Irish jump racing, to improve the sport. It was a marked success, with retiring INHS

Senior Steward John Brennan telling Committee members that it had 'done splendid work' and that 'Already it has led to the improvement of fences on the majority of courses and to a welcome degree of standardization.'[52]

Building on progress made in the 1960s, the governing bodies also gave considerable attention to the physical safety of jockeys and amateur riders in this period, with an increased emphasis on protective gear and safety protocols. This included a growing emphasis on the provision of medical care to injured jockeys, evidenced by the foundation of the Irish Racecourse Medical Officers' Association in 1979.[53] This was a welcome development, with retiring INHS Senior Steward A.D. Wingfield commenting that the new body wanted to work with racecourse executives 'to improve their general arrangements for collection of casualties off the course, rendering First Aid and evacuation to hospital if that is necessary'. Wingfield also reassured Committee members that the medical officers did not 'wish to restrict bruised riders from riding, even if sometimes they feel they must protect the foolish from their folly'.[54] There were other notable developments: the Jockeys' Association initiated the Jockeys' Benevolent Fund to help riders faced with financial hardship through injury, hosting an annual fundraising meeting at Navan in 1969, 1971 and 1972.[55] Professionals at the other end of their career were also given a boost in 1974, when the INHS Rules were changed to allow them to start training while still riding (in the past, some jockeys had circumvented this obstacle by taking out a licence under the name of their head lad).[56] The Stable Lads Pension Scheme also came into force in 1974 and was immediately beneficial to those who worked in the racing industry and found themselves facing hardship. In the scheme's first year, there were six beneficiaries from the fund, while the mother of one man who died while in employment received a lump sum payment.[57]

The majority of stable lads were riders who were not considered good enough to become jockeys. Often, they were caught in a 'vicious circle', as to become apprentices they had to leave school early, but if they did not succeed in the saddle their limited formal education meant they had few options for employment.[58] With little choice, stable lads had to endure squalid living conditions, working for low pay. As Stan Cosgrove later recalled, stable lads and apprentices often had 'to sleep three or four to a bed' and 'put the bed legs in their boots, or they would be stolen by morning'.[59] Along with Michael Osborne, Derek O'Sullivan and others, Cosgrove sought to

Apprentice jockeys muck out at the Racing Academy and Centre of Education (RACE) in Curragh House, just outside Kildare town, in 1980. RACE was established in 1973, as a social project to support apprentices with no background in racing.

address the problem by establishing RACE – a social project to provide support to apprentice jockeys – in 1973. Industry-led and initially funded on a charitable basis, RACE received government support from 1978 and this facilitated its development into a centre of excellence for Irish racing, equipped with stables, an indoor riding school, gymnasia, lecture theatres, classrooms and lodgings.[60] RACE was a timely intervention, as the circumstances of apprentices and stable lads needed to be improved if the racing industry was to withstand an overall decline in Ireland's agricultural workforce. This decline resulted from Ireland's growing industrialization, which introduced greater variety and higher wages to the jobs market. The 'rural industrialization' of horse racing's heartlands caused a marked decline in the number of people employed in agriculture between 1961 and 1971. In Kildare in that period, the agricultural workforce fell from 31.6 per cent to 21.5 per cent, while in Meath it declined from 49.4 per cent to 34.6 per cent. Tipperary also experienced a significant drop, from 49 per cent to 38.7 per cent. While figures for employment in the industry were not available, economist Michael MacCormac observed 'a general feeling … that it has become more difficult to attract people into the industry'. Poor working conditions and industrialization weren't the only factors contributing to a decline in numbers of stable staff. The raising of the school leaving age to 15 and the Youth Employment Act – which limited daily working hours for minors – also had a significant impact on an industry that had long relied on a young workforce.[61]

'I am only a ghost, unrecognized, without respectability, but the fact remains that I train the horses'

The introduction of a minimum school leaving age and youth labour protections indicated that Ireland was becoming an outward looking, modern society. The impact of modernization was apparent elsewhere in horse racing, including in the growing presence of women trainers and riders. Women had a long involvement with horse racing but their contributions were often overlooked or relegated to the footnotes of the sport's history. This was not surprising. In Ireland, women's sport developed in popularity in the late nineteenth and early twentieth century, with hockey, tennis, golf, swimming and cycling proving popular, and with the growth of camogie ensuring that 'more women were engaged in competitive sport … than was the case in most other countries'. At the same time, however, 'women's sport was a marginal presence in the Irish sporting world and its status reflected the status of women in many areas of Irish society'.[62] In some ways, equestrian sport was an outlier. Local hunts were open to both sexes and there was a tradition of women riding against men in point-to-points, stretching right back to the days of the pounding match. In September 1805, a Miss Ousley rode Deceiver to victory over Gyles Eyre, of Eyrescourt Castle, on a bay gelding named Lord Howe. One spectator commented that it was 'a most capital

While women were not allowed to ride in races under INHS Rules until the 1970s, they had long been a presence in point-to-point races. Tipperary-woman Sylvia Frances Masters was an exceptional rider, winning 104 races overall.

race, and won by the lady's extraordinary jockeyship'.[63] Women were successful in Irish point-to-points in the inter-war years, with women like Sylvia Frances Masters (née Perry) to the fore. From Fethard in County Tipperary, Masters was a rider of exceptional ability. She was prolific over a number of years, achieving a season's best seventeen wins and 104 wins overall. She also bred and trained horses and served as joint-Master of the Tipperary Foxhounds from 1935 to 1953.[64] Masters was the best but by no means the only woman in the field in the inter-war period; women's names appeared frequently on race cards and several, like Miss C. Murdock, had impressive records.[65] In later decades, sisters Ann Ferris and Rosemary Stewart (née Rooney) enjoyed stellar point-to-point careers, while Helen Bryce-Smith (McDonagh after marriage) became Ireland's most successful lady rider, partnering 109 winners between the flags – a record that was not broken until February 2022, when Tipperary-woman Liz Lalor reached 110.[66] In a long and decorated career, Bryce-Smith partnered the most successful point-to-point horse in history, Still William, to 33 wins.[67]

While women rode at point-to-points, they were not given official recognition. The attitude of the racing authorities was made clear in England in 1930, when Mrs Arthur Heald applied for and was refused a licence. Heald had based her application on her impressive track record, as she had only been unplaced in three out of sixteen races. Unmoved, the Jockey Club responded to her request by stating that 'the Stewards do not allow ladies to ride in races under their rules'.[68] By the 1960s, with the rise of second wave feminism, women fought to end discrimination on the grounds of sex and to achieve equality in a number of areas, including the workplace. The campaign for equality extended to horse racing. Women were already visible in the sport as owners and breeders, but they were also frequently working – unrecognized – as trainers. While women were granted licences to train in America, France and elsewhere, in Ireland and Britain they were only allowed to take out licences under their head lad's name. In 1948, for example, the INHS Committee stated that 'In the case of ladies wishing to train publicly a licence may be granted in exceptional circumstances only, and to her head lad'. Even then, the licence would only be forthcoming if the Stewards were 'satisfied that the lady has competent knowledge of racing and training'.[69] The effect was to render women trainers across Ireland and Britain invisible. This was evidenced in 1959, when the Irish Grand National was won by Zonda, a horse owned and trained by Peggy St John Nolan, but whose win was attributed to Matt Geraghty.[70] By the time Nolan saddled Drumroan to finish a close third behind Lucius and Sebastian V in the Grand National at Aintree in 1978, however, she did so under her own name.[71]

The tide turned in England in 1965, when Florence Nagle went to war with the Jockey Club for the right to train under her own name. She sought licences for herself and for 76-year-old Norah Wilmot, who had first applied after the death of her father in 1931, and who trained horses for the queen.[72] Nagle summed up her status as a woman trainer in the *Directory of the Turf* thus: 'I should not be in this book, as, like several other women, I am only a ghost, unrecognized, without respectability, but the fact remains that I train the horses, and the mistakes and failures are mine – ditto the rare triumphs'.[73] In 1966, after a twenty-year fight, Nagle became the first woman to be granted a licence by the Jockey Club. In August that year, wealthy American Anne Biddle (née Bullitt) became the first women to receive a licence in Ireland. A fixture of the Irish racing scene, Biddle owned Palmerstown Stud in County Kildare and had some notable successes as an owner, particularly on the flat but also over jumps. She worked as a trainer before being awarded a licence, with her horses instead running under licences granted to her head lads.

Biddle was not particularly impressed by her success in securing a licence, telling the *Irish Field*'s 'Pandora' that she didn't think it was a 'great achievement' or that it would 'make much difference', except to remove 'certain unnecessary complications'.[74] Biddle's unwillingness to be seen as a pioneer in the women's movement may have been a result of her personal experience; she had been estranged from her mother – the noted American suffragette and journalist, Louise Bryant – since childhood.[75] On 31 August 1966, three days after receiving her licence, she saddled a winner with her first runner, Flying Tiger, in a Flat race at Naas.[76] In December 1966, the INHS Committee altered the National Hunt Rules to allow women to train in their own name.[77] It would take some years to turn the tide of history, however, and it was not until the 1990s – with Jessica Harrington's arrival on the scene – that a woman would rank among Ireland's top National Hunt trainers. Harrington took out a training permit in 1989 and had her first winner at Leopardstown in 1991. Based at Commonstown Stud near Moone in Kildare, she has enjoyed enormous success over jumps. In 2017 she became the most successful woman trainer in Cheltenham history; among other notable victories, she claimed the Champion Chase with the great Moscow Flyer in 2003 and 2005, the Champion Hurdle with Jezki in 2014 and the Gold Cup with Sizing John in 2017.[78] Since then, Harrington has turned her attention more to Flat racing and has trained multiple Group 1 winners.

Irish women began to apply for licences to ride on the flat in the 1960s, but the Turf Club were not amenable. By the end of the decade, however, the matter of women being allowed to ride under rules had become a question of 'when', not 'if'. In December 1971, the Jockey Club approved a proposal allowing ladies' races and Meriel Tufnell won the first such race in England, at Kempton Park the following year; two years later Linda Goodwill became the first woman to win a mixed race.[79] The Turf Club followed the English example and the first ladies' race in Ireland was run at the Phoenix Park in October 1972. The Miss Harp Lager Stakes was won by Wacoso, with Belle Bradley on board.[80] Races for women riders were a welcome development, but they were also treated as something of a novelty and were explicitly linked to gender. Harp added the prefix 'Miss' to their sponsorship at the Phoenix Park, while at Navan in November 1972, the ladies' race was sponsored by Revlon. The Revlon Stakes marked the cosmetics firm's first foray into racing sponsorship in Ireland and they provided £400 of the £800 prize pot, as well as presenting each rider with a product from the Revlon range and the winner with a hamper full of cosmetics.[81] While these single-sex races proved to be a success, there was growing pressure to allow women to compete in mixed contests. In 1973, the Jockey Club invited the Stewards of the Turf Club, along with their French and American counterparts, to

Ann Ferris riding Bentom Boy to victory in the Irish Grand National in 1984. © *Healy Racing*

discuss the question of women riding under both rules. On the invitation of the Turf Club, INHS Senior Steward A.D. Wingfield also attended the historic meeting.[82] Following that meeting, the INHS Committee passed a resolution

> That ladies who can satisfy the Stewards as to their experience and competence may be granted permission to ride as Qualified Riders in races in Category A (I.N.H. Flat Races) and in cases of considerable proven ability, in races in Category B (Hunter Chases only), on equal terms with male Qualified Riders.[83]

By opening up hunter chases to women, the Irish turf authorities thus went a step further than their English counterparts, who initially only allowed licenced women jockeys and apprentices to ride against male amateurs on the flat.[84]

Welsh woman Joanna Morgan became the first professional woman jockey in Ireland in 1975, when she signed apprentice papers to Seamus McGrath. Morgan would enjoy a stellar career in Flat racing, becoming the first woman to ride at Royal Ascot and in an Irish Classic, and winning the Irish Cambridgeshire and Irish Lincoln. She also, memorably, bested the great Lester Piggott in a photo finish at the Phoenix Park in 1976.[85] The small number of women riding professionally in the 1970s and 1980s were – like Morgan – focused on the flat, but there was no shortage of talented women riding as amateurs, some of whom scored notable successes, in National Hunt races. Glengormley woman Ann Ferris made history by winning the 1979 Irish Sweeps Hurdle on Irian and the 1984 Irish Grand National on Bentom Boy – a horse trained by her father, legendary point-to-point rider, Willie Rooney. It was an outstanding Irish National for the Rooney family, with Ann's sister Rosemary Stewart finishing third on Dawson Prince.[86] While women amateurs enjoyed some success over fences, it was not until 1983 that Maria Cullen became the first professional woman jockey in Irish National Hunt racing. She rode winners over both hurdles and fences, finishing first on Gerseach in the EBF Mare's Maiden Hurdle at Downpatrick in 1984 and riding Panjanjo to victory in the Old Distillery Novice Chase at Kilbeggan in 1987.[87] In England, after hunter chases were opened to women, the Irish amateur Caroline Beasley (now Robinson) made history by becoming the first woman to win a race at Cheltenham, when she won the 1983 Foxhunter Chase on Eliogarty; three years later, the same pair won the Fox Hunters' Chase at Aintree.[88]

The Blackmore Effect

In April 2021, Rachael Blackmore became the first woman in history to win the Grand National, steering the Henry de Bromhead-trained Minella Times to a famous victory. Seconds after pulling up, Blackmore was asked to comment on her pioneering achievement and responded 'I don't feel male or female right now – I don't even feel human. This is just unbelievable.'[1] Blackmore's Aintree success followed a remarkable performance at Cheltenham, where she became the first woman to claim the Festival's Leading Jockey award after riding six winners. This included the mare Honeysuckle, another of de Bromhead's charges, who partnered with Blackmore to win the Champion Hurdle at Cheltenham in 2021 and 2022 and three Irish Champion Hurdles between 2020 and 2022. Blackmore made more history in 2022, becoming the first woman to win the Cheltenham Gold Cup when riding A Plus Tard to a fifteen-length victory. Her success on the track brought accolades off it; she was crowned RTÉ Sportsperson of the Year in December 2021, before becoming the first Irish person to be named BBC World Sport Star of the Year.[2] To anyone paying attention, Blackmore was no overnight success story. She rode her first winner as an

Rachael Blackmore riding the Henry de Bromhead-trained Minella Times to victory in the Grand National in 2021.
© Healy Racing

Rachael Blackmore signing autographs for young fans at Thurles Racecourse in 2021, shortly after she was crowned RTÉ Sportsperson of the Year. © *Healy Racing*

amateur for John 'Shark' Hanlon at Thurles in 2011. With Hanlon's encouragement, she turned professional in 2015. That year, Nina Carberry piloted On the Fringe to the Foxhunter Chase at Cheltenham and the Fox Hunters' at Aintree, while Katie Walsh followed in the footsteps of Ann Ferris (1984) and Carberry (2011) to become only the third woman to win the Irish Grand National. While Carberry and Walsh made National Hunt history as amateurs, Blackmore became only the second Irish woman (after Maria Cullen in the 1980s) to turn professional. She quickly delivered on her potential, becoming the first woman to win the Conditional Riders' Championship in 2017. Since then, talent and tenacity have propelled her to the first rank of jump jockeys, where her success has been matched or exceeded by very few. As a woman winning regularly in a sport dominated by men, Blackmore – who announced her retirement in May 2025 – became a serial history-maker and an inspiration to a new generation of women riders. She has been reticent to speak about her achievements in terms of her gender,[3] but has helped promote participation in, attendance at and media coverage of women's sport in Ireland through the 20x20 campaign. Speaking at a 20x20 event, Blackmore suggested that other sports can learn a lot 'from the racing industry, in that if I ride a big winner the headline in the paper isn't "lady jockey rides a big winner", it's just "Rachael Blackmore rides a big winner." The achievement isn't the female side of it, it's just an achievement.'[4] She has also highlighted the fact that there is 'equal pay for equal opportunity', with female jockeys being paid the same rates for the same rides as their male counterparts.[5] Racing sets a positive example in many respects, but there are issues that need to be overcome to ensure continued growth in the number of women involved. Research in Britain has found that structural barriers and implicit biases impede women's progress and that it will take almost a century to achieve parity of rides for men and women in National Hunt racing there. It further indicated that the use of female riders varies widely among trainers, that rides for women tend to skew towards older horses and that the betting public underestimates women's ability to win races.[6] No comparable research exists for Ireland, but the picture appears to be more positive there, with a surge in the number of licenced women jockeys in recent years – a development largely attributable to Blackmore's incredible success.

CHAPTER FIVE: 1970–1993

(left) Ann Ferris with her family after winning the Irish Grand National on Bentom Boy, a horse trained by her father, Willie Rooney. He also saddled Dawson's Prince, a horse ridden into third place by Ann's sister, Rosemary. *Left–Right*: Rosemary Stewart, Ann Ferris, Willie Rooney, Caroline Rooney. © *Healy Racing*. (right) Joan Moore celebrating with her granddaughter, Nina Carberry, after Carberry's Irish Grand National win on Organisedconfusion in 2011. © *Healy Racing*

A pioneer of the sport: Joan Moore took over operations at Old Fairyhouse Stud during her husband Dan's illness in the late 1970s, and later became the first woman INHS Steward and the first woman to be appointed as manager of Punchestown. She is pictured at the Turf Club offices on the Curragh with (*left–right*) J.M. Rogers, Lord Hemphill, Denis McCarthy, Captain Simon Walford, Eamon Moloney and Major J.H. Tyrrell – all served as Stewards or Senior Stewards of the INHS Committee.

These pioneering achievements demonstrated that women could ride at the 'sharp end' of the sport, while off the track Joan Moore broke new ground by becoming the first woman member of the INHS Committee in 1985. Retiring Senior Steward Captain Simon Walford viewed Moore's election to the INHS Committee as 'an answer to those outside bodies who think the Committee is not moving with foresight into the 21st century'.[89] Moore's appointment was not an exercise in optics, however, but a recognition of her experience in the industry, her administrative nous and her tremendous energy. These qualities led to her appointment as the first woman Chair of the Point-to-Point Committee in 1988 and the first woman Steward of the INHS Committee in 1992. They were also fundamental to her success as Manager of Punchestown.[90] Moore's career demonstrated that women could have a seat at the top table, but it did not signal a trend toward gender balance in the regulation and administration of Irish racing. Instead, progress in those areas has been uneven. Women have been elected members and Stewards of the Turf Club and INHS Committee, with Meta Osborne becoming the first woman Senior Steward of the Turf Club in 2016. Suzanne Eade was appointed CEO of Horse Racing Ireland (HRI) in 2021, while three women sat on the Irish Horseracing Regulatory Board (IHRB), alongside five men, in 2023.[91] At the same time, however, the number of women working as racing officials remains low, a fact evidenced by the appointment of Tracey O'Meara as Ireland's first female clerk of the course – with responsibility for Down Royal, Downpatrick, and Sligo – in late 2018.[92]

'make sure she's facing the right way when the tape goes up'

As the Irish racing authorities adapted to the realities of a modernizing world, Ireland's tradition of success on the track continued in the 1970s. Between 1970 and 1977, Irish-trained horses won the Cheltenham Gold Cup six times: L'Escargot (1970 and 1971), Glencaraig Lady (1972), Captain Christy (1974), Ten Up (1975) and Davy Lad (1977). First among this winning cohort was L'Escargot, a large and 'quirky' chestnut gelding who was trained by Joan Moore's husband, Dan, and ridden by their son-in-law Tommy Carberry. Owned by the polo-playing American ambassador to Ireland, Raymond R. Guest, L'Escargot claimed the Gold Cup as a 33/1 outsider in 1970 and repeated the feat in waterlogged conditions in 1971. In doing so, he became only the fifth horse in history to win the race consecutively – a feat that would not be repeated until Best Mate's remarkable hat-trick between 2002 and 2004.[93] L'Escargot fell at the third fence in his first Grand National in 1972, before placing third in the storied steeplechase in 1973 and second in 1974. Both editions were won by the greatest horse in Aintree history, the Irish-bred Red Rum, who also finished second in the race in 1975 and 1976, before completing a remarkable hat-trick in 1977. It was the twelve-year-old L'Escargot who interrupted Red Rum's streak in 1975, benefitting from an 11lb advantage and soft ground to storm home fifteen lengths ahead of the Grand National legend. L'Escargot lit up the Liverpool course at a difficult moment in its history. Aintree was run by the Topham family from the 1840s and was managed by the irrepressible Mirabel Topham from the 1930s, but a fall in the number of races at the course in the 1950s impacted on its financial stability. By the mid-1960s, there were legitimate fears that Aintree and the Grand National would disappear forever. After many difficult years, Mirabel Topham sold the course to the Liverpudlian property developer Bill Davies for £3 million in 1973. Davies sought to recoup some of his investment by trebling entry fees but this caused a drop in attendances and L'Escargot's victory in 1975 was witnessed by a record low crowd. By then, however,

Glencaraig Lady remains only one of four mares to have won the Gold Cup. Her performance under a young Frank Berry, who was making his debut at Cheltenham in 1972, was remarkable because it came before the introduction of the mares allowance, meaning that she won at level weights. Serially unsound, the Gold Cup proved to be her last race.

(Clockwise from top left) L'Escargot was a 'quirky' chestnut who delivered some of the greatest moments in Irish racing in the 1970s, winning the Gold Cup in 1970 and 1971 and the Grand National in 1975; L'Escargot and Tommy Carberry jumping neck-and-neck with French Tan and Pat Taaffe in the 1970 Gold Cup. L'Escargot won the race at odds of 33/1; Glencaraig Lady at exercise, ridden by Larry Dunne at Francis Flood's stables. Flood is in the centre of the picture, while his young son Tom is on the right.

bookmakers Ladbrokes had intervened to preserve the National, leasing the course from Davies for seven years. Aintree's future was finally secured in December 1983, after the Jockey Club raised £4 million through a public appeal and purchased the course from Davies.[94]

Under Tommy Carberry, L'Escargot became only the second horse in history – after Golden Miller – to win both the Gold Cup and the Grand National. It was a remarkable achievement for Guest and for the Moore family. By then, Dan was ill and Joan 'had practically taken over training' at their stables in County Meath.[95] Tied

CHAPTER FIVE: 1970–1993

Tied Cottage and owner/rider Tony Robinson on their way to victory in the 1979 Irish Grand National. It was a poignant win, as Robinson was terminally ill with cancer at the time. He passed away the following year.

Cottage would prove to be another star of the Moore stable in the second half of the 1970s. A front-runner of considerable ability, he won the Sun Alliance Novices' Chase at Cheltenham in 1976, finished second in the 1977 Gold Cup, behind the Mick O'Toole-trained Davy Lad, and fell at the last while leading the same race in 1979. Shortly after that, Tied Cottage won the Irish Grand National, being ridden to a poignant victory by his terminally ill owner, Tony Robinson. Tied Cottage would win the Gold Cup on merit in 1980, but was disqualified after trace amounts of theobromine was found in his post-race sample. The drug was believed to have come from contaminated feed and no action was taken against Moore, or against the equally unlucky Mick O'Toole, whose Champion Chase-winning Chinrullah was also disqualified after a positive test resulting from contaminated feed.[96]

One good news story from the 1980 Festival concerned the irrepressible mare, Anaglogs Daughter. Bred to be a Flat horse, her trainer Bill Durkan (working with Ferdy Murphy) switched her first to hurdles and then to steeplechasing, and she finished third in her debut over birch fences at Leopardstown in 1979. A bold front-runner, she followed this up with a twelve-length victory in the PZ Mower Chase at Thurles and a ten-length win in the Arkle Novice Chase at Leopardstown. The mare's ability was not in question and she arrived at the 1980 Cheltenham Festival on short odds to take the Arkle Challenge Trophy. She was not the race favourite, however – that was the English gelding, Beacon Light, a highly talented hurdler who had immediately taken to chasing and won all of his seven starts. Tommy Carberry

A relentless, front-running mare, Anaglogs Daughter won the Arkle Challenge Trophy at Cheltenham by twenty lengths in 1980, but broke down one year later and never fulfilled her potential.

was drafted in to ride Anaglogs Daughter, having never sat on the horse before. On asking whether he should make the running, Carberry was told: 'You won't have any choice Tommy. Just take her down steady and make sure she's facing the right way when the tape goes up.'[97] Carberry followed orders and Anaglogs Daughter sprinted into a lead that she never relinquished. The pace the mare set was phenomenal and in the end she finished twenty lengths clear of the second horse, Corrib Chieftain, who finished another twenty-five lengths ahead of Netherton in third; Beacon Light fell at the third last, when well out of contention. The following season, Anaglogs Daughter – a two-mile specialist – ran her only race over three miles. She took on the first rank in stayers in the King George VI at Kempton and, such was her talent and relentlessness, that she finished second to returning champion, Silver Buck. The mare returned to Cheltenham to contest the Champion Chase in 1981, but was discovered to be lame one day before the race. She recovered in time and raced gamely to finish second, but this marked the beginning of her decline. A number of sub-par performances followed and she eventually broke down when finishing second in the PZ Mower Chase at Thurles in February 1982.[98]

(left) The 1970s brought a changing of the guard, as many of the leading trainers of the mid-twentieth century were succeeded by a new generation. Willie O'Grady, who died suddenly in 1972, aged 58, was succeeded by his son Edward. Pictured (*left–right*) after Great Lark's win in the 1968 Thyestes Chase at Gowran Park are Mrs T.A. Connolly, O'Grady, rider Stan Murphy and owner Mrs A.H. 'Peg' Watt. (right) Tommy Carberry and Jim Dreaper with the three-time Irish Grand National winner, Brown Lad. Dreaper took over the running of Greenogue from his father, Tom, in 1972. © *Sportsfile*.

Anaglogs Daughter burned brightly but briefly a few short years before another mare, Dawn Run, would set National Hunt racing on fire. By then, a number of racing's old guard had stood down, and a new generation stepped forward. Dan Moore died in June 1980, only a couple of months after Tied Cottage's Gold Cup misfortune.[99] Moore's death came five years after that of another great figure of Irish National Hunt racing – Tom Dreaper. Dreaper had retired at the end of 1971, after registering

Gay Trip and Pat Taaffe (centre) jumping the formidable Becher's Brook on the way to winning the 1970 Grand National; this was Taaffe's last big win before he retired and embarked on a successful training career. On the left is Villay, who unseated his owner/rider at the 28th fence, and on the right is Miss Hunter, ridden by Francis Shortt, who finished third. All three horses were Irish-bred.

five winners at the first Sweeps Hurdle meeting held at Leopardstown. He was succeeded at Greenogue by his son Jim, who was champion jumps trainer for each of his first five seasons. Dreaper shared his father's knack for winning at Fairyhouse: he claimed the first of four Irish Grand National titles in five years in 1974, when Arkle's close relation, Colebridge, raced to victory under Eddie Wright. The following year, Tommy Carberry won on the Dreaper-trained Brown Lad, and repeated the feat in 1976. Brown Lad would claim another Irish National in 1978, this time with Gerry Dowd in the saddle. Dreaper also proved successful at Cheltenham, with Ten Up and Carberry delivering another Gold Cup for the Duchess of Westminster in 1975. Around the same time that Jim Dreaper assumed control at Greenogue, Dermot Weld succeeded his father, Charlie, at Rosewell House on the Curragh.[100] Edward O'Grady meanwhile took charge at Killeens Stables in County Tipperary, following the sudden death of his father, W.T. O'Grady.[101]

Having retired from riding after winning the 1970 Grand National on Gay Trip, Pat Taaffe embarked on a successful training career, with Captain Christy delivering a notable success under Bobby Beasley in the 1974 Cheltenham Gold Cup.[102] By the time Taaffe retired, there were other heroes in the saddle. Having shared the champion jockey title with Taaffe, Tony Redmond and Francis Shortt in 1963, Bobby Coonan went on to win six National Hunt jockeys' championships in a row between 1967 and 1972. Coonan had some notable successes in England, too, most notably winning the King George VI Chase at Kempton on board Captain Christy in 1975.[103] Tommy Carberry's exploits in the first half of the 1970s marked him as one of the greatest of his generation and he was crowned Irish champion jockey four times between 1973 and 1976. Carberry had followed Coonan and he, in turn, was succeeded by Frank Berry. Both Carberry and Berry were leading apprentices on the flat, which made them notably stylish riders over fences. They shared the title in 1975, after riding a winner each at the last meeting of the year at Punchestown.[104] Berry's outright dominance began in 1977 and stretched into the late 1980s, as he claimed nine titles in eleven years. Irish professionals also reigned in British National Hunt racing, with Ron Barry (1972–3, 1973–4), Tommy Stack (1974–5, 1976–7) and Jonjo O'Neill (1977–8, 1979–80) following in the footsteps of Bryan Marshall and Tim Molony, by being crowned British National Hunt champion jockey.[105] O'Neill also broke the record for the fastest ever century recorded by a jockey, at Haydock in February 1978.[106]

'For a lot of people, particularly families, the local point-to-point is a real day out'

There were several talented amateur riders in this period, too, including Niall Madden, Michael 'Mouse' Morris, Willie Mullins, Ann Ferris and John Fowler, but it was Ted Walsh who dominated, winning the amateur riders title eleven times between 1972 and 1984.[107] His record of 545 race wins was not overtaken (by Patrick Mullins) until July 2018.[108] Walsh enjoyed notable success on the track, including four wins at the Cheltenham Festival – on Castleruddery and Prolan in the Kim Muir Handicap Chase in 1974 and 1976, respectively, on Hilly Way in the Champion Chase in 1979 and on the Irish hunter chaser and point-to-point star, Attitude Adjuster, in the Foxhunter in 1986. Walsh's success demonstrated the changing nature of the sport and the changing status of qualified riders. Both codes of racing had a long and proud tradition of amateurism, but by the middle of the twentieth century there was a shrinking difference in the abilities of the top professionals and the top amateurs. The improving standard of qualified riders reflected improving standards overall. Perhaps the most dramatic transformation occurred in the traditional home of amateurism, point-to-point racing. The health of point-to-pointing in the Republic

Some leading riders of their day, jumping the last in the Forenaughts Hurdle at Punchestown in February 1975. Left–right: Michael 'Mouse' Morris on Caramore, Frank Berry on Henry-Hall, Tommy Carberry on Troubled Times and Michael Furlong on the very talented winner, Bannow Rambler.

Ted Walsh and Under Way jumping to victory in the Sweet Afton Cup at Dundalk in May 1984. A top-class rider, Walsh won eleven amateur titles between 1972 and 1984. © *Healy Racing*

was a consequence of the financial assistance provided by the Racing Board and a gradual shift in the INHS Committee's attitude to the sport. One of the most significant developments came in 1970, when the INHS Committee sanctioned Sunday meetings for the first time.[109] The number of Sunday point-to-points was increased the following year, with the *Irish Field* reporting that 'The huge crowds that attended ... helped in no small way to give this aspect of the game one of its most successful seasons ever.'[110]

By 1976, almost all of the meetings sanctioned by the INHS Committee were held on a Sunday. Betting was an important feature of point-to-point racing, with the money wagered at some of the larger meetings (especially in County Cork) often reaching between £25,000 and £30,000. In 1977, betting turnover nationally reached £1 million.[111] As the *Irish Field* observed, 'For a lot of people, particularly families, the local point-to-point is a real day out, one to look forward to eagerly and talk about for a week afterwards'. The growing use of motor cars was beneficial to the organizing hunts, as they profited from parking charges. Sponsorship continued to be a feature of meetings, with local companies 'proving all too willing to sponsor individual races'.[112] By 1980, larger sponsors were attracted to point-to-point racing, including Ulster Bank and the prominent bookmaker Sean Graham.[113] Recognizing its 'growing importance' and 'the necessity for greater discipline in its general conduct', the INHS Committee appointed John Harvey as Stewards' Secretary for point-to-point racing in 1977. Harvey was assisted in his role by the Investigation Officer, Joe Walsh.[114] Despite the adverse economic climate in the 1980s, point-to-point meetings remained popular, with betting turnover at meetings in the twenty-six counties rising to a figure well in excess of £2 million.[115]

'borders are but lines on a map and not a division of people'

A strong tradition of point-to-point racing existed in Ulster from the late nineteenth century, when a large number of harrier and foxhound clubs were established across the province. Point-to-points remained popular in Northern Ireland after the partition of the island in 1921, with a columnist in the *Irish Times* noting in 1929 that it was 'famous for its hunters' and that 'many thousands of people travel to the various [point-to-point] venues' there.[116] Point-to-point and National Hunt race meetings in Northern Ireland remained within the INHS Committee's regulatory purview after partition, but

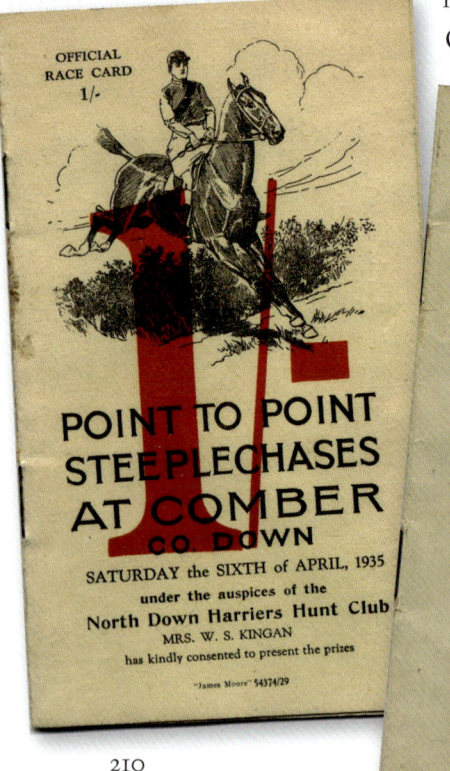

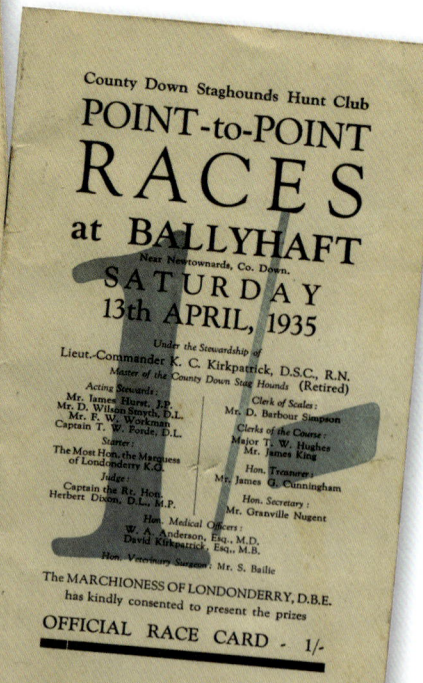

Point-to-point race cards from the Comber and Ballyhaft meetings in County Down, 1935.

A crowd welcomes the Queen Mother to Down Royal Racecourse in 1958.

the establishment of the Racing Board in 1945 placed racing in Northern Ireland between two stools, as the six counties lay outside its jurisdiction. This meant that race and point-to-point meetings were not in receipt of financial support from the Racing Board, but the Turf Club and INHS Committee maintained administrative and regulatory control over them. Instead, horse racing and point-to-pointing were reliant on the Northern Irish administration for financial support. The vulnerable state of racing in Northern Ireland was underlined in the 1970s, when the Jockey Club made a study of the Down Royal and Downpatrick Racecourses and recommended that money should be spent solely on Down Royal. The Northern Irish administration made the decision to stop funding Downpatrick in 1978, but this resulted in a huge outpouring of support for the course, which was used exclusively for National Hunt racing. A supporters club was formed from fourteen breeders and trainers, raising £4,500 by November 1977. Local draper and horse owner Joseph Rea worked to secure sponsorship and local organizations contributed by holding events there.[117]

A sign listing the Stewards of Downpatrick Racecourse, 1980s. Major W.H. Brownlow was chairman of the course for almost thirty years and was instrumental in preventing its closure in the mid-1980s. He was also a long-serving member of the INHS Committee.

With INHS Committee members like Major W.S. Brownlow representing Northern Ireland, that body remained committed to supporting point-to-point and National Hunt racing there throughout the difficult 1980s. When the Racing Board substantially increased its grant to point-to-points in the south in 1983, for example, the INHS Committee provided a grant of £300 to each meeting in the six counties. This was increased by a further £100 in 1984.[118] The same year, the economic downturn threatened the existence of Down Royal and the governing bodies met with Lord Mansfield, Minister of State for Northern Ireland, to gain assurances over the future of the course.[119] The impulse to preserve racing in Northern Ireland was pragmatic, as it had a wider benefit to Irish racing and breeding. It was also rooted in the bonds of association that had resulted in the INHS Committee and the Turf Club retaining all-island authority after partition – bonds that were rooted in history. In 1985, the INHS Committee and the Turf Club marked the tercentenary of Downpatrick and Down Royal by making presentations to the two executives. In early 1986, retiring INHS Senior Steward Eamon Moloney complimented the Northern executives' 'industry and diligence in difficult circumstances'.[120] It was fair praise, as in Northern Ireland the harsh realities of inflation and recession were compounded by ongoing conflict.

In the 1970s, with tensions high, the Troubles had a negative impact on National Hunt racing. In March 1972, less than two months after Bloody Sunday – when the

British army shot twenty-six unarmed civilians during a protest march in Derry – the season-opening meeting at Downpatrick drew a large attendance. It was, however, notable that 'the number of paying customers from across the border could be counted on the fingers of a boxing glove'. The healthy presence of southern-based jockeys and incident-free border checks somewhat undermined the idea that travelling north was now 'a dangerous mission', but it was telling that only two of ten entrants to the £1,000 Ulster National were from the south.[121] Five months later, a meeting at Downpatrick was disrupted by threats made by the Provisional IRA. Two local Provisionals were killed ahead of the meeting, when the bomb they were planting under the grandstand exploded. Racing went ahead but 'Three-quarters of the horses failed to arrive; one race was cancelled; attendance was down by more than half; fully armed British soldiers patrolled the course; and there was a bomb scare in the middle of the afternoon.' Despite an offer of military protection, over thirty horses from the Republic did not travel, with a number of horseboxes turning back from the border because they feared an attack.[122] In March the following year, the Downpatrick executive were forced to abandon the Ulster National meeting when three of eight hurdles on the track were set ablaze by the Provisional IRA, who also claimed to have planted booby traps at the course. The INHS Committee provided support to Downpatrick and worked to rearrange the National's running at a later date.[123] At the same time, the good feeling among the racing community on both sides of the border was demonstrated by an 'extremely generous' donation of £425 from the Northern Ireland Turf Guardians' Association to the injured jockeys fund. A reporter in the *Irish Field* expressed the hope that the gift would 'underline the fact that borders are but lines on a map and not a division of people'.[124]

'the storms of increasing inflation and deepening depression'

In 1977, Fianna Fáil swept to power on a 'bonanza' platform, but the party's policy of cutting tax and increasing public expenditure was disastrous, and was compounded by soaring interest rates that pushed the economy to the brink. Between 1979 and 1986 private consumption barely rose and unemployment increased from 6.8 per cent to 17.1 per cent – the highest level in the history of the State. For the first time in a generation, the population declined and, as in the 1950s, 'the case for the Republic of Ireland being considered a failed economic entity was a strong one'. After three general elections between 1981 and 1982, a Fine Gael-Labour coalition took power but their introduction of higher personal taxation and reduced capital expenditure did little to promote economic growth.[125] Racing felt the pinch before the end of the 1970s. Alongside the bloodstock industry, racing had been so 'adversely affected by inflation' that despite a growth in revenue, the Racing Board was 'unable to meet all the calls made on it for assistance'. Matters were compounded by the government's withdrawal of an annual £100,000 capital grant to the Racing Board and by the imposition of 1.5 per cent Stamp Duty on bookmakers betting, which took £750,000 from the industry annually. To offset the impact of the Stamp Duty, the Board increased the levy on on-course bookmakers from 6 to 7.5 per cent.[126] By 1982, the country's economic decline was such that retiring INHS Senior Steward, Lord Donegall, asked members to 'face the fact that governments, all governments, when desperate for money are not unlike a tiger desperate for food: "a very dangerous animal".'[127] The economic downturn impacted on sponsorship, too, as racing lost several major commercial patrons in 1982. The biggest loss was the Northern Irish bookmaker, Sean Graham, who was forced to temporarily withdraw his support of racing in September that year.[128]

Retiring Senior Steward A.L. Moore stressed the importance of sponsors' goodwill to INHS Committee members in late 1983, telling them that it was 'incumbent on all [racecourse] executives to see that their sponsors get the very maximum publicity, and they should spare no effort in this respect'. He also informed Committee members 'that racing, and especially National Hunt racing has weathered the storms of increasing inflation and deepening depression surprisingly well over the past year'.[129] Amid a worsening economic picture, Moore spoke in relative terms: racing wasn't in terminal decline, but it was in trouble. Prize money and sponsorship increased in the early 1980s, but rocketing inflation made a lie of any growth. With prize money failing to keep pace with inflation, owners and trainers expressed concern that winnings would not cover the cost of keeping horses in training. This was a particular concern for those involved in National Hunt racing, where the stakes were lower than in Flat racing. Alongside low prize money and high costs, falling attendances and a burdensome Betting Tax contributed to the industry's difficulty. Course executives were criticized by racegoers for a lack of attention to facilities, programmes and promotion, all of which negatively impacted on gate receipts and had a knock-on effect on prize money. An analysis of the racing industry undertaken by Goff's Managing Director, Jonathan Irwin, in 1983, highlighted the negative impact the Betting Tax had. Irwin estimated that between £400 million and £600 million was bet illegally every year, far in excess of the amounts wagered legally. Illegal betting was facilitated by bookmakers outside the State, licenced bookmakers in Ireland who did not register all bets, unlicenced bookmakers, and 'runners' for licenced and unlicenced operators.[130]

Racing hit another low in mid-1984, when a period of hard ground impacted on the number of runners and resulted in a decrease in Tote takings; this drop was partly offset by the performance of on-course bookmakers, but any increase in overall takings remained some way below the rate of inflation. While hard ground was temporary, the problems in racing were not. Reduced investment threatened the future of a number of racecourses and the industry as a whole. In 1984 (one year after the racing community in Britain and Ireland rallied to save the Grand National at Aintree), the Association of Irish Racecourses (AIR) invited a number of race-going TDs to a race meeting at Fairyhouse, to illustrate 'at first hand the dilapidated condition of the "condemned stand" at this course and to underline the lack of finance to make such replacements within the industry.'[131] The government took notice of this and other pleas for help. In 1985, steps were taken to alleviate the pressure on the industry, with the government abolishing the 1.5 per cent Stamp Duty and with the Racing Board 'sacrificing short-term gains to achieve long-term gains' by reducing the on-course betting levy to 5 per cent and placing the Tote deduction at 22.5 per cent.[132] These measures helped, but there was some way to go before Irish racing turned a corner. In the end, Fairyhouse only survived through the efforts of a fundraising committee. The Phoenix Park was not so fortunate. Backed by Sir John Arnott, J.H.H. Peard established the course on the outskirts of the Park in 1902, and it was immediately popular with Dublin's fashionable set. It remained under the management of the Peard family until 1969, and it was the property of the Arnott family until 1981, when it was sold to Track Investments Ltd, a company controlled by the Gallagher Group. The collapse of the Gallagher Group in 1982 resulted in the sale of the course to a consortium that included Vincent O'Brien, along with businessmen John Magnier, Robert Sangster and Michael Smurfit. Under the management of Jonathan Irwin, the Phoenix Park boasted a programme of high-value sponsored Flat races. It also became a venue for high-profile non-racing events, including 'A Day at the Races' – a concert headlined by U2 in August 1983. The Phoenix Park was revitalized, but with attendances falling below projected targets, it succumbed to mounting debts and closed its gates in October 1990, leaving Leopardstown as the only course in Dublin.[133]

'And the mare's beginning to get up'

While the 1980s was a difficult decade, it was not without good news stories. Innovations like Sunday racing would help to rejuvenate the sport in the longer term, while the institution of the European Breeders' Fund in 1984 provided a much-needed injection of prize money to Irish Flat and National Hunt meetings. The EBF was (and still is) derived from annual contributions made by stallion owners and proved to be a lifeline for Irish racing, although National Hunt received a smaller allocation from the fund because the majority of subscribers and the largest contributors were owners of Flat stallions.[134] There were moments of magic on the track, too, and one superstar horse who reinforced the Irish public's passion for jump racing. Bred by John Riordan, Dawn Run was a bay mare sired by Deep Run out of Twilight Slave. She was bought by Charmian Hill for 5,800 guineas and put into training with Paddy

Dawn Run was a National Hunt superstar who won multiple Grade 1 hurdles in Ireland, Britain and France. Her greatest moment came at Cheltenham in 1986, when she won the Gold Cup under Jonjo O'Neill, seizing the advantage just yards from the finish. She is the only horse to have won the Gold Cup and Champion Hurdle, and remains the highest rated mare over jumps.
© Healy Racing

From Goresbridge in County Kilkenny, Paddy Mullins started training horses in the 1950s and was leading Irish National Hunt trainer on six occasions in the 1980s. He is pictured here with his sons, Tony, who was joint-champion jockey before a back injury caused his early retirement, and Willie, who was an amateur champion on six occasions.
© *Healy Racing*

Dawn Run with her usual partner, Tony Mullins, and Buck House with Tommy Carmody up, before the 'Match of the Century' at Punchestown in April 1986. By July of that year, these two stars of Irish National Hunt racing were dead. © *Healy Racing*

Mullins in Goresbridge, County Kilkenny. By then, Mullins had already had a long career as a trainer, registering his first winner in 1953. His success in the 1980s saw him named Champion National Hunt Trainer on six occasions.[135] It was Charmian Hill who rode Dawn Run to her first victory – a bumper at Tralee in June 1982 – before Paddy Mullins' son and stable jockey, Tony, became her regular rider, partnering her to 15 of her 21 wins. After success in the 1984 Irish Champion Hurdle at Leopardstown, Dawn Run's owner and trainer set their sights on Cheltenham. At Hill's request, however, Jonjo O'Neill replaced Tony Mullins and piloted Dawn Run to her first major success in England, as she won the 1984 Champion Hurdle by a length from Cima.

Top quality jumpers were a rare commodity in Irish racing in the 1980s and this was reflected in the wild celebrations after the race, with owner Hill carried into the winner's enclosure and 'tossed high into the air by jubilant supporters'.[136] Dawn Run was only getting started. After her first success at Cheltenham, Tony Mullins took over from O'Neill and was onboard as she won the Aintree Hurdle and made a successful foray into France, where she claimed the Prix La Barka and the Grande Course de Haies d'Auteuil (French Champion Hurdle). Dawn Run's chasing inexperience was exposed at Cheltenham's January meeting in 1986, which prompted Hill to replace Mullins with O'Neill for the famous Spring festival. The pair were reunited in triumph, as Dawn Run delivered a sensational performance to win the Gold Cup. Her prospects did not look good at the last, but she rallied up the famous hill, with BBC commentator Peter O'Sullevan famously declaring that 'the mare's beginning to get up'.[137] Yards from the finishing post, she caught Wayward Lad and won the race by three-quarters of a length. The crowd at Prestbury Park went wild, with O'Neill reflecting that it 'was a day in a lifetime … I suppose it wasn't just that she did it – it was the way that she did it. Then it all started; it was unbelievable. All those years I had been riding, this was the first time I could hear the weight of the crowd. I remember thinking if all that lot mobbed me, I was gone – and they almost did.'[138]

After her Cheltenham heroics, Dawn Run appeared at Punchestown, where she emerged victorious in 'the Match of the Century', beating the Mouse Morris-trained Champion Chase winner, Buck House. The mare and the gelding met at level weights over two miles, with Tony Mullins reunited with Dawn Run and Tommy Carmody taking the reins on Buck House. In front of a reported crowd of 40,000 people – the biggest recorded at Punchestown since the royal visit in 1868 – the horses landed over the last fence neck and neck, but the mare pulled away in a thrilling finish to win by two lengths.[139] For those watching on, it was a throwback to the halcyon days of Irish racing in the 1960s and 70s. The gloom soon returned, however; on 27 June 1986, less than three months after her Gold Cup triumph, Dawn Run died after falling and breaking her neck while attempting to win a second French Champion Hurdle.[140] It was a tragedy for National Hunt racing, not just in Ireland, but in Britain and on the Continent. Dawn Run won 21 of 35 races, but her career ended as she entered her prime and she never reached her full potential. It is a testament to her talent that she had already achieved greatness as an eight-year-old. She remains the only horse to have completed the Cheltenham Champion Hurdle–Gold Cup double and the only one to have won the Irish, English and French Champion Hurdles. She was also only the second mare to triumph in the Champion Hurdle, 45 years after African Sister in 1939.[141]

Dawn Run actually outlived her rival from the Punchestown match, as Buck House had died of colic just three weeks before the mare's fatal fall.[142] And with that, Irish National Hunt racing was deprived of its two great stars. Writing in the *Irish Press* in late 1987, Con Power observed that 'The paucity of high class jumpers is one of the most striking aspects of the current National Hunt scene.'[143] A shortage of steeplechasers was not a new complaint in Irish National Hunt circles – the question 'where have all the chasers gone?' was perennial in Irish racing. In 1974, retiring INHS Senior Steward A.D. Wingfield paraphrased a once-popular Marlene Dietrich song to answer: 'Gone to England every one'.[144] Ireland's traditional role as an exporter of high quality chasers continued into the late twentieth century and it was no surprise that the need to sell quality horses increased when times were hard, as the 1980s had been. If Cheltenham is the barometer of success in National Hunt racing, then Ireland hit its nadir in the late 1980s. In 1989, there was no Irish-trained winner for the first time since 1947. This 'dreadful Irish nightmare', as the *Irish Field* described it, was hardly a shock, as there had only been one Irish-trained winner in 1987 and 1988 – the John Mulhern-trained Galmoy. Reflecting on the period some years later, Ted Walsh recalled that, at the time, 'Nobody could see it turning around'.[145]

'an essential adjunct to a successful breeding industry'

Problems on the track reflected problems off it. By the early 1980s, there was already a feeling among racing's stakeholders that an authority should be set up from within the industry, to replace the Racing Board and to control, administer and promote Irish racing.[146] Amid growing discontent, the government appointed a Commission of Inquiry into the Thoroughbred Horse Breeding Industry, with Lord Killanin resigning as a Steward of the Turf Club to serve as chairman. The Commissioners were thorough in their approach, visiting racecourses and stud farms across Ireland, gathering evidence, oral testimony and written submissions, and travelling overseas to study racing, breeding and betting in other countries. The Killanin Report was published in July 1986 and while it found the breeding industry to be in good health as a result of favourable tax provisions, racing required significant reform, with financing proving to be 'the major weakness in the sector'.[147] Despite racing's evident problems, the Commissioners stressed that it had the potential to contribute to Irish economic development, particularly as 'an essential adjunct to a successful breeding industry'. It was an important source of employment (an essential concern at a time of record unemployment), with approximately 12,000 people working full-time and 10,000 part-time in the industry, including in stud farms, at racecourses, racing stables and betting shops. To put racing's importance as an employer into context, the Commissioners pointed out that electronics and pharmaceuticals combined employed fewer people.[148]

The Report contained 123 recommendations to improve the racing and breeding industries, 32 of which would require legislation; this included the dissolution of the Racing Board and its replacement with a Thoroughbred Industry Board (TIB), which would 'be responsible for planning, financing and developing racing, and ... also have additional functions in relation to breeding'. The Commission recommended that the TIB should be given responsibility for the National Stud, RACE, the newly established Equine Centre, the racecourses already under the control of the Racing Board (Leopardstown, Navan and Tipperary), and the Tote, which needed to be made competitive with on- and off-course bookmakers and telephone betting, and modernized through computerization.[149] While the Commission advised that the Racing Board should be replaced, it concluded that the Turf Club and the INHS Committee functioned 'very efficiently and without government influence and control' and should be retained as the governing bodies 'in the interests of the sport'. The Report also noted that the two bodies had established relationships internationally and that 'Disturbing such relationships could be very dangerous and might lead to substantial disadvantages for the industry in a world context'.[150]

A significant portion of the Killanin Report focused on Irish racecourses. The Commission recommended that racecourse improvements be given higher priority than prize money, in order to attract racegoers and punters. At the same time, however, the Commissioners pointed out that the Racing Board had too few resources to support twenty-six courses and noted that 'there is now a greater need than ever for rationalization ... because of the higher standards required by racegoers, the extremely high cost of maintenance and development, coupled with the limited financial

Yellow Sam with Michael Furlong up, leading from Willie Mullins on Silver Road in an amateur riders' hurdle at Bellewstown in June 1975. The seemingly unremarkable race was a vehicle for the most famous betting coup in horse racing history, as Yellow Sam's astute and colourful owner Barney Curley capitalised on his under-handicapped horse and a lack of easy communication between the racecourse and off-course bookmakers. Curley sent out a team of punters to place small bets in 300 betting shops across the country and enlisted a friend to block Bellewstown's one available telephone line, which he did by acting out a phone call to a fictional dying aunt. With the off-course bookies unable to reach their on-course counterparts, Yellow Sam's starting price stayed at 20/1 and the coup earned Curley – a Fermanagh native who had once been a Jesuit seminarian – £306,000, or over £2million in today's money.

resources available'. Without enough money to make the necessary improvements to all courses, it was recommended that 'there should be a concentration of fixtures and finance on those … with the best commercial prospects'. It was also suggested that full-time managers be employed by racecourses, in order to ensure a 'professional approach' and to prevent money going to waste. Smaller courses were urged to pool their resources to secure a manager to run their racing as a group venture, with an ultimate eye on rationalization. To achieve commercial viability, racing would need to be sufficiently funded. To that end, the Commissioners suggested that one-fifth of the taxes raised from off-course betting should be invested in the racing industry.[151]

The Killanin Report was published without any commitment from the government, in order to stimulate public debate on the issues raised. There was debate and some reforms were forthcoming, including the establishment of a subsidiary company to manage the three racecourses owned by the Racing Board; the provision of £500,000 for the refurbishment of racecourse facilities; and the computerization of the Tote. The Report certainly focused 'minds on the issues … demanding attention', but progress on instituting the Report's major recommendations was slow.[152] The government could not ignore the need to restructure and refinance the racing industry for long, however. A major breakthrough came in the 1990 Budget, when Minister for Finance Albert Reynolds announced a grant of £3.5 million to the Racing Board and Bord na gCon (Greyhound Board), 'to accelerate their investment programmes at courses and to enhance generally the attractiveness of, and incentives for, racing'. Reynolds also stated his intention to make a similar provision for the following three years.[153] By 1994, the government had provided grants-in-aid totalling £13.5 million, of which £7.5 million was used for prize money and £4 million to develop racecourse facilities. The balance, meanwhile, was used in the promotion of the sport and the marketing of thoroughbred horses. An important step was taken in that direction in 1991, with the establishment of Irish Thoroughbred Marketing (ITM), to promote Ireland internationally as a producer of top-class bloodstock.[154]

The period between 1970 and 1993 was one of mixed fortunes for Irish racing. The 1970s, like the decade preceding it, represented a period of significant progress and achievement in the sport, not least in National Hunt and point-to-point racing. Irish breeders, owners and trainers continued to produce horses of outstanding ability, while Irish jockeys and amateur riders delivered moments of magic on racetracks across the island of Ireland and in England. The Racing Board pursued financial growth and infrastructural development, while the governing bodies worked to regulate, develop and ultimately modernize the sport. The INHS Committee's growing support for point-to-point meetings altered the landscape of jump racing; traditionally the preserve of local hunts, it became an increasingly important schooling ground for National Hunt horses. At the same time, wider political, social and economic developments challenged and changed the *status quo* in Irish racing, with improved working conditions and protections put in place for stable staff and with women's contributions to the sport becoming more visible. By the early 1990s, however, the industry was in real trouble and in National Hunt racing, the golden era of Irish chasers had become a distant memory. Problems that had emerged in the 1970s, like the oversupply of poor horses, the Racing Board's growing (and related) struggle to properly finance the sport, and the large scale export of good chasers, were exacerbated by high inflation and Ireland's slide into recession in the 1980s. The Killanin Report offered solutions but meaningful change was slow to materialize and when it came, many felt it wasn't enough. In 1994, the Horseracing Industry Bill was introduced to the Oireachtas, to provide a statutory framework for the establishment of the Irish Horseracing Authority (IHA). While the establishment of the IHA was not met with universal enthusiasm, it demonstrated that the racing industry, supported by the State, was desirous of meaningful change. The timing was propitious: as the IHA began its work, Ireland entered a period of unprecedented prosperity. With the necessary infrastructure in place, the thoroughbred industry was ready to capitalize on Ireland's economic miracle. The result was a revolution in Irish racing and breeding.

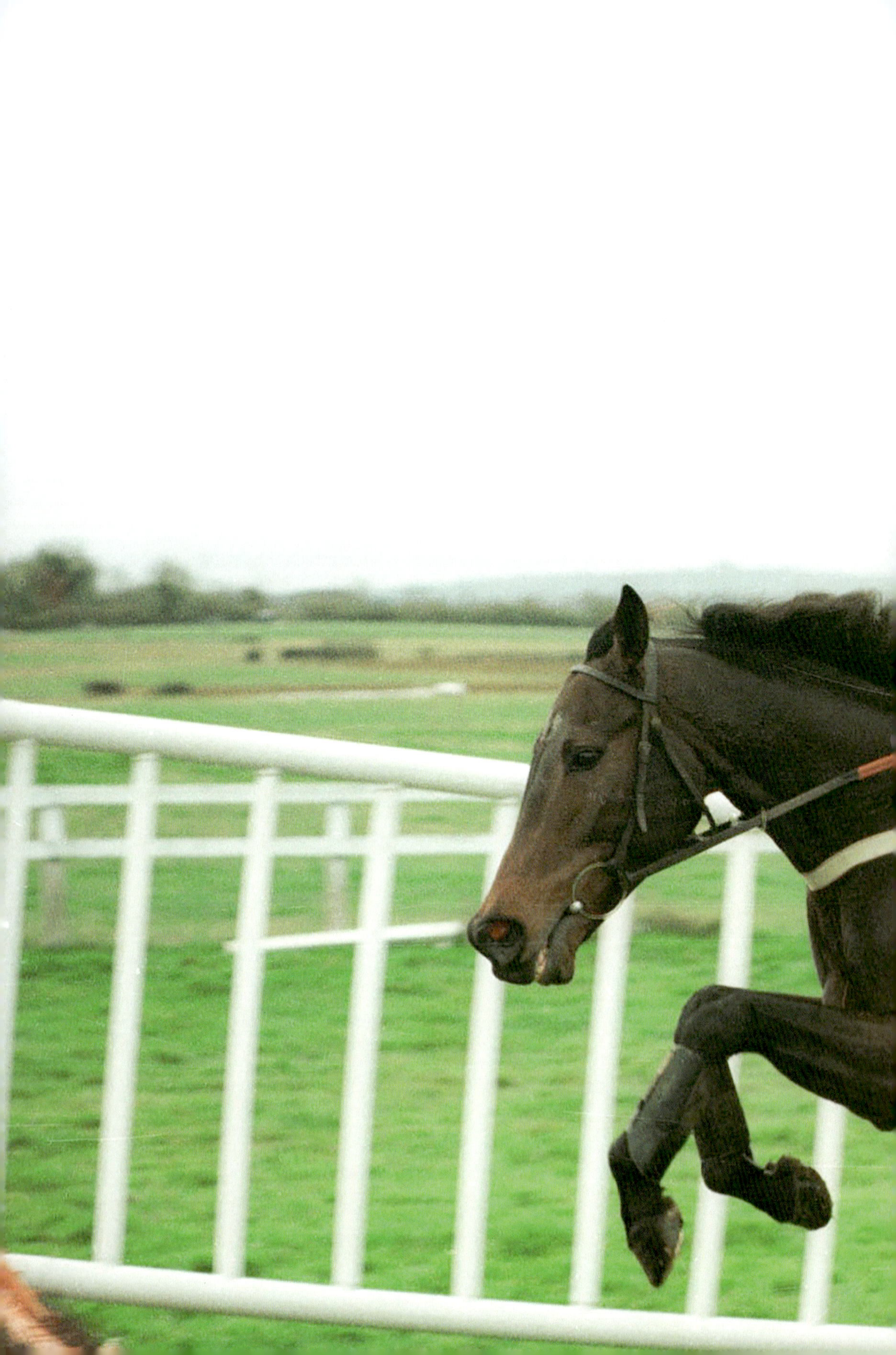

CHAPTER SIX

1994-2022

'One of the distinguishing signs of "Irishness"'

THE HORSERACING INDUSTRY ACT was signed into law in July 1994, and with that the Irish Horseracing Authority (IHA) came into being. Much debate surrounded the IHA at the time of its foundation, but the new body restructured and revitalized the industry. It was helped, no doubt, by a dramatically improved Irish economy. One year after its establishment, the Celtic Tiger began to roar and racing's place in Irish sporting and social life assumed a new importance. Irish people flocked to racecourses across the island and became an ever-growing presence at major meetings in England; betting turnover rose; racecourse facilities were greatly improved; the rise of satellite television revolutionized sports' broadcasting, while the internet transformed gambling; the popularity of syndicates exploded and race meetings like Galway advertised Irish economic success. In National Hunt racing, Danoli's achievements underlined the value of the 'small man' to the sport, while Istabraq demonstrated the importance of world-class stud farms, wealthy owners and talented, well-resourced trainers. At the same time, riders from across the island of Ireland dominated domestic and British National Hunt racing, while point-to-point racing continued to develop, as professional standards were consistently applied to the amateur scene. With the industry expanding in scale and scope, Horse Racing Ireland superseded the IHA in 2001 and developed Irish racing and breeding even further, exceeding the ambitions of the many individuals and groups who worked across decades to ensure its success. Having emerged from the difficult aftermath of the 2008 economic crash, Ireland is now a byword for excellence in racing and particularly National Hunt racing. Even in this golden era, however, there are obstacles to overcome. Much depends on racing's ability to compete for people's leisure time, to retain its character and relevance in an increasingly commercial landscape, and to overcome challenges and controversy.

'to bring the racing and breeding industry in this country to its rightful position as one of the best in the world'

By the early 1990s, the need for a new horse racing authority to replace the Racing Board was impossible to ignore. The man tasked with bringing the IHA into existence was Joe Walsh, the incumbent Minister for Agriculture and a lifelong horse racing enthusiast, who had championed the redevelopment of Mallow Racecourse in the 1990s. Walsh appointed an interim committee on horse racing in October 1993, to advise on the future functions and structure of the new authority and the drafting of necessary legislation.[1] The following February, the Irish Horseracing Industry Bill was introduced to the Dáil, proposing to replace the Racing Board with the IHA. This new body would be tasked with the overall administration of racing, while the Turf Club and INHS Committee would retain responsibility for the regulation of the sport and the provision of integrity services. The IHA would also be made responsible for the development and promotion of the industry; the control of the operations of licenced bookmakers; race-fixtures and race-programmes; the operation of racecourses in the possession of the IHA; the domestic and international promotion of Irish thoroughbred horses; and the provision of grants or loans to authorized racecourses and subsidiary companies.[2] The new authority would be overseen by a fourteen-member board, which included two Stewards from the Turf Club, one from the INHS Committee and representatives from other parts of the industry.

On the urging of the Turf Club and INHS Committee, Walsh recognized that the IHA should award one seat on the board to a representative of the industry from Northern Ireland, 'because the good of the whole industry can only prosper on a 32-county basis'.[3] As Keeper of the Match Book Cahir O'Sullivan pointed out, this was 'the first time for anyone in Northern Ireland to have an input at executive level in the running of the racing industry throughout the island'.[4] At Walsh's request, a review body was appointed by the Northern Ireland Department of Agriculture, to nominate a suitable candidate. A row erupted, however, when the review body's unanimous choice – Down Royal chairperson, Jim Nicholson – was overlooked for Suzy Armstrong, a former Secretary of the Northern Breeders' Association. Review body member Jeremy Hughes wrote to the *Irish Field* that 'Having worked very hard to fulfil Mr Walsh's request to nominate a suitable person for membership of the authority, it is not pleasant to find that the Northern Ireland racing industry has been treated in such a cavalier, contemptuous and dishonourable manner.'[5] The dispute soon entered the political arena, with Ulster Unionist Party leader James Molyneaux tabling a motion in the House of Commons, asking why Walsh had 'apparently – for political reasons – contemptuously ignored the nomination unanimously made by those representing the industry in Northern Ireland'.[6] Liam Cosgrave addressed the fallout in the Seanad, noting that Armstrong's appointment had 'queered the pitch and perhaps soured certain relations' and expressing the hope that 'there was no undue political consideration involved'. In response, Walsh praised Nicholson as a 'fine person who has done a professional job with Down Royal' but stated that Armstrong's selection was directed by government policy on gender balance.[7]

It was not the composition of the board, but the terms of the bill that soured relations elsewhere. In a letter to the editor of the *Irish Times* in March 1994, Lord Killanin was unequivocal in his condemnation of the proposed legislation, writing that 'Unfortunately those responsible for drafting the Irish Horseracing Industry Bill 1994 have patently failed to study or understand the findings of the Commission of Inquiry into the Thoroughbred Horsebreeding Industry – the so-called Killanin Commission. I would like it known that I disagree totally with the content and direction of this proposed Bill'. Killanin suggested that the bill had 'been produced too rapidly, without enough thought given to detail and too little discussion with those deeply involved in the two industries – racing and breeding'. He was particularly dismayed by the omission from the bill of a levy on off-track betting, and the related inclusion of Section 27, which made funding contingent on government support through the Budget or Finance Bills, and left racing vulnerable to shifting political agendas. Section 27 was antithetical to the Killanin Report's recommendation that racing be funded by a levy of twenty per cent on off-course betting, and Killanin himself commented: 'It is to me inconceivable that anyone can think that one of

Ireland's great natural industries, of the highest international repute, can plan its economic future on such a weak premise.'[8]

In the Dáil, meanwhile, opposition TDs criticized the bill as an attempt to nationalize and bureaucratize the industry.[9] Some amendments were made, but the substance of the bill – including Section 27 – passed into law in the summer of 1994. The IHA commenced operations on 1 December that year, at which point the Racing Board ceased to be. The last chairman of the Racing Board and the first chairman of the IHA, Denis Brosnan, thanked all those who had served on the various Boards since 1945 and stated that 'There is little doubt that the development of the industry during this period has been significant.' Brosnan added that 'it is the intention of the IHA to build on this development and to bring the Racing and Breeding Industry in this country to its rightful position as one of the best in the world'.[10] Retiring INHS Senior Steward Alan Lillingston assured the IHA of the 'help and cooperation of the National Hunt Stewards and the Registry Office' and observed that the Authority's teething problems were largely attributable to a lack of funds.[11] A shortage of money was not a long-lived problem, as the IHA was established at a fortuitous moment in Ireland's economic history. The Celtic Tiger was built on previous domestic policy decisions, EEC support, and the advent of the European Single Market in 1992, which allowed the free movement of people, goods, services and money around the bloc. A low Corporation Tax rate stimulated foreign direct investment, 'born global' Irish companies emerged and there was significant growth in the services sector. A rise in employment translated to a growth in income tax and a budget surplus was achieved for the first time in 1996, with surpluses in each of the following ten years. Living standards rose and Ireland moved from being the laggard of Western Europe, to matching and even exceeding some of its neighbours in terms of social and economic indicators.[12]

Despite its perceived faults, the IHA was ready to capitalize on Ireland's sudden prosperity and worked to transform the industry in the 1990s. A rising economic tide lifted all boats, and there was a significant increase in racecourse attendances, betting turnovers, sponsorship and prize money, as well as growth in the domestic and international market for Irish bloodstock. While the IHA was helped by the Celtic Tiger, there was work to do to capture the attention of the Irish public, who had more choice in how to spend their leisure time than ever before. In January 1997, the IHA launched a long-awaited five-year strategic plan for the Irish racing industry, which provided a commitment to upgrading Irish racecourse facilities, with eighty per cent of a £30 million investment from the Capital Development Fund to be spent on eight key racecourses – the Curragh, Punchestown, Leopardstown, Fairyhouse, Mallow, Galway, Listowel, and Greenpark in Limerick (Greenpark closed in 1999, after 130 years, and the course relocated to its current site at Greenmount in Patrickswell). The IHA also announced plans for a concerted marketing campaign, with assistance and incentives given to racecourses to achieve substantial growth in attendances, betting turnover and sponsorship.[13] The promotion of racing stimulated attendances, which rose from 1 million in 1995 to 1.3 million in 1999.[14] A growth in attendances resulted in a rise in on-course betting;[15] this was a particularly welcome development for bookmakers, who had experienced a worrying slide in turnover between 1990 and 1994, with the sum total of bets made falling from £104 million to £67.4 million.[16] The Racing Board's final report predicted that this slide was bottoming out and saw 'grounds for optimism'.[17]

By then, however, bookmakers were feeling decidedly pessimistic and objected strongly to the reopening of a betting shop at Leopardstown in 1995. Paddy Power had opened the first SP shop in Ireland at the south Dublin course in 1989, but it shuttered less than four years later, amid strong opposition from bookmakers. The decision to reopen an SP shop, this time operated by Tote Arena Ltd, resulted in a boycott of Leopardstown by members of the Irish National Bookmakers' Association (INBA).[18] In the late 1990s, however, the government moved to address bookmakers' concerns by abolishing the on-course levy and by reducing the off-course levy from 10 to 5 per cent – a move hastened by the growth of off-shore tax free telephone and online betting.[19] On-course bookmakers were also buoyed by a significant increase in betting turnover.[20] Higher attendances and turnover were part of a wider upward trend. There was marked and related growth in sponsorship and prize money in the latter half of the 1990s, alongside changing models of racehorse ownership and a growth in domestic and international markets for Irish bloodstock. Prize money was a cornerstone of this growth and it increased from £14 to £24.3 million between 1996 and 2000, with input from the IHA, sponsors and racehorse owners. The popularity of National Hunt – the 'poor relation' of Irish horse racing – meant that it received the greatest share of prize money, including a higher contribution from the IHA and from commercial sponsorship. Flat racing only outperformed jump racing in its drawdown from the EBF, which demonstrated the concentration of high-value Flat stallions contributing to the Fund.[21]

'Their guardianship of the rules of racing and of its integrity is recognized domestically and internationally as being first class'

The overarching purpose of the IHA was to impose coherence on the industry. To create the legislation that would establish the new Authority, it was necessary to examine the structures already in place. Like the Jockey Club in Britain, the Turf Club and INHS Committee in Ireland had continued to face questions over the demographic make-up of their membership. In the Dáil in 1991, Fine Gael Spokesperson on Agriculture, Austin Deasy, argued that any new legislation on the racing industry should 'bring a degree of democracy ... into the affairs of horse racing in this country' by implementing a 'proper system that is answerable to this House and to the public in general'.[22] Deasy's comments in the Dáil followed an interview with trainer Jim Bolger in the *Irish Racing Annual*, who took issue with the membership of the Turf Club and INHS Committee.[23] Facing greater scrutiny, the two bodies opted for greater transparency. In April 1993, the Turf Club published its accounts for the first time in its 202-year history, with Senior Steward Brigadier Sam Waller noting that 'Nothing is so important to the racegoer and the racing industry than to be certain that everything is completely above board.'[24] In Waller's words, the published accounts proved there was 'no crock of gold'; instead, the bodies typically operated under a small surplus. Any income derived from the administration of racing, the *Racing Calendar* and the *Form Book*, was swallowed up by the cost of providing integrity services, including the photo finish unit, stewards and the equine forensic unit.[25]

Not for the first time in its history, the INHS Committee had to deal with suggestions that it should amalgamate with the Turf Club. In April 1993, the retiring Senior Steward James Barry reminded members that 'The INHS Committee is a wonderful organization' and concluded by charging all present 'to GUARD IT WELL'.[26] The INHS Committee was not absorbed into the Turf Club, but the IHA relieved the two bodies of some of their traditional functions, including responsibility for race fixtures and race programmes – although the secretariat for these new committees remained in the Turf Club. There was a significant development in programming in this period of transition, as British and Irish racing authorities agreed a pattern of races for National Hunt racing on both islands. Forty-one Grade 1 races were agreed overall, with twenty-five to be run in England and sixteen in Ireland. The first Irish Grade 1s were contested at Fairyhouse in November 1994.[27] While the IHA assumed certain functions that had previously been the province of the Turf Club and INHS Committee, the bodies' importance to the sport and to the wider industry could not be disregarded. In debating the Irish Horseracing Industry Bill in the Dáil, Minister Joe Walsh acknowledged that they had 'done very valuable work in administering Irish racing for over two centuries. Their guardianship of the rules of racing and of its integrity is recognized domestically and internationally as being first class'.[28] It was for that reason that they were statutorily defined in the Irish Horseracing Industry Act as the 'Racing Regulatory Body', with responsibility for the regulation of horse racing and provision of integrity services.[29]

With some coherence established in the industry, the INHS Committee worked to regulate and achieve higher standards in National Hunt and point-to-point

Past INHSC Senior Stewards at the retirement dinner for Registrar Sean Barry, who made a massive contribution to the administration of racing in Ireland through his decades-long service. Back row (left–right): Roy Craigie, William Flood, Michael Doyle, Sean Barry, Leslie Crawford. Front row (left–right): Alan Lillingston, John Moloney, Edward Flannery, Ivo O'Sullivan, David Pim.

CHAPTER SIX: 1994–2022

racing. This was no small job and successive INHS Senior Stewards recognized the contribution of Registrar Michael Keogh, 'a "Niagara" of knowledge and information', and his equally expert successor, Sean Barry, as well as the staff in the Registry Office and racing officials across the island. The Committee's endeavours resulted in a significant improvement to the sport in October 1994, with the introduction of the by-passing of fences. This was after 'a long gestation period', involving consultation with clerks of the course; the Inspector of Courses; the Jockeys' Association; the Turf Club Medical Officer, Dr Walter Halley, and racecourse managers.[30] Bill McLernon, who served as Inspector of Courses from the mid-1980s until 2005, later identified by-passing as the best rule ever introduced to the sport, followed by the replacement of timber with plastic wings and rails.[31] By its nature, racing cannot be entirely without risk, but continuing improvements to Irish racecourses demonstrate the INHS Committee's and Turf Club's regard for rider and animal welfare – a regard that developed in scope and sophistication in the 1980s and 1990s.

With the potential for serious and occasionally fatal injury to occur, rider welfare continued to be of paramount importance. From the mid-1980s, the efforts of Dr Walter Halley helped to give greater definition to Irish racing's safety and medical protocols. By the end of that decade, the compulsory wearing of back protectors had been introduced, a Qualified Riders' Accident Fund (QRAF) was established, the use of Medical Record Books was consistently promoted, the standard of helmets was continuously reviewed and procedures for monitoring injured riders were improved.[32] The INHS Committee also made a concerted effort to improve the skills of National Hunt jockeys and amateur riders. In 1994, retired riders Aubrey Brabazon, Willie Robinson, Ted Walsh, Frank Berry, Michael O'Donoghue, Simon Walford and incumbent INHS Senior Steward Alan Lillingston formed a 'travelling roadshow', appearing at four venues across Ireland and dispensing advice to amateurs, conditionals and professional jockeys.[33] In January 1998, meanwhile, the Committee established the Jockeys' Emergency Fund, after jockey Shane Broderick was paralysed from the neck down in a fall at Fairyhouse on Easter Monday in 1997. The fund was initiated with the assistance owners and jockeys, after it was found that insurance companies 'were unable to provide the level of cover for a future similar accident'. The Jockeys' Accident Fund was also 'revamped' around this time, to provide riders with greater support during periods of injury.[34]

The INHS Committee continued to institute reforms in point-to-pointing, too. This included the extension of the QRAF to amateurs riding at point-to-point meetings across the island, as well as the introduction of further safety measures, including the compulsory wearing of back protectors, the application of instructions on the use of the whip, safety limits on runners, the provision of island fences on all courses and the by-passing of fences where an injured rider or horse caused an obstruction.[35] Rules are only valuable if they are adhered to, of course, and by the early 1990s, there was concern that the organizers of some meetings were not taking the steps necessary to ensure the safety of riders and horses, with one INHS Senior Steward speaking to members of the 'frustrating battle … to restore the standards of fences, courses and safety'.[36] The standard of fences, in particular, continued to present challenges throughout the 1990s, as did a high number of entries, which necessitated the division of races. This was not a sign of irreversible decline, however, with Senior Steward David Pim noting in 1997 that 'Many of the problems faced by the Stewards and others have been a direct result of the huge success of point-to-pointing in general and its attraction to our smaller owners who enjoy Hunt racing as a country pursuit.' It had been a long time since point-to-point racing was just a 'country pursuit', however. As Pim acknowledged, the Stewards had always intended 'to administer and police point-to-point racing on the basis that it is an amateur sport but recognizing its importance as a nursery and introduction to all that is best in National Hunt racing'.[37]

'The cruel treatment of a horse can do naught but give a bad name to racing'

Pim also stressed the importance of horse and rider welfare in drawing public support for point-to-point meetings, with an increase in betting turnover reflecting 'an improvement of the confidence of the public with the supervision of the sport and the entertainment which it offers'.[38] By the 1990s, there was a growing public awareness of animal welfare in horse racing, which was a result of animal rights' activism, particularly in Britain. The animal rights' movement had originated there in the nineteenth-century and there was a long tradition of protest against the Grand National, with particular concern expressed over the number of equine fatalities on the Aintree course.[39] This early activism was peaceful, but the emergence of more militant animal rights' groups at the end of the twentieth century changed the tenor of protest, leading to the physical disruption of equestrian events. Hunting was most affected, but horse racing was also targeted, with activists continuing to protest the Grand National, in particular. In 1993, a demonstration contributed to the abandonment of the historic steeplechase, with protestors running onto the course and blocking the first fence, to delay the start of the race. This was followed by two false starts, the second of which was not properly communicated to the thirty-nine riders, with the result that twenty-three raced on. In the end, Wexford-born jockey John White rode the Jenny Pitman-trained Esha Ness to an invalid victory, with the BBC's Peter O'Sullevan calling the whole affair 'the greatest disaster in the history of the Grand National'.[40]

In Ireland, animal rights' activism developed at a slower pace and on a smaller scale, but organizations concerned with animal welfare did emerge, including groups focused specifically on the welfare of horses.[41] While regulations were frequently improved and expanded to ensure the safety of horses, it was not until the 1970s and 80s that animal welfare was explicitly acknowledged as a public concern. In 1981, the INHS Committee introduced instructions on the use of the whip. This was in response to developments in Britain, where two Irish jockeys had been penalized for excessive use at Cheltenham the previous year. In announcing the instructions, retiring Senior Steward Lord Hemphill reminded INHS Committee members that 'The cruel treatment of a horse can do naught but give a bad name to racing, and will not be tolerated by the racing public of today.'[42] The animal rights' movement in Ireland remained significantly smaller than its British counterpart in the 1990s, but the protesting of the Grand National at Aintree resonated with Irish activists. One group – the Alliance for Animal Rights – protested outside betting shops in Dublin in 1994, on the weekend of the Grand National.[43] These developments did not escape the notice of the INHS Committee, with Lord Harrington calling, in 1995, for the formation of a nationwide committee to address opposition from activist groups, which was 'certain to come within three to four years' and would 'jeopardize the future of equestrian sport'.[44] Public awareness around the welfare of racehorses grew, often following fatalities at high-profile meetings, and some of the criticisms made by animal rights' groups contributed to positive developments in the sport – including continuing revisions on the use of the whip.[45]

'they are a new breed of owner and this can only be good for all of us'

Overall, however, Harrington's concern for the future of racing proved to be unfounded, as protests did little to damage the reputation of horse racing in Ireland. The sport continued to be well-supported by the government and only increased in popularity with the Irish public in the Celtic Tiger era. With racing's – and particularly jump racing's – broad appeal, the IHA recognized the potential public appetite for racehorse ownership in the 1990s. The IHA promoted different models of ownership through its subsidiary company, Irish Thoroughbred Marketing (ITM), which made the purchase and maintenance of a racehorse a realistic prospect for Ireland's increasingly affluent middle class. Shared-ownership was not new: the first racing club in Britain was formed in 1968, but clubs were slower to materialize in Ireland, with the first being established in Dundalk in 1983. Five years later, there were twenty-two clubs in existence.[46] Legendary Flat trainer John Oxx summarized the appeal of shared-ownership, remarking that 'In a country where we have no real base of racehorse ownership, they are a new breed of owner and this can only be good for all of us'.[47] Alongside racing clubs, interested groups also had the option of forming a company, a syndicate or a partnership,[48] and it was also possible for racing clubs to lease horses. This model was used by the North Kildare Racing Club (NKRC), whose sixteen members paid £22 a month to cover trainer Willie Mullins' fees, as well as farrier fees, veterinary fees, insurance and entry fees. The NKRC had a notable success in 1995, when their horse Tourist Attraction won the Supreme Novices' Hurdle at Cheltenham, giving Mullins his first festival success.[49]

The number of group enterprises grew during the 1990s and in the first year of the new millennium, over 700 new owners were introduced to Irish racing. This included the Grand Alliance Racing Club, an Oireachtas syndicate that was comprised of eight Fianna Fáil and eight Fine Gael members, along with one Progressive Democrat – Des O'Malley. One member of the all-male, cross-party syndicate joked that the Grand Alliance operated on the principal of 'gender balance and no socialists'.[50] The syndicate purchased a bay gelding named Arctic Copper and placed him in training with Noel Meade, who was Irish National Hunt champion trainer eight times between 1998/9 and 2006/7.[51] Arctic Copper was reasonably successful for his politician owners before being sold in 2005, with seven wins and twenty-two places under National Hunt Rules.[52] The Oireachtas syndicate's activities served as a symbol of Ireland's newfound economic confidence. With more disposable income, many Irish racing enthusiasts wanted to experience owning a racehorse and syndication was a cost-effective way to achieve that ambition. Syndicate members may have dreamt of the winner's enclosure at Galway or Cheltenham, but they knew that racehorses were expensive, that major (or even minor) success was rare and that their collective enterprise was for pleasure, not profit. As the good times rolled and the Celtic Tiger reached illusory heights in the early 2000s, shared ownership increased significantly and by 2007, there were 1,493 registered syndicates.[53]

'He took us to places we would never have been … and it was great to see what top-class chasing is really like'

The growth in shared ownership in Celtic Tiger Ireland was partly the result of IHA marketing schemes, but it was also rooted in the romance of racehorse ownership, which was ultimately advertised by the success of Irish horses. There was little success to advertise in the late 1980s and early 1990s, when Irish National Hunt racing lacked quality horses and the undisputed superstar over jumps was the English grey, Desert Orchid. Beloved for his fearlessness, front-running and versatility, 'Dessie' won 34

The unforgettable grey, Desert Orchid, at Downpatrick in 1992. An English horse, 'Dessie's' uncompromising style made him a firm favourite with racegoers across the island of Ireland. He won the 1990 edition of the Irish Grand National in memorable fashion, crashing through the last fence after an uncharacteristically poor jump, before racing home twelve lengths ahead.

Adrian Maguire at Dromahane Point-to-Point in 1991. Maguire set the point-to-point scene alight before going on to enjoy great success as a jockey in Britain in the 1990s. © *Healy Racing*.

of his 71 starts and claimed several major chasing prizes, including four King George's and the Cheltenham Gold Cup. He also won the Irish Grand National in 1990, in partnership with Belfast-born jockey and three-time British champion jockey, Richard Dunwoody, who also won two King George's with the hugely popular grey.[54] One of Dunwoody's greatest rivals in the early 1990s was Adrian Maguire, a Meathman who rose to prominence on the Irish point-to-point scene in 1991, when he was crowned champion amateur, having ridden a then-record 38 winners.[55] After switching his focus to British National Hunt racing, Maguire finished just three wins behind Dunwoody in the 1993/4 British National Hunt jockeys' championship. Dunwoody himself was succeeded as British champion by another Northern Irishman, A.P. McCoy, who won the first of a remarkable twenty successive titles in 1995/6. At the same time, Wexford man Mick Fitzgerald broke through to become one of Britain's leading National Hunt jockeys.[56] While Dunwoody, Maguire, McCoy and Fitzgerald dominated in Britain, Charlie Swan reigned in Ireland, winning the first of nine consecutive National Hunt jockeys' championships in 1989/90. Swan was to the fore as Irish National Hunt racing began to turn a corner in the mid-1990s and he was associated with two of the leading lights of Irish jump racing in that period – Danoli and Istabraq. These horses represented the two faces of Irish National Hunt racing, with Danoli proving the value of the 'small man' to the sport and the industry, and with Istabraq demonstrating the importance of Ireland's world-class breeding industry, wealthy owners and well-resourced, talented trainers.

Sired by The Parson out of the mare Blue Gold, Danoli was bred by Francis Austin and sent to Goffs as a three-year-old, where he failed to attract a buyer. The overlooked gelding was later bought by the well-known bonesetter, Dan O'Neill, who combined his own first name with that of his daughter, Olivia, to christen the horse. Danoli was trained by Tom Foley in County Carlow, and opened his National Hunt career with three bumper wins in the 1992/3 season. He triumphed in his first two starts over hurdles and then proved his ability in the top tier of Irish racing by finishing second on level weights to Fortune and Fame in the Grade 1 Irish Champion Hurdle at Leopardstown in early 1994. In March that year, Danoli delivered on his promise by winning the Sun Alliance Novices' Hurdle at Cheltenham. His special place in the hearts of Irish punters was summed up by George Ennor in the *Racing Post*, who wrote that 'They cheered him down to the start, they cheered him as he started, they cheered more loudly as he took the lead, and they raised the roof as

Danoli and Charlie Swan at Punchestown. A resolute style of racing earned Danoli 17 career wins, including the Sun Alliance Novices' Hurdle at Cheltenham (1994), the Aintree Hurdle (1994 and 1995), the Hatton's Grace Hurdle at Fairyhouse (1994) and the Morgiana Hurdle at Punchestown (1994). © *Healy Racing*.

'The people's champion': Danoli captivates a record crowd at his local track, Gowran Park, ahead of the Red Mills Trial Hurdle in 1996. Bred by Francis Austin, Danoli was left unsold at Goffs in 1991, before being purchased by Dan O'Neill, who put him into training with Tom Foley near Bagenalstown in County Carlow. © *Healy Racing.*

he passed the post in front.'[57] Danoli won the Aintree Hurdle in April 1994 and started the following season with victory in the Morgiana Hurdle at Punchestown and the Hatton's Grace Hurdle at Fairyhouse, where he defeated his great rival, the Michael Hourigan-trained Dorans Pride. He finished third in the Champion Hurdle at Cheltenham in March 1995, before winning the Aintree Hurdle. He fractured the cannon-bone in the fetlock joint in that race, however, and had to undergo surgery. Foley believed that Danoli never fully recovered, but he finished third in the Irish Champion Hurdle in early 1996, before drawing a record crowd to Gowran Park where he won the Red Mills Trial Hurdle.

Danoli switched to steeplechasing in the 1996–7 season and registered his first major win at Leopardstown in the Grade 1 Denny Gold Medal Chase. This was followed by another Grade 1 win in the Hennessy Gold Cup at Leopardstown, as Danoli emerged victorious from a field that included the great Irish chaser, Imperial Call. Trained by Fergie Sutherland in County Cork, Imperial Call had won the previous edition of the Hennessy and the Cheltenham Gold Cup in 1996, having formed a fruitful partnership with jockey Conor O'Dwyer. Danoli's career thereafter was affected by injury and he was retired to the Irish National Stud in 2000, where he lived alongside other past stars of Irish racing. He died of colic at Tully in 2006. For Tom Foley, Danoli was a life-changing horse: 'He took us to places we would never have been, like Cheltenham and Liverpool, and it was great to see what top-class racing is really like.'[58] Danoli thus carried the 'small man' to racing's top table and for that reason he was 'The People's Champion'. He was so beloved at the height of his career that he appeared on RTÉ's flagship television programme, the *Late Late Show*, with host Gay Byrne introducing him as 'the most popular person in Ireland'.[59] Like Arkle and Dawn Run before him, Danoli transcended his sport and his species, as his unlikely success resonated in a small country that was just beginning to assert itself on the world stage.

As Danoli's light dimmed, Istabraq began to shine. These two heroes over hurdles shared a jockey in Charlie Swan, but they had little else in common. The son of the legendary champion sire, Sadler's Wells, Istabraq was foaled at Sheikh Al Maktoum's Derrinstown Stud in County Kildare before being sent to trainer John Godsen. With a name derived from the old Arabic for 'lightning', Istabraq did not deliver on his pedigree or his name on the Flat. He was sold to Irish jump racing's greatest patron, J.P. McManus, at the urging of amateur Flat rider, John Durkan, who believed that Istabraq had the makings of a great hurdler. Durkan was not able to fulfil his ambition

Istabraq demonstrating his power and precision when winning the Shell Champion Hurdle under Charlie Swan at Punchestown in 1999. Described by his trainer Aidan O'Brien as 'a horse of a lifetime', he is one of only five horses to have won the Champion Hurdle three times and was only denied a record fourth win by the foot and mouth outbreak in 2001. © *Healy Racing*.

Hardy Eustace and Conor O'Dwyer (right) winning the Champion Hurdle at Cheltenham for the second year in a row from Harchibald and Paul Carberry (centre) and Brave Inca and Barry Cash (left). © *Healy Racing*.

to train the horse, however, as he was diagnosed with leukaemia before he could take out a licence. Five-time National Hunt champion trainer, Aidan O'Brien, took over on what was supposed to be a temporary basis, but Durkan passed away before Istabraq claimed the first of three consecutive Champion Hurdles in 1998. By then, Istabraq was already a successful hurdler, having delivered for McManus, O'Brien and Swan in a number of Grade 1 races, including the RSA Novices' Hurdle, the Hatton's Grace Hurdle, the Punchestown Champion Novice Hurdle and the Irish Champion Hurdle. After trading wins with the up-and-coming Moscow Flyer in early 2001, Istabraq looked primed to win a record fourth Champion Hurdle. It was not to be, however, as an outbreak of foot and mouth disease resulted in the abandonment of that year's Cheltenham Festival.[60]

Danoli and Istabraq were special, but they were not the only stars of Irish National Hunt racing in the 1990s and 2000s. The 2000s proved to be a golden age for Irish hurdlers, with the Dessie Hughes-trained Hardy Eustace winning the Champion Hurdle in 2004 and 2005, followed by the Colm Murphy-trained Brave Inca in 2006.

Three modern masters in the saddle: Barry Geraghty, Paul Carberry and Ruby Walsh. © *Healy Racing*.

Hardy Eustace's 2005 win came at the expense of another hurdling star, the Noel Meade-trained Harchibald, who twice won the Fighting Fifth Hurdle at Newcastle (2004 and 2007) and the Christmas Hurdle at Kempton (2004 and 2008). Harchibald provided jockey Paul Carberry with the most successful partnership of his career, but not his most famous win. That was delivered by Bobbyjo, a horse that stole hearts and headlines when he followed success in the 1998 Irish Grand National by winning the 1999 Grand National. In doing so, he became the first Irish-trained horse to win the marquee race at Aintree since L'Escargot in 1975. This feat was all the more remarkable because Bobbyjo was trained by L'Escargot's National-winning jockey and Paul's father, Tommy Carberry.[61] Another Irish father-son duo took the spoils at Aintree the following year, when Ted and Ruby Walsh combined to claim success with Papillon, before linking up to win the Irish Grand National with Commanche Court.[62] Ruby Walsh's rise to the pinnacle of National Hunt racing was meteoric. Having applied for an amateur licence on his sixteenth birthday, he was a two-time amateur champion by the time he turned twenty, winning back-to-back titles in

Kauto Star and Ruby Walsh jumping to win the JNwine.com Champion Steeplechase at Down Royal in November 2010. © *Healy Racing*.

1996–7 and 1997–8. He followed that achievement by being crowned Irish National Hunt champion jockey in his first season as a professional. It was the beginning of an illustrious career, with Walsh becoming the third-most successful jump jockey in history and the winningest rider at Cheltenham. His concurrent employment as stable jockey for both Willie Mullins and Paul Nicholls and his tally of 59 Cheltenham Festival winners underscores just how special he was.

Walsh partnered some of the greatest hurdlers and chasers of the age and, in some cases, of all time. This cohort included Kauto Star, Denman and Big Buck's for Nicholls, and Hurricane Fly, Douvan, and Faugheen for Mullins. Alongside Walsh and Carberry, Barry Geraghty – whose grandfather bred the exceptional Golden Miller – began to make his mark in the saddle. Geraghty started out pony racing, but his first racecourse ride came in the autumn of 1996, when his father, Tucker, convinced Noel Meade to take a chance on the then teenager. A couple of months later, Geraghty had his first racecourse winner, when the Meade-trained Stagalier claimed a maiden hurdle at Down Royal. A conditional title followed and from there,

The late J.T. McNamara (in the light blue) enjoyed a glittering career as an amateur, winning 602 races before being paralysed in a fall at the Cheltenham Festival in 2013. He rode his 600th winner at Kilfeacle Point-to-Point in County Tipperary in January 2013. © *Healy Racing*.

Geraghty's star continued to rise. He achieved his first Cheltenham success on the Jessica Harrington-trained Moscow Flyer in the 2002 Arkle Challenge Trophy, before partnering the same horse to the Champion Chase in 2003. The same year, Geraghty rode the Jimmy Mangan-trained Monty's Pass to win the Grand National, before delivering for Tom Taaffe on Kicking King in the Cheltenham Gold Cup in 2005.[63] By then, Davy Russell had graduated from a successful career on the point-to-point circuit and was beginning a stellar professional career, which would include Gold Cup success on Lord Windermere in 2014 and two Aintree Grand National wins on Tiger Roll in 2018 and 2019.[64]

As Russell demonstrated, Irish point-to-point racing produced some highly talented riders in the 1990s and 2000s. Among them was Enda Bolger, a banks specialist who trained and rode the great Risk of Thunder on the point-to-point circuit, before leading him to a remarkable seven wins in the La Touche Cup at Punchestown. Owned by film star Sean Connery, Risk of Thunder was a high-profile horse whose flamboyant jumping style reinvigorated public interest in cross-country chasing. On retirement, he moved to J.P. and Noreen McManus' Martinstown Stud, where he became the companion of the great Istabraq.[65] Bolger and McManus partnered to produce one of the outstanding hunter chasers of the era, Elegant Lord, who won all eight of his point-to-point starts between 1992 and 1999 and scored thirteen wins under National Hunt Rules. This included the Foxhunter Chase at Cheltenham in 1996 and the Fox Hunters' Chase at Aintree three years later. It was on Elegant Lord that Bolger surpassed Willie Rooney's longstanding record for point-to-point winning rides, when he reached 402 wins at Ballingarry in County Tipperary in 1998.[66] Bolger's record was broken in 2006, by the late J.T. McNamara, who rode 602 point winners and was named champion amateur rider five times, sharing the accolade with Russell in 2002. McNamara was also highly successful in amateur races on the track, including at Punchestown and Cheltenham, and it was at the latter that he suffered a paralysing fall in 2013, before passing away three years later.[67] McNamara's dominance was matched and then surpassed by Derek O'Connor, the eleven-time champion amateur who to date has ridden over 1300 point-to-point winners and whose rivalry with Jamie Codd in the 2010s 'raised the profile of the sport and indeed the bar in terms of riding quality for generations to come'.[68]

Irish point-to-point meetings continued to function as the 'nursery' of Irish National Hunt racing in the 1990s and 2000s. The versatile Dorans Pride was among

Three-time Gold Cup winner, Best Mate, partnered by Tony Costello, jumping to victory in his maiden race at Belclare Point-to-Point in 1999. He was one of six Gold Cup winners sold by legendary handler, Tom Costello.
© *Healy Racing.*

the equine graduates from the circuit, having won a maiden for Michael Hourigan at Cashel in 1993 before embarking on a highly successful National Hunt career. Hourigan had another notable point-to-point success in Tipperary in 2001, when Beef or Salmon won at Clonmel under the then-amateur Russell. Beef or Salmon went on to win multiple Grade 1 National Hunt races in Ireland and was beloved by the Irish racegoing public.[69] Florida Pearl made a brief and impressive appearance on the circuit in 1996, when he won a maiden at Lismore in County Waterford for handler Tom Costello. After this success, the exciting prospect moved to Willie Mullins' yard and went on to become one of the finest chasers of his generation, winning sixteen of thirty-three starts, including four Hennessy Gold Cups, the RSA Chase and the King George VI Chase. Costello trained the Irish Grand National winner, Tartan Ace, in 1973, but he was best-known as a point-to-point handler and 'pinhooker'. He had an unmatched talent for buying and nurturing future chasing stars, paired with a strong business acumen, which gained him the confidence of his mostly English clientele. He sold a number of former pointers on to highly successful National Hunt careers, including the Cheltenham Gold Cup-winning horses Midnight Court (1978), The Thinker (1987), Cool Ground (1992), Imperial Call (1996) and Cool Dawn (1998).[70] The most famous of Costello's graduates, however, was Best Mate, who pulled up in his first appearance at Lismore, before winning a two-runner maiden point in Belclare, County Galway. He was impressive enough to catch the eye of trainer Henrietta Knight and her husband, former British National Hunt champion jockey, Terry Biddlecombe. He was sold to Jim Lewis and sent into training with Knight in Oxfordshire. Best Mate won fourteen of his twenty-two starts, winning the 2002 King George VI Chase and emulating Arkle by winning three consecutive Gold Cups between 2002 and 2004.[71]

'If all his horses disappeared it would be catastrophic for a great number of people'

Best Mate was not the only Cheltenham Gold Cup winner to emerge from the Irish point-to-point circuit in the 2000s. In 2005, the Adrian Maguire-trained Denman cantered to a twelve-length victory at Liscarroll, County Cork, before the powerful liver chestnut was sold to English owners, who placed him with trainer

(right) J.P. and Noreen McManus with Edward O'Grady and jockey Tommy Ryan after Bit of a Skite won the Irish Grand National in 1983. The McManus's support has been fundamental to the success of Irish National Hunt racing across decades.
© *Healy Racing*.
(below) Don't Push It and A.P. McCoy winning the 2010 Grand National. © *Healy Racing*.

Paul Nicholls. The same year, Imperial Commander made his point-to-point debut at Summerhill, County Meath, and was afterwards sold to an English syndicate and put into training with Nigel Twiston-Davies.[72] While Irish-bred horses continued to be sold into Britain, plenty of jumping talent remained in Irish ownership. That owed significantly to the influence of Limerick businessman, J.P. McManus, who moved from his father's earth-moving company into bookmaking, and parlayed his ability to take calculated risks into a multi-billion euro business empire. McManus began as a racehorse owner in the late 1970s, with the Cesarewitch-winning mare Cill Dara, before he purchased Martinstown Stud in Kilmallock with his wife Noreen in 1982. Since then, the green and gold-hooped McManus silks – chosen in homage to Limerick's South Liberties' GAA club – have been ubiquitous in Irish and British racing. While Flat racing has been the focus of other Irish magnates like John Magnier, McManus has remained devoted to National Hunt racing. With hundreds of horses in training, out of training, being pre-trained or now retired, his importance to the sport in Ireland and Britain cannot be overstated. As trainer Edward O'Grady put it: 'If all his horses disappeared it would be catastrophic for a great number of people'.[73] The great Istabraq stands foremost among McManus' list of winners, but he has enjoyed success with other highly-talented horses, including Binocular, Baracuda, Jezki, Buveur d'Air, Synchronised, Don't Push It and Minella Times. While McManus placed horses with 'an ever-widening group of trainers' across Ireland, he initially concentrated much of his British operation at Jackdaws Castle in Gloucestershire, where Jonjo O'Neill is the resident trainer.[74] McManus was similarly focused in his choice of jockeys for British races, employing A.P. McCoy on retainer from 2004 until his retirement in 2015, when he was succeeded by Barry Geraghty.[75]

McManus continues to be a titanic figure in the sport and recorded his 4,000th winner in January 2022, when Nico de Boinville rode the Nicky Henderson-trained Chantry House to victory in the Cotswold Chase at Cheltenham.[76] In recent years, however, he has been joined at the top table of National Hunt owners by colourful Ryanair CEO, Michael O'Leary, who established Gigginstown House Stud in 2000. With O'Leary's brother, Eddie, in charge of day-to-day operations, Gigginstown has enjoyed huge success and, with all of their horses trained domestically, has contributed significantly to the sport and the industry in Ireland. O'Leary was well-rewarded for his investment in 2006, when the Mouse Morris-trained point-to-point graduate, War of Attrition, delivered a first Cheltenham Gold Cup for his owner, winning by 2½ lengths from the Willie Mullins-trained Grand National winner, Hedgehunter. A successful partnership with Mullins made Gigginstown's maroon and white silks a fixture in winner's enclosures across Ireland and Britain in subsequent years. By 2016, 60 Gigginstown horses were stabled at Mullins' yard in Closutton, County Carlow, including Sir Des Champs, Valseur Lido, Don Poli and Apple's Jade. Gigginstown and Mullins parted company in 2016, however, after a disagreement over training (left) Michael O'Leary with Tiger Roll and Delta Work at the Cheltenham Festival in 2022. The success of O'Leary's Gigginstown Stud, which is managed by his brother Eddie, has further enhanced Ireland's reputation for excellence in National Hunt racing. © *Healy Racing*; (right) Gordon Elliott speaking to reporters after Envoi Allen's win in the Ballymore Novices' Hurdle at Cheltenham in 2020. © *Healy Racing*.

fees. The trainer told At The Races that O'Leary's horses would 'be very hard … to replace. Even with all the money in the world, lots of people try to buy horses like that, but sometimes they just happen … Whoever gets the horses will be a big challenge to me being champion trainer.'[77]

That 'whoever' was Meathman, Gordon Elliott, who had no connection to racing before he became an amateur rider as a teenager. Elliott took out a trainer's licence in 2006 and scored a remarkable success the following year, when 33/1 outsider Silver Birch won the Grand National; incredibly, Elliott had not trained a winner in Ireland at that point. Having underlined his value to O'Leary by winning the 2016 Cheltenham Gold Cup with Don Cossack, Elliott was entrusted with a number of the Gigginstown stars that had been removed from Mullins' yard. He made the most of this windfall of talent and was crowned top trainer at the Cheltenham Festival in 2017 and 2018. Elliott and Gigginstown enjoyed major successes elsewhere that year, with General Principle winning the Irish Grand National and the diminutive Tiger Roll winning the first of back-to-back Grand Nationals.[78] O'Leary shocked the racing world in May 2019, when he announced that he would step back from the sport, reducing the number of horses at Gigginstown over an extended period of five

CHAPTER SIX: 1994–2022

years.[79] O'Leary's departure was expected to be a significant blow, particularly to the industry in Ireland, but the decision to scale down operations appears to have been abandoned, with Gigginstown continuing to be a major presence in the sport and with the O'Learys renewing their partnership with Mullins in 2022.[80]

'It might be a little harder, the next thousand – but we'll give it a go!'

While the loss of his Gigginstown contingent in 2016 was a blow, Mullins could by then boast a stable full of exciting horses, including the Rich Ricci-owned Annie Power, Faugheen and Douvan and Graham Wylie's Yorkhill and Bellshill. This embarrassment of riches was no accident, being instead the result of Mullins' instinct, vision and ambition, his decades-long experience in the sport, his partnership with well-resourced owners and his talented team at Closutton. The son of trainer Paddy Mullins and Maureen (née Doran), who has been described as 'the first lady of Irish racing',[81] Willie Mullins is a member of one of Ireland's great racing dynasties. His brother Tony was a joint-champion jockey – most notably riding his father's famous charge, Dawn Run – and is now a successful trainer; his nephews Emmet (now emerging as a top National Hunt trainer) and Danny have also had success in the saddle; and his son, Patrick, is a multiple champion amateur. Willie Mullins was also a champion amateur, who had notable success on the track with Atha Cliath in the Aintree Fox Hunters' (1983); with Hazy Dawn (1982) and Macks Friendly (1984) in the National Hunt Chase; and with Wither or Which – a horse he also trained – in the Champion Bumper (1996) at Cheltenham.[82] After working as an assistant to his father and Jim Bolger, Mullins took out a trainer's licence in 1988 and claimed his first win with Silver Bachelor at Thurles in February of that year.[83]

Mullins made steady progress as a trainer in the 1990s and 2000s. Tourist Attraction provided him with a first Cheltenham Festival win in the 1995 Supreme Novices, but it was the Violet O'Leary-owned Florida Pearl who delivered his greatest early success, winning nine Grade 1 races.[84] Despite a disappointing season – compounded by the cancellation of the Cheltenham Festival after an outbreak of foot and mouth disease – Florida Pearl helped Mullins to his first Irish jump trainers' championship in 2000/1. Mullins would not repeat that feat until 2007/8, but he has topped the trainers' list in every season since.[85] In 2013, his increasing dominance saw him overhaul Aidan

Florida Pearl, pictured with John Costello, Gráinne Costello, Noel Brennan and Tony Costello, at Lismore Point-to-Point in County Waterford in 1996. A graduate of Tom Costello's yard, Florida Pearl would provide Willie Mullins with his greatest early success as a trainer. © *Healy Racing*.

O'Brien's seventeen-year record for the number of winners trained in an Irish season, with almost three months to spare.[86] To date, he has won the Irish Gold Cup thirteen times, the Punchestown Gold Cup six times, the Irish Champion Hurdle eight times, and the Irish Grand National twice.[87]

Mullins' record at the Cheltenham Festival – the pinnacle of National Hunt racing – is unparalleled. This has made him the trainer of choice for leading National Hunt owners, a circumstance that ensures a continuous supply of high-quality horses to Closutton. He saddled four winners in 2011 – including Quevega in the Mares' Hurdle and Hurricane Fly in the Champion Hurdle – to be crowned leading trainer for the first time. In 2022, Mullins registered ten winners, the highest-ever at a single Festival meeting and equal to the combined number of British-trained winners for that year. He claimed his eleventh leading trainer title at Cheltenham in 2024, finishing with nine winners and taking his Festival total to 103. His son Patrick provided him with a memorable century when combining with Jasmin de Vaux to win the Weatherbys'

CHAPTER SIX: 1994–2022

Willie Mullins pictured at Ballybrit after Poet Power won the bumper at the Galway Races Summer Festival in July 2017. © *Healy Racing*.

Champion Bumper.[88] After enduring a long wait, Mullins claimed the biggest prize in jump racing – the Gold Cup – in 2019, with Al Boum Photo. He has now won that race four times, with Al Boum Photo again claiming victory in 2021, followed by Gallopin Des Champs in 2023 and 2024. Both of those horses point to one of the crucial components of Mullins' success: France. Ever since Quevega and Mikael D'Haguenot made their mark at Prestbury Park in 2009, French-bred horses (scouted for Mullins by Pierre Boulard) have become a big part of the Closutton machine.[89]

Mullins achieved his 4,000th winner at Fairyhouse in January 2023, leaving him second only to Dermot Weld among Irish trainers across both codes. He reacted to that achievement with understated ambition, commenting that 'It might be a little harder, the next thousand – but we'll give it a go!'[90] He has already surpassed Weld, becoming the winning-most trainer in Irish racing history in May 2024, when Ballyburn won the Alanna Homes Novice Hurdle at the Punchestown Festival.[91] This was not Mullins' only history-making turn in 2023/4: his total of 39 Grade 1 winners was the highest total ever recorded in a single season and he also set the record for the highest number of winners – 257 – in an Irish jumps season. And as well as becoming Irish champion trainer for the seventeenth time in 2024, he claimed the British National Hunt title, making him the first Irish-based trainer since Vincent O'Brien in 1954 to do so.[92] At the same time, the success of Mullins' French imports and the extent to which he now dominates National Hunt racing raises some existential questions for the sport and the thoroughbred industry in Ireland. Indeed, while the number of Irish Grade 1 races has increased significantly in recent years, reaching 37 in 2023, Mullins' ascendance has resulted in a relative lack of competition on the track. This is no small concern, but it should not take anything away from his incredible achievements. He has built an empire on talent, experience, drive and determination, taking Irish jump racing to the promised land by repeatedly besting British trainers on their own turf. And he has done so while remaining extremely well-liked within the sport. Mullins is the pre-eminent figure in modern National Hunt racing and he will be remembered as one of, if not *the* greatest jumps trainer of all time.

'a big and major step so that racing would never have to worry about finances'

It is fair to say that Mullins' incredible success could not have been achieved without the rapid development of the industry in Ireland in the Celtic Tiger era. The speed and scale of change meant that by the turn of the millennium, the IHA was no longer fit for purpose. It was superseded – less than a decade after its foundation – by Horse Racing Ireland (HRI), which was established by the Horse and Greyhound Racing Act in 2001, and expanded upon its predecessor's role. HRI was the result of a direct intervention by the Fianna Fáil government, with Minister for Finance Charlie McCreevy offering a significant financial incentive to the Turf Club and INHS Committee, to abjure many of their traditional functions. At the Moyglare Stud dinner in 1999, McCreevy called on the two bodies to merge with the IHA, to ensure greater integration in the racing industry, telling them that 'If you are prepared to make a big and major step, the government is prepared to make a big and major step so that racing would never have to worry about finances'. McCreevy also reminded the two bodies that 'It may not always be that the Minister for Finance and the Minister for Agriculture Joe Walsh are so involved in Irish racing. Others in Dáil Éireann who become ministers may not be so favourably disposed towards racing, particularly those towards the left'.[93] McCreevy and Walsh demonstrated their favourable disposition toward racing in early 2000, approving funds for the construction of a national agricultural and equestrian centre at Punchestown. McCreevy and Walsh agreed to provide 100 per cent grant aid for construction, but did not ensure a full evaluation of the scheme before doing so. An initial budget of just under €7 million was approved, but plans for the centre quickly expanded, and the cost more than doubled, and McCreevy and Walsh drew criticism from some quarters. Punchestown faced further scrutiny in November 2001, when it was found to be on the brink of liquidation, despite receiving significant funding from the government. One year later, HRI proposed a rescue package and assumed responsibility for the day-to-day running of the course.[94]

The Punchestown episode brought some unwanted attention, but the Minister for Finance's unabashed support for horse racing presented the industry with a major opportunity. McCreevy's Moyglare proposition also very publicly placed pressure on the Turf Club and INHS Committee to act in the interests of the wider industry by merging with the IHA. Both bodies initially refused to surrender the majority of their administrative functions, however, and this inflamed tensions in the industry. In October 2000, breeders, owners, trainers, jockeys and stable staff staged a protest outside the Turf Club offices on the Curragh.[95] In the end, the Turf Club and INHS Committee successfully argued their case and resisted pressure to merge with the IHA, but they were compelled to accept a fundamental change to their role in order to survive and ensure funding for the industry. HRI assumed responsibility for many of the functions that had heretofore been provided by the Registry Office, including the registration of owners and horses, entries and declarations, and owners and trainers fees, which had previously been lodged on deposit into Turf Club accounts.[96] In return the government delivered on its promise: it was announced that prize money for National Hunt racing would be increased by forty per cent in the first five months of 2001, while government funding for the industry in the same year would double – rising to €36 million.[97] The HRI Act of 2001 subsequently established the Horse and Greyhound Racing Fund, to distribute funding on an 80:20 percentage ratio. Between 2001 and 2006, a total of €317 million was provided to the horse racing industry by the Horse and Greyhound Racing Fund, with a further €58 million allocated to HRI in 2007 and €61 million the following year.[98] HRI found a permanent home in this period, announcing plans for a €6 million purpose-built headquarters, adjacent to the Curragh, in March 2005.[99]

Increased investment led to industry expansion and horse racing and bloodstock assumed even greater value to the State. Once again, the Turf Club and INHS

Committee had to adapt to navigate the challenges of a changing landscape. In March 2006, the Stewards of the Turf Club broke with tradition in favour of transparency, allowing members of the media into an appeal inquiry for the first time. As Brian O'Connor reported in the *Irish Times*, 'Anyone imagining that skin and hair had been flying behind closed doors all those years would have been dreadfully disappointed.'[100] That hearing – to determine whether a mare named Snowfox deserved to be banned under the non-triers rule – was held in the Stewards' Room at the Curragh Racecourse. Those attending would have passed the charred remains of the Turf Club headquarters, which had been devastated by a fire over four months earlier, on 29 October 2005. The fire caused the collapse of the building's roof, destroying a newly constructed conference centre and Stewards' area. The extent of the damage was summed up by then Turf Club Chief Executive, Denis Egan, who commented that 'All we have left are the walls'. Press Officer Cliff Noone reported that they had 'lost a lot of paperwork and files', adding that 'Whatever is lost, is lost'. The majority of historical records – including minute books and form books – were not lost, however, as they were protected by a fire-proof safe.[101] Staff were relocated to the Turf Club rooms at the Curragh Racecourse until construction of new premises was completed in 2008.[102] During this period, the Turf Club pursued plans for a major redevelopment of the Curragh. The scheme had originated with the Aga Khan, who encouraged the Turf Club to invest in modernizing the home of Irish racing in his address to the Moyglare dinner in 2003, before gifting the Stand House Hotel to the regulatory body.[103] A new ring road was completed in May 2007, but subsequent phases of development were put on hold after the financial crash. Efforts to redevelop the course were resumed in 2015, as the Turf Club joined with private investors and HRI to form Curragh Racecourse Ltd. The cost of redevelopment was initially placed at €65 million but grew significantly in the course of construction, reaching €81 million by the time The Curragh reopened in 2019.[104]

Before boom turned to bust, bloodstock and racing's importance to the Irish economy was undeniable. By the mid-2000s, the Irish bloodstock industry was the third largest in the world. Alongside 390 thoroughbred stallions housed in 89 stud farms, Ireland was home to almost 17,000 broodmares and produced a total of 10,574 foals in 2003.[105] By 2007 this had grown to 12,633 foals, which was the highest number in Europe and the third-largest – behind the US and Australia – in the world.[106] That level of production was viewed by many as unsustainable. As always, the success of the Irish bloodstock was contingent upon the success of Irish horses internationally and on the success of Irish racing. Steps were taken to reduce the number of poor quality horses, including the regulatory bodies' introduction of performance warnings, or 'yellow cards'.[107] Even with ordinary horses on the card, attendances at race meetings across Ireland rose in the first years of the new millennium, reaching 1.3 million and generating €23 million in income in 2003. Higher gate receipts resulted in a combined turnover of €227.3 million for on-course bookmakers and the Tote in the same year, while the growing popularity of off-course betting was evident in a turnover of €1.9 billion – a 228 per cent increase on 1997.[108] The infrastructure at Irish racecourses was improved, with capital grants funding the €22 million Killanin Stand at Galway, and Ireland's only all-weather track at Dundalk.[109] Like the IHA before it, HRI recognized the potential of horse racing as a tourist attraction and collaborated with Fáilte Ireland (previously Bord Fáilte) and Tourism Ireland to market the 'unique horseracing experience' on offer in Ireland. The UK market was of particular importance to the racing tourism sector in Ireland; in the mid-2000s, Irish race meetings attracted an estimated 60,000 visitors from the UK and it was acknowledged that there was room for substantial growth in that market. In 2006, €1.5 million was allocated to promote racing tourism, with the Punchestown Festival identified as having the potential to attract an overseas market.[110] The growth in Irish racing continued until the financial crash in 2008, with attendances at Irish racecourses reaching an all-time high of 1.46 million in 2007, while on-course betting increased by 7.6 per cent on the previous year, off-course betting turnover exceeded €3.6 billion and Tote turnover improved significantly, 'helped by increased co-mingling from Britain and internationally through the At The Races [TV] Channel'.[111]

'satellite television threatens further incursions on our preserve, the rights of which must be jealously guarded'

Reflecting global trends, television assumed ever-greater importance to Irish sport in the 1980s and 90s, becoming an indispensable commercial and promotional asset to racing, as it was to Gaelic games, soccer and rugby. As the national broadcaster, RTÉ dominated the broadcasting of domestic sport until the 2000s, when the Irish media landscape began to change rapidly and radically. Since then, there has been 'a gradual leakage of national sports' away from RTÉ,[112] although it continues to broadcast major Irish race meetings. The racing community had been alive to the challenges that attended broadcasting by the late 1980s, with retiring Senior Steward J.F. Moorhead offering 'a word to the future', by telling INHS Committee members that

> Television has become a double-edged sword. On the one hand it is often made a pre-condition of high sponsorship while on the other it can have a decimating effect on attendances. The advent of satellite television threatens further incursions on our preserve, the rights of which must be jealously guarded. It must be made to contribute accordingly so that in the face of increasing commercialism National Hunt racing may retain its traditional identity and continue to flourish in the years ahead.[113]

It would be some years before the changing TV landscape impacted on Irish racing, but the BBC's struggle to retain sports broadcasting rights in the face of competition from satellite TV companies like BskyB and commercially funded public broadcast networks like Channel 4 and ITV, gave a glimpse of what was to come.[114] As Rouse notes, 'From the 1990s it became clear that the increase in the sums of money paid by broadcasters to secure sports rights was redrawing the relationship between television and sport'.[115] The statutory functions of HRI demonstrated how much the media landscape had changed by 2001. Whereas the IHA had allowed individual racecourses to negotiate broadcast or other media deals, HRI was empowered to negotiate broadcasting rights on behalf of Irish racecourses. This was a lesson learned by looking across the Irish Sea, as by then British racing had been transformed by the Racing Channel, which launched in 1995. The Racing Channel held the broadcast rights to the majority of British race meetings until 2002, when it was pushed out of the market by Go Racing, a consortium consisting of BskyB, Channel 4 and Arena Leisure. Go Racing entered the market with At The Races in 2002 and reduced the Racing Channel's share of the British market to ten small meetings. Trying to survive, the Racing Channel agreed a deal with HRI and the Association of Irish Racecourses (AIR) to broadcast Irish racing on a trial basis.[116] In 2003, however, the Racing Channel failed to renew its deal with Irish racecourses and ceased trading.

When subsequent negotiations with Go Racing broke down, HRI announced that it was considering the possibility of starting its own racing channel.[117] After a relaunch without the involvement of Channel 4 in 2004, however, At The Races began providing coverage of Irish racing, fulfilling a commitment in HRI's strategic plan.[118]

A healthy income from broadcasting has been transformative for Irish racecourses and has added a new dimension to racecourse ownership, but the arrival of pay-per-view TV has given rise to some existential questions in racing. In 2017, HRI – negotiating on behalf of AIR – made a controversial rights deal with Sports Information Services (SIS) and the Racecourse Media Group (RMG), an umbrella organization for the majority of British racecourses. Under the terms of the €40 million deal, SIS and RMG were given international and streaming rights, as well as picture rights for Licensed Betting Offices, but they were also given direct-to-home rights, which lessened public access to the sport by placing much of Irish racing behind a paywall on Racing TV. This provoked criticism from within the racing industry, with J.P. McManus saying he was 'saddened by the development', Michael O'Leary calling it 'a very retrograde step' and Willie Mullins saying he was 'very sorry' to see At The Races go.[119] The negotiation of broadcasting rights for Irish racing has also proven divisive in recent years. In 2023, HRI's role in negotiating media rights for Ireland's twenty-six racecourses was challenged by the executives of Limerick, Kilbeggan, Thurles, Sligo and Roscommon. Acting as United Irish Racecourses (UIR), the quintet of smaller tracks voted against a new five-year deal with SIS/RMG in May 2023, claiming that it favoured larger racecourses and that HRI's distribution of media rights income was unequal.[120] UIR agreed to the €47 million deal the following June, however, having been 'pleased by HRI's willingness to implement a proposed memorandum of understanding for racecourses during future … negotiations, and a review of media rights'.[121]

Satellite television was not the only major technological disruptor in the late twentieth and early twenty-first century. The growing popularity of the internet resulted in concerns that online betting would negatively impact the level of revenue available for the development of the horse racing industry. By 2000, online gambling in Western Europe and the US was worth €86 million, with one UK report predicting that the sector would be worth €11 billion by 2004. The first Irish bookmaker to use an online platform was O'Halloran's Bookmakers in Youghal, County Cork, while in the summer of 2000, Paddy Power provided an early example of its controversial approach to advertising, by inviting rogue trader Nick Leeson to launch paddypower.com.[122] A five per cent off-course levy was extended to online gambling, however, causing fears among bookmakers that they would lose business to overseas competitors. This prompted some to offer an equivalent discount on bets,[123] while in August 2000, O'Halloran's transferred its online operation, luvbet.com, to a subsidiary company in Malta.[124] The government moved to counteract the impact of overseas betting services by reducing the off-course levy from five to two per cent in 2002 and to one per cent four years later (a circumstance that endured until 2019, when the levy was returned to two per cent).[125]

The internet has revolutionized the betting industry and has proven to be highly lucrative for some Irish bookmakers, who expanded in both domestic and international markets. At the same time, it has also transformed the public's relationship with gambling, with the emergence of smartphones and other portable devices making access to betting sites much easier. This has prompted concerns about gambling addiction, with the Minister of State for Law Reform, James Browne, introducing the Gambling Regulation Bill in December 2022. Speaking to the Dáil at that time, Browne stated that 'The advent of the Internet has wrought considerable and rapid changes to gambling activity, with more ease of access to gambling than we could ever have thought possible … It is, therefore, vital … to have a robust regulatory framework with public safety as a cornerstone.'[126] Industry groups expressed concern over some of the provisions in the bill, including a blanket ban on the broadcast of betting advertisements between 5a.m. and 9:30p.m., which many believe will have significant implications for media coverage of racing.[127] The bill passed into law in October 2024 and – among other provisions – it established a new independent statutory body, the Gambling Regulatory Authority of Ireland (GRAI), which is responsible for licensing and the regulation of gambling services in Ireland.[128] The Irish Bookmakers' Association has welcomed the opportunity to work with the GRAI to tackle problem gambling, including on the implementation of a national self-exclusion register for customers.[129] The exponential growth and consolidation of a number of bookmakers has given rise to other potential challenges for the industry, however. This includes bookmakers' sponsorship of individual trainers and jockeys,[130] and their increasing presence as race sponsors. Indeed, the withdrawal of sponsors from other sectors has arguably led to an overreliance on the gambling industry, as horse racing now has a lot of 'eggs in the one sponsorship basket'.[131]

'Access. Influence. Word in the ear. Contacts Forged. Networks Strengthened'.

In 2007, the importance of media rights to the survival of smaller courses was underlined by HRI CEO Brian Kavanagh, who commented that a new and improved five-year deal between AIR and SIS, to supply pictures to betting shops across Britain and Ireland, would help to 'secure the financial future of a number of racecourses'. The importance of this development was underlined by the announcement in September 2007 that Tralee Racecourse would close, after the board decided to sell the property to developers. As Kavanagh concluded, 'The reality is that other Irish racecourses will find themselves in a similar situation … as the potential development value of their land increases'.[132] The sale of Tralee was a sign of the times, as rapid growth in the Irish construction sector underpinned the second act of the Celtic Tiger. A housing bubble was inflated by a proliferation of 'cheap money', with a growing number of available mortgage lenders and products in the market, and a more relaxed attitude towards repayments.[133] Racing's enduring connection to the political class took on a negative connotation in this period, as the 'Galway Tent' – an annual Fianna Fáil fundraiser at the Galway Festival – 'became a byword for corrupt relations between politicians, banks and property interests'. During the Celtic Tiger, Ireland's wealthiest property developers and construction company owners were 'conspicuously present' in Fianna Fáil's hospitality suite, where they socialized with government ministers and other prominent party members.[134] The nature of the hospitality enjoyed there was a matter of speculation and debate, including at the Oireachtas Banking Inquiry in 2015.[135] As journalist Miriam Lord concluded, however, the Tent was not a place where 'shadowy business schemes' were concocted, but was instead part of a wider political culture, with donors benefitting from 'Access. Influence. Word in the ear. Contacts Forged. Networks Strengthened.'[136]

In May 2008, Taoiseach Brian Cowen announced that the Galway Tent was folding with immediate effect.[137] The property bubble had burst in 2007, as demand fell and prices began to drop; this contributed to the contraction of the Irish economy and – amid a global recession – a deep crisis in the Irish banking sector, which was heavily exposed to a property market that had been financed by cheap and easily available credit.[138] As Ireland entered recession, the outlook for Irish horse racing was bleak and by 2009 'the full effects of the recession hit home in all areas of the industry'. Prize money dropped by 12 per cent on 2008, to €52.9 million, and attendances fell to 1.2 million. There was also a 10 per cent decline in the number of racehorse owners, many of whom could no longer afford to pay trainers' and other fees.[139] This had a serious, if unintended impact on horse welfare, as organizations like the ISPCA and the Irish Horse Welfare Trust were overwhelmed by cases of abandoned horses.[140] The impact on the bloodstock industry was seismic, as sales at public auctions plummeted to €67.5 million – a 62 per cent drop on sales of €179 million in 2007.[141] HRI reacted quickly, commissioning economist and former Fine Gael TD and Minister, Alan Dukes, to produce a report to remind the government that 'The bloodstock and racing industry has long been an important part of the Irish economy and also one of the distinguishing signs of "Irishness".'[142] The report cautioned against any reduction in government funding, which would be 'seriously counterproductive' and underlined the thoroughbred industry's importance as a direct employer of 15,000 people, primarily in rural areas. Job losses had already occurred by the time Dukes compiled his analysis,[143] and by 2010, HRI estimated that numbers working in the industry had fallen by 2,000.[144] Amid a financial crisis, however, the government was not dissuaded from cutting its support for the industry, which dropped from €76.3 million in 2008 to €57.3 million in 2011.[145]

'Breeding and racing activities in Ireland are the most prominent and important of any country on a *per capita* basis'

The financial crash damaged horse racing and breeding in Ireland but it amounted to a temporary setback, rather than a terminal blow. While the government was compelled to cut funding in the years succeeding the crash, it remained broadly supportive, with Minister for Agriculture Simon Coveney commissioning Indecon to conduct a review of certain aspects of the horse racing industry in 2012. The resulting report supported 'additional and sustainable funding' to develop the sector, while underlining the accompanying need for greater efficiency, effectiveness and value for money. To that end, recommendations included the slimming down and restructuring of the HRI Board and the 'streamlining of functions between HRI and the Turf Club'.[146] On foot of the Indecon report, HRI established a streamlining taskforce, with consultancy firm Smith and Williamson engaged to facilitate discussions on the steps that could be taken to achieve efficiencies in the industry. Alongside the 2012 Indecon report, Smith and Williamson's findings convinced Coveney to increase funding for the industry from a post-crash low of €43.4 million in 2014, to €54.4 million in 2015. These reports also formed the basis of the Horse Racing Ireland Act 2016. Among other things, the Act had significant implications for the racing regulatory bodies, as it protected their independence, clarified their functions and relationship with HRI, and defined mechanisms by which they could provide accountability to the State.[147] The increasing demands on the two bodies prompted a significant change in 2018, when the Turf Club and the INHS Committee established a limited company known as the Irish Horseracing Regulatory Board (IHRB), to carry out regulatory, integrity and licensing functions for horse racing in Ireland.[148]

The government support for the thoroughbred industry has contributed significantly to its recovery in recent years. A HRI-commissioned report by Deloitte placed the expenditure of the industry in 2016 at €1.84 billion. It also credited racing and breeding with providing 28,900 jobs through direct, indirect and associated employment, and concluded that 'Breeding and Racing activities in Ireland are the most prominent and important of any country on a per capita basis' with '50 thoroughbred horses per 10,000 of population'. The Deloitte report also highlighted the fact that Ireland's world-class bloodstock industry remains steeped in the tradition of the small breeder, with 92 per cent of 6,777 registered breeders in 2016 holding fewer than five thoroughbred broodmares. Horse racing also remained popular with the Irish public after the economic crash; in 2016, it was the second-best attended sport in Ireland, after Gaelic Games.[149] The Deloitte report demonstrated some encouraging trends in the industry, but it was produced in a challenging climate, following the UK's decision to leave the EU in 2016. At the report's launch, HRI chairperson Joe Keeling commented that the industries in the UK and Ireland 'are completely interlinked' and cautioned that a 'No Deal' Brexit would result in higher tariffs on bloodstock sales and a restriction on the free movement of horses.[150] Keeling's fears were well-founded, as the uncertainty caused by Brexit resulted in a decrease in bloodstock sales, from €175.6 million in 2017 to €161.5 million in 2018.[151] While the free movement of horses on the island of Ireland and from Northern Ireland to the EU was maintained, thoroughbreds travelling from Britain to the EU, or vice versa, are now required to obtain an export certificate in both jurisdictions. This has necessitated the creation of Border inspection posts and presented logistical problems for owners and trainers. The logistical issues caused by Brexit have not disappeared, but travel between the two jurisdictions was made easier in 2022, as the payment of a refundable VAT deposit on journeys between Ireland and Britain was dropped.[152]

Brexit also had a direct impact on funding for Irish racing, which was not increased in 2020, as the government adopted a 'wait and see' approach to the end of the EU–UK agreed transition period.[153] The uncertainty introduced by Brexit was followed by the 'devastating impact' of the Covid-19 pandemic.[154] In March 2020, the Cheltenham Festival became a flashpoint for debate, with the British government and the Jockey Club (Cheltenham's owners) facing criticism for allowing the famous meeting to go ahead.[155] Shortly after the meeting at Prestbury Park, Ireland and the UK entered into a period of lockdown that would last until the summer and was followed by restrictions on people mixing and further lockdowns. Overall turnover (derived from the Tote, betting-related charges and racecourse income) fell by over €14 million, to €58.8 million, in 2020. In addition, the number of race meetings fell, racecourse income decreased, and prize money was reduced.[156] Despite the damaging effects of Covid-19, horse racing recovered well. Full-year statistics for 2022 and 2023 showed significant gains in several areas, when compared to pre-pandemic figures from 2019. Bloodstock sales at public auction reached a record high of €215 million in 2022 and this increased to €231 million in 2023. Racehorse ownership increased in 2022 and while the overall number of owners fell marginally in 2023, the number of syndicates rose for the fifth year in a row. This reflects the growing popularity of group ownership, which – along with attracting UK and US-based owners – has been identified as a cornerstone of racing's future success. Owner retention rates and the number of horses in training increased in both 2022 and 2023. Amid an ongoing cost of living crisis, racecourse attendances have not met pre-pandemic levels, but on-course betting turnover for 2023 exceeded that for 2019 and 2022, with increases across the Tote, the betting ring and SP shops.[157]

The industry has withstood the macroeconomic shocks caused by Brexit and Covid-19 and it appears to be thriving once again. Horse racing must contend with other issues to ensure its future success, however. The use of banned substances is not a new challenge in horse racing, but regulatory authorities must maintain pace with scientific developments, and it is proving increasingly difficult to do so.

Internationally, the sport has been rocked by high-profile doping scandals in recent years. In March 2020, twenty-seven people in the US – including trainers and veterinarians – were charged in indictments for 'offences relating to the systematic and covert administration of illegal performance-enhancing drugs ("PEDs") to racehorses competing' in that country and abroad.[158] French racing has also been embroiled in scandal, with the arrest of high-profile trainers in December 2021 and police raids on thirty different equine establishments in March 2022.[159] Instances of PED use have been uncovered in Ireland, too,[160] and claims that doping is a serious problem in Irish racing have resurfaced in recent years. In 2021, Jim Bolger remarked that 'there will be a Lance Armstrong in Irish racing', in reference to the US cyclist who was stripped of seven Tour de France titles after he was discovered to have used PEDs.[161]

Responding to Bolger's remarks, the IHRB – which is responsible for Ireland's Equine Anti-Doping Programme (EADP) – stressed that 'there is a zero tolerance approach to doping in Irish racing'.[162] Bolger's comments nonetheless drew the government's attention to Irish racing, with the Oireachtas Joint Committee on Agriculture, Food and the Marine commissioning an independent review of the IHRB's anti-doping practices. This review was carried out by Dr Craig Suann, who found that the EADP matched 'international best practice in most respects and has made significant advances in recent years'. Suann's report was broadly supportive of the IHRB's approach to drug testing, but made a number of recommendations to enhance 'the robustness of the programme's processes, capabilities and capacities', including the provision of CCTV in racecourse sampling units and the greater traceability of thoroughbreds through all stages of life.[163]

There are other challenges facing the sport and the industry in Ireland. Questions have been asked about the sustainability of Irish racing's current financial model, which has been likened to 'trickle-down economics', with the most successful trainers accruing the vast majority of prize money. While the achievements of leading Irish trainers should be celebrated, the rise of a handful of big yards has made it very difficult for small trainers, who have far fewer resources and are often compelled to sell good horses. This has had a deflating effect on National Hunt racing, with the pressure on the 'small man' leading some to shift their focus to the Flat.[164] In early 2023, the Oireachtas Public Accounts Committee recommended that HRI include a detailed breakdown of the allocation of prize money in its annual report going forward.[165] In the future, HRI may have to change tack and divert more government funding away from prize money, into the promotion of the sport and rider and animal welfare schemes. The welfare of riders has long been a concern for the racing authorities and there has been a growing emphasis on their physical and mental well-being in recent years. Steps have been taken to tackle unhealthy weight-making practices that can have major physical effects, including malnutrition, dehydration and poor bone health. HRI sought to address this issue by establishing a cross-industry Jockey Supports Working Group to make recommendations. In December 2021, it was announced that minimum riding weights in both codes would be increased, with the minimum for National Hunt rising by four lbs, to 10st. A general 2lb increase introduced during the Covid-19 pandemic was also retained, as it was found to be beneficial in reducing instances where overweight is carried. The Working Group recommended a 'holistic approach' to the issue of rider well-being, and HRI have committed to exploring ways to improve racecourse facilities for jockeys and expand non-race day supports.[166] Weigh-room saunas, which were provided by racecourses to help jockeys lose weight, were permanently closed in May 2022.[167]

Concern over the welfare of racehorses presents another challenge, with a growth in public awareness around the issue placing the sport and the wider industry under greater scrutiny. Fatalities in competition continue to draw criticism from animal rights' campaigners, while debates are ongoing over the use of the whip. Beyond these enduring issues, the sport has had to deal with some controversial episodes in recent years. In 2021, the public perception of horse racing was damaged after a photograph emerged showing trainer Gordon Elliott sitting on top of a dead horse while speaking on his phone. Elliott confirmed the picture was genuine, cooperated with the IHRB investigation and issued a statement in which he 'apologized profoundly for any offence' caused.[168] In March 2021, the IHRB banned Elliott from the sport for twelve months, with six months suspended, and this sanction was reciprocated by the BHA.[169] In delivering its decision on the case, the IHRB's Referrals Committee condemned Elliott's actions in the strongest terms, as showing 'the most appalling bad taste' and demonstrating 'a complete absence of respect'.[170] At the same time, the IHRB emphasized that an unannounced stable inspection of Elliott's yard had produced 'no concerns about the welfare of the horses in his care, as has been the case during any other inspection … carried out at his premises'.[171] There have, however, been cases involving other trainers which suggest that expected standards of care are not uniformly adhered to in the industry.[172] As awareness around animal welfare continues to grow, the racing industry must continue to work to convince the public that it has the best interests of horses at heart. The publication by HRI of *Principles of animal welfare in Ireland's horse racing industry* in 2022 was one step in that direction.[173]

Beyond integrity and welfare, horse racing faces a major existential challenge from climate change. An absence of rain during the National Hunt season has already impacted on the sport. In 2019, quick ground conditions delayed the return of some leading jumpers and caused a reduction in the size of entries. With one eye on the April festival, Punchestown spokesman Richie Galway commented that 'It has been a very, very strange season. I can't say there's been a dramatic fall in the number of runners: it's the quality and type of runners.'[174] Strange seasons are projected to become more common, and the thoroughbred industry must respond to ensure the survival of the sport in its current form. HRI has made progress in improving the sector's environmental sustainability. With the need for watering racing surfaces likely to increase, racecourses are prioritizing water conservation by using on-site reservoirs to capture rainwater, with many such schemes part-funded by HRI. Working from a 2009 baseline, furthermore, the thoroughbred industry met public sector targets by reducing energy consumption by 33 per cent by 2020. Looking to the future, HRI have committed to achieving a 51 per cent reduction in carbon emissions by 2030, based on a 2016/18 baseline. A transition to low-carbon biofuel or electric vehicles at racecourses is already underway, and initiatives have also been introduced to reduce waste and promote biodiversity.[175]

The industry's approach to climate change demonstrates its capacity to adapt quickly and at scale. It is that capacity for change that has underpinned a revolution in the industry in Ireland over the past thirty years. The end of the Racing Board and the creation of the IHA coincided with the dawn of the Celtic Tiger and investment in the thoroughbred industry resulted in its rapid expansion and unprecedented success. Indeed, despite the enormous challenges presented by the financial crash, Brexit and Covid-19, the thoroughbred industry has remained strong, providing 30,000 people with full-time employment and contributing €2.46 billion to the Irish economy in 2023.[176] Horse racing is an essential component of that industry, but the Irish people's enduring passion for the sport cannot be explained purely in terms of economic value, annual turnover, or profit.

Modern sport is a commercial concern, but it is driven by a primal impulse. In Ireland, to race a horse is to be woven into the very fabric of the island's long history. It is to become part of a story that is far bigger than the present moment. After all, it is on the track – with 'riders upon the galloping horses' – that dreams are realized and history is made. In the future, when the story of Irish National Hunt and point-to-point racing is rewritten to more fully incorporate the countless achievements of the past decade, it will include the names of influential owners like J.P. McManus, Michael O'Leary and Rich Ricci, alongside those of noted trainers like Willie Mullins, Gordon Elliott and Henry de Bromhead. It will recall the exploits on horseback of professionals like A.P. McCoy, Ruby Walsh, Barry Geraghty, Paul Carberry, Davy Russell, Paul Townend and Rachael Blackmore, and of amateur riders like Derek O'Connor, Jamie Codd, Nina Carberry, Katie Walsh, Patrick Mullins and the late J.T. McNamara. It will trace the careers of Irish-bred stars like Hurricane Fly and Annie Power, and French imports like Quevega and the two-time Cheltenham Gold Cup winners, Al Boum Photo and Galopin des Champs. It will tell the story of Faugheen, who became the first point-to-point graduate to win the Champion Hurdle; of Flooring Porter, who delivered on the dreams of a small-town syndicate; and of Tiger Roll, the pint-sized star who won the Grand National in 2018 and 2019, and who, like Arkle, Dawn Run and Danoli before him, transcended the sport to become a national hero. These names have already joined jump racing's pantheon of greats and, in many cases, stand foremost among its ranks.

As for the future, it remains unknowable. On the evidence of the past, however, there is every reason to expect that horse racing will stand at the centre of the Irish sporting calendar for a long time to come. Ireland's passion for horses and for racing has run through centuries and across political, religious, social, and economic divides. It has been given expression in song and poetry, it has been immortalized in paint and print and it remains central to the lives, livelihoods and culture of Irish people today. There is something spiritual about the Irish connection to horses and there is something magical about the sport that they make possible. And while horse racing is known as the 'sport of kings', jump racing is also the sport of fairy tales, where the 'small man' still has an outside chance. It remains just as it was over one hundred years ago, when Yeats recalled the excitement of a day's racing at Ballybrit and marvelled that 'There where the course is/ Delight makes all of the one mind.'

A modern race meeting: crowds at Killarney in 2019. © *Healy Racing*.

Endword

Martin P. O'Donnell

Senior Steward of the Irish National Hunt
Steeplechase Committee, 2020-3

As the 150th anniversary of the INHSC approached, I believed that it was important to mark that milestone in a manner that would objectively acknowledge and reflect on the development of the Committee over that time.

My initial thoughts around commissioning a book were met with enthusiasm and encouragement from both Emeritus Professor Fergus A. D'Arcy and Professor Paul Rouse, who provided invaluable advice on how best to proceed. It was thanks to them that we were put in contact with Dr Frances Nolan, who as the author of this book, has brought energy, insight, impartiality and academic rigour to the project.

Thanks to Frances's excellent work, we now have a book that guides us through a fascinating time in the development of Ireland as a nation, and demonstrates the accessibility, inclusivity and egalitarianism of National Hunt and point-to-point racing, which continue to make such a valuable contribution to community life throughout the 32 counties.

I hope the book will be a fitting testament to the past 150 years of hard work and commitment by so many, whose individual and collective efforts shaped the future of National Hunt and point-to-point racing. Successive generations have guided the sport with a steady hand, in good times and bad, to ensure its continued development and relevance in modern Ireland.

The value and importance of volunteerism to the success of the INHSC cannot

Former INHS Senior Steward Martin O'Donnell (centre), pictured with INHS Stewards David McCorkell (left) and Philip McLernon.

be overstated; it has been the lifeblood of the organization, which has benefitted from the dedication and commitment of so many members, across so many years. It is a privilege and a pleasure to say that we are still in receipt of much enthusiastic and invaluable support from our Members, whose knowledge and experience of the equine world is shared with such generosity.

There are so many contributors who deserve our thanks and acknowledgement. Foremost among them is Dr Frances Nolan, who has been such a pleasure to work with and who has done such justice to the subject.

Sincere thanks also to Four Courts Press, who have been so co-operative and professional.

I must also acknowledge the unwavering support which the development of this book received from my fellow INHSC Directors, David McCorkell and Philip McLernon; and the subsequent support of the Board of the newly established INHSC CLG, under the stewardship of Jill Farrell, Nicholas Lambert, Tom McDonogh,

Richard Rohan and Robert Steele. Particular thanks to Victor Connolly who took such an active interest in this project and made many valuable contributions.

Thanks also to Paul Murtagh, Registrar of the INHSC, and to his core team of Denise O'Neill and Ray Bergin, for the dedication they bring to all aspects of their work on behalf of National Hunt and point-to-pointing racing.

Over 150 years, there have been many Senior Stewards, Stewards, Registrars of the INHSC and Members of the National Hunt Committee – each one deserves our thanks for their commitment and contribution to the development of the sport, which is so important to us all.

Of course, there would not be any racing were it not for the breeders, owners, trainers and jockeys, and we owe them a debt of gratitude for all they contribute to making National Hunt racing a fabulous spectacle and sport, which continues to attract so much support throughout the country. We are equally indebted to the hunting community, who organize point-to-point meetings on a voluntary basis, and who play such an important role in National Hunt racing.

We must also acknowledge the support which the INHSC has received and continues to receive from successive Ministers for Agriculture, Officials of the Department of Agriculture and Horse Racing Ireland.

Our most heartfelt thanks to our Members, who over successive generations have fostered and overseen the development of National Hunt racing in Ireland, and on whose energy, vision and commitment our organisation is built.

Final thanks is to you, the reader. We hope you have enjoyed this book and that it has earned a place on your bookshelf as a fitting record of the National Hunt racing story so far. It can only be hoped that it will, in time, be joined by a companion publication to mark the next milestone in the development of the sport we all value so much.

'Baldoyle as our artist saw it': a cartoon from the periodical *Irish Life*, depicting a bumper crowd at the north Dublin course in March 1919.

Notes

Introduction

1. James Kelly, *Sport in Ireland, 1600–1840* (Dublin, 2014), pp 101–23; Paul Rouse, *Sport and Ireland: a history* (Oxford, 2015), pp 103–7.
2. Anne Holland, *Horse racing in Britain and Ireland* (London, 2014), p. 17.
3. Rouse, *Sport and Ireland*, p. 1.
4. Arthur Young, *A tour in Ireland, with general observations on the present state of that kingdom in 1776–78* (London, 1897), p. 184.
5. Brendan Behan, *The Hostage* (London, 1958).
6. John Welcome, *Irish horse-racing: an illustrated history* (London, 1982), pp 6–7.
7. Dáithí Ó hÓgáin, 'An capall i mBéaloideaas na hÉireann', *Béaloideas/The Journal of the Folklore of Ireland Society* (Iml. 47/49 1977–1979), pp 199–243; see also Stuart Nassau-Lane, 'The horse in nineteenth-century Ireland: a socio-economic study' (PhD, Maynooth University, 2006).
8. R.F. Foster, *W.B. Yeats: a life* (Oxford, 1998), p. 435.
9. W.B. Yeats, 'At Galway Races' (1908) in *The collected poems of W.B. Yeats*, ed. by Richard J. Finneran (rev. 2nd ed., New York, 1996), p. 97.

Chapter One: 1752–1869

1. Finbar McCormick, 'The horse in early Ireland', *Anthropozoologica*, 42:1 (2007), pp 86, 90; S.J. Watson, *Between the flags: a history of Irish steeplechasing* (Dublin, 1969), pp 1–3; Welcome, *Irish horse-racing*, p. 2.
2. Rouse, *Sport and Ireland*, p. 46.
3. Rouse, *Sport and Ireland*, p. 63.
4. James Kelly, *Sport in Ireland, 1600–1840* (Dublin, 2014), p. 27.
5. Kelly, *Sport*, p. 31; Rouse, *Sport and Ireland*, p. 63.
6. Kelly, *Sport*, p. 31.
7. Welcome, *Irish horse-racing*, p. 5.
8. Rouse, *Sport and Ireland*, p. 64.
9. William Temple, *Miscellanea* (5th ed., London, 1697), pp 131–4; Kelly, *Sport*, p. 32.
10. Kelly, *Sport*, p. 32; Rouse, *Sport and Ireland*, p. 64.
11. Rouse, *Sport and Ireland*, p.65; Fergus D'arcy, *Horses, lords and racing men: the Turf Club, 1790–1990* (The Curragh, 1991), p. 16; Kelly, *Sport*, p. 33.
12. Watson, *Between the flags*, p. 5.
13. Kelly, *Sport*, p. 29.
14. Kelly, *Sport*, p. 34; see also C.I. McGrath, 'The penal laws: origins, purpose, enforcement and impact' in Kevin Costello and Niamh Howlin (eds), *Law and religion in Ireland, 1700–1970* (London, 2021), p. 20.
15. Welcome, *Irish horse-racing*, pp 6–7.
16. *Dublin Intelligence*, 2 and 12 Aug. 1712. A mantua was a type of gown, fashionable at the time.
17. 13 Geo. II, c. 38, quoted in D'arcy, *Horses*, p. 20.
18. *Freeman's Journal*, 12–15 Sept. 1789.
19. Ó hÓgáin, 'An capall i mBéaloideaas na hÉireann', pp 236–7.
20. Quoted in Ó hÓgáin, 'An capall', p. 225.
21. Michael F. Cox, *Notes of the history of the Irish horse* (Dublin, 1897), p. 109; Ó hÓgáin, 'An capall', pp 236–7.
22. *Dublin Intelligence*, 5 Aug. 1731; Kelly, *Sport*, p. 37.
23. Kelly, *Sport*, pp 37–8, 42–3; James Kelly, 'Sport and recreation in the eighteenth and nineteenth centuries' in James Kelly (ed.), *The Cambridge history of Ireland: vol. III: 1730–1880* (4 vols, Cambridge, 2020), pp 491–2.
24. Rouse, *Sport and Ireland*, p. 66; Maighréad Ní Mhurchadha, '"Two hundred men at tennis": sport in north Dublin, 1600–1760', *Dublin Historical Record* (Spring, 2008), p. 89; Kelly, *Sport*, pp 35–7.
25. Rouse, *Sport and Ireland*, p. 6.
26. Martyn J. Powell, 'Hunting clubs and societies' in James Kelly and Martyn J. Powell (eds), *Clubs and societies in eighteenth-century Ireland* (Dublin, 2010), pp 392–408.
27. Rouse, *Sport and Ireland*, pp 66–7.
28. D'arcy, *Horses*, pp 3, 27.
29. D'arcy, *Horses*, pp 12, 31–3.
30. Maurice Moore, *An Irish gentleman, George Henry Moore* (London, 1913), pp 87–8.
31. Heber's *Racing Calendar*, 9 Aug. 1775, quoted in Watson, *Between the flags*, pp 16–17.
32. Watson, *Between the flags*, pp 27–8.
33. Rouse, *Sport and Ireland*, p. 103.
34. D'arcy, *Horses*, pp 36–7, 182.
35. D'arcy, *Horses*, pp 19–22.
36. PRONI D3030/815, Lord Downshire to Lord Castlereagh, 7 June 1799.
37. D'arcy, *Horses*, pp 42–3; Thomas Bartlett, 'Ireland during the Revolutionary and Napoleonic Wars, 1791–1815' in Kelly (ed.), *Cambridge history of Ireland, Vol. III*, p. 77.
38. Rouse, *Sport and Ireland*, p. 103.

39 Watson, *Between the flags*, p. 34; Welcome, *Irish horse-racing*, p. 15.
40 D'arcy, *Horses*, pp 28, 37.
41 NAI, SPOI, SOC, 1562/83, Michael Aylmer to James Trail, 1 Mar. 1807, quoted in D'arcy, *Horses*, p. 24.
42 William Williams, *Creating Irish tourism: the first century, 1750–1850* (London, 2010), p. 14.
43 Conor McNamara, '"This wretched people": the famine of 1822 in the West of Ireland' in McNamara and Carla King (eds), *The West of Ireland: new perspectives on the nineteenth century* (Dublin, 2011), p. 33.
44 McNamara, '"This wretched people"', pp 13–14.
45 D'arcy, *Horses*, p. 343.
46 D'arcy, *Horses*, p. 82.
47 Watson, *Between the flags*, pp 62–3.
48 Watson, *Between the flags*, pp 44–5.
49 Watson, *Between the flags*, p. 45.
50 *The Sporting Magazine*, 6 Feb. 1833.
51 Brian Griffin, '"The more sport the merrier, say we": sport in Ireland during the Great Famine', *Irish Economic and Social History*, 45:1 (2018), p. 94.
52 Watson, *Between the flags*, pp 43, 48.
53 Johann Georg Kohl, *Travels in Ireland* (1844), p. 196, quoted in Rouse, *Sport and Ireland*, pp 104–5.
54 George Henry Moore to Louisa Moore, 6 May 1846.
55 Griffin, '"The more sport the merrier, say we"', p. 94.
56 *Kerry Examiner*, 23 Apr. 1846, quoted in Griffin, '"The more sport the merrier, say we"', p. 94.
57 Watson, *Between the flags*, pp 57, 63.
58 Raymond Smith and Con Costello, *Peerless Punchestown: 150 years of glorious tradition* (Dublin, 2000), p. 21.
59 *Leinster Express*, Apr. 1850, quoted in Smith and Costello, *Peerless Punchestown*, p. 21.
60 Watson, *Between the flags*, p. 63.
61 *Leinster Express*, April 1860, quoted in Smith and Costello, *Peerless Punchestown*, pp 23–4.
62 Queen Victoria to the Prince of Wales, 9 Mar. 1868, in George Earle Buckle (ed.), *The letters of Queen Victoria, volume 4: 1862–1869* (9 vols, London, 1926), iv, p. 514.
63 Prince of Wales to Queen Victoria, 11 Mar. 1868, in Buckle (ed.), *The letters of Queen Victoria, volume 4*, iv, p. 515.
64 Watson, *Between the flags*, p. 79.
65 *Irish Times*, 17 Apr. 1868.
66 D'arcy, *Horses*, pp 192–5.
67 *Irish Times*, 17 Apr. 1868.
68 D'arcy, *Horses*, pp 139–48.
69 *Irish Sportsman and Farmer*, 1 Feb. 1873.
70 D'arcy, *Horses*, p. 148.
71 Watson, *Between the flags*, pp 67–70.
72 Arthur Coventry and A.E.T. Watson, *Racing and steeplechasing* (1887), p. 282.
73 INHSC Minute Book, vol. i, f. 2, n.d.
74 INHSC Minute Books, vol, i, ff 2–3, n.d.
75 INHSC Minute Book, vol. i, f. 4, 21 May 1869.
76 INHSC Minute Books, vol. i, f. 5, 18 May 1869.
77 *Irish Sportsman and Farmer*, 19 Feb. 1870.
78 D'arcy, *Horses*, pp 194–5.
79 *Munster Express*, 22 May 1869.
80 *Freeman's Journal*, 4 Aug. 1869.
81 *Connaught Telegraph*, 25 Aug. 1869.
82 *Freeman's Journal*, 10 Aug. 1869.
83 *Irish Sportsman and Farmer*, 9 Apr. 1870.

Panel: Lord Drogheda and the first IHNS Committee

1 Desmond McCabe, 'Moore, Henry Francis Seymour', *DIB*.
2 INHSC Minutes, vol. i, f. 2, n.d.
3 Tom Hunt, *Sport and society in Victorian Ireland: the case of Westmeath* (Cork, 2007), p. 52.
4 INHSC Minutes, vol. i, f. 2, n.d.

Chapter Two: 1870–1921

1 *Irish Sportsman and Farmer*, 19 Feb. 1870.
2 *Irish Times*, 18 Apr. 1870.
3 *The Field*, 11 Apr. 1874.
4 Watson, *Between the flags*, p. 89; *The Irish Sportsman and Farmer*, 10 Jan. 1874.
5 INHSC Minutes, vol. i, ff 7, 15, 15 Nov. and 2 Dec. 1870.
6 INHSC Minutes, vol. i, ff 11–12, 1 Dec. 1870.
7 INHSC Minutes, vol. i, f. 31, 1 Feb. 1871.
8 Watson, *Between the flags*, pp 113–14.
9 INHSC Minutes, vol. i, f. 61, 13 Dec. 1871.
10 *Irish Times*, 3 Jan. 1876.
11 *Irish Times*, 14 Oct. 1874.
12 Guy St John Williams and Francis P.M. Hyland, *Jameson Irish Grand National: a history of Ireland's premier steeplechase* (Dublin, 1995), pp 19–22, 26–7, 254.
13 Guy St John Williams and Francis P.M. Hyland, *Who was who in Irish racing* (Monasterevin, 2020), p. 255.
14 Williams and Hyland, *Who was who*, p. 255.
15 *Irish Times*, 6 July 1878.
16 INHSC Minutes, vol. i, f. 71, 14 May 1875.
17 *Irish Times*, 14 Aug. 1888.
18 INHSC Minutes, vol. i, f. 288, 26 Aug. 1897.
19 *Irish Times*, 18 Oct. 1877.
20 INHSC Minutes, i, f. 252, 7 Nov. 1892.
21 INHSC Minutes, i, f. 247, 3 Oct. 1892.
22 INHSC Minutes, i, f. 252, 7 Nov. 1892.

23 *Clare Champion*, 1954.
24 *Clare Champion*, 1954.
25 INHSC Minutes, i, f. 256, 1 Mar. 1893.
26 Harry R. Sargent, *Thoughts upon sport: a work dealing shortly with each branch of sport: to which are added, a complete history of the Curraghmore Hunt and memoirs of notable sportsmen* (London, 1895), p. 74.
27 INHSC Minutes, i, 233, 5 Jan. 1893.
28 *Racing Calendar* (1900); Watson, *Between the flags*, pp 132–3.
29 Harry Sargent, quoted in Derek Birley, *Sport and the making of Britain* (Manchester, 1993), p. 299.
30 Birley, *Sport and the making of Britain*, p. 299; Watson, *Between the flags*, p. 103.
31 *Bell's Life*, quoted in *Irish Times*, 6 Mar. 1882.
32 Donnacha Seán Lucey, 'Land and popular politics in County Kerry' (PhD, Maynooth University, 2007), p. 131.
33 *Freeman's Journal*, 23 Dec. 1881.
34 *Irish Times*, quoted in Watson, p. 106.
35 Sargent, *Thoughts upon sport*, p. 75.
36 *Irish Times* quoted in Watson, p. 105.
37 Sargent, *Thoughts upon sport*, p. 75.
38 St Lawrence, quoted in Watson, *Between the flags*, p. 116.
39 INHSC Minutes, vol. i, f. 220, 3 Jan. 1890.
40 House of Lords Debates, 19 July 1898, vol. 62 cc 258–83.
41 Watson, *Between the flags*, p. 130; Paul Rouse, 'Parkinson, James Joseph ("J.J.")', *DIB*.
42 *Irish Sportsman and Farmer*, 6 Sept. 1890, quoted in D'arcy, *Horses*, p. 202.
43 D'arcy, *Horses*, p. 204.
44 INHSC Minutes, vol. i, ff 318–19, 6 May 1904.
45 D'arcy, *Horses*, p. 219.
46 INHSC Minutes, vol. i, f .326, 25 Aug. 1905; f. 329, 30 Aug. 1906.
47 INHSC Minutes, vol. i, f. 318, 6 May 1904.
48 D'arcy, *Horses*, p. 229.
49 William Murphy, 'Croker, Richard ("Boss")', *DIB*.
50 John Cottrell and Marcus Armytage, *A–Z of the Grand National: the official guide to the world's most famous steeplechase* (Newbury, 2008), pp 24, 35, 36, 142, 266, 460.
51 J.M. Richardson and F. Mason, *Gentlemen riders: past and present* (London, 1909), pp 211–14.
52 *The Nationalist and Leinster Times*, 29 Apr. 1893.
53 *The Nationalist and Leinster Times*, 3 Apr. 1897; Watson, *Between the flags*, p. 124.
54 Desmond McCabe, 'Moore, Henry Francis Seymour', *DIB*; INHSC Minutes, vol. i, f. 246, 2 Aug. 1892.
55 INHSC Minutes, vol. i, f. 267, 30 Aug. 1894.

56 *Irish Life*, 9 Aug. 1912.
57 Quoted in Smyth and Costello, *Peerless Punchestown*, p. 44.
58 *Irish Times*, 30 Apr. 1904.
59 *Irish Times*, 30 Apr. 1904.
60 INHSC Minutes, vol. i, f. 340, 21 May [1910].
61 *Irish Times*, 15 July 1911; *Freeman's Journal*, 1 Jan. 1912.
62 *Irish Life*, 2 Aug. 1912.
63 *Irish Life*, 23 Aug. 1912.
64 Rouse, 'Parkinson', *DIB*; Watson, *Between the flags*, p. 155.
65 Quoted in Watson, *Between the flags*, p. 155.
66 INHSC Minutes, vol. i, 28 Aug. 1914. The Turf Club donated 500 *sovs*. See D'arcy, *Horses*, p. 250.
67 Watson, *Between the flags*, p. 158.
68 *Irish Field*, Dec. 1915.
69 Watson, *Between the flags*, p. 162.
70 D'arcy, *Horses*, p. 248.
71 INHSC Minutes, vol. i, f. 352, 3 Jan. 1916.
72 D'arcy, *Horses*, pp 244–5.
73 *Irish Life*, 25 Aug. 1916.
74 D'arcy, *Horses*, pp 245–6.
75 *Irish Life*, 25 Aug. 1916.
76 D'arcy, *Horses*, p. 249.
77 INHSC Minutes, vol. i, f. 353, 14 Apr. 1916.
78 *Irish Field*, 13 May 1916.
79 *Irish Times*, 10 Mar. 1916.
80 Mark Bence-Jones, *Twilight of the Ascendancy* (London, 1987), p. 187.
81 David Murphy, 'Mahon, Sir Bryan Thomas', *DIB*; Watson, *Between the flags*, p. 134.
82 *Irish Field*, 6 & 13 May 1916; D'arcy, *Horses*, pp 251–2.
83 D'arcy, *Horses*, p. 252.
84 University of Galway, LA4/3, Minute Books of Galway Urban District Council, 3 May 1917.
85 *Irish Field*, 19 Dec. 1914; 15 Jan. 1916; 22 Jan. 1916.
86 Watson, *Between the flags*, p. 162.
87 D'arcy, *Horses*, p. 253; Watson, *Between the flags*, p. 162.
88 *Irish Field*, 27 Apr. 1918.
89 D'arcy, *Horses*, p. 253.
90 INHSC Minutes, vol. i, f. 362, 19 Mar. 1919.
91 Watson, *Between the flags*, p. 170.
92 Watson, *Between the flags*, pp 186–7; Cottrell and Armytage, *A–Z of the Grand National*, pp 461–2; Guy St John Williams, *Winner all right: 100 years of Irish racing and breeding* (Kildare, 1999), p. 42.
93 D'arcy, *Horses*, p. 255.
94 INHSC Minutes, vol. i, f. 373, 16 Apr. [1921].
95 Quoted in Watson, *Between the flags*, p. 177.

Panel: The Brothers Beasley

1 Watson, *Between the flags*, pp 110–11.

2 William Murphy, 'Beasley, Thomas (Tommy)', *DIB*.
3 *Irish Times*, 9 Apr. 1910.
4 Murphy, 'Beasley, Thomas (Tommy)', *DIB*.
5 *Irish Times*, 10 May 1892.
6 *Leinster Leader*, 28 Oct. 1939.
7 *Irish Independent*, 20 Jan. 2008.

Panel: 'The Immortal Manifesto'

1 Jim Shanahan, 'Moore, Garrett ("Garry")', *DIB*.
2 Reg Green, *A race apart: the history of the Grand National* (London, 1988), pp 130–53.
3 See 'Manifesto' by John Jacques of London (1911); Red Tape Whisky advert in *The Sphere*, 4 Mar. 1922; Susan McHugh, *Animal stories: narrating across species lines* (Minneapolis, 2011), p. 99.

Chapter Three: 1922–1945

1 Anne Dolan, 'The Irish Free State, 1922–1939' in Thomas Bartlett (ed.), *The Cambridge history of Ireland: volume IV: 1880–present* (Cambridge, 2020), p. 324.
2 D'arcy, *Horses*, p. 258.
3 INHSC Minutes, vol. i, f. 377, 2 [Sept.?] 1922.
4 D'arcy, *Horses*, p. 243.
5 Watson, *Between the flags*, p. 186; Rouse, 'Parkinson', *DIB*.
6 *Irish Life*, Apr. 1923.
7 *Kildare Observer*, 14 Apr. 1923.
8 *Cork Examiner*, 3 Apr. 1923.
9 *Leinster Leader*, 28 Oct. 1939.
10 D'arcy, *Horses*, p. 236.
11 INHSC Minutes, vol.i, f. 381, 19 Nov. [1922]
12 Sir William Goulding, 24 Apr. 1923, quoted in Watson, *Between the flags*, p. 190.
13 Dáil Éireann debate, Friday, 2 Mar. 1923.
14 *Report of the Inter-departmental Committee on Irish Racing* (Dublin, 1928), p. 6.
15 *Report of the Inter-departmental Committee*, p. 7.
16 Cottrell and Armytage, *A–Z of the Grand National*, pp 417–18.
17 Cottrell and Armytage, *A–Z of the Grand National*, pp 459–60; James Lambie, *The story of your life: a history of* Sporting Life *newspaper (1859–1998)* (Leicester, 2010), pp 338–9.
18 Cottrell and Armytage, *A–Z of the Grand National*, pp 312–13.
19 Patricia Smyly, *Encyclopaedia of steeplechasing* (London, 1979), pp 24–5.
20 *Irish Life*, Sept. 1923.
21 Watson, *Between the flags*, p. 191.
22 Cormac Ó Gráda and Kevin H. O'Rourke, 'The Irish economy in the century after partition', *Economic History Review*, 75:2 (2022), p. 342.
23 S.I. No. 65/1926 – Betting Duty Regulations, 1926.
24 NAI, FIN/1/3520, Ernest Blythe to Members of the Executive Council, 14 Jan. 1925; D'arcy, *Horses*, p. 271.
25 D'arcy, *Horses*, p. 270.
26 Joint Committee on the Betting Act, Final Report, 1926.
27 S.I. No. 65/1926 – Betting Duty Regulations, 1926.
28 D'arcy, *Horses*, p. 299.
29 INHSC Minutes, vol. i, f. 388, 5 Jan. 1926. Mahon was appointed manager of Punchestown on 17 Feb. 1925.
30 Quoted in D'arcy, *Horses*, pp 269–70.
31 *Irish Times*, 27 Jan. 1923.
32 *Irish Times*, 14 Feb. 1924; Williams, *Winner all right*, pp 51–2.
33 Quoted in Williams, *Winner all right*, p. 52.
34 D'arcy, *Horses*, pp 272–83.
35 Watson, *Between the flags*, p. 201.
36 Watson, *Between the flags*, p. 201; D'arcy, *Horses*, p. 281.
37 *Report of the Inter-departmental Committee*, 1928, pp 3–4.
38 *Report of the Inter-departmental Committee*, 1928, p. 7.
39 *Report of the Inter-departmental Committee*, 1928, p. 11.
40 *Report of the Inter-departmental Committee*, 1928, p. 7.
41 *Report of the Inter-departmental Committee*, 1928, pp 12–13.
42 *Report of the Inter-departmental Committee*, 1928, pp 18–19, 23.
43 *Report of the Inter-departmental Committee*, 1928, p. 26; Dáil Éireann debate, 25 Apr. 1928.
44 Dáil Éireann debate, 25 Apr. 1928.
45 *Report of the Inter-departmental Committee*, p. 22.
46 D'arcy, *Horses*, pp 282–3.
47 Dáil Éireann debate, 20 June 1929. See *Totalisator Act, 1929*.
48 INHSC Minutes, vol. i, f. 398, 13 Oct. 1928; Watson, *Between the flags*, p. 209.
49 https://www.hri.ie/about-us/subsidiaries/tote/, accessed 20 Jan. 2023.
50 D'arcy, *Horses*, pp 282–3.
51 *Irish Times*, 31 Dec. 1938.
52 Watson, *Between the flags*, pp 367, 378.
53 *Irish Times*, 29 Mar. 1993.
54 *Irish Times*, 15 Dec. 2017.
55 Watson, *Between the flags*, pp 203–5.
56 D'arcy, *Horses*, p. 299.
57 See Roger Munting, *An economic and social history of gambling in Britain and the USA* (Manchester, 1996), pp 116–26; *Pacemaker* (Dec. 1988), pp 86–8.
58 INHSC Minutes, vol. i, f. 405, 12 Jan. 1931.
59 INHSC Minutes, vol. i, f. 397, 21 Apr. 1928.
60 INHSC Minutes, vol. i, f. 299, 7 Jan. 1929.

61 INHSC Minutes, vol. i, f, 422, 8 Jan. 1937.
62 Andy Bielenberg and Raymond Ryan, *An economic history of Ireland since Independence* (Abingdon, 2013), pp 12–13; Ó Gráda and O'Rourke, 'Irish economy', pp 345–7.
63 *Irish Independent*, 9 Oct. 1935.
64 D'arcy, *Horses*, p. 301.
65 Dáil Éireann debate, 15 Nov. 1933.
66 *Report of the Commission of Inquiry into the Horse Breeding Industry* (Dublin, 1935), p. 5.
67 *Report of the Commission*, p. 7.
68 INHSC Minutes, vol. i, f. 416, 4 Jan. 1935.
69 *Report of the Commission*, pp 7–8.
70 INHSC Minutes, f. 458, vol. i, 18 Jan. 1938.
71 Watson, *Between the flags*, 224.
72 Watson, *Between the flags*, p. 378.
73 INHSC Minutes, f. 458, vol. i, 18 Jan. 1938.
74 Smyly, *Encyclopaedia*, pp 103–4.
75 Quoted in Cottrell and Armytage, *A–Z of the Grand National*, p. 209.
76 Cottrell and Armytage, *A–Z of the Grand National*, p. 209.
77 Graham Sharpe and Declan Colley, *Dorothy Paget: the eccentric queen of the sport of kings* (London, 2017), p. 180.
78 Cottrell and Armytage, *A–Z of the Grand National*, p. 209.
79 Smyly, *Encyclopaedia*, p. 104.
80 INHSC Minutes, f. 461, vol. i, 24 Jan. 1939.
81 Smyly, *Encyclopaedia*, p. 219; Cottrell and Armytage, *A–Z of the Grand National*, pp 422–3.
82 Watson, *Between the flags*, pp 252–3.
83 Watson, *Between the flags*, p. 254.
84 Robin Oakley, *The Cheltenham Festival: a centenary history* (London, 2014), pp 69–71.
85 Anne Holland, *The Grand National: a celebration of the world's most famous race* (London, 2019), p. 71.
86 *Irish Press*, 16 Dec. 1940.
87 Watson, *Between the flags*, pp 234–5.
88 *Irish Horse* (1948), p. 30.
89 *Irish Independent*, 25 Sept. 1948.
90 Robert D. Marshall, 'Wylie, William Evelyn', *DIB*. Both men had different recollections after the event.
91 Marshall, 'Wylie', *DIB*.
92 D'arcy, *Horses*, p. 304.
93 INHSC Minutes, vol. i, f. 461, 24 Jan. 1939.
94 INHSC Minutes, vol. i, f. 465, 23 Jan. 1940.
95 *Irish Press*, 28 Nov. 1939.
96 Bryce Evans, *Ireland during the Second World War: farewell to Plato's cave* (Manchester, 2014), p. 75.
97 *Irish Horse* (1945), p. 59.
98 D'arcy, *Horses*, p. 307.
99 Shane Lehane, *A history of the Irish Red Cross* (Dublin, 2019), pp 79–80.
100 *Racing Calendar*, 20 Mar. 1942.
101 Quoted in Watson, *Between the flags*, p. 229.
102 Watson, *Between the flags*, p. 230.
103 INHSC Minutes, vol. i, f. 474, 12 Nov. [1942].
104 INHSC Minutes, vol. i, ff 475–6, 10 Dec. [1942].
105 INHSC Minutes, vol. i, f. 472, 21 Apr. 1942.
106 Marie Coleman, 'McGrath, Joseph ("Joe")', *DIB*.
107 D'arcy, *Horses*, p. 307.
108 *Racing Calendar*, 5 Feb. 1943.
109 D'arcy, *Horses*, p. 308.
110 *Irish Independent*, 21 Sept. 1942.
111 *Irish Independent*, 12 Jan. 1943.
112 D'arcy, *Horses*, pp 308–10.
113 INHSC Minutes, vol. i, f. 479, 11 Sept. [1943].
114 Watson, *Between the flags*, p. 243.
115 Dáil Éireann debate, 19 July 1945.
116 *Irish Horse* (1944).

Panel: Being Seen, Tuning In: Horse Racing and Early Media

1 *Racing Calendar*, 1916.
2 See, for example, *Irish Life*, passim.
3 British Pathé, 'Navan's new racecourse: inaugural meeting at Proudstown Park' (1921).
4 Richard Pine, *2RN: the origins of Irish radio* (Dublin, 2002), p. 172.
5 Quoted in Pine, *2RN*, p. 168.
6 Dáil Éireann debate, 11 May 1928.

Panel: The Early Evolution of Fences

1 See, for example, INHSC Minutes, vol. i, f. 72, 14 May 1875; f. 194, 31 Aug. 1888; f. 509, 23 June 1898.
2 INHSC Minutes, vol. i, f. 388, 5 Jan. [1926].
3 INHSC Minutes, vol. i, f. 409, 6 Aug. 1932.
4 INHSC Minutes, vol. ii, f. 88, 21 Aug. 1959.
5 INHSC Minutes, vol. ii, ff 84–90, 9 Jan. 1959; 21 Apr. 1959; 21 Aug. 1959.
6 *Irish Times*, 30 Jan. 1958.

Chapter Four: 1945–1969

1 Watson, *Between the flags*, p. 261; Dáil Éireann debate, 22 Mar. 1945.
2 *Irish Times*, 17 Feb. 1945.
3 Dáil Éireann debate, 7 Mar. 1945.
4 Rouse, *Sport and Ireland*, p. 315.
5 Dáil Éireann debate, 7 Mar. 1945; *Racing Board and Racecourses Act*, 1945, c.3, s. 27 (6).
6 *Irish Horse* (1950), p. 53.
7 Without the Classics, the combined stakes for National Hunt races was over £1,000 higher. *Irish Horse* (1949), p. 53.

8 *Irish Horse* (1949), pp 51–3; *Irish Horse* (1950), p. 55.
9 *Irish Times*, 21 July 1945; *Irish Horse* (1950), p. 52.
10 *Irish Horse* (1950), p. 55.
11 D'arcy, *Horses*, p. 311.
12 INHSC Minutes, f. 451, 10 Jan. 1945.
13 *Irish Independent*, 14 Nov. 1944; *Irish Examiner*, 18 Nov. 1944.
14 INHSC Minutes, f. 450, 15 Nov. 1944.
15 *The Anglo-Celt*, 14 Apr. 2016.
16 *Irish Horse* (1945), pp 45–7; *Irish Independent*, 13 Mar. 1946.
17 INHSC Minutes, vol. ii, f. 7, 31 Jan. 1947.
18 Williams and Hyland, *Who was who*, p. 136; D'arcy, *Horses*, p. 316.
19 D'arcy, *Horses*, p. 315.
20 INHS Minutes, vol. ii, f. 21, 6 Jan. 1949.
21 *Irish Life*, 6 Jan. 1922.
22 *Irish Times*, 25 Sept. 1959.
23 INHSC Minutes, vol. i, f. 456, 21 Sept. 1945; Watson, *Between the flags*, p. 291.
24 *Irish Times*, 1 Jan. 1974.
25 INHSC Minutes, vol. ii, f. 140, 16 Oct. 1964; ff 172–3, 17 Jan. 1968.
26 INHSC Minutes, vol. ii, f. 7, 31 Jan. 1947; D'arcy, *Horses*, p. 316.
27 D'arcy, *Horses*, p. 327.
28 INHSC Minutes, vol. ii, f. 27, 4 Nov. 1949; D'arcy, *Horses*, p. 320.
29 *Sunday Independent*, 23 Apr. 1950.
30 *Irish Independent*, 26 Apr. 1950.
31 Watson, *Between the flags*, p. 261.
32 *Evening Herald*, 26 Apr. 1950.
33 NAI, PRES/P2257, Michael McDunphy, 26 June 1942. I am grateful to Prof. Bernadette Whelan for this reference.
34 D'arcy, *Horses*, pp 320–1.
35 INHSC Minutes, vol. ii, f. 73, 17 Apr. 1957.
36 *Irish Horse* (1948), p. 39.
37 Jacqueline O'Brien and Ivor Herbert, *Vincent O'Brien: the official biography* (London, 2005), pp 41–50.
38 Guy St John Williams, *Martin Molony: a legend in his lifetime* (Dublin, 2001), pp 107–8.
39 *Irish Times*, 7 July 2020.
40 *Irish Independent*, 8 Mar. 2009; *Irish Times*, 7 July 2020.
41 Córas Iompair Éireann, *Annual reports, nos 1–6* (1950–6), pp 25, 28.
42 O'Brien and Herbert, *Vincent O'Brien*, p. 113.
43 Watson, *Between the flags*, pp 261–73.
44 O'Brien and Herbert, *Vincent O'Brien*, p. 73.
45 Gerry P. McKenna, 'O'Brien, (Michael) Vincent ("M.V.")', *DIB*; *Irish Independent*, 8 Mar. 2009.
46 *Irish Times*, 12 Sept. 2009.

47 *Irish Horse* (1952), pp 29–30, 32.
48 *Irish Horse* (1953), p. 38.
49 D'arcy, *Horses*, pp 316–17.
50 https://irta.ie/history/, accessed 20 May 2023.
51 https://irta.ie/history/, accessed 20 May 2023.
52 Brian Girvin, 'Stability, crisis and change in post-war Ireland, 1945–1973' in Bartlett (ed.), *Cambridge history of Ireland*, p. 396.
53 Girvin, 'Stability, crisis and change, p. 384.
54 Rouse, *Sport and Ireland*, p. 296.
55 Rouse, *Sport and Ireland*, pp 294–5.
56 Watson, *Between the flags*, p. 287.
57 *Irish Horse* (1953), p. 39.
58 Watson, *Between the flags*, pp 287–8.
59 *Racing Calendar* (Dublin, 1954), pp 300–1.
60 *Irish Examiner*, 1 Apr. 1954.
61 McKenna, 'O'Brien, *DIB*.
62 *Irish Examiner*, 1 Apr. 1954.
63 *Irish Press*, 5 Apr. 1954.
64 *Irish Examiner*, 12 Aug. 1954.
65 *Irish Independent*, 12 Aug. 1954; *Irish Press*, 22 Oct. 1954.
66 Herbert and O'Brien, *Vincent O'Brien*, p. 115.
67 Patrick Sharman, 'Runners, riders and risk: safety issues in the history of horseracing' in Stephen Wagg and Allyson M. Pollock (eds), *The Palgrave handbook of sports, politics and harm* (New York, 2021), p. 275. Joyce Kay and Wray Vamplew, *The encyclopaedia of British horse racing* (Abingdon, 2012), p. 358.
68 *Racing Calendar* (Dublin, 1931).
69 Sharman, 'Runners, riders and risk', p. 275.
70 *Irish Independent*, 8 Nov. 1962.
71 *Irish Times*, 20 Dec. 1968.
72 INHS Rule 23, *Racing Calendar*, 12 Dec. 1974.
73 INHSC Minutes, vol. ii, f. 147, 23 Apr. 1965.
74 INHSC Minutes, vol. ii, f. 150, 8 Oct. 1965.
75 Aubrey Brabazon, *Racing through my mind* (Ardmore, 1998), p. 96.
76 Watson, *Between the flags*, p. 312; Oakley, *Sixty years of jump racing*, p. 192.
77 *Racing Calendar* (Dublin, 1952).
78 John Mills, *Life of a racehorse* (London, 1865), p. 94.
79 George Lambton, *Men and horses I have known* (London, 1924), pp 253–4.
80 Charles Adolph Voight, *Famous gentleman riders* (London, 1925), p. 138.
81 *Racing Calendar* (Dublin, 1947).
82 INHSC Minutes, vol. ii, f. 51, 19 Mar. 1954.
83 Quoted in D'arcy, *Horses*, p. 318.
84 O'Brien and Herbert, *Vincent O'Brien*, pp 146–61; D'arcy, *Horses*, pp 318–19.
85 INHSC Minutes, vol. ii, f. 98, 18 July 1960.
86 INHSC Minutes, vol. ii, f. 37, 23 July 1951.

87   INHSC Minutes, vol. ii, f. 40, 11 Jan. 1952.
88   INHSC Minutes, vol. ii, f. 102, 6 Jan. 1961.
89   INHSC Minutes, vol. ii, ff 106–7, 14 Apr. 1961.
90   INHSC Minutes, f. 136, 17 Apr. 1964.
91   INHSC Minutes, f. 148, 8 Oct. 1965.
92   INHSC Minutes, ff 142–3, 8 Jan. 1965.
93   *Irish Field*, 22 July 2016.
94   John Rouse, 'Dreaper, Thomas ("Tom") William', *DIB*.
95   Stewart Peters, *The Irish Grand National: the history of Ireland's premier steeplechase* (Stroud, 2006), pp 48–9.
96   Gary Fishgall, *Gregory Peck: a biography* (New York, 2002), p. 240.
97   *Irish Field*, 24 Dec. 1965.
98   Pat Taaffe, *My life and Arkle's* (London, 1972), p. 65.
99   Robin Oakley, *Sixty years of jump racing: from Arkle to McCoy* (London, 2017), p. 41.
100   Nicholas Godfrey (ed.), *100 favourite racehorses: the Racing Posts' definitive readers' poll* (Wellingborough, 2005).
101   *Irish Horse* (1962), p. 35.
102   https://cheltenhamfestivaluk.com/arkle, accessed 10 Jan. 2023.
103   Sean Magee, *Arkle: the story of the world's greatest steeplechaser* (Newbury, 2009), pp 35–45.
104   *Racing Post*, 3 Aug. 2019.
105   *Irish Independent*, 7 Dec. 1964.
106   *Irish Independent*, 31 Mar. 1964; Magee, *Arkle*, pp 70–1.
107   Magee, *Arkle*, pp 86–7, 118–21.
108   Taaffe, *My life and Arkle's*, p. 59.
109   *Irish Field*, 31 Dec. 1966.
110   Quoted in Watson, *Between the flags*, p. 298.
111   *Racing Post*, 31 May 2010; Taaffe, *My life and Arkle's*, p. 59.
112   *Racing Post*, 13 Nov. 2020.
113   *The Guardian*, 13 Feb. 1965.
114   *The Irish Horseman*, Aug. 1972.
115   Rouse, *Sport and Ireland*, p. 301.
116   Girvin, 'Stability, crisis and change', pp 398–402.
117   Rouse, *Sport and Ireland*, p. 301.
118   Rebecca S. Miller, 'Roseland, Jetland, Cloudland and beyond: Irish showbands and economic change, 1958–1975', *New Hibernia Review/Irish Éireannach Nua*, 18:3 (Autumn 2014), p. 77.
119   *Irish Times*, 10 Aug. 1961.
120   *Irish Examiner*, 8 Apr. 2020.
121   Watson, *Between the flags*, p. 288.
122   *Irish Times*, 10 Aug. 1961.
123   Watson, *Between the flags*, p. 289.
124   *Irish Times*; 23 Feb. 1960; 7 May 1960.
125   D'arcy, *Horses*, pp 323–5.
126   *Irish Times*, 27 Feb. 1965.
127   Dáil Éireann debate, 1 July 1964.
128   Declan Kiberd, *Inventing Ireland: the literature of the modern nation* (Cambridge, MA, 1996), p. 565.
129   Quoted in the *Irish Field*, 11 Dec. 1965.
130   *Irish Field*, 8 Jan. 1966; *Irish Field*, 15 Jan. 1966.
131   *Irish Field*, 13 Mar. 1965; 4 Dec. 1965; 22 Jan. 1966.
132   *Irish Field*, 7 Jan. 1967.
133   INHSC Minutes, vol. ii, f. 173, 17 Jan. 1968.
134   *Irish Examiner*, 18 Nov. 1969.
135   INHSC Minutes, vol. ii, f. 171, [Nov?] 1967.
136   INHSC Minutes, vol. ii, f. 179, 15 Jan. 1969; *Irish Field*, 11 Jan. 1969.
137   *Irish Times*, 13 Aug. 1969.
138   Brian Hanley, *The impact of the Troubles on the Republic of Ireland: boiling volcano?* (Manchester, 2018), p. 43.
139   *Irish Press*, 24 Dec. 1969.
140   *Irish Times*, 30 Dec. 1969.

Panel: Amateur Legends of the Mid-Twentieth Century

1   P2P.ie, accessed 10 Jan. 2023.
2   *Racing Post*, 25 July 2005.
3   *Racing Post*, 12 Jan. 2006.
4   *Irish Field*, 24 June 2022.
5   *Irish Independent*, 9 Feb. 2006.

Panel: The Tóstal Steeplechase

1   *The Journal*, 7 Apr. 2013.
2   Watson, *Between the flags*, p.
3   Interview with Bill McLernon, 24 Feb. 2023; *Racing Post*, 25 July 2005.

Panel: 'Himself' and 'The Black Stuff'

1   GPR/MK03.01/0001.26, Black and white press advertisement 'The first Grand National' as advertised in *Illustrated Sporting & Dramatic*, week ending 22 March 1930, page 57.
2   GPR/MK09/0387, 'Advertising Guinness animals', Bryan Guinness, Lord Moyne, to Robert, 22 Mar. 1966.
3   GPR/MK09/0387, 'Advertising Guinness animals', Letter [5 Apr. 1966]; Magee, *Arkle*, pp 122–3.
4   *Irish Mirror*, 16 Apr. 2024

Chapter Five: 1970–1993

1   INHSC Minutes, vol. ii, f. 186, 14 Jan. 1970.
2   INHSC Minutes, vol. ii, f. 193, 14 Jan. 1971.
3   *Irish Field*, 18 Mar. 1972.
4   *Irish Field*, 20 Nov. 2015; *Meath Chronicle*, 19 Nov. 2015.
5   *Irish Racing Calendar: 'races past' for the year 1970* (Dublin, 1970), pp 959–60.

6. Gary Murphy, *Haughey* (Dublin, 2021), pp 123–34.
7. Gary Murphy in conversation with Michael Moynihan, *Irish Examiner*, 6 Dec. 2021.
8. Guy St John Williams and Francis P.M. Hyland, *Who was who*, p. 196; Murphy, *Haughey*, p. 159.
9. Murphy, *Haughey*, pp 158–9.
10. *National Stud Act, 1969*; *National Stud Act, 1976*.
11. *Irish Field*, 25 Dec. 2020.
12. *Irish Field*, 25 Dec. 2020.
13. *Irish Times*, 24 Dec. 2005.
14. Quoted in https://charlesjhaughey.ie/articles/equestrian, accessed 13 Jan. 2023.
15. *Irish Times*, 28 May 1970; NAI, 2001/6/251, Memorandum for the Government, Racing Board Annual Report and Accounts, 1969.
16. See Seanad Éireann debate, 18 June 1975.
17. Stephen Collins and Ciara Meehan, *Saving the State: Fine Gael from Collins to Varadkar* (Dublin, 2020), p. 106.
18. *Irish Field*, 29 Apr. 1972.
19. *Irish Field*, 12 Feb. 1972.
20. INHSC Minutes, vol. ii, f. 203, 12 Jan. 1972.
21. INHSC Minutes, vol. ii, f. 251, 12 Jan. 1977.
22. INHSC Minutes, vol. ii, f. 277, 18 Jan. 1980.
23. *Irish Times*, 23 June 1976.
24. *Irish Field*, 6 Jan. 1973.
25. *Irish Field*, 6 Jan. 1973.
26. *Irish Field*, 8 Apr. 1972.
27. *Irish Field*, 26 Feb. 1972.
28. Dáil Éireann debate, 29 Apr. 1975.
29. *Irish Examiner*, 6 June 1975.
30. Dáil Éireann debate, 5 June 1975.
31. *Irish Field*, 22 Apr. 1972.
32. The Racing Board, *Report and accounts for the year ending 31 December 1972* (1973); Joseph McNabb, 'Graham, Sean (John) Patrick', *DIB*.
33. *Irish Examiner*, 7 Apr. 1986.
34. Ronan Casey, *Joe Dolan: the official biography* (London, 2008), pp 110–11.
35. INHSC Minutes, vol. ii, f. 187, 14 Jan. 1970.
36. INHSC Minutes, vol. ii, f. 196, 14 Jan. 1971.
37. *Irish Field*, 25 Mar. 1972.
38. Michael J. Hurley, 'Baldoyle as a racecourse village', *Dublin Historical Record*, 59:1 (2006), pp 71–2.
39. *Irish Press*, 9 Nov. 1973.
40. INHSC Minutes, vol. ii, ff 192, 27 Oct. 1970.
41. Neal Garnham, 'Accounting for the early success of the Gaelic Athletic Association', *Irish Historical Studies*, 34 (May 2004), pp 72–3.
42. INHSC Minutes, vol. II, f. 203, 12 Jan. 1972.
43. *Irish Times*, 28 Nov. 1970.
44. Racing Board, *Reports and financial statements for year ending 31st December 1985* (Dublin, 1986); *Irish Times*, 17 July 1985.
45. *Belfast Telegraph*, 22 Mar. 2004.
46. INHSC Minutes, vol. ii, f. 242, 23 Jan. 1976; f. 245, 13 Apr. 1976; f. 249, 26 Oct. 1976; f. 260, 17 Jan. 1978.
47. D'arcy, *Horses*, p. 328.
48. INHSC Minutes, vol. ii, f. 253, 12 Jan. 1977.
49. INHSC Minutes, vol. ii, f. 203, 12 Jan. 1972.
50. INHSC Minutes, vol. ii, f. 223, 29 Jan. 1974.
51. INHSC Minutes, vol. ii, f. 239, 25 Apr. 1975.
52. INHSC Minutes, vol. ii, f. 251, 12 Jan. 1977.
53. *Irish Field*, 13 Dec. 1980.
54. INHSC Minutes, vol. ii, f. 278, 24 Jan. 1980.
55. *Irish Field*, 25 Mar. 1972.
56. INHSC Minutes, vol. ii, f. 227, 7 Aug. 1974; f. 234, 8 Jan. 1975.
57. INHSC Minutes, vol. ii, f. 234, 8 Jan. 1975.
58. Michael MacCormac, *The Irish racing and bloodstock industry: an economic analysis* (Dublin, 1977), p. 227.
59. See https://racingacademy.ie/uploaded_files/8/ce1f6f5ac5296b974c26c7e19_7347_6200.pdf, accessed 12 Feb. 2023 (James Willoughby, 'Ireland's own racing academy driven by passion and pride').
60. https://racingacademy.ie/cms/about-us/history/, accessed 31 Jan. 2023.
61. MacCormac, *Irish racing and bloodstock industry*, p. 227.
62. Rouse, *Sport and Ireland*, pp 198–205.
63. Quoted in Watson, *Between the flags*, p. 38.
64. *Irish Times*, 2 Apr. 1932; 13 Apr. 1935; 7 July 1967.
65. See, for example, *Irish Times*, 1 May 1934; *Irish Independent*, 30 Mar. 1938.
66. https://www.p2p.ie/news_item.php?news_id=18964, accessed 29 Jan. 2023; *Racing Post*, 23 May 2022.
67. Pat Healy and Richard Pugh, *Point to point: the heart of Irish racing* (Dublin, 2022), p. 130.
68. *Irish Times*, 17 May 1930.
69. INHSC Minutes, vol. ii, f. 18, 25 Sept. 1948.
70. *Irish Times*, 27 July 1983.
71. *Irish Times*, 3 Apr. 1978.
72. *Irish Times*, 4 Feb. 1965; *Irish Field*, 20 Feb. 1965.
73. Quoted in the *Irish Field*, 20 Feb. 1965.
74. *Irish Field*, 3 Sept. 1966.
75. *Irish Independent*, 26 Aug. 2007.
76. Watson, *Between the flags*, p. 292.
77. INHSC Minutes, vol. ii, ff 157–8, 2 Dec. 1966.
78. *Irish Farmers' Journal*, 8 Feb. 2023.
79. Kay and Vamplew, *Encyclopedia*, pp 343–4.
80. *Irish Times*, 10 Oct. 1972.
81. *Irish Times*, 6 Oct. 1973.
82. INHSC Minutes, vol. ii, f. 223, 29 Jan. 1974.
83. INHSC Minutes, vol. ii, f. 220, 19 Oct. 1973.
84. *Irish Times*, 17 Oct. 1973.
85. *Irish Times*, 30 Aug. 1997; *Irish Times*, 20 Jan. 2015.

86 *Irish Times*, 24 Apr. 1984.
87 *Irish Independent*, 22 Mar. 1984; *Irish Times*, 23 June 1987.
88 Healy and Pugh, *Point to point*, p. 111.
89 INHSC Minutes, vol. ii, ff 318–19, 25 Jan. 1985.
90 INHSC Minutes, vol. ii, f. 367, 27 Jan. 1989; f.419, 24 Apr. 1992; *Meath Chronicle*, 11 Jan. 2020.
91 *Irish Field*, 15 July 2016; *Irish Field*, 19 May 2023; Joint Committee on Agriculture, Food and the Marine Debate, 13 July 2023.
92 *Irish Field*, 8 Feb. 2019.
93 Oakley, *Sixty years of jump racing*, pp 45–6
94 Oakley, *Sixty years of jump racing*, pp 100–2.
95 Arthur Moore, quoted in the *Racing Post*, 12 July 2017.
96 Oakley, *Sixty years of jump racing*, pp 48–9.
97 Quoted in *Racing Ahead*, 20 Feb. 2016.
98 *Racing Ahead*, 20 Feb. 2016.
99 *Irish Press*, 17 June 1980; *Irish Press*, 4 Aug. 1980.
100 *Irish Field*, 1 Jan. 1972; 8 Jan. 1972.
101 *Irish Field*, 31 July 2020.
102 See Declan Colley, *When Bobby met Christy: the story of Bobby Beasley and a wayward horse* (Cork, 2010).
103 *Irish Field*, 4 Jan. 1975.
104 *Irish Field*, 3 Jan. 1976.
105 https://www.thepja.co.uk/championships/jump-jockeys-championship/, accessed 20 Jan. 2023.
106 *Irish Field*, 11 Feb. 1978.
107 *Irish Field*, 5 May 2023.
108 *Irish Times*, 15 July 2018.
109 INHSC Minutes, vol. ii, f. 186, 14 Jan. 1970.
110 *Irish Field*, 1 Jan. 1972.
111 *Irish Field*, 29 Jan. 1977; INHSC Minutes, vol. ii, f. 259, 6 Dec. 1977.
112 *Irish Field*, 29 Jan. 1977.
113 INHSC Minutes, vol. ii, f. 278, 24 Jan. 1980.
114 Quoted in *Irish Field*, 29 Jan. 1977.
115 INHSC Minutes, vol. ii, f. 361, 11 Nov. 1988.
116 *Irish Times*, 7 Mar. 1929.
117 *Irish Times*, 4 Nov. 1977.
118 INHSC Minutes, vol. ii, f. 265, 17 Oct. 1978; INHSC Minutes, vol. ii, f. 305, 25 Apr. 1983; *Racing Calendar*, 26 Jan. 1984.
119 INHSC Minutes, vol. ii, f. 310, 20 Jan. 1984; *Racing Calendar*, 26 Jan. 1984.
120 INHSC Minutes, vol. ii, f. 327, 23 Jan. 1986; *Racing Calendar*, 30 Jan. 1986.
121 *Irish Field*, 4 Mar. 1972.
122 *Irish Times*, 29 Aug. 1972.
123 *Irish Times*, 7 Mar. 1973; 7 May 1973.
124 *Irish Field*, 10 Mar. 1973
125 Ó Gráda and O'Rourke, 'Irish economy', pp 2, 20–1
126 Racing Board, *Report and financial statements for the year ended 31st December 1979* (Dublin, 1980).
127 INHSC Minutes, vol. ii, f. 294, 29 Jan. 1982.
128 *Racing Calendar*, 20 Nov. 1983.
129 *Racing Calendar*, 20 Nov. 1983.
130 *Analysis of the Irish racing and breeding industry* (Kill, 1983); *Irish Times*, 4 Feb. 1983.
131 *Irish Field*, 15 Dec. 1984.
132 *Report of the Commission of Inquiry into the Thoroughbred Horse Breeding Industry* (Dublin, 1986), p. 78; Frank Smyth, Secretary of the Racing Board, quoted in the *Irish Field*, 23 Feb. 1985.
133 *Irish Times*, 1 Mar. 1988; *Irish Times*, 21 Oct. 1989; *Irish Times* 15 Oct. 1990.
134 This increased from £75,000 in 1984/5 to £120,000 in 1986. See INHSC Minutes, vol. ii, f. 310; *Commission of Inquiry*, p. 127.
135 https://www.goracing.ie/past-champions/, accessed 1 Mar. 2023.
136 *Irish Field*, 17 Mar. 1984.
137 Godfrey (ed.), *100 favourite racehorses*, p. 64.
138 Quoted in Godfrey (ed.), *100 favourite racehorses*, p. 64.
139 *Irish Times*, 24 Apr. 1986.
140 *Irish Times*, 27 June 1986.
141 *Racing Post*, 18 Mar. 2018.
142 *Evening Press*, 4 June 1986.
143 *Irish Press*, 27 Dec. 1987.
144 INHSC Minutes, vol. ii, f. 223, 29 Jan. 1974.
145 *Irish Field*, 18 Mar. 1989; *Irish Times*, 19 Mar. 2019.
146 *Irish Times*, 2 Feb. 1983.
147 *Commission of Inquiry*, p. 12.
148 *Commission of Inquiry*, p. 20.
149 *Commission of Inquiry*, pp 20–2.
150 *Commission of Inquiry*, p. 82.
151 *Commission of Inquiry*, p. 19.
152 Seanad Éireann debate, 12 July 1988.
153 Dáil Éireann debate, 31 Jan. 1990.
154 https://www.itm.ie/About, accessed 1 Feb. 2023.

Panel: The Blackmore Effect

1 *Irish Independent*, 10 Apr. 2021.
2 *Irish Times*, 19 Dec. 2021.
3 *Irish Examiner*, 7 May 2021; https://www.rte.ie/sport/racing/2021/0322/1205384-blackmore-in-racing-gender-isnt-an-issue/, accessed 6 Jan. 2024.
4 *Irish Times*, 22 Oct. 2020.
5 *Irish Farmers' Journal*, 26 May 2021.
6 Vanessa Cashmore, 'Are girls any good? An analysis of gender differentials amongst British thoroughbred horseracing' (Masters Dissertation, University of Liverpool, 2018). For a summary of the report see: https://www.britishhorseracing.com/wp-content/uploads/2018/01/SUMMARY-Female-jockeys-29-01-18-1.pdf, accessed 10 Jan. 2024.

Chapter Six: 1994–2022

1. *Irish Times*, 22 Oct. 1993.
2. *Irish Horseracing Industry Bill, 1994*, s. 10.
3. *Irish Times*, 5 July 1994.
4. Quoted in *Belfast Telegraph*, 29 Sept. 1992.
5. *Irish Field*, 2 July 1994.
6. Quoted in *Irish Times*, 22 July 1994.
7. Seanad Éireann debate, 29 June 1994.
8. *Irish Times*, 19 Mar. 1994.
9. Dáil Éireann debate, 21 Apr. 1994.
10. *The Racing Board: reports and financial statements for the period ended 30 November 1994* (1995), p. 5.
11. INHSC Minutes, vol. ii, f. 470, 11 Apr. 1995.
12. Bielenberg and Ryan, *Economic history*, pp 34–5; John O'Hagan, 'The Irish economy, 1973–2016' in Bartlett (ed.), *Cambridge history of Ireland: Volume IX*, p. 516.
13. *Irish Times*, 9 Jan. 1997; *Irish Times*, 4 Apr. 2022.
14. IHA, *Annual Report 1999*, p. 26.
15. IHA, *Annual Report 1999*, p. 27.
16. Dáil Éireann debate, 21 Apr. 1994; *Reports and Financial Statements … 1994*, p. 6.
17. *Reports and Financial Statements … 1994*, p.4.
18. *Irish Times*, 27 Oct. 1995; 9 Jan. 1997.
19. *Horse and Greyhound Racing (Betting Charges and Levies) Act, 1999*; *Finance Act, 1999*; Dáil Éireann debate, 17 June 1999. A 0.3 per cent charge on on-course bookmakers was introduced when the levy was abolished.
20. IHA, *Annual Report 2000*, p. 21.
21. IHA, *Annual Report 2000*, p. 22.
22. Dáil Éireann debate, 23 May 1991.
23. *Irish Times*, 10 Dec. 1990; *Irish Racing Annual 1990–91* (1990).
24. *Irish Examiner*, 7 Apr. 1993.
25. *Irish Field*, 10 Apr. 1993. The accounts showed a trading loss of £280,000 for 1992, but this resulted from costs incurred refurbishing The Curragh.
26. INHSC Minutes, vol. ii, f. 438, 2 Apr. 1993.
27. *Irish Times*, 24 Nov. 1994.
28. Dáil Éireann debate, 21 Apr. 1994.
29. *Irish Horseracing Industry Act, 1994*, s. 2, c. 10.
30. INHSC Minutes, vol. ii, f. 472, 11 Apr. 1995.
31. *Irish Independent*, 9 Feb. 2006.
32. INHSC Minutes, vol. ii, f. 338, 5 Feb. 1987; f. 366, 27 Jan. 1989; f. 370, 28 July 1989.
33. INHSC Minutes, vol. ii, f. 474, 11 Apr. 1995.
34. INHSC Minutes, vol. iii [no folios], 13 Jan. 1998.
35. INHSC Minutes, vol. ii, f. 426, 8 July 1992.
36. INHSC Minutes, vol. ii, f. 426, 8 July 1992.
37. INHSC Minutes, vol. ii, f. 526, n.d., 1997.
38. INHSC Minutes, vol. ii, f. 526, n.d., 1997.
39. *Belfast Newsletter*, 12 Mar. 1923. See also *Belfast Newsletter*, 31 Jan. 1931; *Irish Examiner*, 30 Mar. 1954.
40. *Independent*, 4 Apr. 1993; *Irish Field*, 10 Apr. 1993.
41. UCDA, P285/254, Correspondence between Lady Eva Forbes and Louisa and W.T. Cosgrave, 5–19 Dec. 1930.
42. INHSC Minutes, vol. ii, f. 285, 16 Jan. 1981.
43. *Irish Times*, 11 Apr. 1994.
44. INHSC Minutes, vol. ii, f. 493, 31 Oct. 1995.
45. INHSC Minutes, vol. ii, f. 517, n.d., 1996.
46. *Irish Times*, 23 Aug. 1988.
47. *Irish Times*, 21 Dec. 1990.
48. *Irish Times*, 11 Jan. 1993.
49. *Irish Independent*, 24 Apr. 1995.
50. *Racing Post*, 24 Apr. 2001.
51. Dáil Éireann debate, 17 May 2001; *Racing Post*, 24 Apr. 2001.
52. https://www.racingpost.com/profile/horse/519615/arctic-copper/form, accessed 1 Mar. 2023.
53. *Irish Times*, 1 Aug. 2018.
54. Quoted in Godfrey (ed.), *100 favourite racehorses*, p. 31.
55. Healy and Pugh, *Point to point*, p. 140.
56. https://www.thepja.co.uk/championships/past-championship-winners/, accessed 1 Mar. 2023.
57. Quoted in the *Racing Post*, 14 Aug. 2000.
58. Quoted in *Irish Times*, 15 Aug. 2000.
59. *Irish Times*, 15 Aug. 2000.
60. Godfrey (ed.), *100 favourite racehorses*, pp 36–7.
61. *Irish Independent*, 12 Apr. 1999.
62. *Racing Post*, 1 May 2019.
63. Brian O'Connor, *Kings of the saddle: Ireland's greatest jockeys* (London, 2010), pp 65–84.
64. Healy and Pugh, *Point to point*, p. 150.
65. *Irish Field*, 1 Feb. 2016; *Irish Examiner*, 2 Feb. 2016.
66. *Racing Post*, 30 Oct. 1999.
67. Healy and Pugh, *Point to point*, p. 150; https://www.p2p.ie/rider.php?rider_id=372, accessed 20 Mar. 2023.
68. Healy and Pugh, *Point to point*, p. 138.
69. Healy and Pugh, *Point to point*, p. 127.
70. Healy and Pugh, *Point to point*, pp 121, 125.
71. Healy and Pugh, *Point to point*, p. 119.
72. Healy and Pugh, *Point to point*, p. 121.
73. *Irish Times*, 10 Mar. 2018.
74. Oakley, *Sixty years of jump racing*, p. 241.
75. *Racing Post*, 30 Apr. 2004; *Irish Independent*, 23 June 2015.
76. *Racing Post*, 29 Jan. 2022.
77. *Irish Field*, 28 Dec. 2016.
78. *Irish Times*, 2 Mar. 2021.
79. *Irish Field*, 14 May 2019.
80. *Irish Times*, 12 Sept. 2022.
81. *Irish Field*, 16 Feb. 2024.
82. Oakley, *Sixty years of jump racing*, p. 242.
83. https://www.hri.ie/statistics/trainer/data/?tid=17185, accessed 2 Jan. 2025.
84. https://www.hri.ie/statistics/horse/data/?hid=26263,

85 https://www.hri.ie/statistics/trainer, accessed 2 Jan. 2025.
86 *Irish Independent*, 24 Feb. 2013.
87 https://www.hri.ie/statistics/trainer/data/?tid=17185, accessed 2 Jan. 2025.
88 *Racing Post*, 13 Mar. 2024.
89 *Racing Post*, 7 Mar. 2016.
90 *Irish Times*, 29 Jan. 2023.
91 *Irish Times*, 3 May 2024.
92 https://www.hri.ie/statistics/trainer/data/?tid=17185, accessed 2 Jan. 2025.
93 *Irish Times*, 13 Dec. 1999.
94 *Irish Times*, 15 Nov. 2003.
95 *Racing Post*, 17 Oct. 2000.
96 *Horseracing Ireland Act, 2001*.
97 *Irish Field*, 25 Nov. 2000.
98 Tony Fahey and Liam Delaney, 'State financial support for horse racing in Ireland', *Budget perspectives 2007* (ESRI, Dublin, 2006), p. 1; Dáil Éireann debate, 15 Feb. 2007; *Analysis of the economic impact of the Irish thoroughbred horse industry* (2009), p. 4.
99 *Irish Times*, 7 Mar. 2005.
100 *Irish Times*, 11 Mar. 2006.
101 *Irish Times*, 30 Oct. 2005; *Irish Times*, 31 Oct. 2005.
102 I am grateful to Mr Ray Bergin for this information.
103 *Irish Times*, 6 Dec. 2003.
104 *Irish Times*, 6 Nov. 2008.
105 *An assessment of the economic contribution of the thoroughbred breeding and horse racing industry in Ireland* (2004), p. i.
106 International Federation of Horseracing Authorities, Annual Report 2007, p. 32.
107 *Irish Times*, 4 Feb. 2009.
108 *Assessment of the economic contribution*, p. ii.
109 HRI Annual Report, 2007.
110 Dáil Éireann debate, 26 Jan. 2006.
111 HRI Annual Report, 2007, p. 10.
112 Roddy Flynn, 'A level playing field? Irish broadcast-sports rights and the decline of the national' in Marcus Free (ed.), *Sport, the media and Ireland: interdisciplinary perspectives* (Cork, 2020), pp 225–6.
113 INHSC Minutes, vol. ii, f. 353, 22 Jan. 1988.
114 *Irish Times*, 24 Dec. 1997.
115 Rouse, *Sport and Ireland*, p. 321.
116 *Irish Examiner*, 1 May 2002.
117 *Irish Times*, 7 Feb. 2003.
118 HRI Annual Report, 2004, p. 4.
119 *Irish Times*, 4 Feb. 2018.
120 *The Irish Field*, 20 Jan. 2023; *Irish Times*, 9 May 2023.
121 *Irish Examiner*, 17 June 2023.
122 *Irish Times*, 10 Mar. 2000.
123 *Irish Times*, 1 Sept. 1999.
124 *Irish Times*, 11 Aug. 2000.
125 *Finance Act, 2002; Finance Act, 2006*.
126 Dáil Éireann debate, 6 Dec. 2022.
127 *Irish Times*, 18 Oct. 2024.
128 *Gambling Regulation Act, 2024*
129 *Irish Times*, 18 Oct. 2024.
130 See *Irish Times*, 13 Jan. 2020.
131 *Irish Times*, 28 Feb. 2022.
132 HRI Annual Report, 2007, p. 10.
133 Andy Bielenberg and Raymond Ryan, *An economic history of Ireland since Independence* (Abingdon, 2013), pp 161–2.
134 Blanaid Clarke and Niamh Hardiman, 'Ireland: hubris and nemesis' in Suzanne J. Konzelmann and Marc Fovargue-Davies (eds), *Banking systems in the crisis: the faces of liberal capitalism* (Abingdon, 2013), p. 126.
135 See, for example, Joint Committee of Inquiry into the Banking Crisis debate, 22 July 2015; 23 July 2015.
136 *Irish Times*, 4 July 2015.
137 *Irish Times*, 23 May 2008.
138 Bielenberg and Ryan, *Economic history of Ireland*, pp 162–4. The troika was formed from three entities – the European Commission, European Central Bank and International Monetary Fund.
139 HRI Annual Report, 2009, pp 9–10.
140 *Irish Times*, 28 Sept. 2010.
141 HRI Annual Report, 2009, p. 9.
142 *Analysis of the economic impact*, p. 3
143 *Analysis of the economic impact*, p. 4.
144 *Analysis of the economic impact*, p. 4; HRI Annual Report, 2010, p. 10.
145 HRI Annual Report, 2010, p. 10.
146 Dáil Éireann debate, 6 Nov. 2012.
147 *Horse Racing Ireland Act 2016*; Dáil Éireann debate, 10 Nov. 2015.
148 https://www.ihrb.ie/about-us/history, accessed 1 Mar. 2023.
149 *Economic impact of Irish breeding and racing 2017* (Dublin, 2018), pp 4–5, 7.
150 *Irish Times*, 8 Sept. 2017.
151 *Irish Times*, 31 Jan. 2019.
152 https://www.revenue.ie/en/customs/documents/temporary-import-export-of-horses.pdf, accessed 10 June 2023; *Racing Post*, 16 Aug. 2022.
153 *Irish Times*, 12 Oct. 2020.
154 HRI Annual Report, 2020, pp 6–7.
155 *The Guardian*, 2 Apr. 2020; *The Telegraph*, 3 Apr. 2020.
156 HRI Annual Report, 2020, p. 8.
157 *HRI Factbook 2022*, p. 2; https://www.hri.ie/corporate/press-office/press-release/2023-statistics-point-to-an-underlying-stability-in-irish-racing-and-breeding#, accessed 4 Mar. 2024.

158 https://www.justice.gov/usao-sdny/pr/manhattan-us-attorney-charges-27-defendants-racehorse-doping-rings, accessed 5 Mar. 2023.
159 *Racing Post*, 7 Dec. 2021; *Irish Field*, 8 Apr. 2022.
160 See, for example, *Irish Examiner*, 24 Oct. 2014; *Irish Times*, 24 Nov. 2014; *The Guardian*, 18 July 2018; https://www.ihrb.ie/referrals-appeals/john-hughes-racing-establishment-employee-card-holder-referral-2–february-2012, accessed 3 Mar. 2023; https://www.ihrb.ie/referrals-appeals/philip-fenton-trainer-referral-18–january-2012, accessed 3 Mar. 2023.
161 *Sunday Independent*, 4 July 2021.
162 https://www.ihrb.ie/general-press-releases/ihrb-statement, 14 June 2021, accessed 3 Mar. 2023.
163 Dr Craig Suann, *Independent review of the Irish Horseracing Regulatory Board (IHRB) Equine Anti-Doping Programme* (2021), pp 6, 13, 25.
164 *Irish Times*, 27 Jan. 2023.
165 *Irish Independent*, 29 Jan. 2023.
166 *Racing Post*, 21 Dec. 2021.
167 *Irish Times*, 7 Mar. 2022.
168 *Racing Post*, 27 Feb. 2021.
169 https://www.ihrb.ie/referrals appeals referral-hearing-of-gordon-elliott trainer, 5 Mar. 2021, accessed 2 Mar. 2023; https://www.britishhorseracing.com/press_releases/bha-response-to-penalty-imposed-by-irish-horseracing-regulatory-board-on-trainer-gordon-elliott/, 5 Mar. 2021, accessed 2 Mar. 2023.
170 https://www.ihrb.ie/referrals-appeals/referral-hearing-of-gordon-elliott-trainer, 5 Mar. 2021, accessed 2 Mar. 2023.
171 https://www.ihrb.ie/general-press-releases/irish-horseracing-regulatory-board-statement-on-outcome-of-gordon-elliott-disciplinary-hearing, 5 Mar. 2021, accessed 2 Mar. 2023.
172 *Irish Times*, 13 May 2022; *Irish Independent*, 12 Feb. 2023.
173 HRI, *Principles of animal welfare in Ireland's horse racing industry* (2022).
174 *Irish Times*, 9 Jan. 2019.
175 HRI, *Racing toward a better world: sustainability strategy 2024* (2024), pp 12–15. See https://www.hri.ie/HRI/media/HRI/common/Documents/HRI-2024–Sustainability-Strategy.pdf, accessed 20 Oct. 2024.
176 https://www.hri.ie/corporate/press-office/press-release/prize-money-increased-for-2024–as-horse-racing-ireland-budget-includes-supports-for-integrity,-equin#, accessed 10 Feb. 2024.

A crowded field in the Sweet Afton Cup at Dundalk in 1962. The eventual winner, Mr Romford, ridden by Captain Simon Walford, is the grey on the far right. Walford devoted his life to racing and he later served as Senior Steward of the INHS Committee.

Bibliography

PRIMARY SOURCES

British Pathé
Film ID: 244.13, 'Navan's new racecourse: inaugural meeting at Proudstown Park' (28/9/1921).

Guinness Archives
GPR/MK, Guinness Park Royal, Marketing Material

Irish National Hunt Steeplechase Committee (INHSC) Minute Books
vol. i (1869–1945)
vol. ii (1946–97)
vol. iii (1998–2010)

National Archives of Ireland
FIN, Department of Finance, early series, 1896–1958
PRES, Office of the Secretary to the President, 1937–80
TSCH, Department of the Taoiseach

National Library of Ireland
MS 8489, Colonel Maurice Moore Papers, 1841–1939

Public Record Office of Northern Ireland
D3030, Castlereagh Papers

University College Dublin Archives
P285, W.T. Cosgrave Papers

University of Galway Archives
LA4, Galway Urban District Council, Minute Books of

287

Interviews
Sean Barry, 15 Feb. 2022
Bill McLernon, 24 Feb. 2023

Printed Primary Sources

Parliamentary Debates
Dáil Éireann debates
House of Lords Debates
Seanad Éireann debates

Legislation and Statutory Instruments
Betting Act, 1926
Betting Duty Regulations, 1926 – S.I. No. 65/1926
Finance Act, 1999
Finance Act, 2002
Finance Act, 2006
Gambling Regulation Act, 2024
Horse and Greyhound Racing (Betting Charges and Levies) Act, 1999
Horse Racing Ireland Act, 2016
Horseracing Ireland Act, 2001
Irish Horseracing Industry Act, 1994.
Irish Horseracing Industry Bill, 1994
National Stud Act, 1969
National Stud Act, 1976
Racing Board and Racecourses Act, 1945
Totalisator Act, 1929

Reports
An assessment of the economic contribution of the thoroughbred breeding and horse racing industry in Ireland. 2004.
Analysis of the economic impact of the Irish thoroughbred horse industry. 2009.
Analysis of the Irish racing and breeding industry. Kill, 1983.
Córas Iompair Éireann, *Annual reports, nos 1–6.* 1950–6.
Economic impact of Irish breeding and racing 2017. Dublin, 2018.
Final report of the Joint Committee on the Betting Act, 1926.

Horse Racing Ireland:
Annual Reports
> *Our industry, our standards: principles of animal welfare in Ireland's horse racing industry,* 2022.
> *Racing toward a better world: sustainability strategy 2024*
> *Factbook 2022*
> *Independent review of the Irish Horseracing Regulatory Board (IHRB) Equine Anti-Doping Programme 2021.*

International Federation of Horseracing Authorities, Annual Reports
Irish Horseracing Authority (IHA), Annual Reports
Racing Board, Annual Reports and Accounts
Report of the Commission of Inquiry into the Horse Breeding Industry. Dublin, 1935.
Report of the Commission of Inquiry into the Thoroughbred Horse Breeding Industry. Dublin, 1986.
Report of the Inter-departmental Committee on Irish Racing. Dublin, 1928.

Newspapers and Periodicals

Belfast Telegraph
Clare Champion
Connaught Telegraph
Cork Examiner
Dublin Intelligence
Evening Herald
Evening Press
The Field
Freeman's Journal
The Guardian
The Independent
Irish Examiner
Irish Farmers' Journal
The Irish Field
The Irish Horse
The Irish Horseman
Irish Independent
Irish Life
Irish Mirror
The Irish Press
Irish Racing Annual 1990–91. Dublin, 1990.
Irish Racing Calendar: 'races past' for the year 1970. Dublin, 1970.
Irish Sportsman and Farmer
The Irish Times
The Journal
Kildare Observer
Leinster Leader
Meath Chronicle
Munster Express
The Nationalist and Leinster Times
Pacemaker
Racing Calendar
Racing Post
The Sphere
The Sporting Magazine
Sunday Independent
The Telegraph

SECONDARY SOURCES

Books

Bartlett, Thomas, 'Ireland during the Revolutionary and Napoleonic Wars, 1791–1815', in James Kelly (ed.), *The Cambridge history of Ireland, volume III: 1730–1880*, 4 vols (Cambridge, 2020), pp 74–101.

Behan, Brendan, *The Hostage* (London, 1958).

Bence-Jones, Mark, *Twilight of the Ascendancy* (London, 1987).

Bielenberg, Andy and Raymond Ryan, *An economic history of Ireland since Independence* (Abingdon, 2013).

Birley, Derek, *Sport and the making of Britain* (Manchester, 1993).

Brabazon, Aubrey, *Racing through my mind* (Ardmore, 1998).

Buckle, George Earle (ed.), *The letters of Queen Victoria, volume 4: 1862–1869*, 9 vols (London, 1926).

Casey, Ronan, *Joe Dolan: the official biography* (London, 2008).

Clarke, Blanaid and Niamh Hardiman, 'Ireland: hubris and nemesis' in Suzanne J. Konzelmann and Marc Fovargue-Davies (eds), *Banking systems in the crisis: the faces of liberal capitalism* (Abingdon, 2013), pp 107–33.

Coleman, Marie, 'McGrath, Joseph ("Joe")', *Dictionary of Irish biography*.

Colley, Declan, *When Bobby met Christy: the story of Bobby Beasley and a wayward horse* (Cork, 2010).

Collins, Stephen and Ciara Meehan, *Saving the State: Fine Gael from Collins to Varadkar* (Dublin, 2020).

Costello, Kevin and Niamh Howlin (eds), *Law and religion in Ireland, 1700–1970* (London, 2021).

Cottrell, John and Marcus Armytage, *A–Z of the Grand National: the official guide to the world's most famous steeplechase* (Newbury, 2008).

Coventry, Arthur and A.E.T. Watson, *Racing and steeplechasing* (London, 1887).

Cox, Michael F., *Notes of the history of the Irish horse* (Dublin, 1897).

D'arcy, Fergus, *Horses, lords and racing men: the Turf Club, 1790–1990* (The Curragh, 1991).

Dolan, Anne, 'The Irish Free State, 1922–1939' in Thomas Bartlett (ed.), *The Cambridge history of Ireland: volume IV: 1880–present*, 4 vols (Cambridge, 2020), pp 323–48.

Evans, Bryce, *Ireland during the Second World War: farewell to Plato's cave* (Manchester, 2014).

Fahey, Tony and Liam Delaney, 'State financial support for horse racing in Ireland', *Budget Perspectives 2007* (ESRI, Dublin, 2006).

Finneran, Richard J. (ed.), *The collected poems of W.B. Yeats*, rev. 2nd ed. (New York, 1996).

Flynn, Roddy. 'A level playing field? Irish broadcast-sports rights and the decline of the national' in Marcus Free (ed.), *Sport, the media and Ireland: interdisciplinary perspectives* (Cork, 2020), pp 227–46.

Foster, R.F., *W.B. Yeats: a life* (Oxford, 1998).

Fuller, Bryony, *Vincent O'Brien: the National Hunt years* (Punchestown, 1992).

Fuller, Bryony, *Tom Dreaper & his horses* (1991).

Garnham, Neal, 'Accounting for the early success of the Gaelic Athletic Association', *Irish Historical Studies*, 34:133 (May 2004), pp 65–78.

Girvin, Brian, 'Stability, crisis and change in post-war Ireland, 1945–1973' in Thomas Bartlett (ed.), *The Cambridge history of Ireland, volume IV: 1880–present*, 4 vols (Cambridge, 2020), pp 381–406.

Godfrey, Nicholas (ed.), *100 favourite racehorses: the 'Racing Post' definitive readers' poll* (Wellingborough, 2005).

Green, Reg, *A race apart: the history of the Grand National* (London, 1988).

Griffin, Brian, '"The more sport the merrier, say we": sport in Ireland during the Great Famine', *Irish Economic and Social History*, 45:1 (2018), pp 90–114.

Hanley, Brian, *The impact of the Troubles on the Republic of Ireland: boiling volcano?* (Manchester, 2018).

Healy, Pat and Richard Pugh, *Point to point: the heart of Irish racing* (Dublin, 2022).

Holland, Anne, *Horse racing in Britain and Ireland* (London, 2014).

Holland, Anne, *The Grand National: a celebration of the world's most famous race* (London, 2019).

Hunt, Tom, *Sport and society in Victorian Ireland: the case of Westmeath* (Cork, 2007).

Hurley, Michael J., 'Baldoyle as a racecourse village', *Dublin Historical Record*, 59:1 (2006), pp 65–80.

Hyland, Francis P.M., *History of Galway Races* (London, 2008).

Kay, Joyce and Wray Vamplew, *The encyclopaedia of British horse racing* (Abingdon, 2012).

Kelly, James, 'Sport and recreation in the eighteenth and nineteenth centuries' in Kelly (ed.), *The Cambridge history of Ireland, volume III: 1730–1880*, 4 vols (Cambridge, 2020), pp 489–516.

Kelly, James (ed.), *The Cambridge history of Ireland, volume III: 1730–1880*, 4 vols (Cambridge, 2020).

Kelly, James, *Sport in Ireland, 1600–1840* (Dublin, 2014).

Kelly, James and Martyn J. Powell (eds), *Clubs and societies in eighteenth-century Ireland* (Dublin, 2010).

Kiberd, Declan, *Inventing Ireland: the literature of the modern nation* (Cambridge, MA, 1996).

Konzelmann, Suzanne J. and Marc Fovargue-Davies (eds), *Banking systems in the crisis: the faces of liberal capitalism* (Abingdon, 2013).

Lambie, James, *The story of your life: a history of the Sporting Life newspaper (1859–1998)* (Leicester, 2010).

Lambton, George, *Men and horses I have known* (London, 1924).

Lehane, Shane, *A history of the Irish Red Cross* (Dublin, 2019).

Lyons, Emma, 'Ladies Day at Punchestown: 150 years of festival fashion', *West Wicklow Historical Society Journal*, 11 (2021), pp 7–14.

MacCormac, Michael, *The Irish racing and bloodstock industry: an economic analysis* (Dublin, 1977).

Magee, Sean, *Arkle: the story of the world's greatest steeplechaser* (Newbury, 2009).

Marshall, Robert D., 'Wylie, William Evelyn', *Dictionary of Irish biography*.

McCabe, Desmond, 'Moore, Henry Francis Seymour', *Dictionary of Irish biography*.

McCormick, Finbar, 'The horse in early Ireland', *Anthropozoologica*, 42:1 (2007), pp 85–104.

McGrath, C.I., 'The penal laws: origins, purpose, enforcement and impact' in Kevin Costello and Niamh Howlin (eds), *Law and religion in Ireland, 1700–1970* (London, 2021), pp 13–48.

McHugh, Susan, *Animal stories: narrating across species lines* (Minneapolis, 2011).

McKenna, Gerry P., 'O'Brien, (Michael) Vincent ("M.V.")', *Dictionary of Irish biography*.

McNabb, Joseph, 'Graham, Sean (John) Patric', *Dictionary of Irish biography*.

McNamara, Conor, '"This wretched people": the famine of 1822 in the West of Ireland' in Conor McNamara and Carla King (eds), *The West of Ireland: new perspectives on the nineteenth century* (Dublin, 2011), pp 13–34.

McNamara, Conor and Carla King (eds), *The West of Ireland: new perspectives on the nineteenth century* (Dublin, 2011).

Miller, Rebecca S., 'Roseland, Jetland, Cloudland and beyond: Irish showbands and economic change, 1958–1975', *New Hibernia Review/Irish Éireannach Nua*, 18:3 (Autumn 2014), pp 77–92.

Mills, John, *Life of a racehorse* (London, 1865).

Moore, Maurice, *An Irish gentleman, George Henry Moore* (London, 1913).

Munting, Roger, *An economic and social history of gambling in Britain and the USA* (Manchester, 1996).

Murphy, David, 'Mahon, Sir Bryan Thomas', *Dictionary of Irish biography*

Murphy, Gary, *Haughey* (Dublin, 2021).

Murphy, William, 'Beasley, Thomas (Tommy)', *Dictionary of Irish biography*.

Murphy, William, 'Croker, Richard ("Boss")', *Dictionary of Irish biography*.

Ní Mhurchadha, Maighréad, '"Two hundred men at tennis": sport in north Dublin, 1600–1760', *Dublin Historical Record* (Spring 2008), pp 87–106.

O'Brien, Jacqueline and Ivor Herbert, *Vincent O'Brien: the official biography* (London, 2005).

O'Connor, Brian, *Kings of the saddle: Ireland's greatest jockeys* (London, 2010).

Ó Gráda, Cormac and Kevin H. O'Rourke, 'The Irish economy in the century after partition', *Economic History Review,* 75:2 (May 2022), pp 336–70.

O'Hagan, John, 'The Irish economy, 1973–2016' in Bartlett (ed.), *Cambridge history of Ireland, volume IV,* pp 500–26.

Ó hÓgáin, Dáithí, 'An capall i mBéaloideas na hÉireann', *Béaloideas/The Journal of the Folklore of Ireland Society,* 47/49 (1977–9).

Oakley, Robin, *Sixty years of jump racing: from Arkle to McCoy* (London, 2017).

Oakley, Robin, *The Cheltenham Festival: a centenary history* (London, 2014).

Peters, Stewart, *The Irish Grand National: the history of Ireland's premier steeplechase* (Stroud, 2006).

Pine, Richard, *2RN: the origins of Irish radio* (Dublin, 2002).

Powell, Martyn J., 'Hunting clubs and societies' in James Kelly and Martyn J. Powell (eds), *Clubs and societies in eighteenth-century Ireland* (Dublin, 2010), pp 392–8.

Richardson, J.M. and F. Mason, *Gentlemen riders: past and present* (London, 1909).

Rouse, John, 'Dreaper, Thomas ("Tom") William', *Dictionary of Irish biography.*

Rouse, Paul, 'Parkinson, James Joseph ("J.J")', *Dictionary of Irish biography.*

Rouse, Paul, *Sport and Ireland: a history* (Oxford, 2015).

Sargent, Harry R., *Thoughts upon sport: a work dealing shortly with each branch of sport: to which are added, a complete history of the Curraghmore Hunt and memoirs of notable sportsmen* (London, 1895).

Shanahan, Jim, 'Moore, Garrett ("Garry")', *Dictionary of Irish biography.*

Sharman, Patrick, 'Runners, riders and risk: safety issues in the history of horseracing' in Stephen Wagg and Allyson M. Pollock (eds), *The Palgrave handbook of sports, politics and harm* (New York, 2021), pp 267–91.

Sharpe, Graham and Declan Colley, *Dorothy Paget: the eccentric queen of the sport of kings* (London, 2017).

Smith, Raymond and Con Costello, *Peerless Punchestown: 150 years of glorious tradition* (Dublin, 2000).

Smyly, Patricia, *Encyclopaedia of steeplechasing* (London, 1979).

Taaffe, Pat, *My life and Arkle's* (London, 1972).

Temple, William, *Miscellanea*. 5th ed. (London, 1697).

Voight, Charles Adolph, *Famous gentleman riders* (London, 1925).

Wagg, Stephen and Allyson M. Pollock (eds), *The Palgrave handbook of sports, politics and harm* (New York, 2021).
Watson, S.J., *Between the flags: a history of Irish steeplechasing* (Dublin, 1969).
Welcome, John, *Irish horse racing: an illustrated history* (London, 1982).
Williams, Guy St John and Francis P.M. Hyland, *Who was who in Irish racing* (Monasterevin, 2020).
Williams, Guy St John, *Martin Molony: a legend in his lifetime* (Dublin, 2001).
Williams, Guy St John, *Winner all right: 100 years of Irish racing and breeding* (Kildare, 1999).
Williams, Guy St John and Francis P.M. Hyland, *Jameson Irish Grand National: a history of Ireland's premier steeplechase* (Dublin, 1995).
Williams, John and Gavin Hall, "A good girl is worth their weight in gold": gender relations in British horseracing', *International Review for the Sociology of Sport*, 55:4 (Dec. 2018), pp 453–70.
Young, Arthur, *A tour in Ireland, with general observations on the present state of that kingdom in 1776–78* (London, 1897).

Theses

Cashmore, Vanessa, 'Are girls any good? An analysis of gender differentials amongst British thoroughbred horseracing' (Masters Dissertation, University of Liverpool, 2018).
Lucey, Donnacha Seán, 'Land and popular politics in County Kerry' (PhD, Maynooth University, 2007).
Nassau-Lane, Stuart, 'The horse in nineteenth-century Ireland: a socio-economic study' (PhD, Maynooth University, 2006).

Online sources

https://www.britishhorseracing.com.
https://charlesjhaughey.ie
https://cheltenhamfestivaluk.com
https://dib.ie
https://www.goracing.ie
https://www.hri.ie
https://www.ihrb.ie
https://irta.ie
https://www.itm.ie
https://www.justice.gov
https://www.p2p.ie
https://racingacademy.ie
https://www.racingpost.com
https://www.revenue.ie
https://www.rte.ie
https://www.thepja.co.uk

Index

The names of horses mentioned in the book are given in *italic* type here.
Entries in **bold** type refer to images.

1798 Rebellion, 19–20
2RN, *see* Radio Teilifís Éireann
A Plus Tard, 198
Abd-el-Kader, 23, 116
Absentee, 36
Adare Commission, 124–7, 132
African Sister, 219
Aga Khan III, 92, 257
Aintree Racecourse, race meeting, 23, 60, 61, 69, 93, 114, 199, 202–3, 235–6
    Aintree Hurdle, 218, 241
    Champion Chase, 76
    Fox Hunters' Chase, 199, 247, 252
    Grand National (Aintree), **4**, **5**, 23, 25, **44**, 45, **54**, 55, **56**, 56, 57, **58**, 58, 59, **60**, 60, 61, 64, 69, **77**, **78**, **79**, 92–3, 103, **112**, 115, 117, **118**, 135, 143, **148**, 149, **150**, **151**, 160, 170, 195, **198**, 202, **203**, 203, **206**, 206, 207, 235–6, 244, 246, **249**, 250, 251
    Grand Sefton Steeplechase, 93
    Stanley Steeplechase, 76
Al Boum Photo, 254
Alberoni, 149
Albert Edward, Prince of Wales, *later* Edward VII, 27–8, 51, 55, 64–5, **65**, 90, **90**
Alexander, J.S., 35
Alexandra, Princess of Wales, *later* Alexandra, queen consort of Edward VII, 28, 51, 64–5, **65**
All Sorts, 72
Ambush II, 55, 64
An Tóstal Festival, 146–7
Anaglogs Daughter, 204–5, **205**, 206
Anglo-Irish, 2, 3, 5, 11, 13, 132–3, 16, 17, 20, 21, 23, 25, 32, 36, 42, 43, 50, 65, 79, 91, 172
Anne Grosvenor, duchess of Westminster, 162, 207
Annie Power, 252
Another Flash, 159
Anthony, Algy, 55, 76, **79**
Anthony, J.R. 'Jack', 76
Anthony, Owen, 92
anti-Treaty IRA, 83, 87

Apple's Jade, 250
Archive, 162
Arctic Copper, 237
Arkle, 6, 114, 115, 160–1, 162–6, **163**, **164**, **168–9**, 168–9, 171–3, 179, 187, 248
Armstrong, Suzy, 229
Arnott, Sir John, 36, 65, 215
Ascetic, 55
Ascetic's Silver, 55
Ascot Racecourse, race meeting, 165, 197
Association of Irish Racecourses (AIR), 215, 259–60, 262
At The Races (tv channel), 258, 259–60
Atha Cliath, 252
Attitude Adjuster, 208
Austin, Francis, 240
Australia, 3, 98, 105, 153, 257
Auteuil Racecourse, race meeting
    Grand Course de Haies d'Auteuil (French Champion Hurdle), 218
    Grand Steeple-Chase de Paris, 45, 56, 76, **78**

Baggallay, Captain Denis, **138**, 138
Baker, Mary, 162
Baldoyle Racecourse, race meeting, **30**, 31, 36, 44, 53, 56, 62, **64**, 68, 74, 76, 99, 110, 111, 187
Ball, Dick, 114
Ballinode, 93
Ballsbridge Bloodstock Sales, 112, 162
Ballyburn, 254
Ballydoyle House, stables, 149, **150**, 152
Ballyhaft Point-to-Point, **210**
Ballylinch Stud, 92, 103
Ballymacad, 69
Ballymacoll Stud, 114
Bannow Rambler, **208**
Barbour Cup (Westmeath Point-to-Point), 106
Barbour, E.L.M., 102
Barbour, Frank, 106
Barry, J.H., 35
Barry, James, 232

295

Barry, Ron, 207
Barry, Sean, **233**, 234
Bartlemy Point-to-Point, **157**
Battleship, 117
Baxier, 143
Be Careful, 102
Beacon Light, 204
Beasley, Bobby, 57, 159, 207
Beasley, Caroline, 197
Beasley, H.H., 57
Beasley, Harry, 45, 56–7, **57**, 58, 87–8
Beasley, Johnny, 45, 56, 58
Beasley, Tommy, 45, **56**, 56, 58
Beasley, Willie, 45, 56, 59
Beef or Salmon, 248
Belclare Point-to-Point, 247, 248
Belfast, 12, 185
Bellewstown Racecourse, race meeting, 12, 31, **221**
Bennet, Captain G.H. 'Tuppy', 92, **93**, 153
Bennett, George Cecil, 133
Bentley, Joss, 93
Bentom Boy, **196**, 197, **200**
Beresford, Henry de la Poer, third marquess of Waterford, **28**, 32
Beresford, John de la Poer, fifth Baron Decies, 73
Beresford, John Henry, fifth marquess of Waterford, 48, 50
Berry, Frank, **202**, 207, **208**, 234
Best Mate, 202, **247**, 248
Betting and Gaming Act (UK, 1961), 105
Betting Tax (1926), **94**, 95, 98, 104
Betting Tax (1931), 104
Biddle, Anne, 195
Biddlecombe, Terry, 248
Bit of a Skite, **249**
Blacker, Mrs Freddie, 92, 102
Blackmore, Rachael, 198–9, **198, 199**
Blackwell, George, **93**
Blake, Edmund, 1, 17, 146, 147
Blancona, 102
Blennerhassett, Arthur, 53
Bloodstock Breeders' and Horse Owners' Association, 123
Blythe, Ernest, **94**, 95, 97–8, 99–101, 103–4
Bobbyjo, 244
Bolger, Enda, 246, 247
Bolger, Jim, 66, 232, 252, 266
Boulard, Pierre, 254
Bourke, Dermot, seventh earl of Mayo, 85, 87
Bourke, Richard Southwell, sixth earl of Mayo, 28

Boylan, Brigadier E.T., 137, 138
Brabazon, Aubrey, **135**, 140, **144**, 144, **151**, 154, 234
Brabazon, Cecil, 150
Brabazon, Leslie, 67, **68**
Bradley, Belle, 196
Brave Inca, **243**, 243
Brennan, John, 180, 184, 187, 190, 191
Brexit, 264–5
Bright Cherry, 162
Brindley, Thomas 'Judge', 53
Briscoe, Basil, 112–14
Briscoe, Henry W., 35
Briscoe, Robert, 132–3
Britain, 2, 16, 18, 20, 23, 33, 43, 68, 69–70, 72, 75–6, 98, 105, 109, 134, 166–7, 172, 180, 184, 185, 194, 229, 235, 236, 237, 249, 258, 262, 264–5
    ownership of National Stud, 92, 110, 126
British administration in Ireland, 19, 63–4, 72, 91
British army, 34, 72, 212–13
    Army Remount Department, 73, 89–90
British Broadcasting Corporation (BBC), 167, 170, 259
British Broadcasting Corporation (BBC) Northern Ireland, 166
British empire, export of horses from Ireland, 3, 66–7, 73–4
British Horseracing Authority (BHA), 267
Broderick, Shane, 234
Brooke, Frank, 77
Brown Lad, **206**, 207
Browne, James, 261
Brownlow, Major W.S., **212**, 212
Brownstown Stud, 124
Bryanstown House, 165–6
Bryce-Smith, Helen, 194
Buck House, **217**, 218
Buckingham, John, 170
Bulger, Dan, 138
Bulteel, J.G., 61
Butler, James, twelfth earl of Ormond, 13
Byerley Turk, **15**
Byrne, W.J., 150

Canty, Joseph 'Joe', 76
Captain Christy, 57, 201, 207
Carberry, Nina, 199, **200**
Carberry, Paul, 147, 244, **244**, 245
Carberry, Tommy, 201, **203**, 203, 204–5, **206**, 207, **208**, 244

Carey's Cottage, 149
Carmody, Tommy, **217**, 218
Carr, Philip, 113
Carrickfergus Strand, County Antrim, race meeting, 12
Cash, Barry, **243**
Castledermot, **145**
Castleruddery, 208
Caughoo, **135**, 135
Central Racing Advisory Committee (CRAC), 123, 124
Chamier, 149
Chamour, 155
Chantry House, 250
Cheltenham Racecourse, Festival, race meeting, 23, 96, 114, 135, 141, 142, 144, **145**, 149, 160, 161, 162, 195, 197, 198, **202**, **203**, 204, 217, 218, 219, 237, 243, 245, **251**, 251, 252, 253–4, 265
    Arkle Challenge Trophy (Cheltenham), 204–5, 246
    Broadway Novices' Chase, *or* Sun Alliance *or* RSA Novices' Chase, 162, 204, 248
    Champion Bumper, *or* Weatherby's Champion Bumper, 252, 253–4
    Champion Chase, 142, 160, 161, 195, 204, 205, 208, 218, 246
    Champion Hurdle, 57, 96, 135, 144, **148**, 149, 159, 161, 196, 198, 217, **243**, 243, 253
    Cotswold Chase, 160, **162**, 250
    Foxhunters' Chase, 197, 199, 208, 247
    Gloucestershire Hurdle, *or* Supreme Novices' Hurdle, 149, 160, 237, 252
    Gold Cup (Cheltenham), 57, 93, 96, 103, 114, 115, 117, 135, 141, 144, 149, 159, 160, 163, **164**, 164, 168, 180, 196, 198, 201–2, **202**, **203**, 203, 204, 206, 207, **216**, 239, 246, 248, 250, 251, 254
    Grand Annual Steeplechase, 23
    Kim Muir Handicap Chase, **138**, 208
    Sun Alliance Novices' Hurdle, *or* RSA *or* Ballymore Novices' Hurdle, 240, 243, **251**
Chichester, Dermot, seventh marquess of Donegall, 214
China Cottage, **145**
Chinrullah, 204
Cill Dara, 250
Cima, 217
Civil War (horse), 72
Clarke, F. Harold, 106, 137, **137**
Cleary, Dick, 72

Clonmel Racecourse, race meeting (Powerstown Park), 69
Closutton stables, 250, 252, 253
Codd, Jamie, 247
Cole, Lowry Egerton, fourth earl of Enniskillen, 71
Collins, General Michael, Turf Club and INHS Committee condolences, 85
Collins, Michael C. (trainer), 124, 150
Comber Point-to-Point, 210
Come Away, 56, **57**
Commanche Court, 244
Commission of Inquiry into the Horse Breeding Industry (1935), 110–11, 119
Commission on Horse-Breeding, Ireland (1896–7), 52
Connolly, Mrs T.A., **206**
Connolly, T.A., **137**, **157**
Conolly, Tom, 16
Controller, 45
Conyngham, Francis, second Marquess, 27, 28, 35
Cool Dawn, 248
Cool Ground, 248
Coonan, Bobby, 207
Coote, Captain Richard, 35
Coranna, 25
Corduff Stud, 116
Cork Park Racecourse, race meeting, **29**, 36, 37, 44
Cosgrave, Liam, 183, 185, 229
Cosgrave, W.T., **84**, 85, 86–7, 95, 101, 109, 119, 133, 175, 181, 183
Cosgrove, Stan, 191
Costello, John A., 139
Costello, Tom, 248
Costello, Tony, **247**, **253**
Cottage Rake, 141, **144**, 144, **145**
Coveney, Simon, 263–4
Covertcoat, 69
Covid-19 pandemic, 265, 267
Cowen, Brian, 262
Cox, John Richard 'Bunny', 140, 142
Craigie, Alec, 160
Craigie, Roy, **233**
Crawford, Leslie, **233**
Croker, H.S., 33, 35, 36
Croker, Richard 'Boss', 54
Crumlin, Dublin city, race meeting, 14, 19
Cullen, Maria, 197, 199
Cumann na nGaedheal, 94, 124
Curley, Barney, **221**
Curragh Coffee House, 16

INDEX   297

Curragh Racecourse, race meeting, 12–13, 14, 18, 42, 53, 74, 152, 155, 167, 170, 182, 231, 257
    Drogheda Memorial Stakes, 53
    Irish Cambridgeshire, 141, 197
    Irish Cesarewitch, 141, 159, 250
    Irish Derby, 53, 55, 56, 149–50, 170
    Irish Lincolnshire, 197
    Irish Oaks, 53
    King's Plate, 13, 53
Curragh, The, County Kildare, 21, 23, 45, 52, 70, 76, 79, 89, 93, 96–7, 189, 256,
Curraghmore Hunt, 49, 50
Córas Iompair Éireann (CIÉ), 144, 188

Danoli, 239–42, **240**, **241**
Davy Jones, 116
Davy Lad, 201, 204
Dawn Run, 6, 180, 206, **216**, **217**, 216–19, 252
Dawson Prince, 197
de Boinville, Nico, 250
de Bromhead, Henry, 198
de Burgh, Major J.H., 122, 124, 158
de Stacpoole, Eileen Constance, Duchess, 118
de Stacpoole, George, fifth Duc, 124
de Valera, Eamon, 74, 75, 109, 119, 133, 166
Deasy, Austin, 232
Delta Work, **251**
Dempsey, Eddie, 135
Denman, 245, 248–9
Derrinstown Stud, 242
Desert Orchid, **238**, 238
Digby, Robert, first Baron, 13
Distel, 135
Dixon, Captain Herbert, 77
Dolan, Joe, 187
Don Cossack, 251
Don't Push It, **249**, 250
Donnelly, Charlie, 102
Dorans Pride, 241, 247
Dormant, 164, 165
Douvan, 245, 252
Dowd, Gerry, 207
Down Royal Corporation of Horse Breeders, 13, 20
Down Royal Racecourse, *also* Maze Racecourse, **26**, **86**, 88, 111, 201, 211, 211, 212, **245**, 245
    King's Plate (Down Royal), 13
Downpatrick Racecourse, race meeting, **6–7**, 76, **135**, 189, 197, 201, 211, **212**, 212, 213, 229, 238
    Ulster National, **135**, 135, 213
Doyle, Michael, **233**

Dreaper, Betty, **161**
Dreaper, Jim, **206**, 207
Dreaper, Tom, 116–17, 140, **145**, 159–60, 163, 166, 169, 180, 189, 206–7
Drogheda Memorial Fund (Irish Trainers' and Jockeys' Benevolent and Provident Fund), 59, 62, 180
Dromahane Point-to-Point, **239**
Drumcree, 55
Dublin and Drogheda Railway Company, 31
Dublin and South Eastern Railway, 63, 77
Dublin Horse Show, 119, 138
Duggan, Jack, 136, 137, **137**, 175
Dukes, Alan, 263
Dundalk Racecourse, race meeting, 116, 258
    Sweet Afton Cup, 143, **209**
Dunne Cullinan, Paddy, 124
Dunne, Captain Gerald, **108**
Dunne, L., 37
Dunne, Larry, **203**
Dunshauglin, 136
Dunwoody, Richard, **181**, 239
Durkan, Bill, 204
Durkan, John, 242–3
Dyas, Harry, 60–1

Eade, Suzanne, 201
Early Mist, **4**, **148**, 148, 149, 152
Easter Hero, 103, 115
Easter Rising, 72–3, 74, 91
Economic War, 109, 126
Edward VII, *see* Albert Edward, Prince of Wales
Egan, Denis, 257
Eliogarty, 197
Elizabeth, Queen Mother, **211**
Elliott, Gordon, **251**, 251, 267
Emergency, the (Second World War, Ireland) 84, 116, 120, 121–6, 134
Empress, 45, 56
England, 23, 24, 32, 52, 58, 117, 134, 172, 195, 207
Entertainment Tax (1916), 70–1, 88, 94–5, 97, 99, 104
Envoi Allen, **251**
Epsom Derby, 23, 55
Equine Anti-Doping Programme (EADP), 266
Esha Ness, 236
European Breeders' Fund (EBF), 216, 232
European Economic Community (EEC), 183
European Union (EU), 264–5
Excess Profits Duty (1915), 70, 88, 94
Eyre, Gyles, 193

Eyrefield Lodge, 45, 55, 56

Fairyhouse Racecourse, race meeting, 26, 36–7, **71**, 72, 75, 87, 97, 101, **115**, **116**, 121, 158, 159–60, **159**, 170, 174, 207, 215, 231, 233, 234, 254
    Hatton's Grace Hurdle (Fairyhouse), 241, 243
    Irish Grand National, 42, 45, 56, 57, **102**, 102, 103, 111, **115**, **116**, 141, 149, 153, **159**, 159–60, 161, 163, 167, 180, 182, 185, 194, **196**, 197, 199, 200, **204**, 204, 207, 244, 248, **249**, 251, 253
    Powers Gold Cup, 162, 170, **181**, 182, 185
Farmer, Captain Dick, 112
Faugheen, 245, 252
Fearless Fred, 142, 143
Ferris, Ann, 194, **196**, 197, 199, **200**, 208
Fianna Fáil, 109, 132, 134, 150, 181, 213, 237, 255
Fine Gael, 133, 172, 183, 214, 232, 237
Fingal Harriers, 171
Finlay, Barbara, **181**
Finlay, Jimmy, **181**
First World War, 5, 42, 68–74, 76, 88, 89, 93, 120, 122
    Red Cross Race Meetings, 69
    War National, 69, 92
Fitzgerald, Mick, 239
Fitzwilliam, Henry W., 33, 35
Flannery, Edward, **233**
Flashing Steel, **181**, 182
Flood, Francis, 142, 180, **203**
Flood, William, **233**
Florida Pearl, 248, 252, **253**
Flyingbolt, 160–1, **161**, 162, **162**, 163, 166
Foinavon, 170
Foley, Tom, 240–2
Forbes, Bernard, eighth earl of Granard, 85
Forbes, Lady Eva, 102
Forster, Lt Col. F.R., 35
Fort Leney, **165**
Fortria, 159, **159**, 160
Fowler, John, 208
France, 194, 254, 266
French, Field Marshal Viscount John, 74, 77
Frigate, 56
Furlong, Frank, 115
Furlong, Major Noel, 115
Furlong, Michael, **208**, **221**
Furness, Marmaduke, first Viscount, 92

Gaelic Athletic Association (GAA), 151, 188, 264
Gallopin des Champs, 254

Galmoy, 219
Galway Racecourse, Festival, race meeting (Ballybrit), **4**, 5, 36, 73, 149, 159, 231, 258, 262
    Galway Hurdle, 143, 159, 180
    Galway Plate, 36, 56, 57, 102, 103, 111, 143, 149, 159
Galway, Richie, 268
Gambling Regulation Act (2024), 261
Gambling Regulatory Authority of Ireland (GRAI), 261
Gargan, Captain E.A., 125
Garristown, County Dublin, race meeting, 14
Gay Trip, **206**, 207
General Principle, 251
George V, *also* George, duke of York, 63, 65, 78
Geraghty, Barry, 112, 147, **244**, 245–6, 250
Geraghty, Laurence, 112
Geraghty, Matt, 195
Geraghty, Tucker, 245
Gerrard, Major T.G.C., 101
Gigginstown House Stud, 250–2, 251
Glencairn Stud, stables, 54, 124
Glencaraig Lady, 180, 201, **202**, 203
Go Racing (media consortium), 259–60
Godsen, John, 242
Goff, Robert J., 52
Goffs, 89, 162, 215, 240
Golden Miller, **112**, 112–14, **113**, 115, 203, 245
Golden View II, 161
Goodwill, Linda, 196
Goulding, Sir William, 88
Gowran Park Racecourse, race meeting, 74, 76, 88, 118, 136, **136**, 137, 158, 161, 162, 163, 170, 173, **241**, 241
    Thyestes Chase, 136, 161, 163, 180, 206
Graham, Sean, **186**, 186, 189, 210, 214
Grand Alliance Racing Club (Oireachtas syndicate), 237
Grand National (horse), 45
Great Famine, 24–6, 41, 51
Great Northern Railways, 30
Great Southern and Western Railway (GSWR), 31–2
Great Southern Railways, **145**
Greenogue stables, 140, 160, **161**, 161, **206**, 207
Greer, Captain Henry, 85
Gregalach, 115
Griffin, Joe 'Mincemeat', **148**
Griffith, Arthur, condolences of Turf Club and INHS Committee, 85
Grosvenor, Anne, duchess of Westminster, 162, 165

Guest, Raymond R., 201, 203
Guest, Sir Ivor Churchill, first Viscount Wimborne, 72
Guinness, **168**, 168–9, **169**

Halley, Dr Walter, 234
Hallowment, **145**
Hamilton, James, first duke of Abercorn, 28
Hamilton, James, third Baron Holmpatrick, 138
Hamilton, Letitia Marion, 2
Hanlon, John 'Shark', 199
Hanway, William, 51
Happy Home, 144
Harchibald, **243**, 244
Hardy Eustace, **243**, 243–4
Harrington, Jessica, 195–196
Hartigan, Hubert, 96, 150
Harvey, John, 210
Hatton's Grace, 144, **145**, 145, **148**, 148, 149
Haughey, Charles J., **181**, 181–3
Haughey, Maureen, **181**
Havasnack, 159
Hawkins, Charles, 92
Haydock Park Racecourse, race meeting, 207
Hazy Dawn, 252
Heald, Mrs Arthur, 194
Healy, T.M., 86–7, **87**
Hedgehunter, 250
Height O'Fashion, 161, 163
Henderson, Nicky, 250
Hill, Arthur, fifth marquess of Downshire, 35
Hill, Charmian, 216–18
Hill-Dillon, Colonel Stephen S., **108**, 109, 111–12
Hobbs, Bruce, 117
Hogan, P.P., 116, 140, **142**, 142, **143**, **145**, 147
Honeysuckle, 198
Horse and Greyhound Racing Act (2001), 255
Horse Breeding Act (1934), 109
Horse Racing Ireland (HRI), 6, 182, 183, 201, 255–6, 258, 259–60, 262, 263, 264, 266, 267, 268
Horsebreeders' Association, 119
Hourigan, Michael, 241, 248
Hughes, Dessie, 243
Hunter, J.R., 21
Hunter, Robert, 21
Hunter, Robert J., 33, 34–5, **35**
Hurricane Fly, 245, 253
Huston, John, 147
Hyde, Douglas, 139
Hyde, Henry, **168**

Hyde, Tim, **115**, **116**

Ilchester Report, 126
Imperial Call, 241, 248
Imperial Commander, 249
Interdepartmental Committee on Irish Racing (1927), 98–101
Irian, 197
Irish Bookmakers' Association, 261
Irish Breeders', Owners' and Trainers' Association (IBOTA), 73–4, 95, 96, 101
Irish Civil War, 84, 87, 91, 115
Irish Horse Welfare Trust, 263
Irish Horseracing Authority (IHA), 6, 182, 223, 228–31, 233, 237, 238, 255–6, 258, 259
Irish Horseracing Industry Bill (1994), 228–9, 233
Irish Horseracing Regulatory Board (IHRB), 201, 264, 266, 267
Irish Hospitals' Sweepstake, **120**, 121, **123**, 124, **125**, 175
Irish Hospitals' Trust, **120**, 170, 174
Irish Jockey Club, 11, 16–17
Irish Lass ('*Podareen Mare*'), 15
Irish National Bookmakers' Association, 231
Irish National Hunt Steeplechase (INHS) Committee, 2, 12, 27, 33, 34–5, 36, 37, 41, 42–7, 49–50, 52–4, 56, 58–9, 62, 70, 71, 73, 75, 77, 79, 84–5, **86**, 95–8, 100–1, **105**, 106–7, 108–9, 110–12, 119–21, 121–3, 124–6, 132, 134, 136–40, 151–8, **155**, 173, 174, 184, 186, 187, 189–90, **190**, 191, 194, 195, 197, 201, 209, 210, 211, 211, 212, 213, 220, 223, 228, 232–5, 236, 255–7, 259, 264
  centenary year, 180–1, 183
  clerks of the course, 45, 50, 90, 106, 190, 201, 234
  Inspector of Courses (with Turf Club), 45–6, 53, 106, 143, 234
  Keeper of the Match Book, 17, 21, 33, 35, 53, **137**, **138**, 138, 189, 228
  Point-to-Point Committee, 190, 201
  Registrar, 106, 137, 138, 233, 234
  Registry Office (with Turf Club), 138, 189, **200**, 256
  Senior Steward, 35, 53, 69, 88, 95, **108**, 109, 110, 111, 122–3, 134, 137, 157, 158, 173, 174, 179, 180, 184, 188, 189, 190, 191, 197, **200**, 212, 214, 219, 230, 232, 233, 234, 235, 236, 259
  Stewards, 35, 41, 43, 45, 47, 50, 53, 65, 71, 72, 90–1, 103, 106, 108, 111, 118–19, 122–3, 125–6, 137, 152, 153, 180, 200, 201, 230
Irish National Hunt Steeplechase (INHS) Rules, 33, 34, 43–7, 49–50, 103, 108, 118, 133, 152, 155,

193, 195
Irish National Stud (Tully Stud), 52, 85, 89, 92, 110, 126–7, 182, 220, 242
Irish Provincial Racecourse Executives' Association (IPREA), 97–8, 100–1, 103, 111
Irish Racecourse Executives' Association, 184
Irish Racecourse Medical Officers' Association, 191
Irish Racehorse Trainers' Association (IRTA), 150
Irish Red Cross Steeplechase, 120, 121
Irish Republican Army (Irish Volunteers), 68, 72, 75
Irish Rugby Football Union (IRFU), 85
Irish Society for the Prevention of Cruelty to Animals (ISPCA), 263
Irish Sweeps Hurdle, 174–5, **175**, 197, 207
Irish Thoroughbred Marketing (ITM) 222, 237
Irish Transport and General Workers' Union (ITGWU), 96
Irwin, Jonathan, 215
Istabraq, 239–40, **242**, 242–3, 246

Jackdaws Castle, 250
Jasmin de Vaux, 253
Jerry M., 76, 77
Jezki, 196, 250
Jockey Club, 11, 16, 32, 33, 34, 70, 85, 152, 153, 155, 194, 195, 196, 203, 211, 232, 265
Jockey Supports Working Group, 267
Jockeys' Accident Fund, 105, 111, 234
Jockeys' Association, 174, 188, 191, 234
Jockeys' Benevolent Fund, 191
Jockeys' Emergency Fund, 234

Kauto Star, **245**, 245
Kavanagh, Brian, 183, 262
Kavanagh, Terry, 59, 60–1
Keeling, Joe, 264
Kellistown Point-to-Point, **157**
Kempton Park Racecourse, **168**, 196, 244
  King George VI Chase, 141, **144**, 165, 239, 205, 207, 248
Kennedy, Edward 'Cub', 73, **89**
Keogh, Michael, 234
Keogh, Moya, **148**
Kicking King, 246
Kiernan, James, 72
Kilbarry, 102
Kilbeggan Racecourse, race meeting, 197, 260
Kilcock, County Kildare, race meeting, 18
Kildangan Stud, 182
Kildare Hunt Ball, 27

Kildare Hunt Club, 27, 51, 85, 96, 147
Kilkenny city, race meeting, 24–5
Kilkenny Foxhounds, 102
Killanin Commission (Commission of Inquiry into the Thoroughbred Horse Breeding Industry, 1986), 219–20, 229
Killanin Report (Report of the Commission of Inquiry into the Thoroughbred Horse Breeding Industry, 1986), 180, 219–20, 229
Killarney Racecourse, race meeting, 136
Killeagh Harriers, **146**, 147
King, Larry, 103
King-Harman, Sir Cecil, 133
Kingsbridge Station (now Heuston Station), **145**
Kirkland, 55
Kirwan, Dan, **102**
Knight Errant, 159
Knight, Henrietta, 248
Knock Hard, 149, 152, 159

L'Escargot, 201–2, **203**, 244
La Touche, Percy, 53, 72, 77, 78
Labour Party, 183, 214
Lalor, Liz, 194
Land League, 50, 51
Lavery, Cecil, 140
Lemass, Seán, 122, 166–7
Lennon, May, 138
Leopardstown Racecourse, race meeting, **62–3** 63, 64, 65, 69, 70, 77, 110, **163**, 170, 187, **188**, 189, 195, 204, 216, 231, 241
  Arkle Novice Chase, *or* Milltown Novice Chase (Leopardstown), 162, 204
  Irish Champion Hurdle, 143, 160, 198, 217, 240, 241, 253
  Irish Gold Cup, *or* Hennessy Gold Cup, 241, 248, 253
  Leopardstown Chase, 141, 149, **163**, 163, 165
Lewis, Jim, 248
Lillingston, Alan, **233**, 234
Limerick Junction Racecourse, race meeting, *also* Tipperary Racecourse, 73, 74, 153
Limerick Racecourse, race meeting, 99, 231, 260
Linde, Henry Eyre, **44**, 45, 55, 56, 59
Lindsay, Lady Kathleen, **67**
Lismore Point-to-Point, 248, **253**
Listowel Racecourse, race meeting, 101, 113, **113**, 231
  Kerry National, 143
Loder, Eustace 'Lucky', 55
Lord Windermere, 246

Louth Hunt, 54
Luan Casca, 151
Lucky Dome, 149, 152
Lushington, G.W., 55
Lynn, Jackie, 72

Macks Friendly, 252
Mad Tom, 18
Madden, Niall, 208
Maddenstown Lodge, 66
Maffey, Dorothy, 139
Magnier, Clem, 180
Magnier, John, 215, 250
Maguire, Adrian, **239**, 239, 248
Maher, J.J., 69, 88
Mahon, Sir Bryan, 72–3, 85, 87, 96, 101
Mallow Racecourse, race meeting, 94, 97, 185, 228, 231
Man O'War, 60, 118
Mandarin, 160
Mangan, Jimmy, 246
Manifesto, 59, **60**, 60–1
Manly, Joe, 76
Marshall, Bryan, **148**, 149, 207
Martin, Captain Gerald, 119
Martin, J.M., 133
Martinstown Stud, 246, 250
Martyn-Hemphill, Patrick, fifth Baron Hemphill, 189, 200, 236
Mary, duchess of York, *later* Mary, queen consort of George V, 63, 65
Master Robert, 93
Masters of Foxhounds Association, 108
Masters, Sylvia Frances, **193**, 194
Mathew, 23
Maze Racecourse, race meeting, *see* Down Royal Racecourse
McAlpine, Sir Malcolm, 76
McAuliffe, Willie, 60
McCabe, F.F., 97
McCalmont, Harry, 103
McCalmont, Lady Helen, **102**, 102–3
McCalmont, Major Dermot, 102–3, 124, 139–40
McCalmont, Major Victor, 103
McCarthy, Denis, 200
McCoy, A.P., 239, **249**, 250
McCreevy, Charlie, 255–6
McDonough, Allen, 56, 58
McDowell, Herbert, 135
McDowell, Jack, 135
McDowell, Mary, **135**

McDunphy, Michael, 139
McGrath, Joseph 'Joe' 123–5, **125**, 133, 175
McGrath, Seamus, 124, 197
McKeever, R.W., 173, 174
McKenna, Patrick, 76
McKinlay, Robert, 93
McLernon, Brian, **146**, 147
McLernon, W.A. 'Bill', 142–3, **143**, **146**, 147
McLoughlin, Liam, **161**
McManus, J.P., 242, 243, 246–7, **249**, 249–50, 260
McManus, Noreen, 246, **249**, 250
McNamara, J.T., **246**, 247
McNeile, A.J., 35
Meade, Noel, 237, 244, 245
Mellor, Stan, 143
Messrs Weatherby, 52, 194
Midland Great Western Railway (MGWR), 31, 36
Midnight Court, 248
Mill House, 160, 163, **164**, 164
Minella Times, **198**, 250
Moloney, Eamon, **200**, 212
Moloney, John, 233
Molony, Martin, 140, **141**, 144
Molony, Tim, 118, 140, **141**, 149, 207
Montgomery, Captain John, 35
Monty's Pass, 246
Moore, A.L., 134, 157, 214
Moore, Arthur, **141**
Moore, Augustus, 25
Moore, Colonel Maurice, 85, 87
Moore, Dan, 117–19, **48**, **117**, **118**, **141**, 180, **200**, 201, 203, 206
Moore, Garrett 'Garry', **58**, 58, 61, 155
Moore, George Henry, 25, 85
Moore, Henry Francis Seymour, third marquess of Drogheda, 12, 27, **28**, 33, **34**, 34–5, 36–7, 49–50, 59, 62
Moore, Joan, 119, **141**, **200**, 201, 203
Moore, John Hubert, 46, 56, 58, 58, 61
Moore, Louisa, 25
Moore, Tom Levins, **48**
Moore, Willie, 61
Moorhead, J.F., 259
Morgan, Danny, 150
Morgan, Frank, 93
Morgan, Joanna, 197
Morris, Michael 'Mouse', **208**, 208, 218, 250
Morris, Michael, third Baron Killanin, 219, 229
Morris, T.A., 123
Moscow Flyer, 196, 243, 246

Moyglare Stud dinner, 255, 257
Mr What, **5**
Mulcahy, Major-Gen. P.A., 140
Mulhern, John, 182, 219
Mullingar Racecourse, race meeting, 187
Mullins, Danny, 252
Mullins, Jim, **157**
Mullins, Maureen, 252
Mullins, Paddy, **157**, 216–18, **217**, 252
Mullins, Patrick, 67, 252, 253–4
Mullins, Tony, **217**, 217, 218, 252
Mullins, Willie, 208, **217**, **221**, 237, 245, 248, 250–1, 252–5, **254**, 260
Murdock, C., 194
Murphy, Colm, 243
Murphy, Ferdy, 204
Murphy, John, 23
Murphy, Martin J., 66
Murphy, Stan, 206
Murray, William, eighth earl of Mansfield, 212
Music Hall, 92
My Prince, 115

Naas Racecourse, race meeting, 88, **89**, 141, 152, **164**, 165, 195
Nagle, Florence, 195
National Hunt Committee (Britain), 33, 52, 153, 155
Navan Racecourse, race meeting, (Proudstown Park), 78, 88, 91, 111, 116, 191, 196
Nelson, Sir James, 122–3
Newbury Racecourse, race meeting, 113, 162–3, 164, 165
Newcastle, County Limerick, race meeting, 31
Newmarket Racecourse, race meeting, 13, 70
Nicholls, Paul, 245, 249
Nicholson, Jim, 229
Nolan, Peggy St John, 194
Normandy, 174
Northern Breeders' Association, 229
Northern Ireland, 78, 85–7, **86**, 121, 166, 174, 180, 181, 189, 210–13, 229, 264–5
Northern Ireland Turf Guardians' Association, 213
Norton, William, 139
Nugent, Sir Walter, 96, 101

O'Beirne, F., 133
O'Brien, Aidan, **242**, 243, 253
O'Brien, Alphonsus 'Phonsie', 143, 153
O'Brien, Dan, 141, **145**
O'Brien, Jackie, **145**

O'Brien, Jacqueline, 149, 153
O'Brien, John E., 114
O'Brien, Vincent, 6, 135, 140–1, **144**, 144, **145**, **148**, 148, 149–50, **150**, 152–3, 155–6, 215, 254
O'Callaghan, Cornelius, 1, 17, 147, 148
O'Callaghan, Maurice, **148**
O'Connor, Derek, 247
O'Donnell, A.S. 'Wren', **157**
O'Donoghue, Michael, 234
O'Dwyer, Conor, 242, **243**
O'Ferrall, Roderic 'Roddy' More, 127
O'Grady, Edward, 207, **249**, 250
O'Grady, Willie, **206**, 207
O'Hehir, Michael, 136, 139, **167**, 167, 170
O'Kelly, Phyllis, **137**
O'Kelly, Seán T., 132, 136, **137**, 139
O'Leary, Eddie, 250
O'Leary, Michael, 250–2, **251**, 260
O'Leary, Violet, 252
O'Malley, Desmond 'Des', 237
O'Meara, Tracey, 201
O'Neill, Dan, 240
O'Neill, Jonjo, 207, **216**, 217, 218, 250
O'Sullevan, Peter, 218, 236
O'Sullivan, Cahir, 189, 228
O'Sullivan, Derek, 191
O'Sullivan, Ivo, **233**
O'Toole, Mick, 204
Old Fairyhouse Stud, **141**
Old Rock and Chichester Hunt race meeting, 35
Oldtown Point-to-Point, 171
On the Fringe, 198
Orby, 55
Organisedconfusion, **200**
Osborne, Henry, 23
Osborne, Meta, 201
Osborne, Michael, 182, 191
Othello ('Black and All Black'), 15
Ousley, Miss, 193
Owen's Sedge, **160**, 160
Oxx, John, 237

Paddy Power, 231, 260
Paget, Dorothy, **113**, 114, 135–6, **138**
Palmerstown Stud, 195
Papillon, 244
Parkinson, Billy, 67, **68**, 68, 76
Parkinson, J.C., 118
Parkinson, James J. (J.J.), 52, 66–7, **67**, **68**, 76, 85, 87, 89

INDEX

Peard, J.H.H., 215
Peck, Gregory, **160**, 160
Persse, Burton, 35
Phoenix Park Racecourse, race meeting, 64–5, 77, 84, 152, 171, 182, 187, 196, 197, 215–16
    IRA Meeting, 84
Pim, David, **233**
Pitman, Jenny, 236
Plunkett, Oliver, twelfth earl of Fingall, 137, 158
Pride of Arras, 57, 87–8
Prince Regent, **115**, **116**, 116–17, 134, 135, 160
Prolan, 208
Punch, 72
Punchestown Racecourse, Festival, race meeting, **3**, 27–9, **28**, 31, 34, 36, 37, 45, 51–2, 56–7, 59, 64, 74, 75, 86–8, 90, 91, 96, 102, 103, 121, 124, 139, 180, 185, **186**, 201, 207, **208**, **217**, 218, 231, **240**, 241, **242**, 243, 254, 255–6, 258, 268
    Conyngham Cup, 51, 56, 57, 102, 103
    Corinthian Cup, 27, **28**
    Downshire Plate, **142**
    Drogheda Stakes, 51
    Kildare Hunt Cup, 34
    La Touche Cup, 77, 246
    Maiden Plate, 57, 87
    Morgiana Hurdle, 241
    Prince of Wales' Plate, 56, 57, 64, 103
    Punchestown Champion Novices' Hurdle, 243
    Punchestown Gold Cup, 162, 253

Qualified Riders' Accident Fund (QRAF), 234, 235
Quare Times, 148, 149, 150, 153
Quevega, 253, 254
Quin, Captain George, 63, 137
Quinn, Captain W., 35
Quirke, Martin, 150
Quita Que, 142

Racecourse (Amendment) Bill (1975), 185
Racecourse Executives' Association, 173
Racecourse Media Group (RMG), 260
Racing Academy and Centre of Education (RACE), 182, **192**, 192, 220
Racing Board, 6, 119, 124, 132–4, 136, 151–2, 156, 171–2, 173, 179, 180, 183, 185, 187, 188, 189, 209, 211, 212, 214, 215, 219, 220, 222, 223, 228, 230, 231
Racing Calendar (English), 52
Racing Calendar (Irish), 17, 19–20, 21, 24, 33, 34, 34–5, 97, 100, 122, 156, 232
Racing Channel, 259

Radio Éireann, *see* Radio Teilifís Éireann
Radio Teilifís Éireann (RTÉ), 91, 166, 167, 170, 184, 258–9
Rank, J. Arthur, 116
Rank, J.V., **116**, 160
Rea, Joseph, 211
Red Park, **102**, 103
Red Rum, 202
Redmond, Tony, 207
Rees, Fred, 76, 92
Rees, Lewis, 92
Reynolds, A.P., 133
Reynolds, Albert, 222
Reynoldstown, 114–16
Ricci, Rich, 252
Rimell, Fred, 174
Riordan, John, 216
Risk of Thunder, 246–7
Robinson, Anthony 'Tony', **204**, 204
Robinson, Willie, 234
Roche, Sir David, 35
Roddy Owen, 159
Rogers, Charlie, 135, 150
Rogers, Darby, 150
Rogers, J.M., **200**
Rooney, Caroline, **200**
Rooney, Willie, 142, 197, **200**, 247
Roscommon Racecourse, race meeting, 136, 260
Roscommon, county, race meeting, 18
Rosewell House, 207
Royal Approach, 160
Royal Danieli, 117, **118**
Royal Dublin Society (RDS), 119, 138
Royal Mail, 115
Royal Tan, 149, **150**, 152–3
Russell, Davy, 246, 247, 248
Ruttledge, P.J., 119, 123, 134
Ryan, James, 110, 120, 122, 172
Ryan, Richie, 183
Ryan, Tommy, **249**

Sadler's Wells, 242
Sandford, Stephen 'Laddie', 92
Sandown Park Racecourse, race meeting, 63, **141**, 165, 169
Sangster, Robert, 215
Sargent, Harry, 55
Scottish Grand National, 92
Seanad Éireann, 85, 229
Second World War, 134–5, 137

Sergeant Murphy, 92, **93**
Shagreen, 160
Shannon Lass, 55, 135
Shaun Spadah, 76, 79, 92
Sheila's Cottage, 135
Shelbourne Football Club, 169
Shirley, Lt Col. Evelyn, 110, 133
Shortt, Francis, 154, **206**, 207
Silver Bachelor, 252
Silver Birch, 251
Silver Fame, 144
Sinn Féin, 74–5
Sir Des Champs, 250
Sir Robert Peel, 37
Sir William, 58
Sizing John, 196
Sleator, Paddy, 150, 158–9, **159**, 180
Sligo Racecourse, race meeting, 201, 260
Smith, William, 92
Smurfit, Michael, 215
Smyth, Mrs H., 102
South and West of Ireland Breeders' and Owners' Association, 123
Spencer, John Poyntz, fifth Earl Spencer, 37
Sports Information Services (SIS), 260, 262
St Lawrence, Thomas, third earl of Howth, 28, 36
St Lawrence, William, Viscount, fourth earl of Howth, 27, **28**, 35, 36, 43–4
Stable Lads' Pension Scheme, 191
Stack, Tommy, 207
Stagalier, 245
Stanhope, William, eleventh earl of Harrington, 236
Stewart, Robert, Viscount Castlereagh 20
Stewart, Rosemary, 194, 197, **200**
Still William, 194
Stokes, Molly, 92
Suann, Dr Craig, 266
Sutherland, Fergie, 241
Swan, Charlie, 239, **240**, 242, 242, 243
Sweepstakes Bill (1923), 88
Sweetman, Gerard, 140, 172
Sword Flash, 159
Symaethis, 111

Taaffe, Pat, 140, 149, **159**, 160, 162–3, **163**, **164**, 166, **168–9**, 169, **203**, **206**, 207
Taaffe, Thomas 'Toss', 149
Taaffe, Tom, **5**
Taaffe, Tom (jnr), 246
Tartan Ace, 248

Tattersalls Bloodstock Auctioneers, 141
Temple, Sir William, 13
Ten Up, 201
The Colonel, 116
The Liberator, 58
The Soarer, 61
The Tetrarch, 89, 103
The Thinker, 248
Thiggin-thue, 45
Thomond II, 114
Thoroughbred Breeders' and Owners' Association, 96
Thoroughbred Industry Board (TIB), 220
Thurles Racecourse, race meeting, 74, 198, 199, 204, 205, 252, 260
Tied Cottage, 203–4, **204**, 206
Tiger Roll, 246, **251**, 251
Tipperary Foxhounds, 194
Tipperary Tim, 103
Tolka Park, 168
Too Good, 45
Topham, Mirabel, 202
Totalisator Act (1929), 101
Tote, totalisator system, 100, 101, 104–5, 109, 111, 119, 120, 121, 123, 124, 125, 132, 133, 136, 171, 173, 174, 183, 185, 215, 220, 222, 231, 258, 265, 97–8
Tourist Attraction, 237, 252
Trainers' Association, 188, 96–7
Tralee Racecourse, race meeting, 217, 262
Tramore Racecourse, race meeting, 66, 69, 91, 153
Tramore, County Waterford, **66**
Troytown, 76, 78, 79
Tuam Racecourse, race meeting, 187
Tufnell, Meriel, 196
Tully Stud, *see* Irish National Stud
Turf Club, 2, 11, 12, 17, 18, 21, 24, 32, 33, 34, 41, 52, 65, 68–9, 71, 73–4, 75, 79, 84–5, 86, 96–101, 105, 108, 110–11, 119–20, 122–3, 124–6, 132, 138, 139–40, 143, 152–6, 159, 173, 180, 186, 187, 189–90, 196, 201, 211, 212, 219, 220, 228, 232–3, 255–7, 263–4
  Senior Steward, 182, 201, 232
Twiston-Davies, Nigel, 249
Twomey, John, **146**
Tymon Castle, 159
Tyrrell, Major, J.H., 200

Under Way, 142, 209
United Hunt Club, 147, **157**
United Irish Racecourses (UIR), 260

United Kingdom (UK), 258, 264–5
United States (US), 98, 153, 166, 194, 257, 260, 265, 266
Ussher, Christopher, 35

Vae Victus, 60
Vaughan, R.J., 141
Vermouth, 69
Vickerman, Frank, 141
Victoria, Queen, 27–8, 64
Vigors, T.C., 184, 190
Vulforo, **181**, 181, 182

Waddington, N.W., 157
Waldron, General Francis, **89**
Walford, Simon, Captain, **200**, 201, 2334
Walker, Colonel William Hall, 52, 89, 92
Walker, G.L., 92
Waller, Brigadier Sam, 232
Walsh, J.J., 91
Walsh, Joe, 210, 228, 229, 233, 255–6
Walsh, Katie, 199
Walsh, Ruby, 147, **244**, 244, **245**, 245
Walsh, Ted, 208, **209**, 219, 234, 244
Walwyn, Fulke, 116
War of Attrition, 250
War of Independence, 74–7, 88, 91
Ward Union Hunt, 26, 36–7, 48, 53, **71**, 158, 171
Waters, Thomas G., 27, 37
Watson, Col. S.J., 180
Watt, Mrs A.H. 'Peg', **206**
Watt, Major A.H., 125
Wayward Lad, 218
Welcome, John, 107
Weld, Charlie, 207
Weld, Dermot, 66, 207, 254
Wellesley, Gerald, 150

Westenra Lodge, 76, **79**
Westmeath Point-to-Point, 106
Wetherby Racecourse, race meeting, 117
Wexford Hunt Point-to-Point, **104–5**
Wexford Racecourse, race meeting, 136
Whelan, Thomas, **89**
Whisper Low, 45
White, John, 236
Whitney, John Hay 'Jock', 103, 114
Whitney, Pauline Payne, 114
Why Not, 61
Widger, Joe, **54**, 60
Widger, Tom, **54**
Wild Man from Borneo, **54**, 60
Williamson, George, 61
Wilmot, Norah, 195
Wilson, Gerry, **112**
Wingfield, A.D., 190, 191, 197, 219
Winter, Fred, 143
Wither or Which, 252
Woodbrook, 45
Wright's *Steeple Chase Calendar*, 32
Wright, Eddie, 207
Wylie, Graham, 252
Wylie, William E., **108**, 110, 119, 133
Wyndham-Quin, Richard, Viscount Adare, sixth earl of Dunraven and Mount Earl, 124, 133

Yeats, W.B., 5, 269
Yellow Furze, 111
Yellow Sam, **221**
Youghal Strand, County Cork, race meeting, 12
Young Arthur, **23**

Zonda, 194